THE
CALIFORNIA
CONNECTION

POLITICS IN THE GOLDEN STATE

THE
CALIFORNIA
CONNECTION

TERRY CHRISTENSEN
LARRY N. GERSTON

San Jose State University

LITTLE, BROWN AND COMPANY
Boston   Toronto

Library of Congress Cataloging in Publication Data

Christensen, Terry.
    Politics in the Golden State.

    Includes index.
    1. California—Politics and government—1951–
I. Gerston, Larry N.   II. Title.
JK8716.C47   1984   320.9794   83-24387
ISBN 0-316-13901-7

Library of Congress Catalog Card Number 83-24387

ISBN 0-316-13901-7

9 8 7 6 5 4 3 2 1

BP

Published simultaneously in Canada
by Little, Brown & Company (Canada) Limited

Printed in the United States of America

Produced by Ron Newcomer & Associates

Cartoons by Signe Wilkinson

Acknowledgments, page 340.

Preface

California politics can be bewildering. Some things appear to change before they can be understood, while others seem to be unshakable remnants of California's past. Personalities weigh as heavily on the state as formal institutions, and the environment in which they operate can shift like quicksand. The state's voters routinely express contradictory opinions, providing something for everyone. Few things about California are stable or predictable.

Some people throw up their hands at all this, dismissing California politics as nothing but a bizarre aberration, a sideshow. Others, perhaps exaggerating its importance, see California as a sort of mystical trend-setter for the nation and the world. Whether it's a political circus or the harbinger of things to come, what happens in California matters, not only to the state's residents, but to people elsewhere.

California is connected. It's connected economically, socially, politically —in every sense—to the rest of the United States and the world. These connections are part of what makes California so vital to others; they also are part of what shapes the state. Both the subtle and obvious qualities of California politics can be understood by grasping California's connections.

In this book, we explore California's varied connections. We do this by telling stories about the people, institutions, and policies that make California so unique. Partly, we've chosen this approach because, aside from dismissing it as trivial, the greatest offense against California politics is to make it boring. No place has such a wealth of characters, plot-twists, and surprise endings.

We hope readers will find the stories interesting in themselves, but that's not the only reason we're telling them. We think the complexities of California politics can be appreciated best by seeing the state's formal and informal institutions at work. That's one way we've learned about California politics ourselves. One of us has a long record of activity in community organizing and campaign work, supplemented by a stint as a member of the Democratic Party State Central Committee. The other has worked as an aide to a State Assemblyman and a County Supervisor, and also as a television commentator on California politics.

The work for this book was partially funded by research grants from San Jose State University and greatly assisted by Chairman Roy E. Young and the Department of Political Science. The tedious work of typing and retyping the manuscript for impatient authors was done with grace by Patti Mackay, Linda Garcia, Linda Chromik, Gayle Yasutake, Emi Nobuhiro, Nancy Sanderson, and Leslie Brand.

Cari Beauchamp, Alvin Sokolow, and Roy Young reviewed parts of the manuscript, and Katherine Bishop and Susy Elfving provided ready assistance. Their insights were invaluable, although each of them will argue with our conclusions and interpretations. Several people, mostly in Washington, D.C., granted interviews that were essential for the chapter on the California congressional delegation. Their comments are not footnoted because some interviews were not for attribution, but we are grateful for their time and cooperation. Paul Brett Hammond of the University of California, Los Angeles and Elizabeth Moulds of the California State University at Sacramento both made important contributions as reviewers for Little, Brown. Will Ethridge, former political science editor at Little, Brown, gave us the necessary "go" early on. Don Palm, Ethridge's successor, deserves special thanks for his unflagging faith and support of our project from its conception to the final product.

Our students functioned as a sort of test market and helped more than they know in the shaping of *Politics in the Golden State: The California Connection*. A select few and very special students will know when they read certain chapters just how much they contributed. We were fortunate to have superb research assistance from Julie Bonds, Jan Eric Fjeld, Russ Fung, Stephanie Gutowski, Joyce Jeffrey, Teresa Johnson, Sonya Johnson, Carolyn Kennedy, John Laffey, Cassie McDuff, Arthur L. Smith, Jr., Robert Schwab, Eric Strahl, Jackie Toth, Jim Ungvarsky, and John Wright.

We set out to write a book with a certain feel and tone, one that would make learning about California politics as interesting and enjoyable as it should be. Now that the book has been put together, it's obvious that Signe Wilkinson's cartoons contribute as much to that end as our writing. This San Jose *Mercury News* political cartoonist was a clever, talented, and enthusiastic participant throughout the writing of *Politics in the Golden State: The California Connection*.

Finally, we had personal support from people who are special to each of us.

Ray Allen is one of the few people connected with this book who isn't a Californian. His persistent demands for explanations of the mysterious phenomena of California politics drove Terry Christensen on, while at the same time he managed to be both a ruthless task-master and a patient and sympathetic listener to an author's laments.

Adam, Larry Gerston's three-year old son, gave his father a sense of purpose and perspective. Just a "Hi, Daddy," at the end of a long day provided the author all the reason in the world to pass something on to his little third generation Californian.

Terry Christensen
Larry N. Gerston

Contents

1
CALIFORNIA CONNECTIONS

Toto, I Have a Feeling We're Not in Kansas Anymore

It's not like Kansas or any other state either. Some people are so mystified by California that all they can do is joke about it. It's a "munchkin-land," says filmmaker Woody Allen, where the "only cultural advantage" is that drivers can make right turns on red lights.[1] Columnist Mike Royko says "You name it. If it babbles and its eyeballs are glazed, it probably comes from California."[2]

Others try to make more sense of California's complexity. Carey McWilliams, the greatest of the writers about California, admits it's "no ordinary state. It is an anomaly, a freak, the great exception among the American states."[3] "There has never been a state quite like California," writer John Gunther declares. It is "the one about all others that could exist alone."[4] But Curt Gentry, another writer, adds that "California is important not just for its size, or for what it produces, but because its most important function is to act as a huge testing laboratory for the American experience . . . an extension of the American dream, a feeler into the future."[5] California has acquired this role because it always seems to carry things one step further, often to extremes. Novelist Wallace Stegner observes

> in a prosperous country, we [Californians] are more prosperous than most; in an urban country, more urban than most; in a mobile country, more mobile; in a tasteless country, more tasteless; in a creative country, more energetically creative; in an optimistic society, more optimistic; in an anxious society, more anxious. Contribute regionally to the national culture? We *are* the national culture, at its most energetic end.[6]

California produced Charles Manson, Rev. Jim Jones, the Symbionese Liberation Army, Patty Hearst, and the "me" decade, but California also produces more Nobel Prize winners than any place else. California marketed the pet rock, EST, hot tubs, and the Valley Girl, but California industry leads the world in agriculture, aerospace, electronics, and entertainment. Only eight countries have larger economies than California's.

2

Critics joke about California politics, but this state produced two of the last four presidents and the most influential chief justice of the United States Supreme Court in this century. The state's media-oriented politics is sneered at, but the techniques pioneered in California campaigns are copied elsewhere. Vintage California controversies like the tax revolt and gay liberation are scoffed at, but other places soon find themselves confronting the same issues. Besides, California has too many voters and too much money to be ignored. That's why every national candidate turns up early and often in California.

People who dismiss California politics as merely silly simply don't understand them. California is different, perhaps even strange, and that makes it more difficult to figure out than most other states. Traditions and institutions are less stable than in other states. Even the great economic powers in California, seemingly the most stable forces of all, have been challenged and defeated.

To understand California politics, we need to look back over two centuries and examine the way the state has developed. Most of what is bewildering about California reflects constant change, a series of explosions that have propelled the state through history to make it what it is today. Wave after wave of immigrants and virtual revolutions in the state's economy have always kept California in flux. People tend to think of California in the present, having no history, but these historical connections made California the unique state it is and shape its politics today.

Most Californians Aren't . . .

Not since 1846 have a majority of Californians been natives of the state. Immigrants have arrived in California for two centuries: the Spanish in the 1770s; the Mexicans; then Yankees and various Europeans with the gold rush; then more Yankees and Europeans as the transcontinental railroad was completed; Chinese, Japanese, and Filipinos brought as laborers; then another wave of Mexicans; then Arkies, Okies, and other Dust Bowl refugees; then blacks, more Mexicans, and people from all over the United States; and most recently, Iranians, Central Americans, and Indochinese.

This brief list is far from complete, but it illustrates the constant change in California's population mix. The state has never settled into a stable, relatively homogeneous population like most other states; this is one reason for California's unpredictable politics. With each election, as many as 33 percent of California's voters may be participating for the first time.

All these people didn't come to California by chance. Two forces drew them: the myth and the reality of California. The myth, which dates back to the Spanish exploration, is California as the golden land, El Dorado, a land of wealth and opportunity. But the myth also has an element of truth. Each wave of immigrants was pushed to California by depression and stagnation wherever they were and pulled by California's opportunity. Economic development and technological change—from gold to railroads to missiles to video games—have given millions of people the opportunity they hoped for. They came for gold, land, silver, oil, the movies, farming, Silicon Valley—goals as diverse as the state's population itself. They came for good weather and the good life.

THE FIRST IMMIGRANTS

California's first natives were also its first immigrants. The Indian population of California probably came here thousands of years ago, crossing the Bering Strait from Asia. Small groups and villages were spread mainly through the coastal valleys and, being a disparate people, they spoke 130 dialects. There were perhaps as many as 300,000 Indians when the next immigrants arrived.

The Spanish began colonizing California in 1769, establishing a string of missions and military bases *(presidios)* along the coast from San Diego to San Francisco. The first civilian settlements *(pueblos)* were San Jose in 1777 and Los Angeles in 1781. The Spanish recruited the peaceful Indians, who put up virtually no resistance, as religious converts and workers for the missions. That proved more devastating to the Indian population than warfare: white men's diseases and the loss of their own culture led to a precipitous decline in the Indians' numbers. By 1849 there were only about 100,000 left. This was probably the only time California experienced a net population loss.

The Spanish never got around to doing much with their California colony. It was far away and they were preoccupied with other matters, including the Napoleonic Wars. As a consequence, Spain soon found its empire in ruins as the colonies won their independence.

Mexico freed itself of Spain in 1822, taking California with it. Under Mexican rule, land became the central issue in California politics. California's pattern of large-scale ownership was established by the Mexicans as they awarded huge land grants for *ranchos*. That fit the tradition they had inherited from aristocratic Spain. It also suited California's sparse population, which grew slowly from about 3,700 non-Indians in 1820 to 9,000 in 1846. The large tracts also were appropriate for the sort of farming being done at the time. The main products were hides and tallow from cattle—products easily shipped to distant markets and requiring little water, but lots of grazing land.

Even as this type of land ownership was being established, change was on its way. Non-Hispanic foreigners were coming to California, first for the fur of sea otters, which they nearly made extinct, and later for trade and farming. The first wagons made it over the Sierra in 1844; 2 years later the infamous Donner Party proved the trail was still pretty rough. By then, about 10 percent of the state's population, other than Indians, was non-Hispanic. Some of the new immigrants adapted to what they found, marrying into Mexican families (usually large landowners) and changing their names. Others didn't adapt so well. They resented Mexican rule and saw greater commercial opportunities in a closer association with the United States.

The United States Connection

The influx of Yankees weakened Mexico's tenuous hold on California, but American foreign policy broke it. The young nation was feeling its oats and California's lush lands and access to the Pacific were inviting. President Andrew Jackson made an unsuccessful offer to buy California in 1835, but a rebellion in Texas and war with Mexico soon accomplished what Jackson could not.

The Texans broke with Mexico in 1836, setting up their own republic. Ten years later the United States annexed Texas, provoking war with Mexico. That gave California, stimulated by a little Yankee agitation, an opportunity to break away from Mexico. The Bear Flag Revolt, a rather modest insurrection directed by American military agents, began in 1846. There was some fighting in California, but the defeat of Mexican forces in Texas proved decisive.

The Mexican-American War ended with the signing of the Treaty of Guadalupe-Hidalgo in 1848. Mexico lost Texas, California, New Mexico, Arizona, and substantial parts of Utah, Nevada, and Colorado. In return, the Mexicans were given $15 million and the assurance that the rights of Mexican citizens residing in the annexed areas would be respected; such rights included land-ownership and official use of the Spanish language. These guarantees reflect a significant difference between Mexican-Americans and every other American minority except Indians: they were not immigrants to the United States; they were conquered and annexed. As Carey McWilliams puts it, "their cultural autonomy was guaranteed by a treaty"[7]—a fact that is frequently forgotten today.

THE GOLD RUSH

What happened next is unparalleled in history. Just 9 days before the signing of the Treaty of Guadalupe-Hidalgo, gold was discovered in California, and in a few weeks the rush was on. The state was instantly populated, growing from 9,000 in 1846 to 264,435 in 1852. Many of the new immigrants were from other parts of the United States, but even more came from other places, especially Ireland, Germany, and Italy. James McClatchy, founder of one of California's great newspaper dynasties, for example, arrived from Ireland, via New York. The first Chinese were brought to California as laborers in the mines. The gold rush also pulled settlers away from the coast for the first time, made San Francisco a major port and the dominant city on the West Coast, and gave California a head start on the rest of the West, which was still virtually unpopulated.

THE FIRST CONSTITUTION

Rapid population growth and economic development precipitated an equally rapid political development. The anxious newcomers pounded out a constitution in 1849 and presented the federal government with demands for statehood. Slavery, the major issue of the day, had caused delays in the admission of other states, but not in California. Plantation agriculture was not forseen in this case, and was too lucrative to put off. California worked it out, demanded admission and won it in 1850, just 4 years after Mexican rule. Precocious California became a state without going through a period as a territory like other western states.

The pattern of California politics had been set: rapid change wrought by economic development and masses of immigrants. The importance of the immigrants' connections and California's willingness to adapt whatever seemed useful from other places to its own purposes is illustrated by the state's first constitutional convention and the document it produced. The average age of the delegates was just thirty-eight, and only seven of the forty-eight were natives of California. Thirteen had been in the state less than a year; twelve were from New York; eight were foreign-born.

In their haste they lifted freely from the constitutions of other states, especially Iowa and New York. They established a fragmented executive, including a governor, lieutenant governor, controller, attorney general, superintendent of public instruction, and surveyor general. The governor was given powers of appointment and veto. The legislature was bicameral, and representation in both houses was based on population. The third branch of government, dominated by a supreme court, was composed of district, county, and local justice courts. Basic rights of citizens were written into the constitution, but only white males were given the right to vote. San Jose was designated the state capital, and the Hispanic population was recognized by provision for all documents to be bilingual. Amendment of this constitution was to be by legislative recommendation and voter ratification.

THE LAND RUSH

By 1852 the gold rush had peaked. Development shifted to other forms and the land rush was on. But immigrants to California who expected to homestead on small parcels of land like immigrants in other states were in for a bitter disappointment. In the established states the United States government owned most of the land and sold it cheaply in small parcels to individual farmers; this policy did much to implement the American dream. California, however, was different. Almost 9 million acres of the best land had been distributed by Spanish and Mexican land grants and more had been hastily handed out in the last days of Mexican rule.

The new arrivals had to risk squatting or use devious means to get their land. Forged land grants were common. Many grants were legally challenged. Others were disputed on grounds that their boundaries were vague. In some cases landmarks were moved so that boundaries could be altered. A land commission, established in 1857, finally reviewed the challenges and—amid charges of corruption and illicit influence—upheld 75 percent of the grants. More land was made available by a brutal drive against the Indians. Between 1848 and 1865, 15,000 Indians were killed in usually bogus Indian wars; others were simply driven off their land.

Some individuals did very well despite these difficulties. Henry Miller, a young German immigrant, began buying up cheap land, often without water. He also took advantage of an 1859 federal action that released 2 million acres of what was loosely defined as swampland. By 1873 Miller and his partner, another German named Charles Lux, owned 22,500 square miles of California, becoming "America's first cattle kings."[8] Miller and Lux and others proved that land was available in California, but only to the rich or clever, not the sort of homesteaders who settled other states. California seemed to be for speculators, not homesteaders.

By 1870 a few hundred men owned most of California's farmland. Great fortunes were made and many of California's landowning families still hold enormous power today. California's social structure had been established, partially by legal means and partially by brute force and deceit. The unhappy homesteaders experienced only frustration. Some were allowed to settle and develop parcels of land and then, after they had done the hard work of developing it, were driven off or offered the land at a high price. Their efforts to change the system often resulted in violence, but in the end they lost. California was, again, different from other states. It was a farm state, but not a state of yeoman farmers. Rather, its agriculture was based on huge ranchos, later to become agribusinesses. This not only established the pattern of rural development, it hastened urbanization by driving homesteaders off the land and into the cities, thus providing a ready force for California's expanding industry.

The Railroads: A New Connection

California's next great transformation was wrought by transportation technology: the arrival of the railroad. The railroad changed the pattern of immigration, the relations between rich and poor, and the politics of the state—all this barely 10 years after admission to the Union.

The Central Pacific Railroad was incorporated in 1861. It was financed by four Sacramento merchants, who had been immigrants from the Northeast and who had made their initial fortunes supplying goldseekers. Their names—Crocker, Hopkins, Huntington, and Stanford—are prominent in California today, for they became the "Big Four," dominating California's economy and politics for half a century through their railroad company.

In a spectacular feat of engineering and politics, California was linked to the eastern United States by rail in just 6 years. The project was particularly daring because between the two coasts was mostly undeveloped wilderness. It would have made more sense to extend the railroad gradually, as development occurred. But California has never done anything gradually. The state's politicians pushed hard for the project. There were even rumors that California might take advantage of the Civil War to declare its independence if the railroad wasn't built. But the railroad also gave the Union better access to California's wealth, a sufficiently attractive prospect to justify a considerable government investment in the middle of a war.

Congress passed the Pacific Railway Act in 1862, providing millions of dollars in loans and land grants to subsidize the building of the transcontinental railway. Stanford became governor of California in 1862, just in time to see that financial aid from the state would also be available. Cities and counties also chipped in, sometimes under threat that the railroad would bypass them. The frenzy to complete the project was so great that the railroad was built from both directions, east and west.

Getting enough workers to complete the project in such a hurry was a problem, especially because silver had just been discovered in Nevada and another rush was on. Like the big gold mine operators before them, the railroad builders solved the problem by importing 15,000 Chinese laborers. By 1860 the Chinese were 10 percent of California's population. The number climbed to 150,000 in the 1870s, solidly entrenching another substantial minority in California.

The transcontinental line was completed in 1869, by which time the Big Four's Central Pacific Railroad had become the Southern Pacific, after acquiring a line to Southern California. During the 1870s they extended their network throughout the state, by either building new lines or buying up those built by others. When competitors resisted such acquisitions, the Big Four slashed their own rates until they drove the others out of business. By the 1880s the Big Four's Southern Pacific controlled not just railroads but 85 percent of the state's entire transportation system.

Through control of freight rates, the Southern Pacific organization could not only break competitors, but control the economic development of the state, affecting farmers in the countryside and industries in the cities. If that wasn't enough, the railroad was also California's biggest landowner, holding 11.5 million acres, about 12 percent of the state's area. Their economic power and their statewide organization enabled them to build a political machine unparalleled in California history and unrivaled in its time. It easily put allies in city, county, and state office. The machine was usually assisted by the newspapers, which cooperated out of prudence or because they were subsidized by the railroads.

This overwhelming power, labeled "the Octopus" by novelist Frank Norris, had developed in just a few years. But as early as 1875 problems were emerging for the machine. The railroad and a few dozen men owned so much land that there wasn't much left for homesteaders. The shortage forced immigrants in pursuit of the California dream to the cities, where they were often disappointed. Industries like the Union Iron Works in San Francisco were growing and fledgling unions were organized. A depression in the 1870s, however, created stiff competition for jobs and considerable discontent.

As a result, the first organized opposition to the railroads emerged—the Workingmen's party led by Denis Kearney, an Irish immigrant and demagogue. The railroad was a primary target, but Kearney soon found that a more potent rallying cry was "the Chinese must go." By this time the Chinese had half the factory jobs in San Francisco and in 1875 the Chinatown population was 47,000.[9]

THE SECOND CONSTITUTION

Antagonism to the Octopus and hatred of the Chinese fueled the Workingmen's Party, which managed to elect a mayor in San Francisco and several state legislators. They also precipitated a revision of the state constitution and elected a third of the delegates to the convention. Along with allies from the Grange, an organization of small farmers, they were able to revise the constitution to include regulation of railroads, utilities, banks, and other corporations. The new constitution also deleted Spanish as an official language and made it illegal for Chinese to work on public projects, own land, or be employed by state-chartered corporations.

The Workingmen and the Grange weren't the only ones at the constitutional convention, however. Other special interests managed to get their concerns written into the constitution as well. Limits on taxing and spending were imposed on the legislature. The Bill of Rights was extended and the courts were reorganized. The result was a very long and detailed constitution.

The Workingmen's party had faded away by 1883, perhaps because its mission had been accomplished or because the depression that had produced it had ended. But like the Bear Flag Revolt of the 1840s, the gold rush of the 1850s, and the building of the railroad in the 1860s, it had disrupted and altered the state. As Carey McWilliams points out, whatever its short-term effects, the Workingmen's party fits the California pattern of political movements:

> Both the ease with which this movement arose and the swiftness with which it collapsed were essentially aspects of the feebly rooted character of social organization in California. There was nothing to break or check the rise of the movement and by the same token, there was nothing to hold it together once its initial objects had been achieved. Deeply rooted political traditions would have kept such a movement in check in other states; but the traditional factor was almost wholly lacking in California politics.[10]

THE SOUTHERN CALIFORNIA CONNECTION

The railroads faced another sort of problem at about the same time. They controlled the transportation system and 11.5 million acres of the state's most valuable land, but they needed development to profit from their holdings. Development required workers to harvest the crops and work in the factories, but depression and the railroad monopoly were discouraging immigration.

This problem was solved by the "rate wars" and "land booms" of the 1880s, both of which were largely created and promoted by the railroads. Both the Santa Fe and Southern Pacific Railroads had completed lines from the Midwest to Southern California. The two railroads launched a rate war in which fares from the Midwest dropped to a dollar. Their low rates subsidized immigration, bringing workers and business to California and thus—in the long term—great benefits to themselves. The new immigrants were a bit different from their predecessors, most of whom had traveled great distances from foreign countries and from the northeastern United States. The new wave was from the American Midwest. They were the makings of an emerging middle class and also of Southern California as a major population center.

The 1880s also brought aggressive boosters and speculators like Harrison Gray Otis, who came to Los Angeles, bought the *Los Angeles Times*, and in 1888 founded the city's chamber of commerce. The chamber was soon the largest and most ambitious in the United States. Between 1888 and 1891 this organization distributed 2 million pieces of promotional literature throughout the country, especially in the Midwest.[11]

Through vigorous promotion, the chamber ensured a growing market for the land the members owned and the housing they built. They also ensured a steady influx of workers, which, combined with the good climate and favorable business conditions, helped attract new industry. To further that cause, the chamber, led by Otis, staunchly resisted unionization. Between 1890 and 1911 they succeeded in keeping wages as much as 40 percent lower than in unionized San Francisco.[12] The flow of immigrants assisted this cause by maintaining a constant surplus of workers.

Another discovery did even more than the boosters' propaganda to fuel the boom in Southern California. This time the gold was black: oil. California had been producing oil in small quantities since the 1860s, but when Edward L. Doheny, the son of an Irish immigrant, discovered oil in Los Angeles, the boom really took off. By 1899, 3,000 wells had been drilled in the Los Angeles area, and by 1900 the state was producing 4,320,000 barrels; 10 years later production was up to 77,698,000 barrels.[13] Oil was to Southern California what gold was to the northern half of the state. The railroads and the Los Angeles Chamber of Commerce were its promotional handmaidens.

The Progressive Challenge

Meanwhile the reforms wrought by the Workingmen's party had not achieved lasting change. The Southern Pacific retained control of California politics. Rather than being regulated by the reformers' railroad commission, the railroad took over the commission. The Southern Pacific and its allies—the banks, the utility companies, several newspapers, and other major landowners—continued to rule in California. Together, they formed a formidable political machine with agents in virtually every city and county. They controlled the political parties and rewarded themselves and their supporters while penalizing their opponents.

At the turn of the century a new challenge arose, this time not from the urban working class but from the growing urban middle class. That such a challenge was mounted at all indicates another precipitous change in California's social and economic structures. The state was becoming more urban, and its population was not so rigidly divided between wage earners and owners, whether on farms or in factories. The new challengers were lawyers, doctors, teachers, merchants, and some crusading journalists. Another revolution was brewing in California.

In 1907 middle-class malcontents in San Francisco, Sacramento, Fresno, and Los Angeles organized the Lincoln-Roosevelt League as a reform group within the Republican party. They became part of the national Progressive movement, led by Theodore Roosevelt among others. In just a few years and with surprising ease, they vanquished the Southern Pacific Octopus and left a lasting mark on California politics.

In 1908 many of the Lincoln-Roosevelt League candidates were elected to the state legislature. Once in office, they set about weakening the machine by changing the way political parties selected candidates. Instead of nomination by party conventions, which were easily controlled by the machine, they introduced the direct primary, a system by which the voters choose party nominees in elections.

Hiram Johnson, a San Francisco attorney who gained statewide fame for successfully prosecuting that city's corrupt leaders, became the Progressive reform candidate for governor in 1910. Johnson found a campaign gimmick, another California tradition, when he toured the state by automobile. He was applying a new technology—one that ultimately contributed greatly to the downfall of the railroads—but he was also pointedly rejecting the evil railroads.

When Johnson won, the Progressives were in the driver's seat and they introduced sweeping reforms. The Public Utilities Commission was established to regulate the railroads and other utilities. Women, an important part of the Progressive movement, gained the right to vote. Child labor and workmen's compensation laws to protect workers and conservation acts to protect natural resources were also approved. But the main target of the Progressives was the machine and they set about destroying it by weakening the political parties through which it operated. They began with the direct primary as a permanent replacement for party caucuses. They tried to remove party labels from the ballot altogether and succeeded in doing this at the local level through nonpartisan elections, although efforts to make state elections nonpartisan failed. The Progressives also introduced cross-filing, a system in which candidates could seek nomination by any political party without designating which they belonged to. Party structures and rules were also closely regulated by law. Eventually, they introduced the civil service system for state workers, a system whereby employees are selected on the basis of education or skills rather than under the old patronage system, which awarded jobs based on party membership. All these things helped break the machine, but they also left a legacy of weak and ineffective political parties, which helps keep California politics confusing and unpredictable even now.

Just to make sure they never got stuck with unresponsive government, the Progressives also introduced something called direct democracy. Three different devices were established: initiative, referendum, and recall. The initiative gave citizens the means to make laws by signing petitions and putting issues on the ballot. Currently, petitioners are required to collect signatures of registered voters equivalent to 8 percent of the number who voted in the preceding gubernatorial election to qualify an initiative constitutional amendment for the ballot and 5 percent to qualify ordinary laws. Voters were also given the right to petition to revoke laws passed by the legislature. Such referenda require signatures equivalent in number to 5 percent of those voting in the previous gubernatorial election. Certain acts of the legislature, including proposals to borrow money or amend the constitution, must also be referred to the voters. Finally, voters were given the right to fire public officials by petitioning for their recall; signatures equal to 12–20 percent of those voting for candidates for the office in question are required to put a recall on the ballot. Then a majority must vote for the recall to succeed.

The darker side of Progressivism, as of the Workingmen's party earlier, was its racism. The Chinese "problem" had been solved by halting Chinese immigration in 1882. The big farmers who had relied on Chinese workers then turned to the Japanese. By 1910 the Japanese nearly equaled the Chinese in population (72,156). Racial antagonism soon arose and the Progressives responded by making it illegal for aliens to own land in California. The Progressives also supported the national Immigration Act of 1924, which virtually stopped the flow of Japanese immigrants. Of course that meant farmworkers had to come from somewhere else, and eventually the growers turned to nearby Mexico.

The Progressive movement transformed the state, changing everything from its population mix to its political parties. They also influenced the nation. Hiram Johnson was Theodore Roosevelt's vice-presidential candidate on the Progressive (Bull Moose) ticket in 1912. It was the only election he ever lost. He went on to be reelected governor in 1914 and then to serve in the United States Senate from 1916 to 1945, becoming California's first national leader.

He exemplifies the California tendency to personalize its politics, for Hiram Johnson virtually *became* the Progressive movement and was the dominant figure in state politics for 26 years, long after the movement faded away.

Southern California Comes of Age

One of the largest internal migrations in American history took place between 1920 and 1930, as 2 million people moved to California. The state grew by 65.7 percent, a rate exceeded in California history only by the gold rush era, and nearly three-fourths of the new arrivals came to Southern California. In 1920 just 20 percent of California's population lived in or around Los Angeles; by 1940 half the state's population lived there.

These masses of people were drawn by jobs. The oil boom was on, and the Panama Canal and Los Angeles Harbor had been completed, making shipping a major industry. Clothing, automobile, and aircraft manufacturers were emerging as major employers. The movies were also part of the draw. Filmmakers came to Southern California for its fine climate and cheap labor, and perhaps also to be near the Mexican border for quick getaways from creditors and the tax collector.[14] They provided a modest number of jobs, but they contributed greatly to the building of the California myth.

Such growth wouldn't have been possible in the arid Los Angeles basin if the business leaders of the area hadn't ensured a supply of water. Men like Harrison Gray Otis and his son-in-law Harry Chandler, with the aid of engineer William Mulholland, engaged in what has been called "water imperialism,"[15] first tapping the water of the distant Owens Valley, then reaching to the Colorado River.

THE GREAT DEPRESSION

California's boom was slowed by the Great Depression of the 1930s, but it also brought a new wave of American immigrants. Okies and Arkies—refugees from the Dust Bowl states of the Midwest—swarmed into Southern and Central California hoping for work. So many arrived in Los Angeles that the city police went considerably out of their jurisdiction to set up border patrols at the state line to keep these "undesirables" out.

Thousands of refugee families—like the Joads in John Steinbeck's classic *The Grapes of Wrath*—sought work in the Central Valley. By 1935 California, the promised land, had 13.5 percent of the transients in America, and an estimated 50,000 were homeless and starving in the Central Valley. In the 1930s, for the first time, more than half the farmworkers in California were native-born Americans. This produced the biggest farm labor strikes in the state's history, although unionization was decades away.

The availability of native-born Americans as farm labor produced hostility to Mexican workers, who had been the primary source of farm labor since World War I, and California turned against the Mexicans, just as it had turned against the Chinese and Japanese before. Hostility was greatest in the cities, where many Mexican farmworkers lived in the off-season. In 1931 Los Angeles County initiated a repatriation program, citing the fact that although Mexicans comprised 7 percent of the population, they used more than 25 percent of the county's charity and hospital funds. To get rid of these welfare recipients, the county worked out a deal with the Southern Pacific Railroad to return them to Mexico for just $14.70 each.[16]

A NEW REVOLT

The Depression and the new wave of immigrants had their impact on California politics, almost upsetting the Republican apple cart. California had been virtually a one-party Republican state throughout its history. Both the Southern Pacific machine and the Progressive reformers had worked through the Republican party. But things were changing by the 1930s. Democratic voter registration was growing and the new immigrants gave it a boost just as the widespread unemployment of the Depression was radicalizing workers.

Upton Sinclair, a novelist and socialist, saw what was happening. He registered as a Democrat, and in 1934, ran for governor on a program called "End Poverty in California" (EPIC), which advocated radical tax reform. Sinclair easily won the Democratic nomination and swiftly built a popular mass movement with EPIC chapters all over the state.

The dominant powers in California politics got nervous enough to raise $10 million, mostly contributed by banks and businesses, to defeat Sinclair. That was the most that had ever been spent on a campaign in California and marked the beginning of the state's tradition of costly media campaigns. The anti-Sinclair cause was also aided and abetted by the state's mostly conservative Republican newspapers, which spread rumors that he was a communist, an atheist, and a homosexual. Despite this massive opposition, Sinclair lost by only 200,000 votes. Sinclair's efforts strengthened the Democratic party in California enough to elect Culbert Olson, an EPIC supporter, as California's first Democratic governor in this century. Olson served only one term, however, and the EPIC movement soon faded away. Once again, a mass movement had arisen virtually from nowhere, shaken the state, and then disappeared.

WORLD WAR II: NEW INDUSTRY AND RACIAL CONFLICT

Although California had been industrializing for a century, it took World War II to complete the process. Several pioneer California industries—most notably radio, electronics, and aircraft manufacturing—expanded dramatically. Employment by aircraft makers like Douglas, Northrup, and Lockheed grew from 20,000 workers in 1939 to 243,000 in 1943.[17] The boom drew the Dust Bowl refugees off the farms and into the cities and brought in a new wave of immigrants, including many blacks, doubling their numbers from 2 percent to 4.4 percent during the 1940s. The total growth rate hit 53.3 percent with 4 million people arriving, but the most lasting effect of the war years was the strengthening of the California economy by industrial diversification. Today aircraft, aerospace, electronics, and defense manufacturing ranks second only to agriculture in California's economy.

But the war years also brought a new round of racial antagonism, leading to the "internment" of Japanese-Americans. Whole families, like that of Norman Y. Mineta, now a congressman, were packed off to what some people refer to as concentration camps. Many lost their farms and businesses. This shameful chapter of California history—as with previous persecutions and deportations of minority groups—took place with virtually no dissent from the state's political leaders of either party.

With the Okies in the factories and the Japanese in the camps, yet another shortage of farm labor arose. This time the problem was solved by a federal program to import Mexican citizens (braceros). At its peak in 1945, the program brought in 120,000 workers; it continued until 1964.

Mexican-Americans, meanwhile, were settling in cities and growing more assertive. The war years saw the emergence of pachuquismo, a style of dress, talk, and dance that was uniquely Mexican-American. It signified the growing confidence of California's largest and oldest minority group, and the reaction by the white majority was intensely hostile. With the Japanese out of the way, racial antagonism focused on Mexican-Americans. The pachucos in their distinctive "zoot suits" were an easy target. The press ridiculed them. The Los Angeles City Council made wearing a zoot suit a misdemeanor. One night in 1943 a convoy of taxis full of sailors launched an attack on the zoot suiters. The police helped the sailors rather than their victims and the press applauded the attacks. The "Zoot Suit Riots" went on for days, and the victims included not only zoot suiters, but blacks and Mexican-Americans dressed in normal clothing.

The Making of the Central Valley

Agriculture had replaced gold mining as California's most important industry by 1870. The completion of the railroads vastly expanded the markets available for California's produce, and as a consequence, farming grew more intensive. By that time wheat growing had supplemented cattle and sheep ranching. After the railroads were completed, farmers diversified to orchards and vineyards. The first trainload of fruit was shipped east in 1886; many more followed and cities like San Jose thrived on fruit drying and canning as well as shipping.

But the expansion and intensification of California's farms always faced the problem of water. Without it, whole regions were useless. It's not that California doesn't have plenty of water—it's just not evenly distributed. Northern California has plenty; Southern California and the San Francisco Bay Area have far too little to support agricultural development and urbanization. As previously noted, in order to develop Los Angeles, its boosters had to acquire water from elsewhere.

In the middle of the state is the great Central Valley, 100 miles wide and 500 miles long, with mountains on all sides. Two mighty rivers flow through the valley, the Sacramento and the San Joaquin, both emptying into the San Francisco Bay. In order to develop agriculture at the southern end, a way was needed to move the water south. The Central Valley Project, a network of dams and canals, was born as a state effort in 1935 and soon taken over by the federal government. Parts of the project were completed during World War II, though most of it took much longer. What was once desert land in the San Joaquin Valley now produces cotton, tomatoes, grapes, sugar beets, and dozens of other agricultural products.

The Central Valley Project was to Central California what the gold rush was to Northern California and the oil boom was to Southern California. The major difference was that the California tradition of large-scale landownership and factory-style farming kept the number of jobs down; so although the economy boomed, the population expanded more slowly.

Postwar Boom and Political Change

California continued to grow through the 1950s, adding 5 million to its population during that decade. Many war veterans who had passed through California on their way to the Pacific Front liked what they saw and returned when the war was over. The aircraft and defense industry slumped briefly, but bounced back vigorously as the federal government accelerated defense spending during the Korean War and the Cold War. The big aircraft companies diversified into missiles and aerospace, and small electronics companies were growing south of San Francisco in what was to become Silicon Valley.

California was led during and after the war by Earl Warren, who succeeded Hiram Johnson as the father figure in California politics, establishing an image that was above party politics and based on what he called "personal accountability." For a Republican like Warren in a state with an emerging Democratic majority, that was a shrewd tactic. He was assisted by the cross-filing system, which enabled him to win the nominations of both the Republican and Democratic parties. First elected governor in 1942, Warren was reelected in 1946 and 1950, the only California governor to win three terms. He soon became a national political figure, and was the Republican nominee for vice-president in 1948 and a contender for the presidential nomination in 1952. President Dwight Eisenhower made him chief justice of the United States Supreme Court in 1953, where he was the leader of the liberal majority until his retirement in 1969.

Warren probably got out of California just in time, for the Democratic party was on the rise in 1950. The resurrection began with the founding of the California Democratic Council (CDC) in 1953 as a statewide organization of local Democratic clubs. The CDC endorsed candidates in primary elections in an effort to prevent Republicans like Warren from using the cross-filing system to win the Democratic nomination. Alan Cranston, now a senator from California, was the first president of the CDC.

By 1958 the CDC had 40,000 members and a strong and dynamic statewide organization. Edmund G. "Pat" Brown, the state's attorney general, won the Democratic nomination for governor with the assistance of the CDC. His opponent in the general election was Senator William Knowland, who, in a game of political musical chairs, had forced Republican Governor Goodwin Knight to run for the Senate. Knowland and his mentors at the *Los Angeles Times* hoped that a term as governor would advance his presidential ambitions. The voters were unenthusiastic about these blatant maneuvers, and Brown picked up support. He was also assisted by a major get-out-the-vote effort by organized labor, which was opposing an antiunion initiative on the same ballot. Brown won the election and the Republican stranglehold on California politics was broken. Two-party competition has been the rule in the state ever since. Just to be sure of that, the Democrats, now in control of both the executive and legislature, swiftly got rid of cross-filing.

THE 1960S AND 1970S

By 1963 California had surpassed New York as the most populous state in the Union. The state's strong economy continued to attract immigrants, and its politics were as tumultuous as at any time in its history. Minority groups grew assertive, demanding equal rights and economic opportunity, and rioting in the 1960s out of sheer frustration. In 1964 the voters turned against the minorities, approving an initiative that overturned fair housing legislation, though the voters were later overruled by the Supreme Court. But eventually, black, Asian, and Hispanic politicians were elected to state and local office, and the anger subsided. The legislation that had permitted the importation of Mexican citizens as braceros to work on the farms was allowed to lapse. Ending this program helped the unionization of farmworkers, led by Arizona-born Cesar Chavez, to succeed in the 1970s.

The voters reelected liberal Democrat Pat Brown in 1962, rejecting former Vice-President Richard Nixon. Then they did an about-face in 1966, denying Brown a third term and choosing conservative actor Ronald Reagan. Republican Reagan was elected just as California seemed at its most liberal, with the civil rights, farmworker, student, and antiwar movements at their strongest. But there has always been a strong conservative streak in California voters, and they may have been fed up with these seemingly radical movements.

While all this was going on, a rather more modest reform movement was also under way. By 1966 California's constitution had been amended 350 times and was the third longest in the world. A wordy document, it included protections for everything from prize fighting to walnut trees, thanks to the strength of California's interest groups and the initiative amendment process. Efforts to streamline the constitution were begun in 1947 and accelerated with the establishment of a special commission in 1963. The voters approved most of the commission's recommendations to simplify and tighten the constitution without altering its basic structure. Still, with every election, the voters consider new amendments to the constitution, and its length and complexity continue to grow.

After 8 years with Ronald Reagan as governor, Californians did another about-face, choosing someone as unlike him as possible, young Jerry Brown. Pat Brown's son was a Democrat whose politics, though hard to define, later were branded "neoliberal." As California's boom slowed down, Brown declared an "era of limits." By the end of his two terms, Brown had become an advocate of California's high-technology industry as the salvation of the state's economy, earning him the label of an "Atari Democrat."

While Brown governed, California's traditions of instant political revolutions and immigrant waves continued. In 1978 a Utah-born realtor named Howard Jarvis got an initiative on the ballot to slash property taxes. Proposition 13 was overwhelmingly approved and the taxpayers' revolt was under way. In the meantime yet another wave of refugees hit, this time from Southeast Asia. By 1980 California found itself host to half of the nation's Indochinese refugees, with 90,000 from Vietnam alone.

Then in 1982, after 8 years with Jerry Brown as governor, the continually shifting sands of California politics produced a conservative Republican governor, George Deukmejian. Nothing could better illustrate the volatility of California politics than the flip-flopping from Brown to Reagan to Brown to Deukmejian.

California Now

California's population has doubled every 20 years for more than a century. New immigrant groups arrive regularly from different parts of the United States and the world. Simultaneously, technological and industrial changes—from gold to silicon chips—have transformed the state every decade or two. These explosive forces of change have kept California politics explosive as well.

THE ECONOMY

Although change is the norm in California, there are stable forces and constant political powers through it all. In a state where natural resources— gold, silver, timber, oil, and fertile land—are so abundant, possession of these resources amounts to lasting economic and political clout, most of which is in the hands of a few families and large corporations.

Landownership remains crucial to understanding the state. Although about half of California is owned by the state and federal governments, most of this land is mountains and desert. The other half, most of the farmland and urban areas, is in private hands. And the biggest landowner after government is still the Southern Pacific Railroad, which has 2 million acres or 2 percent of

California. Their holdings include 20 percent of the Central Valley. Other great farm corporations, like J. G. Boswell, with its 147,505 acres, also own huge tracts. In fact, the average farm in California today is 15 square miles; every year there are fewer and fewer farms, and those that remain are larger and larger.[18]

These great landholders have long been involved in politics, because they need certain governmental policies to exploit their investment. A supply of cheap labor helps, and the growers have always been involved in immigration policy and opposed to unionization. Even more important, much of their land would be of little value without irrigation, so getting water has long been a top priority for agribusiness. The Central Valley Project is a monument to their power. Indeed, agriculture soaks up 90 percent of the water collected and distributed by state and federal water projects,[19] and the price they pay for it is well below what it costs the government to supply. All this adds up to a formidable industry, the biggest in California. Over 250 products are grown and over 300,000 people are employed in the $13.7 billion business. With just 3 percent of the nation's farmland, California collects 10 percent of the country's farm income.

As important as agriculture is in California, it's not simply a farm state like Kansas. Over 2 million people work in manufacturing, predominantly in aerospace, defense, and electronics. A third of all United States aerospace companies are in California and the state boasts 20 percent of the country's jobs in aircraft manufacture. In the Los Angeles area alone, 200,000 people work in aerospace, and the electronics industry accounts for 170,000 jobs in San Jose's Silicon Valley and over 400,000 statewide.

These industries are even more dependent on government than agribusiness. Aircraft and aerospace companies get their work from government contracts. They've done well for California, which, with 10.5 percent of the United States population, gets over 20 percent of all defense contracts. Electronics companies are less dependent on government, but in the past few years they've emerged as a political force seeking to protect themselves from foreign competition and heavy taxation.

Although agribusiness and manufacturing provide the firm base for California's economy, 78 percent of the state's work force is involved in neither industry. Known as service workers, they make up such a large part of California's work force that it's been called the first postindustrial society. Two million people work in wholesale and retail trade. Government employs another 1.7 million, 17 percent of the workers in the state. More than half a million work in finance, insurance, and real estate. Another half million work in the $21 billion tourist industry. Construction remains an important industry in ever-booming California, with 431,000 workers in 1980.

California's vibrant economy is further strengthened by its strategic geographical position. Nearby Mexico has provided a source of workers and a market for California-produced goods, and recently discovered oil reserves in Mexico may one day fuel California's automobiles. California also commands American access to the Pacific basin. Asian immigrants have long supplied California with workers, wars in Asia have fueled the California economy, and Asian nations are important trading partners and sometimes competitors. Former Senator S. I. Hayakawa observed that "what happens in the Philippines, Japan and Korea has a greater impact on us [in California] and is of more immediate interest than most events in Massachusetts."[20]

All this adds up to a strong, highly diversified economy—the ninth largest in the world, with an annual gross product of $351 billion. A. W. Clausen, former president of the second largest bank in the world, California-based Bank of America, boasted that "California's economy is a different story altogether from that of the rest of the country. At the worst, we won't slip into a recession."[21] Recent events have proven him wrong. California has always been hit by national economic trends, but the state's economy is so strong and diversified that it usually suffers less.

Just as the California economy is not independent from the nation's, the state's industries are not independent of government. In fact, all of the state's major industries need government badly. Agriculture needs water. Aerospace and defense manufacturers need government contracts. Electronics needs protection from international competition and industrial espionage. Construction needs building permits. Tourism needs parks and transportation systems. That adds up to an amazing array of economic interests clamoring for government attention and aid, deeply affecting the politics of both the state and the nation.

THE PEOPLE

If California's economy is varied, so is its population, partly because the development of different industries has drawn people from different parts of the world at different times. Most states settle into a pattern: a wave of immigrants arrives, settles or assimilates, and a dominant culture takes hold. But the constant assault of new groups of immigrants has prevented such stabilization in California. The only thing stable about California's population is its diversity.

Every decade since the gold rush has brought a huge increase in population, although growth was tapering off a bit in the 1970s, which brought the smallest increase in the state's history. Still, by 1980, California's population of 23,667,902 was 10.5 percent of the nation's total, and it continued to increase in diversity. California led the country in foreign-born residents, with 3.5 million of 14.8 percent of the state's population. More than 200,000 Indochinese arrived, a third of all the Indochinese in the United States. There were also 200,000 Iranians, 200,000 Salvadorans, and 150,000 Koreans. The state's minority population continued to grow. By 1980, 19 percent of Californians were Hispanic, 7.7 percent were black, and 5.3 percent were Asian, leading some demographers to predict that California would have a Third World majority by the year 2000. At the same time, California continued to attract so many people from other states that in 1980 only 45 percent of the state's population had been born here (see Table 1–1).

The way Californians live is also a bit different from other states. Ninety-two percent of the California population resides in what the Census Bureau calls "urban places," as compared to 74 percent nationally. More Californians have high school or university degrees than the national average. The median income of Californians in 1980 was $18,170, also higher than the national average. More women worked and more people lived alone. There was one car

TABLE 1-1   California Population Growth

	California population	California growth rate (%)	National growth rate (%)
1820	3,720		
1846	9,000*		
1852	264,435		35.9
1860	379,994	70.0	35.6
1870	560,247	47.4	26.6
1880	864,694	54.3	26.0
1890	1,213,398	40.3	25.5
1900	1,485,053	22.4	20.7
1910	2,377,549	60.1	21.0
1920	3,426,861	44.1	14.9
1930	5,677,251	65.7	16.1
1940	6,907,387	21.7	7.2
1950	10,586,223	53.3	14.5
1960	15,717,204	48.5	18.5
1970	19,971,069	27.0	13.3
1980	23,667,902	18.5	11.4

*Estimate.

for every two persons and almost one telephone for every person in the state. It's a mixed, affluent, sophisticated, and mobile population that reinforces the diversity of the state's economy and the volatility of its politics.

THE REGIONS

If a mixed economy and population aren't enough to complicate California's politics, that diversity is exacerbated by the fact that both are unevenly distributed through the state. As we've seen, different parts of the state grew at different periods for different reasons. And different sorts of people came to the varied regions of the state, attracted by their climates or the sort of work they offered.

The differences between Northern and Southern California are probably best known. They're so pronounced that the idea of dividing the state into two parts has been discussed throughout California history. Joel Garreau, author of *The Nine Nations of North America,* claims that "San Francisco and Los Angeles are not just two cities. They represent two value structures. Indeed, they are the capitals of two different nations. Los Angeles the capital of MexAmerica and San Francisco that of Ecotopia."[22]

San Francisco and the Bay Area are traditionally liberal, Democratic, urban, Catholic, and unionized, with strong contingents of European and Asian ethnic groups. "The City" is the state's corporate and financial headquarters; just 50 miles south, San Jose is the high-tech capital of the world.

And then there is Southern California, from Santa Barbara to San Diego, dominated by sprawling Los Angeles. The white population is more likely to be from Iowa than from Italy. The economy is based on oil, aircraft, and entertainment. Voters tend to be conservative and Republican, especially in Orange and San Diego Counties, but the minority population is large and liberal. Los Angeles County contains 45 percent of the state's Hispanic population and whites are a minority of 48 percent in the City of Los Angeles itself. The area's newspapers and radio and television broadcasts now reach over half the voters in the state, and most statewide politicians—even those from the North— spend a lot of time there.

But North-South is not the only important division in the state. Writer Tom De Vries says the real division is not North and South, but East and West. He sees the West as the urbanized coastal area, from Marin to San Diego, and the East as the rest. The East, he claims, is treated as a "colony" by the West, a sort of agricultural and recreational "preserve." To coastal Californians, the East is "out there. Where people are named Clyde, Jose or Darlene. In the Western

Strip everybody is named Jennifer or Jason, just as they are in New York. . . .
[The East does] the logging and [the West] gets the wood, then makes speeches
against people who cut down trees for a living." From the colony's point of
view, there's no difference between San Francisco and Los Angeles. Both
import water. Neither understands the colony. The 1981 battle over spraying
urban areas to get rid of the Mediterranean fruit fly exemplifies the division.
The West worried about ecology; the East worried about economic survival.[23]

The "colonial" California De Vries is talking about is really the great Central
Valley—one-sixth of the state's territory and the home of its biggest business,
agriculture. Its cities include Stockton, Fresno, Modesto, Bakersfield, and
Sacramento, the state capital. Water and farming are the big concerns, and
politics tends to be even more conservative than in Southern California.

Besides the San Francisco Bay Area and Southern and Central California,
three other regions are distinctive: the North Coast, the Sierra, and the desert.
The coast north of San Francisco is lumber and fishing country. In an area
where 2 million acres of redwoods have been reduced to just 270,000, conservation is a constant issue. The population and the cities are small and
politics is conservative. Even more sparsely populated is the Sierra—430 miles
of mountains that wall off California from the rest of the nation. Here politics
often centers on development of recreational facilities and housing. Both the
North Coast and the Sierra have the water the rest of California needs, but
taking it means changing the rivers and the lakes of these regions. One such
thirsty area is the Imperial Valley desert on the Mexican border, which gets just
2 inches of rain a year. This 3,000-square-mile area is now valuable farmland
thanks to the importation of water. Just to its north, however, is the Mojave,
25,000 square miles of desert.

What's It All Add Up To?

Today's California is a product of repeated shock waves of economic and
demographic change made more complicated by the sheer physical scale and
geographic variety of the state. From the gold rush to the silicon chip, from the
Spanish to the Indochinese, change is the norm in California. Each change
has had an impact and then been absorbed by California's incredible diversity,
adding to the complexity and fluidity of the state's politics.

After taking a look at California's history and at the kind of place it is today,
we shouldn't be surprised that its politics are in constant flux. That's not only
because of the new people who come here, drawn by the California dream.
Sociologist Neil Smelser says California is seen as a "wide-open place where

newcomers believe they can be reborn."[24] It's a place of opportunity, of possibilities. Many immigrants bring their traditions with them, but many more leave them behind and make something else of themselves. German butcherboys like Henry Miller become cattle kings. Irish peasants like Denis Kearney build political movements. Children of sharecroppers like Tom Bradley become mayors. Children of Armenian immigrants like George Deukmejian become governor.

Openness, absence of tradition, rootlessness, and opportunity characterize California society and politics. They also make Californians willing to experiment, to try out new leaders, and to invent new institutions and policies. "California," Carey McWilliams wrote, "the giant adolescent, has been outgrowing its governmental clothes, now, for a hundred years. . . . Other states have gone through this phase too, but California has never emerged from it."[25]

Constant change can be bewildering, though, and it often produces a backlash. California's renowned openness and tolerance, for example, have not always extended to the state's minorities, who have been convenient scapegoats for social and economic problems. And as Curt Gentry points out, Californians occasionally get "tired of constant change . . . tired of being in the forefront of every battle; tired of living on the edge of tomorrow" and want a "pause," [26] so they elect a Ronald Reagan or a George Deukmejian.

California's political institutions are too weak and diverse to control these varied social and economic forces. The institutions *reflect*, rather than contain, the social system. California's political parties, for example, are notoriously weak. Even as long ago as the nineteenth century, California voters showed little loyalty to political parties. Masses of voters readily bolted to the entirely new, though short-lived, Workingmen's party. Three decades later, the Progressives institutionalized weak parties with their election reforms. High percentages of new voters in every election also made it difficult for strong party organizations to evolve.

The weakness of the parties opened up opportunities for other political forces. During the first half of this century, a half dozen Republican newspapers exercised enormous power in California elections. Later, television became an important medium for politicians to reach voters. Interest groups, from liquor distributors to unions and utilities, replaced parties as sources of support for candidates, and they lobbied government directly, with no need for the parties as intermediaries.

As a consequence of all these things—constant change, diversity, rootless voters with weak party loyalty, impotent parties, strong interest groups, and a heavy media orientation—personalities become more important in California politics than they are elsewhere. In a state without fixed patterns of politics or strong organizations, opportunities for individuals with flair, imagination, skill, good timing, or just good luck are enormous. Could any other state have produced Hiram Johnson, Earl Warren, Richard Nixon, Ronald Reagan, Jerry Brown, Rose Bird, Howard Jarvis, and Willie Brown? Other states might boast one or two like these, but no place else could rival that entire group of highly individualistic politicians.

California politics is so varied that these diverse politicians cannot only be elected by the same voters at different times, they can win at the *same* time. In June 1978, California voters approved Howard Jarvis's tax-cutting Proposition 13. In November of that same year, they overwhelmingly reelected Governor Jerry Brown. In 1982 they chose a Republican governor and put Democrats in charge of all the other executive offices and the state legislature. In that same year, they voted *for* a nuclear freeze but *against* gun control, apparently fearful of genocide but comfortable with homocide.

Waves of change, diversity, instability, weak traditions, and open structures create California's volatile politics. It may seem confusing, but keeping these characteristics in mind as we examine specific aspects of California politics makes understanding possible, for California's present and future are connected to its past.

Notes

[1]Woody Allen (writer and director), *Annie Hall*, 1977.

[2]*Newsweek*, September 17, 1979, p. 34.

[3]Carey McWilliams, *California: The Great Exception* (Westport, New York: Greenwood Press, 1971), p. 24.

[4]Neal R. Peirce, *The Pacific States of America* (New York: Norton, 1972), p. 20.

[5]Curt Gentry, *The Last Days of the Late Great State of California* (New York: Ballantine, 1968), p. 123.

[6]Peirce, p. 24.

[7]Carey McWilliams, *North from Mexico* (Westport, New York: Greenwood Press, 1968), p. 207.

[8]Stephen Birmingham, *California Rich* (New York: Simon and Schuster, 1980), p. 41.

[9]James D. Hart, *A Companion to California* (New York: Oxford, 1978), p. 80.

[10]McWilliams, *California: The Great Exception*, p. 176.

[11]Carey McWilliams, *Southern California* (Santa Barbara, Calif.: Peregrine Smith, 1973), p. 129.

[12]Ibid., p. 277

[13]Hart, p. 308.

[14]McWilliams, *Southern California*, p. 331.

[15]McWilliams, *California: The Great Exception*, p. 297.

[16]Carey McWilliams, *Factories in the Field* (Santa Barbara, Calif.: Peregrine Smith, 1971), p. 148,

[17]Hart, p. 5.

[18]Hal Rubin, "Who Owns California," *California Journal* Vol. XII, no. 6 (June 1981): 121.

[19]Ibid., p. 122.

[20]*Newsweek*, September 17, 1979, p. 33.

[21]*Time*, June 9, 1980, p. 57.

[22]Joel Garreau, *The Nine Nations of North America* (New York: Houghton Mifflin, 1981), p. 5.

[23]Tom De Vries, "Westword," *California*, November 1982, p. 180.

[24]*San Jose Mercury*, October 9, 1980.

[25]McWilliams, *California: The Great Exception*, p. 17.

[26]Gentry, p. 283.

2
CAMPAIGNS, POLITICAL PARTIES, AND ELECTIONS

Unconventional Politics at Work

In theory, political parties relate to politics as the sun connects to the solar system: both are the center of all activity. But, if the sun is predictable, parties are not. Political parties once satisfied all needs as organizers of candidate selection, campaign management, election finance, and voter turnout. Political reforms and the media age, however, have weakened party structures and allowed individuals to work from their own bases of power. As Robert Agranoff writes, "once powerful party organizations that mobilized a pre-existing bloc of voters behind a party ticket have given way to a new politics dominated by personal cliques, based on 'stars' of politics who employ new means to mobilize a more fluid electorate."[1] With partisan values at a minimum and individualism at a maximum, California is the home of explosive, frenetic, and unpredictable politics.

More than other Americans, Californians place party recommendations a distant second to personal choices. Party "labels" have an incredibly transparent quality. In place of political roots and well-established traditions, the state's voters are "influenced by a candidate's manner, style, and appearance rather than his message."[2] These attitudes have led to the development of campaign management firms that specialize in getting out political messages through public relations, direct mailing, slick newspaper and billboard ads, and expensive television commercials.

The battle for the 44th Assembly district seat in 1982 shows all the drama and idiosyncracies of California campaigns, parties, and elections. Although the district had a lopsided Democratic registration margin of 59 percent to 29 percent, party loyalties took a backseat to the personalities of Democratic candidate Tom Hayden and his Republican counterpart, Bill Hawkins. As the result of countless brochures, extensive door-to-door canvassing, and Hollywood celebrities, the Hayden-Hawkins campaign became the most publicized and expensive legislative race in California history.

The 44th Assembly District Election—
Referendum on Tom Hayden

When Tom Hayden announced his candidacy for the Democratic nomination in the 44th Assembly district, he became the single most important issue in the race. Hayden's past was that of a self-proclaimed left-wing radical. As a founder of the Students for a Democratic Society in the mid-1960s, Hayden led demonstrations against American involvement in Vietnam and, at one point, was arrested for disrupting the 1968 Democratic National Convention. Three years after he married antiwar activist and actress Jane Fonda in 1973, Hayden founded the Campaign for Economic Democracy, a broad-based liberal group that argued for redress of a number of economic disparities through political action. Although Hayden's new organizational network brought him closer to traditional means of political action, most veteran politicians and members of the press continued to view him as antiestablishment.

In 1976 a brazen young Hayden challenged incumbent United States Senator John Tunney in the Democratic primary. With little more than a radical reputation, he succeeded in capturing 37 percent of the vote, not enough to defeat Tunney (54 percent), but more than enough to split the always fragile ranks in the Democratic party. Tunney lost his seat in November 1976 to Republican S. I. Hayakawa and, although much of the blame was undeserved, Hayden was chastised by mainstream Democrats for making Tunney vulnerable. Six years later Hayden was determined to be part of that mainstream, but he had an uphill battle in making his point.

ROUND ONE: THE DEMOCRATIC PRIMARY

The 44th Assembly district seat became a free-for-all when Democratic incumbent Mel Levine decided to run for Congress. By late 1981, three Democrats—Alan Katz, an attorney; Steve Saltzman, a field deputy to Los Angeles Mayor Tom Bradley; and Hayden—announced their candidacies. Shortly into the primary race, Katz dropped out, leaving Saltzman and Hayden in a one-on-one contest. For the Republicans the primary represented an opportunity to get an early organizational jump on the fall campaign. Bill Hawkins, an insurance executive, had token opposition and widespread support among the party leadership. With little in doubt for the Republicans, most attention focused on the Hayden-Saltzman contest.

Tom Hayden was seeking elective office for only the second time. Yet his background was so colorful that he had almost 100 percent name identification among the district's voters.[3] Most of the time, high name recognition is a plus in an election, especially one with no incumbent.[4] But in Hayden's case, his name worked both for and against him. On the one hand, he had a base of support with his 12,000-member Campaign for Economic Democracy (CED), many members of whom were active in the 44th Assembly district. Because party organizations have no preprimary clout in California, Hayden had the benefit of rare, structural assistance. On the other hand, he encountered a great deal of distrust from prominent officials in his own party. As Assemblyman Mel Levine put it, "so many people don't like or trust him and they can't even articulate why."[5] The then neighboring Assemblyman Herschel Rosenthal was more direct in noting that "Hayden is not perceived well in the Legislature . . . Republicans just hate him, and Democrats fear he will embarrass them, first as a candidate and then as a legislator."[6] Like most candidates seeking an open seat, Hayden found precious little support from party leaders other than Governor Jerry Brown. He did encounter substantial resistance, however, so much so that an effort (largely unsuccessful) was made to weaken the liberal composition of the 44th district as part of the state's new reapportionment map.[7]

The Saltzman Strategy: Emphasizing the Virtues of Establishment Politics. Steve Saltzman's candidacy sharply contrasted with the Hayden effort. If Hayden's acceptability was related to his becoming connected with the establishment, Saltzman *was* the establishment. One newspaper account described him as a "textbook model of a liberal Westside Democratic candidate."[8] Attractive and athletic looking, the 32 year old Saltzman was a longtime district resident with nearly ideal vocational, political, and ethnic roots for his constituency. He taught at a Head Start school in Venice, started a summer camp for underprivileged children, worked as an aide to former Senator John Tunney prior to his association with Mayor Bradley, and was an active member in the Jewish community. In a district where 30 percent of the voters were Jewish, the latter connection was thought to be helpful if not an outright necessity.

Somehow Saltzman's attributes were not as important as his possibility for being an alternative to Hayden. He seized upon Hayden's radical past as a framework for Hayden's current political values. Said Saltzman, "I'm committed to the free enterprise system."[9] Saltzman's support came from the business community along with homeowners and landlords who opposed the strict Santa Monica rent-control initiative, which had been passed largely through the efforts of Hayden's CED in 1979. In all, he raised over $300,000, with much of it (over $125,000) coming from himself and his family. Yet money and establishment ties were not enough for Saltzman, for he could not compete with Hayden's larger campaign fund, excellent organization, and glittery Hollywood connection.

The Hayden Primary Strategy—Making New Politics Work.   Tom Hayden had a number of campaign assets that worked to offset his liabilities. Superior fund raising was one of them. Before the primary season ended, Hayden raised an unprecedented $500,000. Much of it came from his wife, actress Jane Fonda, who donated nearly $50,000 and loaned another $125,000 to the Hayden campaign. Hayden's Campaign for Economic Democracy was another important source of money, contributing $43,000 between October 1981 and March 1982.[10] Fonda and the CED proved helpful to Hayden throughout the primary and general election campaigns.

Campaign organization was a second factor that benefited Hayden. Although he took to the airwaves for the general election, Hayden and his campaign workers walked the district in a most thorough fashion. Hayden himself went door to door every day for 2 to 3 hours at a time. One account pointed to how Hayden's connections with the Hollywood community paid dividends in his primary nomination effort. The morning after the Academy Awards, where he was seen on television with Fonda, he was back to his door-to-door campaigning. "Hi, I'm Tom Hayden, and I'm running for the state legislature in your district," he told one constituent. "I know who you are," she laughed. "There you were on television last night, and here you are again."[11] Fonda herself was an integral part of the door-to-door work. In one typical incident she was quoted as saying to a constituent, "Hi, I'm Jane Fonda, and I'm walking the precinct for my husband, Tom Hayden. I'd like to give you something to read." When the constituent expressed near disbelief and awe that it was Fonda, she shot back, "Would I kid?"[12] Although Hayden and Fonda were the best-known individuals in the door-to-door effort, the campaign was known for sizable daily walking precinct activities from hundreds of volunteers.

The Hollywood connection was particularly helpful to the Hayden effort. With Jane Fonda as the nucleus, the Hayden campaign drew the money and endorsements of some of Hollywood's most recognizable personalities. Father-in-law Henry Fonda, a popular actor, joined the Hayden team early, along with singers Bonnie Raitt, Jackson Browne, and Linda Ronstadt. Yet this was only the beginning. After the primary the Hollywood connection became a crucial component of the Hayden campaign.

The Primary Results.   The Hayden forces had too many weapons for Steve Saltzman. At the primary's end Hayden outdistanced Saltzman by a 51 to 41 percent margin. However, because his victory was so narrow in a polarized campaign, Democrats feared and Republicans hoped that the Hayden controversy would cost him in the end.

ROUND TWO: THE FALL CAMPAIGN

With their party primary victories behind them, Tom Hayden and Bill Hawkins set out to battle for the 44th Assembly district seat. Both prepared for a campaign focusing on Hayden's personality rather than any substantive issues. Said Hawkins, "Tom Hayden's past and things he has authored are public record and open to debate. [The election represents] a campaign for the free enterprise system versus the Campaign for Economic Democracy." For his part Hayden said he expected to face "a vicious campaign of character assassination."[13] With these opening salvos, so began the most expensive legislative contest in California history.

Hawkins on the Attack. As a moderate Republican in a liberal district, Hawkins attempted to position himself in the center, while branding Hayden as an unacceptable radical alternative. One Hawkins campaign billboard quoted Hayden as saying, "Give prison inmates the right to unionize."[14] Another ad quoted Hayden as saying, "I believe that violence should never be ruled out of change."[15] Both quotes were out of context as well as more than a dozen years old, but Hawkins used them anyway.

A key aspect of the Hawkins campaign centered on Hayden's anti-Vietnam record. Recalling that Hayden traveled to North Vietnam in 1967 against the wishes of the State Department, Hawkins referred to a number of former POWs who attacked Hayden's actions as harmful to the United States efforts in Vietnam.[16] Lost in the shuffle was the simple fact that the California legislature does not make "foreign policy," at least not in any official sense. Then again Hawkins's point was that Hayden's Vietnam activity was as much an indication of bad (and, perhaps, immoral) judgment as anything else.

The Hawkins candidacy was a rallying point for Republicans throughout the state. So helpful were his contributors that by the campaign's end, Hawkins raised over $800,000, eclipsing the previous record for a California state legislative race. (Only Hayden would surpass this amount.) Although some of his larger donations came from the California Republican party ($15,000) and the Assembly Republican Action Committee ($25,000), the most important sources of support had "Kitchen Cabinet" connections with the Reagan White House. Among these were Henry Salvatori ($6,000), Justin Dart's Dart and Kraft, Incorporated ($5,000), Welton Becket Group ($4,000), Fluor Corporation ($2,000), and Holmes Tuttle Ford ($2,000). In addition to the Reagan allies, other support came from Los Angeles County Republican Supervisor Deane Dana ($25,000) and Friends of Los Angeles County Republican Supervisor Mike Antonovich ($10,000). Traditional Republican contributors such as

United for California, a coalition of major corporations ($35,000), California Real Estate Association ($5,000), and the California Apartment Association ($10,000) played major financial roles in the Hawkins campaign.[17]

Hayden on the Attack.   Tom Hayden knew that his image posed a serious threat to electoral success. Aware that he couldn't change the past, Hayden set out to convince the voters that *he* had changed. To accomplish such a goal required issue development, money, skill, and luck—all of which jelled in the closing days of the fall campaign.

His first objective was to convince the voters that Hayden was neither a radical nor a single-issue (peace) candidate. Known as an advocate of alternative energy, tenants' rights, full employment, and environmentalism, Hayden attempted to create a respectable distance between himself and his adversary. If Hawkins sought to present Hayden as part of the "Fonda–Hayden" team, Hayden attempted to label Hawkins as an apologist for fellow Republican Ronald Reagan. Referring to the Hawkins-Reagan connection, Hayden said, "I intend to hold [Hawkins] responsible for unemployment, high interest rates, business bankruptcy, environmental contamination, the exploitation of the Santa Monica mountains, oil drilling in Santa Monica Bay, and not allow him to merely get off with the claim that he is not 'Fonda Hayden.'"[18] That Hawkins had no direct association with the president was not important. Putting Hawkins on the defensive, however, may have neutralized some of the negative portraits of Hayden and allowed the campaign to center on substantive issue differences.

As with any election, money raising became imperative to the Hayden campaign. The candidate was all too aware that a number of strategies would be necessary to convince the voters of his credibility. Most of these strategies, aside from door-to-door canvassing, cost money—lots of it. Before he was through, Hayden raised more than $1,300,000 for his fall campaign, making his total the largest amount ever generated in a state legislative race. Jane Fonda provided nearly half of the money ($615,000) by giving contributions of more than $200,000 and loans for another $400,000. Much of the remaining fund raising came via the Hollywood connection. Steve Binder, an independent television producer, gave $50,000 for cable television rights to a Fonda fashion show. Contributors included musician Herb Alpert; actors Ed Asner ("Lou Grant"), Mike Farrell ("MASH"), George Takei ("Star Trek"), John Ritter ("Three's Company"), and Jon Voight; actresses Margot Kidder (*Superman*), Pam Dawber ("Mork and Mindy"), and Valerie Harper ("Rhoda"); and poet Rod McKuen. Hayden also received money from traditional groups like the

California AFL-CIO and the California State Employees Association.[19] Still it was the entertainment community that gave the campaign a kind of glamorous visibility. These people were important not only for their own money but for their ability to attract contributors at various events.

Use of the mass media and accurate target mailings became well-known traits of the Hayden campaign. Mass media is an expensive proposition in Los Angeles when a local election advertisement is beamed to a potential audience of 11,700,000 people. Given an assembly district of less than 275,000, the Hayden strategists decided to advertise extensively through radio and television, even though their "target" was less than 3 percent of the total audience! In the final 2 weeks alone, the Hayden campaign spent $250,000 on television and nearly $40,000 on radio spots—more than is usually spent for all costs in an assembly candidate's entire campaign. One typical ad packaged Hayden, Fonda, and their son as a "typical" Santa Monica family. Before the ad ended, Hayden said "I am not the same angry young man I was in the 1960s. I've changed."[20] These and other ideas were components in Hayden's adept use of "target mail," in which specific messages are sent to particular audiences. In the words of one account, "women received a post card showing women's leaders endorsing him. Mailers from renter's rights leaders tell tenants they can trust Hayden. Senior citizens are told his opponent wants to cut social security benefits."[21] In the final days of the campaign the sophisticated Hayden organization complemented the mass media blitz with more than twenty specialized mailers.

Although a campaign should never rely on luck as a basis for victory, it doesn't hurt. The Hayden candidacy received a dose of luck from, of all places, the Hawkins camp. When his Republican opponent purchased the controversial billboard messages, Hayden expressed indignation over their misrepresentation of his views. Such counterarguments are common in political campaigns. But Hayden's rebuttal gained respect when Richard Buck, runner-up to Hawkins in the Republican primary, withdrew his support from Hawkins because of the messages. An even more significant defection occurred in late September when Hawkins' research director, Darrell Whitman, resigned from the campaign on the basis that Hawkins was intentionally smearing Hayden with the billboard ads. These negative remarks helped to place a cloud over Hawkins's integrity and Hayden was the prime beneficiary.

Counting the Votes.   Tom Hayden was the beneficiary of a lot more than luck by the election's end. His superior fund-raising skills, Hollywood connection, mass media work, and mastery of target mailing gave him an arsenal of weapons for fighting his opponent. As the campaign progressed, Hayden convinced enough voters that his politics were not so outrageous, that he had matured, and that his opponent was no bargain.

In the final analysis Hayden did what any Democrat in the Democrat-laden 44th Assembly district should have done: he won by a margin of 53 to 44 percent. But then again Hayden was not *any* Democrat; rather, he was the once fiercely antiestablishment maverick who had come full circle to hook up with the establishment. Because of an initial handicap related to a negative image and the resources used to overcome that handicap, Hayden's success was not the typical victory. In many ways his campaign was almost a caricature— certainly an exaggeration—of the methods and tactics that make California political campaigns unique.

Party Organizations—What They Are, What They Are Not

Myth and reality come face to face when we attempt to make sense of the connection between political parties and California politics. One well-known traditional account of California holds that "through the recruitment of candidates, their advocacy of policies and political campaigning, parties organize political competition for the citizen."[22] Colorful? Yes. Accurate? No. Our account of the 44th Assembly district race typifies the role parties play in election campaigns. To describe their function as "minimal" overstates the case.

The fact is that California has a political party system on paper, and that's about it. Any success obtained by the candidate is due not to the party, but to the candidate, his or her supporters, and perhaps a key legislator or two. As for policies and competition, about the only place they appear is in the legislature, a body that has become far more partisan and politically organized than the public-at-large. Nevertheless, party organizations do exist, even if in a condition that makes them marginally valuable at best. What we need to know is how political parties work and why they have a peripheral role in California.

THE "TEXTBOOK" ACCOUNT

If voter sentiment is any indication, California is a two-party state dominated by Democrats and Republicans. Every single statewide and legislative office-holder belongs to one of these two parties. Despite a lack of electoral success, other parties also have candidates on the ballot. In the 1982 election, for example, the American Independent, Peace and Freedom, and Libertarian parties had candidates running for statewide and, in some cases, legislative offices. The gubernatorial election results typify the vote-getting abilities of the major and minor parties. Republican George Deukmejian and Democrat Tom Bradley shared 97 percent of the vote, while the minor party candidates each collected about 1 percent.

The California State Elections Code stipulates three ways in which a political group can become a political party on the ballot: (1) if in the previous gubernatorial election at least one of its candidates for statewide office received 2 percent of the votes cast; (2) if enrolled party membership equals 1 percent of the state vote in the previous gubernatorial election; or (3) if the group obtains signatures or petitions that amount to 10 percent of the preceding state vote. Although many political parties have come and gone, the Democrats and Republicans have each secured the minimum vote for more than 100 years. In the 1982 elections the three minor parties also managed to capture 2 percent of the vote in at least one of the statewide contests, thereby making it unnecessary to requalify through registration or petition in 1986.

The Voters—Where They Stand.   California voters identify with the major political parties in much the same ways as voters in other states. In any given year about 90 percent choose between the Democratic and Republican parties. Once an individual registers as a member of a political party, registration remains permanent until either the individual fails to vote in a major (primary or general) election or the registrant decides to switch affiliations by re-registering in a different capacity. Being a "member" of a political party means little more than participation in the party primary. When the general elections occur, individuals may vote how they wish regardless of their registration.

Prior to the Great Depression Californians were overwhelmingly partial to the Republicans. These sentiments changed during the 1930s when the state went through the same political realignment that happened throughout the nation. From that point until the present Democrats have maintained sizable registration advantages. Table 2-1 shows the consistent pattern of Democratic registration success. Registration, however, does not necessarily translate into victory at the polls.

Despite their success with registration, the Democrats did not capture control of both houses in the state legislature until 1958; moreover, they yielded that control to the Republicans in the late 1960s despite continued registration advantages. In the twelve gubernatorial elections between 1938 and 1982, Republicans won the top spot seven times including 1982 when, despite a 53 to 35 percent disadvantage, George Deukmejian won a narrow victory over Tom Bradley. Although the party machines may be able to churn out the votes in well-organized states like New York, Pennsylvania, or Illinois, the machines just don't work in California.

TABLE 2-1   Party Registration During Gubernatorial Election Years,
1930-1982

Year	Democrat (%)	Republican (%)	Minor parties (%)	Decline to state (%)
1930	20.3	73.3	1.1	5.6
1934	49.5	45.5	1.0	3.9
1938	59.4	35.8	1.6	3.2
1942	60.2	35.9	0.6	3.4
1946	58.0	37.3	0.3	4.4
1950	58.4	37.1	0.6	4.0
1954	55.5	41.0	0.5	3.0
1958	57.4	39.6	0.5	2.5
1962	56.9	39.8	0.1	3.0
1966	56.6	40.2	0.5	2.7
1970	54.9	39.8	1.4	3.9
1974	56.6	36.0	1.1	6.8
1978	56.6	34.2	1.4	7.8
1982	53.2	34.9	2.5	9.4

Internal Organization.   The Elections Code provides detailed rules for the party organizations. These rules periodically are changed in the state legislature, where Democrats and Republicans usually defer to each other for the operation of their respective parties. For the most part the parties function under similar guidelines, although the Democrats elect more members to the State Central Committee than the Republicans, who place greater reliance on appointments.

The state central committee is the highest level of party organization. The Democratic and Republican State Central Committees each have about a thousand members. These include all county chairpersons, statewide and legislative incumbents, statewide and legislative nominees, and, in the case of the Democrats, elected members from each assembly district. The main responsibility of the State Central Committee is to elect the state chairperson, who must rotate between the north and south portions of the state every 2 years. Although chairpersons have the vague function of "conducting party campaigns," they have no means (other than charm!) to carry out their task.

Each of the fifty-eight counties has a central committee serving as the party organization at the local level. These seats are filled through elections that are incorporated into the primaries every 2 years. Small counties elect committee members on an at-large basis, while the more populated counties divide elections into assembly districts.

Two interesting facts come to mind about the state and local central committee organizations. First, there is little linkage between the two units, thus reinforcing fragmentation in the party system. The exceptions exist with county committee chairpersons who, because of their position, are automatically placed on the state committee. Also legislative and statewide incumbents and nominees are entitled to membership on both committees, usually making this group the largest block serving both levels. For this reason, state committees often have been criticized as extensions of elected officials.

Second, the Elections Code provides that the County Central Committees manage the affairs of the political party under the direction of the State Central Committee. This responsibility looks great on paper, but in actuality, there is nothing for the state or county organizations to do. With little money for year-round staffs, preprimary endorsements forbidden, and fund raising splintered among the various candidates, party organizations do little more than rationalize the campaign efforts of individuals.

UNOFFICIAL PARTY GROUPS

When the Progressives dominated California politics early in the twentieth century, they restructured state election methods so that the voters no longer would be in the hands of corrupt party organizations. In their place the Progressives emphasized the best-qualified individuals for office, irrespective of any party affiliation. They introduced cross-filing so that candidates could run for and capture the primary nominations of more than one party; they forbade party organizations from endorsing candidates prior to the primaries; and they weakened party conventions while placing virtually all nominating responsibilities in the hands of the voters. The official party organizations were nearly devastated, as new unpredictable power relationships flooded the state. In effect, the Progressive reformers "created a power vacuum that has never been filled adequately. The parties, with their ineffective organization, limited funding, and legal restrictions have been unable to perform the necessary functions of candidate recruitment and support."[23]

Because parties were no longer effective, candidates for office had difficulty winning elections without the support of large groups or monied interests. As a result of these relationships, those who won often were beholden to the narrow interests who put them in office. These conditions did not sit well with those who viewed political parties as desirable sources of candidate recruitment, support, and election.

In the mid-1930s frustrated Californians focused on a new kind of partisan collaboration, unofficial party organizations, as a way to restore the accountability of office seekers and officeholders to a broad political constituency. Although dozens of such organizations have come and gone since that time, three stand out for their unique contributions to California politics: the California

Republican Assembly (CRA), the California Democratic Council (CDC), and the Campaign for Economic Democracy (CED).

California Republican Assembly.   The CRA is important as the first unofficial party organization in California. The group was created in 1934 in response to Democrat Franklin Delano Roosevelt's 1932 presidential victory and the new Democratic majority elected to the state Assembly. As an unofficial group not bound by the legal prohibition on endorsements, the new organization endorsed and supported candidates early in the election campaign, "using its political muscle to head off the entry of other candidates into the party's primaries."[24] Such unity allowed Republicans to keep control of their own party nominations and get a leg up on the divided Democrats. The CRA had about 20,000 members in its prime (late 1940s and 1950s), a substantial number of activists, considering the skeletonlike nature of the official Republican party. It lost much of its punch during the 1960s, when other Republican groups, notably the United Republicans of California and California Republican League, were formed. Nevertheless, it remains important as the prototype of unofficial party groups in California.

California Democratic Council.   Although they held healthy voter registration advantages beginning in the 1930s, Democrats were not able to convert that support into electoral victories. Ravaged by cross-filing, party leaders and activists formed the CDC in 1953. Like the CRA, the CDC specialized in preprimary endorsements, although it soon added "year-round activities, including panels, forums, and social events."[25] The latter functions were designed to keep members involved between elections as well as during them. By the early 1960s the CDC had about 80,000 members in 200 local clubs throughout the state. No other unofficial party organization has ever reached this level of popularity. It was tremendously successful in electing Democrats to office. But the very success of the CDC also contributed to its demise. Elected Democrats, no longer in need of the CDC endorsement, began to attack the body for its increasingly liberal views. Incumbents also resented the necessity of asking for the CDC endorsement. By the mid-1960s the love affair between Democratic leaders and the CDC was over, and CDC membership dwindled. Today it has less than 10,000 members.

Campaign for Economic Democracy.   Shortly after Tom Hayden's bid for the 1976 Democratic nomination to the United States Senate, he established the Campaign for Economic Democracy. Early support came from Fonda, Democratic Congressman Ron Dellums, and United Farm Workers President

Cesar Chavez. In 1977 the foursome sent off a letter to former Hayden supporters, asking them "to change the face of power in California over the next decade."[26] At first the new organization shied away from party politics; electoral success came with city council victories in Bakersfield, Chico, Berkeley, and Santa Monica. By 1978, however, the CED restricted its support to a select few Democrats in the party primaries.

CED has had one advantage not commonly found inside or outside of party organizations: money. When Fonda formed a series of health salons known as "Workout" in 1979, she channeled all the profits to CED. Profits from *Jane Fonda's Workout Book* were sent in the same direction. About $300,000 in profits went to the CED in 1982 for operating expenses.[27] Membership dues ($15 per person) and fund-raising concerts via the Hollywood connection (Jackson Browne, Bonnie Raitt, the Grateful Dead, and the Doobie Brothers) have boosted coffers as well. Between January 1981 and March 1982, CED made political contributions of more than $50,000, most of which went to Hayden's efforts in the 44th Assembly district. With 12,000 members and plenty of funding, the organization has become a potent force in state politics.

Unofficial Party Organizations—More Than Fluff.   One political scientist recently wrote that unofficial party groups "still provide forums for candidates running for office . . . but their impact on the nomination process is virtually gone."[28] Such words are reminiscent of Mark Twain's suggestion that reports regarding his death were greatly exaggerated. Unofficial party organizations do not have the statewide clout enjoyed by the CRA and the CDC in their respective heydays, but they do have selective successes. The Hayden-CED victory in 1982 clearly shows that these groups can provide many of the tangible resources commonly found in states with well-developed political parties: namely, money, talent, and campaign workers.

Campaigning in the 1980s

The absence of strong parties has made it easy for a new type of campaign format to dominate California politics. Whistle-stop tours, precinct walking, and individually addressed campaign literature—all traditional election tools— have given way to a new generation of strategies. These tactics include political rock concerts, professional campaign firms, and computer-organized target mailers. Such changes have led at least one observer to describe the modern campaign as a politics of fleeting images rather than substance: "It is a politics of every candidate for himself, each with an individual campaign organization loyal only to the candidate and disbanded after the election. . . . It is a politics with no core, no sense of collective effort."[29] If these campaign characteristics are breaking ground in other states, they are well-established techniques in contemporary California politics.

CANDIDATE-CENTERED CAMPAIGNS

When the direct primary was introduced to California politics at the turn of the century, it also directed the center of campaign activity away from the party leaderships and into the hands of the respective candidates. The past three quarters of a century solidifed the individualistic nature of campaigns. Modern state party organizations in California have precious little staff assistance and few financial resources for distribution to candidates. Things are not much different at the local level, although the Republicans have year-round paid staff members in less than a dozen of the state's fifty-eight counties. Given the lack of party assistance, virtually all of the fund raising, organization, and issues research fall on the shoulders of the individual candidates.

Candidate-centered campaigns are expensive affairs. Because political parties have no way of preventing any number of candidates from entering a contest, primary elections can be every bit as costly as the general election contest. In other words, the successful primary candidate has the unenviable chore of gearing up for two expensive elections within a 6 month period. Thus, Tom Hayden spent $1.3 million to defeat Republican Bill Hawkins after he had spent $500,000 to defeat primary opponent Steve Saltzman. Of course, in Hayden's case, he had access to both money and organization. Other candidates are not equally fortunate.

High campaign costs have forced candidates to rely less on small donors and more on uncomfortable alliances with special interest groups. Former Fair Political Practices Commission chairman Daniel Lowenstein writes that such arrangements may cost more than money: "The willingness of ordinary citizens to contribute money has not kept up with the candidates' need. Accordingly, contributions from special interest groups are escalating rapidly."[30] The combination of candidate-centered campaigns and their high costs has decreased the candidates' attention on partisan questions and increased concern for the values of the special interests who support him or her.

CAMPAIGN MANAGEMENT FIRMS

Few individuals have the necessary expertise to run their own election campaigns. In the absence of party organizations many candidates turn to management firms for guidance and direction. The wise candidate makes such a

choice only after careful thought. "Next to choosing a marriage partner," the
National Journal writes, "the most critical decision for a contemporary politician may be the selection of a professional campaign consultant."[31]

Campaign management firms have a 50 year history in California politics.
Their necessity was dictated by the impotence of party organizations particularly during the primaries, by nonpartisan local elections, and by the large number of ballot propositions that are regularly placed before the state's voters. Early
campaign management firms, the creation of newspaper and advertising company experts, centered their efforts on brochures and clever ads. But their
modern counterparts play an even larger role in the political process. These
massive storehouses of expertise include services in "organization, polling,
advertising, direct mail operations, issue research and analysis, telephone solic-
itation and volunteer recruitment."[32] What once seemed to be a simple
democratic exercise—a candidate's search for voter support—has become a
complicated, scientific operation.

In the 1982 elections every serious candidate for statewide office, as well as a
sizable number in legislative races, employed the services of a campaign management firm. In many cases the candidates gave these organizations virtual
carte blanche authority for managing the campaign. For their part the management experts demanded full responsibility for their clients' affairs. As David
Garth, political architect of Tom Bradley's gubernatorial campaign, put it,
election strategy "can't be separate from the fundraising or the press or the paid
media. We make sure all the press statements have the same tone as the
commercials and that everyone in every corner of the campaign is talking the
same language, the same themes."[33]

Campaign management firms are modern-day equivalents to party machines
with two exceptions: many are nonpartisan "guns for hire" in that they work for
whoever employs them; also, they avail their services to individual candidates
rather than broad party slates. Other than these differences, campaign firms
have assumed a surrogate party leadership role for political candidacies. Nevertheless, these organizations remain concerned more with their own marketing
success than the virtues of a candidate.

COMPUTERS AND TARGET MAILING

The computer age has revolutionized virtually every facet of American society, including contemporary election campaigns. On the surface, computers
represent a breakthrough for politics, because of their ability to digest and dissect
voter registration lists in a fraction of the time it would take dozens of campaign

workers to do the same thing. Computers are models of efficiency; they can be programmed to search out long lists for select groups in certain parts of a legislative district. They are the weapons for candidates and their managers to "target" mail to constituents with unique voter traits.

Mailers have been part of California politics for 50 years; the state's dispersed population almost demands them. During the 1940s and 1950s the CRA and CDC routinely flooded their respective partisans with mailers prior to the primary and general election contests. Unsophisticated by modern standards, these efforts usually consisted of sending the same message to all voters. In the 1960s computer experts began to apply new advances in the industry to political campaigns. By tailoring the right kind of mailer for the right constituents, programmers could personalize the campaign to the needs of different voters.

Today computer specialists are critical ingredients for the management firm's overall campaign strategy. They are used to identify various populations within an election district in terms of their special characteristics that might relate to pressing campaign issues. For example, to isolate a bloc of gay voters, a computer specialist "will search a gay neighborhood's voting rolls, identify households where two or more unrelated men live together, then assume they're gay."[34] Similar success can be found with liberals or conservatives, students and/or veterans, homeowners or renters, males or females, and ethnic minorities. Although the computer selections are not always correct, they are right enough of the time that the few mistakes they make are more than offset by the large numbers of voters successfully reached.

Isolating a voter group is one thing; doing something with the information is another. Here is where computers and campaign management strategists make a potent political combination. Once the data are produced, "it then takes a shrewd campaign manager to target the 'pitch' right into the voter's strike zone"[35] so renters will receive a message on why candidate X looks out for them. Meanwhile, homeowners will get a mailer stating why the same candidate is on their side.

Target mailers were used repeatedly throughout the 1982 election campaigns. In the closing days of the governor's race, Tom Bradley made a strong pitch for the women's vote by sending a letter to a half million Californians who used *Ms.* next to their names when they registered to vote. The simple message was "that Bradley was committed to women's issues and his Republican opponent, Attorney General George Deukmejian, was not."[36]

Computer-assisted target mailers and campaign management strategists have one thing in common: they tend to surface before an election season and disappear when the election is over. But at least one target-mail organization,

Computer Caging Corporation, has developed a set of connections unique even to California politics. Owned by conservative Republican state Senator H. L. Richardson, this enterprise operates on a year-round basis. Richardson has used his computer business to accomplish several goals simultaneously. Aside from the traditional mail-campaign services available to issues and candidates with a decidedly conservative bent, the company regularly recruits members and donations for Richardson's favorite causes: Gun Owners of America, Law and Order Campaign Committee, and the Free Market Political Action Committee. With millions of dollars flowing in annually, the state senator "targets his organization's funds and political expertise on contested races in marginal districts."[37] Current Republican legislators Ed Davis, Ollie Speraw, and John Doolittle (all in the Senate) along with William Baker, John Lewis, and Nolan Frizell (all in the Assembly) have benefited from Richardson's golden hand. In addition, Computer Caging Corporation has been in the conservative forefront of such issues as gun control, reapportionment, and the state's supreme court appointees. It is the only direct-mail organization to have direct ties with a member of the legislature.

MASS MEDIA

The candidate's time is at a premium during an election campaign. Given California's size and population, it is impossible for candidates seeking major offices to reach millions of voters personally. Similar difficulties occur in congressional districts (which average approximately 550,000 voters) and assembly districts (approximately 275,000). Moreover, it is impossible for the candidate to rely on the party to provide workers for door-to-door activities. Parties are forbidden from any activity in the primaries and have few resources for general election assistance. How, then, does the candidate get to the voters? The most economical way is through the media.

Use of the mass media, particularly television, gives the candidate instant access to the voters that he or she would never have otherwise. Political scientist William Crotty writes that television is so important to our lives that "it has supplanted the political party as the main conduit between candidate and voter."[38] In California, television has not supplanted the party as much as it has filled the void created long ago by the Progressive reforms. Thus, candidates will do anything, including television, to get their messages to the people. But it's not cheap. In the last week of the 1982 general election campaign, gubernatorial candidate Bradley spent nearly $600,000 on television and radio commercials.

Mass media ads represent the most ambitious effort in candidate packaging for popular consumption. "For 30 seconds in television and radio, the candidates can say what they want, unchallenged, to millions of viewers or listeners. . . . They can look their very best, never showing a blemish or a stumble. After all, there's always Take 2. Or 3. Or however many takes for the candidate to say it right."[39] Thirty seconds give the candidates just enough time to drop the appropriate buzzwords and catchy phrases into the voters' laps before "The Love Boat" returns to its cruise or "Dallas" continues with the Ewing brothers' struggle. Thus, the Bradley commercials focused on such topics as coastline protection, his crime-fighting record as a policeman, and the 200,000 jobs he brought to Los Angeles as mayor. The Deukmejian commercials concentrated on his former state senatorial record on anticrime legislation, senior citizen property tax relief, and the need to reverse liberal court decisions. In many cases the messages were distortions of reality. Bradley didn't bring 200,000 jobs to Los Angeles any more than Deukmejian could change court decisions. Then again, accuracy was not a particularly important criterion in these or any other ads. Moreover, usually opponents could do little more than threaten to sue, a response most voters have come to expect as part of the "dirty business" of politics.

Some of the best-packaged commercials were used in Tom Hayden's run for the assembly. With a record of left-wing activism during the sixties and seventies, Hayden sought to convince voters that *he* was now the victim of irresponsible attacks. One of his commercials showed Hayden and his 9 year old son walking the 44th Assembly district in the thick of right-wing demonstrators. Among other epithets, the demonstrators screamed to the child, "Your mother's [Jane Fonda] scum." Hayden's son then turned to his father and asked, "Dad, why is everyone so mean?" Hayden then looked at his son compassionately and said, "Not everybody is like that." He then turned to the camera and concluded, "I still care about people."[40] The commercial was designed to show the voters that Hayden was the caring family man who wanted to overcome the evil carried out by rowdies. Although its message was unique to Hayden's image problem, the commercial typified the "spontaneous dramas" that unfolded before television audiences again and again.

CAMPAIGNING IN CALIFORNIA: OUT OF STEP OR A STEP AHEAD?

Recently, an experienced professional campaign manager and media consultant suggested that three prerequisites are necessary to ensure election victories: "No. 1 is television, No. 2 is television, No. 3 is television."[41]

Campaigning techniques have changed with the evolution of society. In California, however, the changes have been more extreme than other places. The absence of strong, formal party organizations has left an environment ripe for selling candidates in the most expeditious, economical way possible. To this extent, television has come to the rescue, providing a sure way to get a candidate controlled exposure to a lot of people in a short time.

Television, however, is only part of the contemporary campaign style in California. Without talented management firms to market the candidate, television would be useless. Even then, the experts can commit costly mistakes—mistakes seen by millions. One such error in judgment may have helped Governor Jerry Brown lose his bid to win the United States Senate election over San Diego Mayor Pete Wilson. The spot began with famous Hollywood celebrities expressing their desire for peace, then showed a nuclear bomb explosion and mushroom cloud, and then cut away to a small child who declared, "I want to go on living." The commercial ended with an announcer saying, "Pete Wilson opposes the nuclear arms freeze. Jerry Brown supports it. Vote for your life. Elect Jerry Brown to the U.S. Senate."[42] The ad was so unpopular that the Brown campaign was forced to pull it off the air.

Computer-organized target mailers are yet another ingredient in modern elections. By flooding voters with messages tailored to their particular values, these campaign devices have tried to reconnect once lost bonds between the candidates and the electorate. They are significant tools not for merely getting out the vote, but for encouraging the "right" elements to vote.

Candidates, Campaigns, and Constituents— Understanding the Relationship

Running for office has become big business in California. The days of candidates stumping the district with one-to-one conversation and handshakes are now almost as rare as an old-fashioned campaign rally in the local park. Both continue to exist, but as exceptions rather than the rule. In some ways the Hayden Assembly campaign harkened to these traditions hand in hand with its sophisticated management and media blitz. Perhaps an even better example is Dan McCorquodale's Senatorial campaign, in which, as a candidate in the reapportioned twelfth district, he personally visited 75,000 homes en route to unseating incumbent Dan O'Keefe. Even these successes, however, were benefited not by party work but rather the efforts of particular candidates and their personal organizations.

Political parties continue to have a place in California, although the extent of their value is open to debate. They are still the principal vehicles for organizing political ideas. They are still important sources of division in the legislature. Lastly, parties remain valuable as the basic means by which voters select officeholders on election day, especially when they have no other way of assessing the candidates. All these factors point to political parties as viable entities in California politics. Then again, their utility may offer more of a symbolic than concrete benefit in campaigns.

The fact is that parties are not very good at helping candidates in running campaigns. Instead, those seeking office must rely on personal followings, special interest groups, and, increasingly, established legislators for organizational and financial support. Such sources of assistance leave candidates with unusual sets of IOUs should they be lucky enough to win. Although ostensibly accountable to their districts and voters, they also may be beholden to groups and organizations far removed from both.

More than ever, political campaigns are candidate-centered activities in California. The free-for-all environment existing in the primaries extends to the general election. The candidate is responsible for securing campaign assistance, management, and disbursement of information. If you multiply this phenomenon by 80 Assembly, 20 State Senate, and 45 congressional contests and the statewide contests that take place every 4 years, you'll realize that the state becomes witness to more than 150 campaigns, many of which overlap into neighboring districts. Remember, when Tom Hayden used television to promote his candidacy, his message was transmitted to 11,425,000 people *outside* his district. Similar events occurred with regularity in congressional races, along with the expected statewide campaigning for executive branch offices.

Use of campaign management firms and computer-organized target mail is also organized on an individual basis. Several candidates in the same general area and from the same political party (for example, governor, state senator, and assembly member) may share a number of views, but each will target mail through his or her own campaign management firm. It keeps a lot of experts in business, but it also leaves the voters nearly paralyzed with assorted literature, media messages, and door knocking.

All of the preceding points to a major contradiction in California politics. Although the process for seeking office is more open than ever, the costs of getting there may now be so great that only a few can afford to make the attempt. To the extent that this is true, California may be paying a high price for the state's approach to parties, elections, and campaigns.

Notes

[1] Robert Agranoff, *The New Style of Election Campaigns* (Boston: Holbrook Press, 1976), p. 10.

[2] John R. Owens, Edmund Costantini, and Louis F. Weschler, *California Politics and Parties* (New York: Macmillan, 1970), p. 144.

[3] "At 41, Tom Hayden and His Politics Are Coming of Age," *San Francisco Chronicle*, April 4, 1982.

[4] In their rather exhaustive study of the legislative process, Malcolm E. Jewell and Samuel Patterson write that in legislative races, "the level of information about candidates is relatively low, and in many cases is nothing more than name identification." See *The Legislative Process in the United States*, 3rd ed. (New York: Random House, 1977), p. 96.

[5] Michelle Willens, "The Democrats' Dilemma: How to Stop Hating Tom Hayden," *California Journal* 13, no. 1 (January 1982): 15.

[6] Ibid., p. 14.

[7] "Hayden Sends Shudders Through Democratic Ranks," *Los Angeles Times*, February 11, 1982.

[8] "Radical Image Follows Candidate Hayden," *Los Angeles Times*, April 26, 1982.

[9] Ibid.

[10] Ibid.

[11] "At 41, Tom Hayden."

[12] "Fonda Takes Her Act on the Road to Aid Hayden's Drive," *Los Angeles Times*, May 3, 1982.

[13] "Hayden Appears Headed For Even Rougher Fight," *Los Angeles Times*, June 10, 1982.

[14] "Hayden Unleashes Costly TV, Radio Blitz," *Los Angeles Times*, October 25, 1982.

[15] "Hayden's Radical Past Gets Spotlight in Assembly Race," *San Francisco Chronicle*, October 23, 1982.

[16] "Hayden-Hawkins Race Draws POWs," *Los Angeles Times*, October 29, 1982.

[17] "Spending in Hayden Race Tops $1 Million," *Los Angeles Times*, October 1, 1982 and "Hayden-Hawkins Funds Set Record," *Los Angeles Times*, November 2, 1982.

[18] "Hayden Appears Headed."

[19] "Hayden-Hawkins Funds" and "Spending in Hayden Race."

[20] "'New' Hayden's TV Campaign," *San Francisco Chronicle*, October 12, 1982.

[21] "Hayden Unleashes."

[22] Eugene C. Lee and Willis D. Hawley, *The Challenge of California* (Boston: Little, Brown, 1970), p. 11.

[23] Ruth A. Ross, *California's Political Process* (New York: Random House, 1973), p. 67.

[24] Ibid., p. 201.

[25] Ibid., p. 69.

[26] Quoted from Tom Bourne, "The Prop. 13 Boost to the Hayden-Fonda Team," *California Journal* 10, no. 8 (August 1979): 269.

[27] "Fonda Plan to Extend Workout, Share Profits," *Los Angeles Times*, January 26, 1983.

[28]Charles G. Bell, *California Government Today* (Homewood, Ill.: Dorsey Press, 1980), p. 144.

[29]William J. Crotty, *The Party Symbol* (San Francisco: W.H. Freeman, 1980), p. 13.

[30]Daniel Lowenstein, "Money Talks in Politics, and We Must Cut Its Jabbering," *Los Angeles Times*, November 9, 1982.

[31]"Are You Planning To Run For Office? Then A Political Consultant Is A Must," *National Journal*, January 16, 1982, p. 101.

[32]Ibid.

[33]Michelle Willens, "The Real '82 Opponents: Garth, Haglund and Rietz," *California Journal* 12, no. 12 (December 1981): 413.

[34]Jeff Gillenkirk, "Target Practice: Their Aim Is True," *New West*, January 14, 1980, p. 65.

[35]Ibid.

[36]"Bradley 'Ms.' Mailing seeks Female Vote," *Los Angeles Times*, October 26, 1982.

[37]Lillianne Chase, "A Guided Tour of The Seven H. L. Richardson Enterprises," *California Journal* 13, no. 8 (August 1982): 272.

[38]William J. Crotty, *American Parties in Decline* (Boston: Little, Brown, 1980), p. 67.

[39]Michelle Willens, "The Advertising Arms Race," *California Journal* 9, no. 10 (October 1979): 316.

[40]"Hayden's Radical Past."

[41]Quoted in Mary Ellen Leary, *Phantom Politics* (Washington, D.C.: Public Affairs Press, 1977), p. 20.

[42]"Brown Pulls A-Bomb TV Commercial Off Air," *Los Angeles Times*, October 6, 1982.

3
INTEREST GROUPS
AND LOBBYISTS

Will the Real Power Brokers
Please Stand Up?

From the anti-Chinese Coolie Association of the 1850s to the United Farm Workers in the 1980s, individuals with shared values have established California interest groups. Throughout the state's history thousands of such organizations representing commerce, labor, agriculture, and individuals have made claims on the state's political machinery.

Interest groups have long enjoyed a special role in California politics. Their high visibility and hyperactivism make them virtual partners in the state's legislative operation. One political scientist has written that interest groups "supplement and reinforce governmental policy relationships."[1] Such a contention would suggest that groups play a secondary role in the governmental process. But in California, groups are so powerful that, in some ways, they appear to be "the tail wagging the dog." Perhaps this is why one study refers to group activity in California as a classic example of "the triumph of many interests."[2]

Today's interest groups spend a sizable proportion of their resources attempting to influence state politics, particularly in Sacramento where so many important political decisions are made. The battle between the Teamsters and the California Highway Patrol (CHP) over whether the latter should be allowed to use radar illustrates the open legislative environment in which interest groups assert their needs. Indeed, to fully understand California's policymaking machinery, one must come to terms with the relationship between interest groups and the state's political process.

Showdown Over Radar: Interest Group Politics in Action

Throughout the 1970s the CHP leadership repeatedly stressed the virtues of radar as a means of controlling California's speed-happy motorists. They pointed to a nearly 50 percent increase in highway fatalities between 1974 (the year the national speed limit of 55 mph was initiated) and 1979; to the increasing percentage of the population who routinely exceeded the 55 mph speed; to the decline in CHP manpower precisely at the time when more patrol officers were needed to keep motorists from violating the law.[3] Although the CHP was not required to get legislative approval as a condition for radar adoption, the commissioner felt that a show of legislative support might quell the controversy surrounding the equipment. Such support, however, never came.

Between 1970 and 1980 ten separate bills were introduced in the California legislature with the sole intention of acquiring radar for the CHP. Some were introduced by Democrats, while others were brought forward by Republicans; some originated in the Assembly, and others were first sponsored in the Senate. Despite varied histories, these ten bills shared the same fate—not one of them was enacted into law. By 1980 California had the distinction as the *only* state in the Union without radar for its state police.

At first, opponents came out against radar because of the expense. When the energy crisis of the mid-1970s threatened the United States oil supply, the federal government offered to pick up 90 percent of the radar cost in the hope of reducing fuel consumption as vehicles traveled at slower speeds. In 1978 the federal government volunteered to pay the entire radar tab of $3.25 million if the measure was adopted by the state. Still the California legislature refused the offer.

Failing to win California's cooperation through generosity, in 1978 the United States Congress enacted the Highway Safety Act to force state compliance of the national 55 mph law. The legislation's primary objective was to get larger percentages of each state's driver population to fall within the 55 mph range over a 5 year period. For 1979, 30 percent of all drivers could not exceed 55 mph; future percentages increased to 40 percent in 1980, 50 percent in 1981, 60 percent in 1982, and 70 percent in 1983. Failure to meet these standards would jeopardize 5 percent of a state's grants from the federal Department of Transportation.

Although most states had little difficulty in meeting the federal targets, a few sparsely populated western states offered token compliance. Nevada exemplified the western attitude by imposing a "stiff" $5 fine for anyone caught speeding between 55 and 70 mph! California, however, did not even bother with pretense. The national speed limit became a state joke. In 1977, 59 percent of the state's drivers exceeded the speed limit, and the figure grew to 67 percent by 1979. In other words, the state's motorists were moving contrary to the national government's goals. By December 1980 the state clearly was in violation of the law, thus jeopardizing $11 million in federal highway aid.[4] Only the patience of the new Reagan administration prevented the Department of Transportation from imposing the mandated cuts—and no one could predict with any certainty how long the patience would last. Even this threat, however, did not move the California state legislature.

Why the resistance? A sizable alliance pressured the state legislature to approve radar for the CHP, but this force was offset by powerful opposition mainly from the Teamsters Union. With the trucking industry as the nucleus of its political and economic muscle, the union's three-member lobbying team worked diligently to dissuade the legislature from approving radar. By relying on press releases, legislative connections, and sizable campaign contributions, the leadership of the 350,000 member Teamsters showed tremendous ability to overcome impressive proradar forces.

THE PROPONENTS

For 10 years radar advocates struggled without success to include radar as part of the CHP's traffic patrol arsenal. In pursuit of its goals the state police agency referred to speed–traffic fatality relationships and their connected costs, and a diverse coalition of supporters and public opinion.

The California Highway Patrol. The CHP based much of its radar argument on the direct correlation between traffic speed and death rates. For those accidents occurring at speeds between 41 and 50 mph, 4.5 fatalities were found for every 100 collisions. Impact speeds of 51–60 mph generated a 6.0 per 100 rate, while automobiles impacting at the 61–70 mph bracket induced a fatality rate of 8.2 per 100 accidents.[5] When Congress passed the 55 mph national speed limit law in 1974, the number of automobile-caused deaths plummeted in California. Every year thereafter, however, the number of statewide fatalities increased as larger percentages of the driver population traveled in excess of 55 mph (see Table 3-1). California's fatality rate far surpassed the national increases. In the 5 year period between 1974 and 1978, for example, the number of traffic-related fatalities nationwide increased by 12.9 percent. During the same period in California the state's traffic deaths accelerated by a staggering 32.7 percent.

According to the CHP, the fatalities and increased speeds were linked. Given limited resources, radar was the only viable means left to enforce the law and reduce highway deaths. The agency concluded that in those states and local communities using radar, "both the highest and the average speeds, as well as speed-related accidents, decreased significantly. . . . Consequently, to assist

TABLE 3-1   The Relationship Between Fatal Accidents and Speed

Year	Fatal accidents statewide	Average speed (mph)	Vehicles exceeding 55 mph (%)
1973*	4318		
1974†	3550		
1975	3751		
1976	3980		
1977	4443	56.2	59.4
1978	4712	56.8	63.2
1979	4941	57.4	67.0

*Last year of the 65 mph basic speed limit in California.
†First year of the national 55 mph speed limit.
Source: CHP Booklet prepared for SCR 55 (1980), p. 15.

the California Highway Patrol in gaining compliance with the law, as well as maintaining a satisfactory level of service, we believe the use of speed measuring instruments is essential."[6]

Two additional arguments accompanied the speed–highway fatality theme. These centered on the unnecessary cost of dollars for fuel and the CHP's manpower problems under the current "pacing" system. The CHP pointed out that reductions in speed would increase automobile gasoline mileage and, hence, reduce fuel costs. Each 1 mph statewide decrease in speed would result in a fuel savings of 50 million gallons. At $1.20 per gallon, this savings amounted to $60 million annually. Moreover, a 5 mph reduction in highway travel speed meant a total fuel reduction of 250 million gallons and $300 million each year. With energy at a premium both in terms of availability and expense, such figures appeared helpful to radar advocates.

The CHP also argued that radar adoption would allow the same number of officers to increase their effectiveness. Use of radar instead of "pacing" would reduce the average pursuit time from 1:57 minutes to 34 seconds. With nearly a million speed stops in 1979 alone, CHP projections indicated that officers would have reduced exposure to injury by 22,489 personnel hours or 12.5 personnel years. In a state where only 900 officers patrol 100,000 miles of highway during a typical 8 hour shift, radar deployment offered the hope that limited staffing would generate greater efficiency.

The data relating to saved lives, dollars, and personnel seemed to build a strong case for radar. The federal government's offer to pay the cost of the new speed detection devices seemed only to increase the attractiveness of radar. Yet the legislature was not convinced.

The Proradar Coalition.   The diverse core of radar boosters incorporated some of the state's leading politicans as well as the state's major law enforcement officials. In addition to CHP Commissioner Glen Craig, the list of proponents included:

Governors Ronald Reagan and Jerry Brown

Assembly Speaker Leo McCarthy

Senate President Pro-Tem James Mills

California State Peace Officers Association

State Sheriffs Association

California Association of Highway Patrolmen

California Trucking Association

County Supervisors Association

Southern California Automobile Club

In most political environments such widespread support would seem enough to bowl over the opposition. The proposal appeared to have the necessary consensus for an idea to become law. The consensus, however, was both shaky and incomplete.

Public Opinion.   Radar proponents also claimed that their goals were backed by strong public support. The CHP mailed out 13,000 questionnaires to randomly selected drivers in late 1975. By January 1976 more than 5,000 replies were received in Sacramento. The results showed that a convincing margin of 63 percent to 37 percent approved of radar.[7]

The CHP survey compared favorably with the results of a California poll conducted in December 1980. Although the poll focused on the problems associated with gasoline shortages, the respondents were asked a number of questions on the best ways to cope with inadequate supplies of fuel. When asked if the 55 mph speed law should be strictly enforced, 76 percent said "yes," 22 percent said "no," and 2 percent had no opinion.[8] The data suggest general public acceptance of the 55 mph concept *along with* radar as a means for enforcing the speed limit. In both cases, moreover, responses have been unusually one-sided.

The radar proponents seemed to command the necessary ingredients for pressuring the legislature into positive action. Objective data clearly showed that reductions in auto speeds meant fewer fatalities; the coalition of proponents had support both in and out of government; finally, even public opinion fell into line on the radar issue. Despite all these advantages, other interests were sufficiently persuasive to neutralize the proradar coalition.

THE OPPONENTS

Given the apparent widespread support for radar at no cost to the state, it is hard to imagine how so many efforts between 1970 and 1980 fell short of becoming law. Yet part of California's political environment includes 600 registered lobbyists representing more than a thousand clients. These representatives make claims before relevant legislative committees, judicial bodies, and various agencies within the executive branch. Because the CHP requested legislative approval prior to statewide use of radar, antiradar interest group activity focused on the legislature and its members.

The radar issue has drawn opposition from both the private and public sectors. The most conspicuous interest group resistance has come from the Teamsters. Inside the legislature, Assemblyman Louis Papan (D–Daly City) has complemented the Teamster effort with his own active crusade against radar. Together, these two forces have more than offset the CHP's data, prominent groups, and public opinion. The ability of the antiradar elements to repel the proponents has been remarkable.

The Teamsters.   With 350,000 members and an annual political action budget of about $500,000, the Teamsters Union is among the most active interest groups in Sacramento. Concerned with a variety of issues ranging from the minimum wage to working conditions, the union takes active positions on about six hundred bills per year. Inasmuch as the Teamsters are the principal union for organized truck drivers in the state, they have had more than a passing interest in preventing the adoption of radar. Truck drivers depend upon the ability to make speedy deliveries so that they can go from one assignment to the next. The union correctly perceived radar as a threat to fast-paced delivery schedules. Accordingly, the Teamsters surfaced as the key interest group against radar in any shape or form. In the words of chief lobbyist Gerald O'Hara, "We [the Teamsters] are the only active, most visible organization against radar." [9]

Respected as a powerful political force, the Teamsters have enjoyed a special relationship with key public leaders in California. When the union opened its new state headquarters in 1977, then Governor Jerry Brown gave a closed-door address to 900 key officials. In 1978 the Teamsters gave more than $150,000 to selected statewide and legislative candidates, forty-four of whom were incumbents in the Assembly or Senate. Shrewdly assessing where power truly lies, the union gave its largest donations to State Senate President Pro-Tem James Mills and then Assembly Ways and Means Committee Chairman Willie Brown. Despite its huge campaign war chest, the union gave no more than $2,750 to any single legislator—sizable sums, perhaps, but not the kind of money one might assume necessary to "buy an election." Governor Jerry Brown, Secretary of State March Fong Eu, Treasurer Jesse Unruh, and Controller Ken Cory received contributions varying between $3,000 and $15,000 (Brown received the latter). Not surprisingly, a disproportionate amount of Teamster money went to members of the transportation committees in the Assembly and Senate. These committees have principal jurisdiction over radar-related questions.

Most labor groups have fairly close connections with the California Democratic party and its key members. In many ways, however, the Teamsters do not represent the typical labor group. The union's members are a diverse lot, ranging from farm employees to policemen. The union's connections with state politicians have been equally diverse. Lobbtist O'Hara describes the Teamsters as having "the best staffed labor lobby in the capital."[10] Indeed, one example of the union's bipartisan clout lies in O'Hara himself, who was one of a handful of appointees to survive the transition from the Reagan administration to the Brown administration. Reagan appointed O'Hara to the Cal-OSHA Standards Board in 1973. When O'Hara's 6 year term expired in 1979, Brown reappointed the Teamster lobbyist to the board, this time as its chairman.

The political makeup of the Teamsters has little in common with the state's primary labor organization, the California AFL-CIO. Although dominant in numbers (1.8 million members as of July 1981, compared with the Teamsters' 350,000), the California AFL-CIO actually spends slightly less than the Teamsters for campaign influence.[11] Serving as an umbrella organization for several dozen smaller unions, the California AFL-CIO maintains only one full-time lobbyist in Sacramento. Since 1970 that task has fallen to Executive Officer John Henning. Although once removed from partisan politics, the AFL-CIO closed ranks with the state Democratic party in 1958, when they jointly opposed an antilabor "right to work" initiative designed to eliminate closed union shops. Since that time the California AFL-CIO has forged an alliance with Democratic leaders on a nearly exclusive basis. For their part the Teamsters have worked equally well with both political party leaderships.

Teamster opposition to radar springs from the union's relationship with the trucking industry drivers. In the words of one Teamster official, the union not only speaks for "many professional truck drivers, but we also represent our members as consumers of insurance policies. . . . [We] believe that the use of radar, very simply, will not reduce the number of traffic infractions nor improve highway safety, but rather result in an increase in citations which will adversely affect driving records. . . ."[12] With highway safety as its highest priority, the union repeatedly has advocated more uniformed CHP officers and marked patrol cars as the best way to protect all drivers. Given pressures on the state's limited resources, however, the CHP has had a difficult enough time in keeping the force from suffering reductions.

As the first line of defense against radar, the Teamsters have worked hard to keep the CHP from adopting the speed detection devices. Skillful lobbying, campaign donations, and an active public relations campaign have helped to neutralize the efforts of radar proponents. Interest groups, however, cannot make legislation; that task lies solely with the Assembly and Senate. Given this necessary connection, the union's success has come in conjunction with the work of key leaders in the legislature, most notably Assemblyman Louis J. Papan.

Louis J. Papan.   Normally, legislators and interest groups find common ground on important issues in the committees. But Louis Papan, the legislature's leading opponent of radar, spent little time on the Assembly Transportation Committee between 1971 and 1980. Moreover, for most of the same period, Papan received relatively little financial assistance from the Teamsters.

First elected to the Assembly in 1972, Papan was appointed to and made vice-chair of the Transportation Committee in 1973; he left the committee in 1975. Papan received only token Teamster support during his 2 year stint on the committee. In 1974, for example, the Teamsters gave Papan $500, ranking him a dismal seventh of the eight members on the committee who received union money (Assemblyman John Foran, a San Francisco Democrat, received the highest amount at $2,250). Only when Papan assumed the chairmanship of the powerful Assembly Rules Committee did his prominence meet with generous Teamster contributions. Of the five Rules Committee members receiving Teamster money in 1980, Papan led the group with $3,250, while the four others were given amounts ranging from $1,000 to $2,250. Because the Rules Committee established the committee assignments for all bills, it is probable that the Teamsters had more than radar on their minds when contributing to Papan. Before 1980 Papan never received more than $1,250 in any single year, placing him well down the list to Teamster favorites.

Papan's absence from the Transportation Committee and his lukewarm Teamster support suggest that his antiradar ambitions were a result of his own politics, which paralleled those of the Teamsters. But the alignment appears to have been one of coincidence rather than intent.

There are two explanations for Louis Papan's constant opposition to radar. The first stems from a run-in between the Assemblyman and the CHP in 1975.

Papan was issued a speeding citation for traveling 90 mph, well beyond the 55 mph limit. After receiving the ticket, Papan demanded that the CHP rescind the citation because the CHP officer who chased him did a "poor clocking job." At first, the ticket was voided by a CHP captain who was a 21 year veteran of the force. When the reversal caught the public's attention, the CHP reinstated the ticket. Given this experience, Papan's critics contend that he became committed forever to preventing any improvement of the CHP's speed law enforcement abilities.[13]

The Assemblyman himself simply asserts that there are better ways than radar to promote highway safety. Papan argued that less than 2,000 of the 318,000 injuries suffered on California roads in 1979 could have been prevented with radar. Furthermore, he questioned whether radar would work well on busy freeways, where speed detection devices would have difficulty pinpointing violators in clusters of closely bunched vehicles. Given these facts and the loss of 900 positions in the CHP between 1975 and 1980, Papan proposed that the best way to ensure highway safety would be through expansion of the force with the addition of 300 officers.[14] A study by the Brown administration in 1979, however, determined that 300 officers would cost $14 million annually in salary and benefits, compared to the free radar.[15] These doubts were enough to prevent the Papan proposal from receiving serious consideration.

Over the years, Papan's antiradar position has received the necessary minimal support from his legislative colleagues at the right moments. In 1976, as a case in point, two state Senate Finance Committee members deleted radar from the budget at the last moment without any explanation. In 1979 the Assembly Transportation Committee reversed itself after approving radar a few weeks earlier in the session. Each time the legislature considered radar, a new combination of opponents joined Papan in blocking the measure. Although Papan did not necessarily participate in the votes, he was somewhere near the action. As one Senate radar proponent so aptly put the matter, "Louis Papan has almost single-handedly defeated the radar measures. . . . The consensus is that as long as he is in office, legislative authorization of radar will not be granted."[16] Apparently, enough of his colleagues were willing to defer to Papan when he called upon them for support, evidence of the legislature's elaborate inside lobbying network.

THE RADAR FIGHT IN PERSPECTIVE

The radar issue in California helps explain the prominence of interest groups in the state's unofficial power structure. Whatever the direct impact of the Teamsters, the union asserted itself with authority in adamant opposition to a plethora of interests on the other side of the radar issue. Inasmuch as the California political map is fraught with numerous pressure points, this opposition, coupled with just enough doubt in the legislature, managed to prevent any changes in the status quo.

The Influence of Interest Groups

The relationship between interest groups and California's official policymaking machinery differs from the way vested interests operate in the national political arena. Nationally, interest groups are assertive; however, their information may be challenged by a massive federal bureaucracy, congressional committee staffs, and political party organizations. Thus, when making legislation, Congress relies on information from both inside and outside of government. In California an open, undisciplined political environment guarantees a wide berth for those who wish to influence decision makers, with little challenge from either the legislature or state bureaucracy. The result is a political climate that shines on not only the state in general but on interest groups in particular.

That California serves as a haven for interest group representation is not new to the Golden State. The state's constitution is replete with built-in guarantees for crucial interest group beneficiaries, including special tax exemptions for fruit and nut producers (agriculture), trees less than 40 years old (timber), and freight or passenger vessels (shipping). Some lobbyists have also used the political process to gain favorable treatment by the legislature. Their staying power is so formidable that even the fiscal crisis of the early 1980s has not jarred the government from its pattern of accommodation. As California began the 1983–84 fiscal year with a state deficit of 1.5 billion dollars, the wine tax of one cent per gallon was 47.6 cents below the national average (unchanged in 45 years), the hard liquor tax of 2 dollars per gallon was 64 cents below the national average (unchanged since 1967), the 10 cent per package cigarette tax was 3 cents below the national average (also unchanged since 1967), and the beer tax rate of 4 cents per gallon was 13 cents less than the national average (unchanged since 1959).[17] California also remained as the *only* oil-producing state with a severance tax.

These policies aren't the result of public pressure. They reflect the state's responses to organized group demands and needs. In fact, California has a history of accommodating those groups perceived as important to its economic health.

THE EMERGENCE OF GROUP POWER—THREE-STAGE EVOLUTION

Throughout California history interest group activities have paralleled the state's political development. Back in 1849 it was the mining industry that first stimulated concern in California. After mining lost its importance, other interest groups came to dominate the state's political activity. The evolution of interest group clout in California can be broken down into three stages: the Railroad period (1870–1910), the Industrial period (1911–60), and the Ratification period (1961–present).

The Railroad Period.   During the last third of the nineteenth century and the first decade of the twentieth, the Southern Pacific Railroad enjoyed a monopoly on California's political destiny. The most observable form of its political domination came with the election of railroad baron Leland Stanford to the governorship in 1861. But the railroad's clout extended beyond Stanford to virtually every important politician in the state. As historian Walton Bean puts it, when a lawyer was elected to the legislature for the first time, he received a letter from the Southern Pacific legal department "stating that the railroad wished to retain an outstanding attorney from his region during a period which happened to coincide with that of the upcoming session in Sacramento."[18] Regardless of political party affiliation, each new attorney-legislator received an accompanying retainer fee, which continued as long as he remained in office. Interest groups that were dominant in other states, notably agriculture and the print media, cowered in the railroad's wake. Until its Progressive-orchestrated demise, the railroad virtually controlled the state.

The Industrial Period.   The most comprehensive era of interest group activity occurred between 1911 and 1960. With the railroad now defeated, the state was open for domination by other interests. Such control was not about to fall into the hands of political parties, because these institutions were also weakened by the Progressives. Instead the growing economic diversity of California provided the opportunity for countless interest groups to emerge and assert their needs. Agriculture became the state's leading industry, and with its elevation, the California Farm Bureau grew accordingly. As manufacturing increased, interest groups developed to represent automobiles, the defense, electronics, and labor. So important were interest groups that one political scientist, William Buchanan, argues that all major legislation passed during this period was in response to the pressure of organized groups.[19]

The Ratification Period.   Since the early 1960s, interest group activity in
California has settled into a mode of "live and let live." Rather than engage in a
costly war for domination, groups have worked out informal agreements with
each other and then gone to government for ratification. For their part the
legislature and other policymaking authorities have minimized independent
choices in order to preserve political equilibrium among the state's major
interests.

There are numerous examples that point to the state's ability to accommo-
date interest groups. Passage of the Agricultural Labor Relations Act of 1975 is
particularly noteworthy because both the legislative and executive branches
worked to satisfy competing goals of farmers and farmworkers.

After 40 years of clashes in the fields, the last 10 of which saw repeated
boycotts and strikes, the farmworkers and growers decided they would be better
off making peace rather than continuing a costly fight. Although Governor
Jerry Brown and his staff shouldered much of the day-to-day negotiating responsibilities, the terms of the legislation were such that both adversaries, the
250,000 member United Farm Workers and the state's growers, felt vindicated.
In the words of one analysis at the time, "for the growers, the bill will be some
help because [UFW leader Cesar] Chavez's prime tool, the secondary boycott,
will be weakened somewhat. . . . For Chavez, the compromise is a victory if he
can win the representation elections. He can still call strikes at harvest time.
. . ."[20] Hence, the battle between two interest groups was put to rest—at least
for the time being.

Who They Are, What They Do

California interest groups come in all shapes and sizes. Some, like the
Teamsters, are both large and well funded; they bring to life the perceptions
most of us have about organized private power. Most interest groups, however,
do not bask in such two-sided strength. Greenpeace, for example, has a sizable
membership approaching 100,000, but a comparatively modest annual operating budget in the $500,000 range. However, the Gun Owners of California
spends over $1.5 million each year, although the organization has only about a
dozen members.

Each interest group is unique, but all have the fundamental objective of
influencing decision makers. Some are more successful than others. Money, of
course, is a crude—and important—measure of that influence. Yet money
alone will not automatically lead to positive legislative response if a group's goal
is not considered reasonable. Perhaps former Assembly Speaker (now State

Treasurer) Jesse Unruh put it best when he said: "If you can't eat their [interest group's] food, drink their booze, screw their women and then vote against them, you have no business being up here."[21]

Lobbying skills, combined with money, go far toward explaining a group's success. Some, like the California Real Estate Association, are reputed to have an ambitious and effective lobbying staff. Others, like the California State Employees Association (CSEA), are known for being less successful in turning money and influence into favorable policies. Thus, in 1982 when the CSEA contributed more than $550,000 to statewide and legislative campaigns, the state employees emerged from the budget process with no cost-of-living increase.

MAKING MONEY TALK

Of the more than 1,000 interest groups in California, approximately 200 are in the "big league" category of spending at least $500 each year for political influence. According to the Fair Political Practices Commission's final report on 1978 state elections, the major interests who spent the most money for lobbying and election campaigns fell into eleven major categories. The lion's share of contributions came from business (55 percent).[22] In 1980 interest groups increased their spending by about 50 percent to a total of $31.2 million.[23]

For the most part the same groups surface every year as the state's leading financial contributors. Between 1980 and 1982, however, some movement did occur among the top ten interest group donors in California. After more than a decade in the limelight, the Teamsters were absent from the list, an event that coincided with the absence of any radar-related bills in the legislature. In the "rising star" department the United Farm Workers Political Action Committee contributed $750,000 in 1982, placing the organization in a virtual dead heat for first place honors with the California Medical Association's Political Action Committee, which gave $750,667. The UFW's contributions were two and one half times as much as the union gave in 1980, when the organization had Democratic Governor Jerry Brown's support. Less certain of that support from newly elected Republican Governor George Deukmejian in 1982, the union pumped its money into Democratic legislative contests. Table 3-2 lists the top ten contributors in 1982 and the amounts they gave, and compares them with their standing in 1980.

Ironically, both interest group lobbyists and recipients seem to be uncomfortable with the expanded role of money in politics. From a politician's perspective, Assembly Speaker Willie Brown, the state's leading money raiser, has

TABLE 3-2   Top Ten Interest Group Contributors, 1982

Group	Amount	1980 rank
1. California Medical Association	$750,667	1
2. United Farm Workers	750,000	—
3. California State Employees Assn.	554,138	2
4. United for California (Business)	551,500	4
5. California Teachers Association	520,914	5
6. California Real Estate Assn.	482,827	3
7. Operating Engineers Local No. 3	481,333	—
8. California Trial Lawyers Assoc. Comm.	381,640	—
9. Bankers for Responsible Government	381,640	9
10. Fund for Insurance Education	344,457	—

Sources: San Francisco Chronicle, November 27, 1981, and Los Angeles Times, November 10, 1982.

expressed unhappiness about the need to rely on interest group support: "Let me tell you, it is an incredibly humiliating experience to go around and beg people for money," Brown has been quoted as saying.[24] Such remarks have also been uttered from those who give money as well. In the words of one of the state's leading lobbyists, "From a lobbyist's point of view, the most nauseating thing that can happen is for a legislator to tell you in thinly veiled terms that his support is going to cost your clients so much money."[25] Interest groups don't like it; legislators don't like it. However, given escalating campaign costs and a proliferation of organized interest, the relationship between policymakers and interest groups has become indispensable.

THE IMPORTANCE OF ACCESS

Money may be an indicator of interest group activity, but it's not the *only* indicator. An organized interest is successful when, in the face of countless pressures on a policymaking authority, it manages to influence that individual successfully. Teamster lobbyist Gerald O'Hara's "high visibility" approach is one such way to reach key leaders. But sometimes even this isn't enough, and the interest groups members may be solicited in order to demonstrate a strong show of opinion. Various techniques ranging from mass letter writing to personal meetings between legislators and interest group members go far toward augmenting the lobbyist's own role.

Taking Their Case to the Legislature.   The efforts employed by the California Association of Realtors (CAR) on property tax relief show just how important an interest group's members can be on the state's political process. When

Howard Jarvis's Proposition 13 initiative qualified for the June 1978 ballot, the legislature hastily designed a counterproposal that offered a limited version of tax relief. As the legislature worked toward its objective, CAR lobbyist Doug Gillies and his staff labored hard to influence the outcome of the final package. But the six-member lobbying team remained unsure over whether the legislature would heed their pleas as the tax relief bill went from committee to committee. The principal worry for the CAR lobbyists centered on the legislature's interest in a "transfer tax" upon sale of property as a way of making up for the revenues lost from property tax relief. Because lavish campaign donations and professional lobbying had not discouraged the legislature from this possibility, Gillies used other techniques to reach his objective.

Shortly before the legislature was scheduled to decide on the transfer tax concept, Gillies and his staff called CAR district officers, asking them to send one or two representatives from each area of the state on a designated day. Although the organization's membership topped 100,000, the lobbyist wanted no more than 500 to show up. Said Gillies, "We didn't want it to look like Cesar Chavez's army on the lawn of the Capitol. A small number can be just as effective. Sometimes you get too many people and annoy the heck out of legislators."[26] The realtors came to Sacramento and met with their individual legislators in small groups. Two days after their show of force, the transfer tax was tossed out of the bill. In this instance, money was less important to the interest group's success than access.

Taking Their Case to the Governor.   Hardly aloof from the legislative fray, the governor can be a critical source of influence for interest groups. California's Mediterranean fruit fly crisis of 1980–81 placed Governor Jerry Brown between farmers and a coalition of local government leaders and environmentalists over the best means of eradicating this serious threat to the state's agriculture.

The "medfly" insect deposits its eggs in a wide variety of "host" plants. When subsequent larvae develop, the affected produce becomes unsalable. Malathion, a commonly used pesticide, is the chemical generally used for eradication of the medfly.

During the summer of 1980 organized agriculture urged Brown to order, through his executive powers, aerial malathion spraying of the original 500 square mile quarantine area in the Santa Clara Valley. Local officials and environmentalists countered that house-to-house ground spraying would do the job. At first, Brown sided with the locals, but by the summer of 1981 the pest had spread eastward to the fringe of the Central Valley, causing panic among the state's farmers, quarantines of California produce by other states, and alarm in the federal government. Again the farm interests pressured Brown. Warned the president of a Sacramento produce cooperative, "We've been playing games. We've got to get going with the spraying."[27] By June 1981 the federal government joined the agricultural interests in pressuring Governor Brown. This time the governor gave in and the state conducted a 6 month aerial spraying program.

Taking Their Case to the Courts. The judicial system, once thought to be removed from politics, increasingly has become the target of interest group activity. Groups of all sizes and shapes have sought redress, and particularly those with limited resources have found relief that they might not find elsewhere.

State reductions in welfare payments exemplify the interest group–court connection. When the Reagan administration reduced the national government's commitment to the Aid to Families with Dependent Children (AFDC) program in 1981, states had the choice of spending more of their own money or scaling down their commitments to fit in with national government funding. Like most states California opted for the latter alternative by developing tightened eligibility rules for AFDC money.

In response to the changes, the Coalition of California Welfare Rights Organizations challenged the state in a class action suit, arguing that the state's new rules were an overzealous interpretation of the new federal law. The welfare coalition chose the courts because it was clear that the legislature and governor, participants in the decision to change the rules, were not about to change their minds. In April 1983 the state supreme court held for the welfare group, ordering the state to return to its previous eligibility system. Thus, the court responded to an interest group claim.

Taking Their Case to "The People." Most interest groups focus their attention and resources on the three traditional institutions just discussed. The wide open politics of California, however, include initiatives and referenda as a regular part of the political process. In such cases, the voters—not the legislature—become the state's policymakers and, not surprisingly, interest groups react in the necessary manner to protect themselves.

In the November 1982 state elections, fifteen propositions were included on the ballot, up slightly from the twelve propositions that were part of the June election. As is the case with a bill moving through the legislature, organized interests made their feelings known about the issues of concern to them. Two such propositions, 11 (requiring a 5 cent deposit on all beer and soft drink containers) and 15 (making handgun registration mandatory) drew tremendous interest and amounts of money during the campaign.

The "no" side on Proposition 11 outspent the "yes" side by a ratio of nine to one. Interest groups played a prominent role in raising nearly $6 million to fight mandatory bottle and can deposits. The biggest anti-11 contributors included the Glass Packaging Institute ($750,000), the Can Manufacturers Institute ($425,000), and the Anheuser-Busch Company ($260,000).[28] In the case of gun control, supporters of the initiative raised $2,800,000, while opponents collected $8,600,000—a closer ratio of slightly more than three to one. But the most interesting information about this political tussle was that the National Rifle Association *alone* came up with $3,700,000 to fight Proposition 15, or far more than the entire war chest assembled by the "yes" on 15 side.[29]

In the mandatory container deposits and gun control examples, the most pronounced interest group activity organized defensive campaigns to defeat undesirable measures. There are occasions, however, when special interests use the initiative process to get voter support for their goals. One persistent effort by state financial institutions (primarily banks, savings and loans, and mortgage companies) to end the state's 10 percent ceiling on interest rates succeeded only after three initiative attempts. In June 1976 the electorate turned down the proposal by 600,000 votes, even though the initiative had no organized opposition. Undaunted, the financial institutions secured enough signatures to place the issue back on the ballot in November 1976; this time the measure failed by 400,000. Finally, in November 1979, the financial industry once again qualified the interest rate ceiling issue for the ballot. With a more effective campaign and low voter turnout (less than 40 percent), the financial interests won by a landslide majority of more than a million votes.

These two instances point out the importance of interest groups to the state's political process. Aware that ballot propositions can change the status quo, interest groups participate in these elections much as they would in a legislative committee deciding on the same issues. The only difference is that instead of confining their activities to a select group of legislators, interest groups must respond to ballot propositions by soliciting the votes of state voters. Most of the time they succeed, although recent initiatives such as Proposition 20 of 1972 (the Coastal Protection Initiative) show that interest groups and their money can be beaten.

The Lobbyists' Environment

Just as interest group activity has changed over time, lobby techniques also have become increasingly sophisticated and diverse. In the past, lobbyists were not held in high regard by either the legislature or the public. Rather, they were perceived as narrow-minded people who preyed on legislators' weaknesses to manipulate the political system for their own private goals. Today's lobbyists are viewed in a considerably different light, at least by legislators. Instead of relying on money, vice, and other illegal means to ply their trade, modern lobbyists work with different tools in a very public setting. Although they are increasingly generous in campaign donations, lobbyists realize more than ever that their most important service is to provide legislators with information, something that the latter constantly find in short supply.

OLD-STYLE LOBBYING

Prior to the 1950s, lobbyists enjoyed a "no holds barred" existence in Sacramento. The most successful among their ranks set up shop in some of the capital's better-known eateries, inviting legislators to take advantage of endless food and liquor. These arrangements, coupled with generous cash contributions at propitious moments, provided lobbyists with incredible clout.

If one lobbyist could be said to personify this era, he was Artie Samish. A rags-to-riches story of an individual whose formal education ended at the sixth grade, Samish became the state's most learned man in the field of influence. He began his lobbying apprenticeship as an engrossing and enrolling clerk in the legislature in 1921, staying in the position just long enough to get an insider's crash course on the legislative process. In 1923 Samish left the legislature to become a lobbyist for S and H Greenstamps. By the mid-1930s he easily emerged as the king of California's Third House.

It's not that Samish worked in different ways than the state's other lobbyists; he just did his work on a grand scale to the point where he had no peer. At one point during Samish's colorful career, Governor Warren paid him a left-handed compliment of sorts in acknowledging that "on matters that affect his clients, Artie unquestionably has more power than the governor."[30] If anything, Warren understated the case, for in some ways Samish was the *government*.

With a staff of twenty-five operatives scattered in strategic capital locations, Samish could trace and intersect legislation at virtually any point from its starting place to the governor's signature. He maintained dossiers on each of the state's legislators and executive branch members, paying close attention to their vulnerabilities. As a result of his meticulous detective work and generous campaign contributions, Samish became indispensable to (and feared by) legislators and interest groups alike. Before his career was short-circuited by a federal income tax evasion conviction in 1953, Samish's clients included breweries, hard liquor interests, bus companies, railroads, tobacco corporations, banks, building and loan companies, racetracks, the chemical industry, and major unions.

Samish may have been a lobbyist of the early twentieth century tradition, but he set the pattern for his modern counterparts. Like the Southern Pacific's famed legal counsel W. F. Herrin, who dominated the state around the turn of the century, Samish realized the importance of dealing with lawmakers as individuals irrespective of their political party affiliation. In addition, he was one of the state's first lobbyists to realize that in order to run the legislature, you must learn how it works. His brief stint as an Assembly clerk gave him tremendous insight into the pressure points of the legislative process.

MODERN LOBBYING

When California voters passed the Political Reform Act of 1974 by a whopping 70 percent approval, state reformers hoped that the Samish-related abuses of the past would be put to rest once and for all. They had reason to be optimistic because the act provided rigid disclosure requirements for lobbyists and legislators alike, a $10 limit on lobbyists' personal gifts to politicians (not to be confused with unlimited donations for political campaigns), and a Fair Political Practices Commission to oversee the new law. Despite these changes, interest groups and their lobbyists remain alive and well in California politics.

In some ways today's lobbyists are second-generation refinements of the Artie Samish era. Quite a number of them are individuals who served as legislators before embracing the lobbyist's profession. To this extent they have used their understanding of the legislature to help influence the legislative process. Moreover, it doesn't hurt for former legislators to keep close associations with their past allies. As one legislator-turned-lobbyist has stated, "[L]egislators look at a former member as somebody they want to talk to—someone whom they trust to protect confidences and not to use information to beat them over the head politically. . . . They feel a former member understands that sensitivity better than perhaps somebody else."[31] Although the jobs may change, friendships do not.

If the lobbyists of the past were adept at realizing the superficial importance of political parties in the legislature, today's lobbyists have reached new levels of sophistication. No longer feeling the need to capture legislative majorities, the astute lobbyists focus on the "juice committees," those particular committees in the legislature that handle the most sensitive questions regarding health, horse racing, liquor, agriculture, real estate, and banking. Such has been the pattern of the Teamsters in their close association with the legislature's transportation committees when fighting the radar issue. Moreover, the modern lobbyist is critically aware that money alone will not capture votes. Rather, money is but a means to gaining influence. "We are buying access," a key savings and loan lobbyist has noted. "Anyone who assumes you can buy votes is a dummy."[32]

Perhaps the best example of the successful modern-day lobbyist is James Garibaldi. As a former legislator and attorney, Garibaldi earns more than $250,000 annually from lobbying activities alone. His clients include the Wine and Spirit Wholesalers of California, Hollywood Park racetrack, Blue Chip Stamps, Leslie Salt Company, Pacific Outdoor Advertising, and the California Association of Highway Patrolmen. Although his clients combine for annual campaign contributions in the $100,000 range, Garibaldi is known for winning votes with logic as well as money. In the words of a fellow lobbyist, "He never walks in and says, 'Do it for the Gipper.' He walks in with 14 reasons and says, 'If you want I'll give you another 14.'"[33]

Modern-day lobbyists have not stopped giving money, but they have added persuasion as part of their repertoire. This new level of awareness separates them from lobbyists of the past.

Interest Groups and California Politics— A Powerful Connection

Interest group influence long has been intimately connected with California politics. Whereas such activity was once conducted in "smoke-filled rooms," today it is readily accessible to public scrutiny. Despite the increasing publicity surrounding interest group behavior, little has been done to stem the role of groups in the state's political process. If anything, each attempt to regulate group behavior has left them better equipped to compete with official institutions.

En route to becoming a state, California provided a comfortable constitutional environment for numerous interests. Angered by the benefits awarded to special interests, reformers rewrote the constitution in 1879 with the hope, in part, of controlling these groups. But in the wake of all the reform hoopla, special interests, notably the railroad, enjoyed a stronger position than ever.

Determined to place some constraints on private power, the Progressives attempted to remove them and their political party lackeys from the state's political process. Yet, when the new laws were finally in place, interest groups merely skirted party organizations to deal with policymakers directly.

In the most recent reform effort the state's voters approved the Political Reform Act in 1974, intending to set limits on private influence. Shortly thereafter, the state supreme court declared that limits on campaign contributions were unconstitutional, and the state was left with a cumbersome law that requested public disclosure of receipts and expenditures but little else.

Today interest groups enjoy a special place in the state's political environment. Because party organization has been rendered virtually powerless and legislative campaign costs are frightfully high, an inevitable relationship has developed between politicians and special interest. Given the state's political and economic diversity, one would expect nothing less. In the words of one assessment of the 1982 California elections, "candidates use expensive polls, television commercials and mailings. . . . With no party to support them, candidates, who must finance their campaigns, seek help from lobbyists."[34] That help is certain to be there. The question regarding what interest groups get in return for their help, however, is more difficult to answer.

Notes

[1]Carol S. Greenwald, *Group Power* (New York: Praeger, 1977), p. 12.

[2]See L. Harmon Zeigler and Hendrik van Dalen, "Interest Groups in State Politics," in Herbert Jacob and Kenneth Vines, eds., *Politics in the American States*, 3rd ed. (Boston: Little, Brown, 1976), Chapter 3.

[3]See CHP booklet prepared in support of SCR 55 (1980), pp. 14–15, unpublished document.

[4]"Speeding to a Loss," *Los Angeles Times*, December 1, 1980.

[5]CHP booklet, p. 14.

[6]Ibid., p. 4.

[7]*Los Angeles Times*, January 14, 1976.

[8]"The California Poll," release no. 1106, December 17, 1980, p. 3.

[9]Telephone interview with Gerald P. O'Hara, Legislative Representative, California Teamster Public Affairs Council, February 3, 1983.

[10]Ibid.

[11]In 1980, a representative year, the Teamsters ranked eighth in campaign contributions of $491,000. The California AFL-CIO ranked 10th with contributions of $446,000. See "Sacramento Lobbyists Still Have Their Clout," *San Francisco Chronicle*, November 27, 1981.

[12]Letter from Larry J. Kurbatoff, Assistant Legislative Representative, California Teamsters Public Affairs Council, March 9, 1982.

[13]"Fast Lane Lou Pulls a Fast One," editorial, *Los Angeles Times*, July 3, 1980.

[14]"Papan Defends His Radar Position," letter to the editor, *Los Angeles Times*, October 3, 1980.

[15]*Los Angeles Times*, June 13, 1979.

[16]Letter from State Senator Jim Ellis, 39th district (D–El Cajon), April 23, 1982.

[17]"State's Revenue Crunch Worries Lobbyists," *Los Angeles Times*, December 21, 1981.

[18]Walton Bean, *California: An Interpretive History* (New York: McGraw-Hill, 1968), p. 305.

[19]William Buchanan, *Legislative Partisanship: The Deviant Case of California* (Berkeley: University of California Press, 1963), p. 22.

[20]Chris Bowman, "Brown's Farm-Labor Coup," *California Journal* 6, no. 6 (June 1975): 192.

[21]Quoted in Lou Cannon, *Ronnie and Jesse* (Garden City, N.Y.: Doubleday, 1969), p. 101.

[22]State of California, Fair Political Practices Commission, "Campaign Contribution and Spending Report," November 7, 1978 General Election, May 15, 1979, p. D-17.

[23]"Lobbyists' Spending Keeps Pace with Inflation," *San Jose Mercury*, January 29, 1982.

[24]"Sacramento Lobbyists Still Have Their Clout," *San Francisco Chronicle*, November 27, 1981.

[25]Ibid.

[26]"Lobbyist Had Key Role in Tax Relief," *Los Angeles Times*, March 7, 1978.

[27]Quoted in Eric Brazil, "The Political Stakes in the Medfly Infestation," *California Journal* 12, no. 4 (April 1981): 139.

[28]See "Foes Deposit Big Sums Against 'Bottle Bill,'" *San Jose Mercury*, September 28, 1982 and "How Money Talks in State Elections," *San Jose Mercury-News*, November 7, 1982.

[29]"National Spending Mark Set in Campaign on Handgun Control," *Los Angeles Times*, February 15, 1983.

[30]Quoted in Lester Velie, "The Secret Boss of California," *Collier's*, August 13, 1949, p. 13.

[31]Kerry Drager, "The New Breed of Sacramento Lobbyist," *California Journal* 11, no. 10 (October 1980): 394.

[32]"The 'Juice' Committees in Capitol" *Los Angeles Times*, December 2, 1981.

[33]"He Survived Reformers—and He's Still the Judge," *Los Angeles Times*, October 26, 1981.

[34]"In California's 'New Politics,' Campaign Reform Is Spelled M-O-N-E-Y," *Los Angeles Times*, August 1, 1982.

4

THE MEDIA IN CALIFORNIA POLITICS

Citizen McClatchy and Others

The media—newspapers, radio, and television—are the principal means of communication between the public and decision makers. How the media perform this task has a major impact on the fate of policies, politicians, and the public. The media shape ideas, information, and debate through their control of information. They can push issues into the public forum or suppress them. They can create or destroy leaders.

This is especially true in California. A constant stream of immigrants and mobility within the state give California a population lacking fixed patterns of political behavior and knowledge of the state's history and traditions. Weak political parties and an open political system deny politicians an organizational base for communicating with their constituents. The power of the media in California politics has always been great because most of what Californians know about politics comes from the media. In the first half of this century, a few newspaper-owning families virtually ran the state. The advent of television altered that, but with fewer newspapers and greater concentration of ownership today, the power of the press remains great. A handful of media conglomerates now controls most of what we know about our state's politics. A look at how they have used their power historically and how they have changed tells us a great deal not only about them, but also about politics and power in California.

The Founders of California's Newspaper Dynasties

James McClatchy was an orphaned teenager when he left Ireland in 1840, but the seeds of his politics had already been implanted by observing the wealth of the landed few in Ireland and the hopeless poverty of the masses. Soon he was working for Horace Greeley at the *New York Tribune* and, like his mentor, active in land reform politics. It was Greeley who said, "Go West, young man," and James McClatchy took his advice, joining the gold rush.

Like many other immigrants, McClatchy's passage to California was a rough one. He sailed from New York to Mexico, crossing to Mazatlán where he joined a group of other immigrants on a boat bound for San Diego. Unfortunately, none of them knew how to sail. After 36 days tossed by storms, stilled on a becalmed sea, and lost, they were running out of supplies. Most of the party, including McClatchy, landed and set out for San Diego by foot. Trudging across the desert of Baja California, they gradually threw away all their possessions except their guns. Starving, they ate a horse, then resorted to snakes and toads. But with the determination of many other immigrants to California's promised land, the hungry, barefoot band made it to San Diego and McClatchy proceeded to Sacramento and the gold country.

Unlike his fellow immigrants, however, James McClatchy wasn't interested in gold. He went to work for a Sacramento newspaper and covered California's first constitutional convention in Monterey. He soon found that the same patterns of landownership that had outraged him in Ireland and New York existed in California, and he became involved in the battle between squatters who were settling land and speculators who had acquired huge land grants at the end of Mexican rule in California. The struggle was bitter and sometimes violent: eight men were killed in fights between the settlers and speculators in Sacramento before the courts settled ownership, and McClatchy himself was jailed for resisting authority.

By 1857 McClatchy was editor of the *Sacramento Bee*, where he continued his land reform campaign by advocating imposition of an acreage limitation on ownership. In the 1860s his interests shifted to the Union cause in the Civil War. The pro-Confederate "Copperheads" were strong in California and plotted to gain control by electing sheriffs in as many counties as possible. McClatchy thwarted them in Sacramento County by running for sheriff himself, and winning. He also used connections in Washington to have the commandant of the Union army in California, a Southern sympathizer, replaced.

Over the years James McClatchy bought shares of the *Sacramento Bee*, but it was left to his family to attain complete ownership after his death in 1883. His heirs still control the newspaper. In addition to land reform and the Union cause, McClatchy used his newspaper to push for completion of a railroad across the Sierra Nevada and for public ownership of utilities. He was an early conservationist, promoting reclamation, and campaigning against hydraulic mining because it spoiled rivers. He made beautification of Sacramento a pet cause, and that city owes its pleasantly shaded streets at least in part to his persistence. He endorsed labor unions as a legitimate device for the expression of the concerns of working people, though he advocated compulsory arbitration as a fair solution for both sides. He was also an ardent political reformer, supporting fair and efficient government and primary elections rather than party nomination of candidates. Yet land was always McClatchy's special interest, from the time he left Ireland to his death, and he relentlessly campaigned against monopoly ownership and for conservation.

McClatchy's progressive views distinguished him from the owners of the other great California papers, who were in the business to advance themselves and their friends. Highly conservative, they almost always aligned themselves with the establishment rather than fighting it like McClatchy. While he took the side of small farmers and workers, his competitors took the side of land barons, railroads, and commercial interests. While he was for conservation, they were for exploitation.

The *Los Angeles Times*, for example, was committed less to journalism than to the promotion and development of Los Angeles. Harrison Gray Otis bought the paper in 1886, shortly after the completion of the railroad connection to the East started the Los Angeles land boom. Otis was a vigorous entrepreneur with extensive business interests, especially in land development. He used the *Times* to promote his conservative political views and his vested interests in the growth of Los Angeles and became the dominant force in local politics. It was Otis who formed the Los Angeles Chamber of Commerce to promote the city. It was Otis who led the successful fight against labor unions, breaking the union at the *Times* in a bitter and sometimes violent battle that lasted almost 20 years. By crushing the unions and ensuring a steady stream of job-seeking immigrants, Otis hoped to create an acquiescent work force that would put Southern California at a competitive advantage with unionized Northern California in attracting industry. "Among her splendid material assets," he boasted of Los Angeles, "none is so valuable . . . as her possession of that priceless boon, industrial freedom."[1]

At about the same time San Francisco's great newspapers were founded. The de Young brothers, an unscrupulous pair, were willing to suppress stories in their *San Francisco Chronicle* for a price, and their sensational style got one of them shot by an outraged victim in 1880. One of their competitors was the *San Francisco Examiner*, which Montana mining millionaire George Hearst bought to further his political career. In 1887 he gave control of the newspaper to his son, William Randolph Hearst. Like the de Youngs, he wanted to sell newspapers, but he also wanted power. His newspapers became the very model of "yellow journalism," creating news where none existed and playing up issues that drew readers. Hearst latched onto the spirit of manifest destiny, flogging up public support for the Spanish-American War. With his success at the *Examiner* and his immense family fortune, Hearst became the first of the California newspaper moguls, extending his power by acquiring other newspapers around California and the country. *Citizen Kane*, Orson Welles's film classic, is a slightly fictionalized version of Hearst's amazing career.

What all these newspapers had in common was power and family ownership.

Newspapers in the Era of Reform

From the turn of the century to the end of World War I, California and much of the nation were caught up in a furor of reform. At the base of the reform movement was a changing economic structure. As the cities grew, there emerged an urban commercial class—merchants, doctors, lawyers, and realtors—which wanted their money's worth for the taxes they paid. They also wanted efficient government that would make the improvements necessary for growth that would benefit themselves and their businesses. They were the Progressives.

The Progressives organized to destroy the Southern Pacific Railroad's political machine, which dominated California and its cities at the time. Led by Hiram Johnson, the Progressives elected reformers to state and local offices. Campaigning up and down the state by automobile, rather than railroad, Johnson inveighed against the railroad "Octopus." He took his case directly to the voters because so many newspapers were allied with the machine. In San Jose the reformers solved this problem by buying one of the newspapers. In other cities they attacked the publishers as agents of the machine or worse. Johnson's attack on Harrison Gray Otis of the *Los Angeles Times* was particularly bitter:

> In our city we have drunk to the dregs the cup of infamy; we have been betrayed by public officials; we have been disgraced before the world of crimes unspeakable; but with all the criminals who have disgraced us, we have never had anything so degraded, so disreputable, and so vile as Harrison Gray Otis and the *Los Angeles Times*. The one blot on the fame of Southern California, and the bar sinister on the escutcheon of Los Angeles, is Harrison Gray Otis, a creature who is vile, infamous, degraded and putrescent. Here he sits in senile dementia, with gangrened heart and rotting brain, grimacing at every reform and chattering in impotent rage against decency and morality, while he is going down to his grave in snarling infamy.[2]

Otis, in turn, denounced Johnson as "a born mob leader—a whooper—a howler—a roarer."[3]

The Progressives found some sympathetic publishers, however. Hearst's *San Francisco Examiner* had long been a flamboyant opponent of the Southern Pacific and its machine. The *Sacramento Bee* also was a prominent voice of Progressivism. By this time the *Bee* was under the control of C. K. McClatchy, James' son and Hiram Johnson's great friend. Born in 1858, C. K. grew up close to his father and acquired his hatred of monopolistic power and his commitment to good government. He was just 24 years old when he became editor of the *Bee* on his father's death in 1883. Unlike his father, C. K. was never active in politics beyond his role as editor, but he used that position with great vigor, attacking corrupt government wherever he saw it. Enemies in Sacramento accused the *Bee* of "trying to run this city," and labeled C. K. the "town bully," but he campaigned relentlessly through his widely-read column, "Private Thinks."[4]

C. K. carried on his father's campaign for conservation and continued to support organized labor, but he was most enthusiastic in the Progressive cause. His newspaper consistently supported Progressive candidates and their reforms. He vigorously attacked monopolies and crusaded for public ownership of utilities. The Southern Pacific machine was a special target. Governors, C. K. wrote, "shouldn't be the chosen favorite of the Southern Pacific."[5] Unlike Otis, Hearst, and other self-interested publishers, C. K. McClatchy genuinely seemed to want his newspapers to be "real tribunes of the people, always fighting for the right no matter how powerfully entrenched wrong may be . . . the friend of the underdog when the underdog is in the right . . . just at all times."[6]

Growing Chains and Growing Power

When the reformers finally triumphed over the machine, California settled into a half century of Republican party dominance. Until 1958 Democrats held the governor's office only once, even though Democrats constituted a majority of the voters long before that. Republicans stayed in power because of the popularity Hiram Johnson had built and because the Progressives had so weakened party structures with primaries and cross-filing that Democrats often didn't know they were voting for Republicans. The popularity of moderate governors like Earl Warren also seems to have transcended partisanship.

Another reason for the long reign of the Republicans was the domination of the newspapers by a few staunchly conservative, Republican publishers in San Francisco, Oakland, San Jose, San Diego, and Los Angeles. The reforms that weakened the parties strengthened the newspapers, which became the voters' primary source of information. By endorsing and playing up their favorites and ignoring opponents, the Republican newspaper owners helped keep their party in power for half a century. At the same time the number of newspapers declined and ownership was consolidated. In some cities, like San Diego and San Jose, the remaining two newspapers were owned by the same company. Most newspapers also became parts of chains, following the Hearst pattern.

THE INLAND EMPIRE

The McClatchy family was busy building its "Inland Empire"—founding the *Fresno Bee* (in 1922), buying the *Sacramento Star* and the *Fresno Republican*, and merging them with their *Bee* papers in each city. The *Modesto News-Herald* became the *Modesto Bee*. C. K.'s son Carlos managed the expansion and was editor of the Fresno paper. The empire also bought radio stations in each of the three cities. C. K. remained at the helm, approving every editorial, until his death in 1936 at the age of 77. His demise, the *San Francisco Chronicle* declared, brought "to its close the career of almost the last survivor of the colorful old-time journalists of California. Even while the picturesque band were alive and in their prime, C. K. was easily the most vivid and the most influential."[7]

C. K.'s death and the expansion of the empire brought change, but no lessening of influence. Because his son Carlos, who had been groomed to succeed him, died before him, C. K.'s daughter Eleanor was his chosen heir. Whereas James and C. K. were active in politics and journalism, and Carlos gravitated to the management side of the business, Eleanor left both to professionals, preferring a background role as representative of the family tradition. "When you are in this business," she announced, "you should be out back, not up front. . . . I was taught that newspaper people should never push themselves forward, but should stand on the sidelines and report the doings of others."[8] Although Miss Eleanor was not directly involved in running the newspapers, she exhibited the family's power through donations to hospitals and cultural organizations.

She hired Walter P. Jones, a "journalistic powerhouse of legendary proportions," to succeed her father as editor of the *Bee*.[9] He kept the job until his death in 1974, carrying on the family advocacy of good government, conservation, public ownership of utilities, and liberal policies in general. His editorials also favored military bases for the Sacramento area (they brought in business) and water projects to irrigate the Inland Empire, both areas of great importance to the development of California at the time. Under his leadership the *Bee* continued to support liberal candidates.

OTHER EMPIRES

Newspapers in other cities were also going through changes. In 1901, the Hayes family had acquired the *San Jose Mercury* and *Herald*, which were soon consolidated as the *Mercury*; in 1942, they bought the evening *San Jose News*, giving them a virtual newspaper monopoly in San Jose. The Hayeses were Progressives like the McClatchys, but when the first generation of publishers died, however, the papers were sold to the Ridder family, which was building a small chain of newspapers, each run by a brother. Joe Ridder was sent to San Jose in 1952 to punch up the newspapers, which soon became unabashed propaganda organs for the pro-growth local power structure. Criticized by environmentalists for the destruction of the orchards of the "Valley of Heart's Delight," Ridder responded, "Trees don't read newspapers."[10] He kept his papers' endorsements Republican and used the news pages to play up his favorites.

The situation in San Diego was almost identical to that of San Jose. Both the morning *Union* and the evening *Tribune* were owned by the Copley family, which also owned nine other dailies and nineteen weeklies. "Their news control has made the Copleys the major political force in town for more than a generation," one local observed.[11] Arch-conservative publisher James Copley used the news pages to flaunt candidates he favored while ignoring others. Copley and his editors were even more directly involved in politics than their peers in other cities, serving on campaign committees for San Diego Mayor Pete Wilson and presidential candidate Gerald Ford. Largely as a consequence of the paper's right-wing intransigence, the *San Diego Union* was rated one of the worst newspapers in the country by a national journalism review.[12]

The *Oakland Tribune*, published by the Knowland family since 1915, had a similar record. Joseph Knowland, a wealthy lumberman, bought the paper and used it to further his career in the state legislature and Congress. His son, William, had an even more promising career, serving in the state legislature, then winning the appointment to fill the United States Senate seat left vacant by the death of Hiram Johnson in 1945. After an unsuccessful bid for the governorship in 1958, Knowland returned to run the *Tribune*. He committed suicide in 1974 and was succeeded by his son, Joseph, Jr. The Knowlands' *Tribune* was a fixture in Oakland's conservative establishment, promoting its candidates and causes, like urban renewal, the sports complex, and the Bay Area Rapid Transit System. The newspaper helped keep Oakland and Alameda County Republican long after Democrats predominated in registration.

Across the bay the Hearst family was busy building a national media empire. By 1923 they owned twenty-two daily newspapers and nine magazines and had become the biggest consumer of paper in the world. The *San Francisco Ex-*

aminer and the *Los Angeles Herald-Examiner* were the Hearsts' lead papers in California. Although they sometimes endorsed Democrats, their sensational journalistic style was conservative to reactionary. They remained ultranationalistic, inflaming racist passions against the Japanese and Mexicans in the 1940s. They became increasingly antilabor; Hearst himself ended San Francisco's 1934 General Strike by aligning all five of the city's newspapers against it.[13] By the 1950s their reputation had declined to the point that author David Halberstam says, "The narrowness and shallowness of the political view was exceeded only by the incompetence of the corporate side."[14]

Meanwhile the *San Francisco Chronicle* was on the rise. In 1937 the de Young family had hired a respected journalist as editor. His intention was to transform the *Chronicle* into the "*New York Times* of the West," and although he made progress in that direction, circulation did not increase enough to satisfy his publishers. When Charles de Young Thierot became publisher in 1952, he hired a new editor named Scott Newhall. Described by newspaper critic Richard Reinhard as "an absolute wacko,"[15] Newhall turned the *Chronicle* into an entertaining, if lightweight, newspaper. "All we did," Newhall said, "was put on a floor show of fairy tales to get readers. . . . My mission with the *Chronicle* was to destroy Hearst."[16] Newhall's "floor show" included frivolous and sensational news coverage and Herb Caen, the most widely read columnist in the San Francisco Bay Area. Though Caen is liberal, the *Chronicle* editorial pages remain solidly Republican and conservative. Newhall's strategy worked. Under his leadership, circulation climbed from 150,000 to half a million, far surpassing the *Examiner* and second only to the *Los Angeles Times* in California. At the same time the *Chronicle* was rated one of the ten worst newspapers in the United States by a national journalism review.[17]

Although nominally in competition, the *San Francisco Chronicle* and *Examiner* had worked out an accommodation by the 1960s, making San Francisco almost as much a one-owner, two-newspaper town as San Diego and San Jose. The de Youngs and the Hearsts formed a joint operating company, sharing printing and distribution of the newspapers, combining their Sunday editions, and giving the *Chronicle* a morning monopoly and the *Examiner* an evening monopoly. They also split profits, a considerable boon to the far weaker *Examiner*. Their journalistic staffs remain separate, as do their editorial positions. The *Examiner* is not so adamantly Republican in its endorsement of candidates as the *Chronicle*, but both newspapers support the San Francisco establishment on local issues.

If these newspapers exercised great influence, none matched the record of the *Los Angeles Times*, much to the benefit of the family that owned it. "They did not so much foster the growth of Southern California as, more simply, invent it . . . ," writes David Halberstam. "No single family dominates any major region of the country as the Chandlers have dominated Southern California."[18] Harry Chandler, Harrison Gray Otis's son-in-law, worked closely with the publisher who made his family into a dynasty. They put together the coalition of businessmen that promoted the growth of greater Los Angeles, using the *Times* as their propaganda organ, and they were themselves heavily involved in the business of land development. Perhaps their greatest coup involved buying land in the Owens Valley to get water rights, then using the *Times* to persuade Los Angeles voters to fund a system to transport the water to Los Angeles, where it was needed only to allow the development of more land Chandler and his cohorts owned.

Conservative through and through, the *Times* opposed public ownership of utilities (except, of course, water), sided with the Southern Pacific machine against Hiram Johnson's reformers, helped kill public transport in Los Angeles because the automobile facilitated more extensive land development, and constantly fought and red-baited unions to keep the labor market in Los Angeles subservient and attractive to new industry. The *Times* also contributed to the anti-Japanese and anti-Mexican hysteria in the 1940s, helping to inflame the Zoot Suit Riots of 1943.

The succession of Harry Chandler's son Norman as publisher in 1944 moderated the tone of the *Times*, though its politics were unchanged. Norman entrusted the political operations to correspondent Kyle Palmer, who was the family's political agent for 40 years. The Chandlers and Palmer used the paper to promote conservative politicians, almost all of whom were Republicans. They were equally willing to use their power to destroy opponents. The *Times* virtually created the career of Richard Nixon, and Senator William Knowland's run for governor in 1958 was part of a *Times*-Knowland presidential strategy, the failure of which was the beginning of the end for Kyle Palmer.

With the outstanding exception of the McClatchys, the families that owned the major California newspapers were staunch conservatives who used their power to maintain Republican dominance in state politics well past its time. But change was coming. By the 1970s a new generation had come to power in all of the great publishing families, and the newspaper business had changed with the advent of television and corporate journalism.

Corporate Journalism

Every major newspaper in California went through major changes in the 1960s and 1970s. Virtually all of them became part of larger multimedia corporations and newspaper chains. In the process their journalistic style became more professional and objective, and their political influence grew more subtle.

McCLATCHY'S GROWING EMPIRE

Although still firmly under family control, the McClatchy empire exemplifies many of changes in the style and power of the California media. James McClatchy's great-grandson, another C. K., became editor of the *Sacramento Bee* on the death of Walter Jones in 1974 and took charge of the whole Inland Empire. Born in Fresno, educated at Stanford, this C. K. worked briefly for the *Washington Post*, presidential candidate Adlai Stevenson, and the American Broadcasting Company before joining the *Bee* as a reporter in 1958 and working his way up through the ranks.

Like his ancestors, C. K. sees his roots in the Central Valley: "I find this Valley—plain and flat and conservative as it is—one of the most thrilling places to be alive in that I know."[19] He inherits his family's clout, yet like his Aunt Eleanor, C. K. remains "intensely private," maintaining a "low community profile."[20] He's carried on the family tradition, turning the newspapers "into a nationally respected chain. He is as well-known and as highly thought of in the newspaper world as Otis Chandler or Katherine Graham, and he has done all this from a relatively obscure part of the country."[21] In the judgment of one media observer, C. K. made the *Bee* into "the poor man's *Washington Post*."[22]

As editor, C. K. brought in a new generation of editors and reporters, who have been credited with rejuvenating the *Bee* newspapers. Political coverage expanded to include more investigative reporting, longer interpretive pieces, and more coverage outside the *Bees'* immediate territory. Unlike other newspapers, the *Bees* have not confined their political coverage to the traditional focus on the out-front politicians—elected officials and candidates. Along with the opposition *Sacramento Union*, the *Sacramento Bee* has been ranked as providing the best coverage of what goes on in the state bureaucracy, an area only superficially reported by other newspapers.[23] The *Bee* also ran a five-part study of power in Sacramento, including those who exercise influence behind the scenes. Not surprisingly C. K. McClatchy was ranked second most powerful in the area.[24] The *California Journal* gave the *Bee* "the highest marks . . . for consistent excellence and effort" in covering politics in Washington, especially as they affect the home state.[25]

Election endorsements have been taken off the front page and put on the editorial page, the opinion section where most professional journalists believe they belong. The traditional command for readers to clip the list and take it to the polls has been replaced by a more reserved *"The Bee's* Recommendations." The political preferences of the *Bee* have not changed, however. The newspapers choose mostly liberal and Democratic candidates and have been ranked as the most liberal papers in the state by the *California Journal*.[26] On issues they continue their liberal, conservationist, good government lines. Although reporters have had difficulty when they've done stories critical of water projects, the *Bee* came out against the peripheral canal.

Unlike most of the other great newspapers in the state, the McClatchy papers have not issued public stock, and C. K. still controls 52 percent himself. Still the operations of the company have become more corporate in style. C. K. gave up his Aunt Eleanor's style of philanthropy, making sure it's known when the *Bee* gives money. "When our name doesn't appear . . . on a donor's list, people may become antagonistic toward us, thinking we didn't give," he said.[27] At the papers themselves, old reporters complain of "more middle management,"[28] and the *Bee's* traditional sympathy for labor unions, dating from its founding father, has been tarnished by new management practices. In 1978 the *Bee's* mailers' union went out on strike—the paper's first in 66 years, shattering its "amazing history of labor peace" according to one observer "and [bringing] about a change in the image of the paper from a liberal, benevolent, community-minded newspaper to a careful, if coldly managed, daily where profitability has gotten the upper hand."[29] Within 48 hours of the walkout, the *Bee* had changed to mechanized handling.

At the same time, the Sacramento paper switched from afternoon to morning publication like its sister newspapers, bringing it into head-on competition with the *Sacramento Union* and immediately increasing circulation by 12 percent.[30] McClatchy's new management team forged ahead in an effort to "streamline the paper and put some punch in the profit picture. . . . The old paternalistic McClatchy is now one where the character is that of an efficient newspaper operation. They brought in people from the South and non-union environments."[31]

Meanwhile the little chain of newspapers was changing into a media conglomerate. Already in possession of radio stations in Sacramento, Modesto, Fresno, and Reno, the McClatchys also acquired television stations in Fresno and Sacramento, lessening media competition in those cities even more and thereby increasing their own power by creating near-monopolies on information and communication. Their newspaper chain also expanded. They made a bid for the *Oakland Tribune* in 1977, but it failed, largely because of difficulties with the *Trib's* unions. But between 1978 and 1981 the McClatchys bought newspapers in Idaho, Washington, Alaska, and five small California cities.

And that's not all. In an effort to stay in the forefront of the communications industry, the McClatchys prepared to follow the example of other newspaper chains by expanding into cable television in the 1980s. To make sure the Federal Communications Commission would not object—and perhaps to raise the money—they began by selling their Fresno and Sacramento television stations for $13.5 and $65 million, respectively. The Fresno station went to a group of conservative Central Valley growers delighted to gain control of a medium that could give them a voice to counter McClatchy's.[32] Allegations by the *Wall Street Journal* that the *Bee* had suppressed an investigative story about the growers to facilitate the sale,[33] though denied and unproven, put a blemish on the *Bee's* impeccable journalistic reputation and enhanced its emerging image as a corporate operation. The company already had control of cable systems in Reno, Fresno, and half a dozen smaller California cities. C. K., described by a critic as "the media man of the future," called cable "a very important local news instrument,"[34] but for undisclosed reasons, dropped out of the bidding for the Sacramento system in 1981.

As the empire expanded, the *Bee's* reputation and power changed. The family operation became corporate in style. Troubles with labor unions and expansionism marred its once benign image. Competition from television and from a rejuvenated *Sacramento Union* lessened its power. The move into cable television may be a way of recouping these losses. But even with its new blemishes, the *Sacramento Bee* remains one of the most influential newspapers in the state, and the McClatchy family continues to be a formidable force in the Central Valley and in California.

MERGERS AND TAKEOVERS

Other newspapers in the state went through similar changes. The *San Francisco Chronicle* remained family-owned, with a younger generation, Richard Thierot, in the publisher's ofice. With business degrees from Yale and Stanford, the new publisher is a more professional manager than his predecessors, and he has a slightly larger media empire to oversee. In addition to the joint operating agreement with the *Examiner*, the *Chronicle* expanded into television, having acquired San Francisco television station KRON and a cable system with over 70,000 subscribers in Northern California.

Despite commanding the second highest circulation in the state (see Table 4-1), the *Chronicle* is still considered by many critics to be "more deficient in serious news than almost any other [newspaper] in its class."[35] Increasing competition from the *San Francisco Examiner*, the *Oakland Tribune*, and the *San Jose Mercury*, all of which have made more substantial improvements,

TABLE 4-1   Major California Newspapers, their Circulation, Owner,
and Liberal Ranking

Newspaper	Daily circulation	Ownership: family/corporate	Liberal ranking[a]
Los Angeles Times	1,011,798	Chandler/Times Mirror	8
San Francisco Chronicle	510,955	de Young-Thierot/Chronicle Pub.	32
Sacramento Bee	210,002	McClatchy	1
Fresno Bee	129,955		
Modesto Bee	69,994		
San Diego Union	205,788	Copley Press	24
San Diego Tribune	125,566		19
Los Angeles Herald-Examiner	281,533	Hearst	9
San Francisco Examiner	152,401	Hearst	25
San Jose Mercury	159,512	Knight-Ridder	6
San Jose News	66,464		
The Register (Orange County)	238,133	Freedom Papers Inc.	45
Van Nuys Daily News	121,327		7
Oakland Tribune	131,273	Gannett	10

Source: Editor and Publisher Yearbook, 1982. Reprinted with permission.
[a]"Political Ratings of California Newspapers—1980," California Journal 12, no. 10 (October 1981): 366. Based on endorsements of candidates and propositions, with a ranking of 1 being the most liberal.

have, however, driven the *Chronicle* to hire better editors and more enterprising reporters. At the same time, the entertainment values of the newspaper's critics and columnists remains high. "If you live on a street where every householder gets busy painting, fixing up and modernizing," a new editor admitted, "after a while you begin to look at your own house."[36] The *Chronicle*'s endorsement policies, however, have remained staunchly conservative Republican.

The *San Francisco Examiner* remains part of the Hearst chain, which had shrunk from thirty-three newspapers to just thirteen until the recent acquisition of thirty small Los Angeles County newspapers (twenty-eight weeklies and two dailies). But the empire now includes twenty magazines, seven radio stations, three television stations, and a developing cable system. The *Examiner* itself changed and improved with the arrival of a new editor in 1976. He introduced zoned editions and hired new columnists and younger, more aggressive reporters. Political coverage was expanded, and the *Examiner* now boasts the best court and labor reporters in the state. Although fourteen members of the Hearst family still work for the corporation, none is as directly involved in daily journalism as the founder.[37] Those responsibilities are now left to professional journalists.

In San Diego, James Copley, conservative publisher of the *Union* and *Tribune*, died in 1973. The papers were then taken over by his wife, Helen, who moderated their politics. Competition from the *Los Angeles Times*, which was trying to move into the huge San Diego market also gave the Copley papers impetus for change. According to the *California Journal*, Mrs. Copley "has told reporters that the sacred cows of her husband are now fair game, and the papers have become noticeably more evenhanded. Still not fair game for Copley reporters, however, are Helen Copley's own sacred cows, which seem to include the Chamber of Commerce [and] Mayor [now United States Senator] Pete Wilson. . . ."[38] And in 1982, the *Union* published no fewer than six editorials pushing its candidate in a crucial Congressional race.

The Oakland and San Jose newspapers were absorbed by the two largest chains in the country and change was more substantial. The Ridder's San Jose newspapers merged with the Knight chain in 1977, forming a corporation that ranked 295 in the Fortune 500. The chain owns thirty-three newspapers (in San Jose, Long Beach, Pasadena, Anaheim, Miami, Philadelphia, Detroit, and many smaller cities) with the largest combined circulation in the country. Like the other newspaper chains, they are moving into cable television. When the corporation took over, they ousted the old publisher, but replaced him with a younger member of the Ridder family, one who more readily fit the corporate mold. They also brought in new, highly professional editors who, in turn, recruited younger, more aggressive, and more talented reporters. Political news, previously treated superficially and often as a joke or twisted to suit the bias and interests of the publisher, suddenly became serious business. Editorials turned mildly liberal and critical of growth, disturbing the old-guard power structure.

In Oakland the Knowland family was unable to agree on the future of the *Tribune* and in 1977 sold it to Combined Communications, which soon passed it on to the Gannett corporation. Ranked 426 in *Fortune* magazine's listing of the 500 largest corporations in America, Gannett owns eighty-three dailies and fourteen weeklies as well as seven television and thirteen radio stations. Seven of the newspapers and three of the radio stations are in California. Gannett transformed the stodgy old *Tribune*, hiring Robert Maynard of the *Washington Post* as its editor. Maynard is black, like almost half of the citizens of Oakland, something the *Tribune* no longer ignores. Unlike all the other major dailies in the state, the *Tribune* pays as much attention to its traditional inner-city base as to the more lucrative suburbs. According to the *Columbia Journalism Review*,

> The most significant change has been in the paper's approach to its readers and potential readers. Instead of writing off the poor and working-class residents of the city, as so many newspapers have done in recent years, Maynard is making a brave try at turning the *Tribune* into a true community newspaper—one that will serve (and perhaps even explain to one another) the mainly white East Bay suburbanites and the largely black and Hispanic population of the city proper.[39]

Corporate management undoubtedly improved the *Tribune*, but one problem with corporate takeovers is that newspapers become pawns in a much larger game. That was made plain in 1982 when the Gannett chain announced it was buying San Francisco television station KRON from the *Chronicle*, although the sale ultimately fell through. To conform to federal regulations prohibiting ownership of both a newspaper and a television station in the same market, Gannet announced it would sell the *Tribune*. Editor Robert Maynard borrowed enough money to buy the paper, but its future remains in doubt. If the *Tribune* fails, the primary beneficiary will be the *Chronicle-Examiner* partnership, which will have one less competitor with which to contend.

THE *L.A. TIMES* GOES NATIONAL AND CORPORATE

As much as these newspapers changed, none changed more than the *Los Angeles Times*. In the 1970s it became not only *the* newspaper of Southern California, but a respected national journal and the crowning glory of a major media conglomerate. The change coincided with the coming to power of a new generation in the Chandler family. The modernization of the *Times* began with Norman Chandler's wife, Buffy, whose cultural and philanthropic activity was calculated to change the public image of the newspaper and who encouraged her husband, an able businessman but a complacent publisher, to bring the newspaper into step with the times. In 1960 Mrs. Chandler persuaded her husband to step down as publisher and give the job to their son, Otis, over the objections of more conservative members of the family.

Otis Chandler took a mediocre newspaper, long used to further the business interests of the family and its friends, and made it serious, simultaneously shifting the family business interests from real estate to a new media empire. Chandler, like his mother, wanted "to make the rest of the country" take the *Times*—and himself—"seriously."[40] He brought on new, highly respected editors and reporters who began a tradition of long feature articles and investigative reporting. Political coverage expanded. By election day in 1974, for example, the *Times* had sixteen reporters covering California campaigns. The Republican slant of the news pages was moderated and coverage of candidates became balanced. The *Times* bureaus in Washington and Sacramento were lavishly expanded. The *Times* reporters in the capitals also function differently than they did in the past. "There was a total transformation," one veteran reporter declared. "Under Norman, the Sacramento bureau chief was the Chandler family's emissary to the governor's office, giving orders, not really reporting. Now their reporting of California and national politics is excellent."[41]

At the local level the paper slowly began covering minority issues and recognizing environmental problems, even advocating some controls on growth. Editorials became more liberal on social issues, though still probusiness. Usually, however, the editorials were thoughtful discussions of issues without strong viewpoints of their own. "The positions we adopt," one *Times* editorial writer said, "are so objective as to be utterly indifferent."[42] The *Times* even stopped endorsing candidates for major offices in 1974. The newspaper was more objective than in the old days, but some critics believe it had gone beyond objectivity to boredom.[43]

But the success of the *Times* can't be denied. Circulation is over a million a day, the paper runs more ads than any other, and 1978 profits were $83 million—not bad at a time when other papers were going under. One of the *Times'* advantages was the absence of unions, enabling it to adapt more rapidly than other papers to the new technology and economies in production. The *Times* also led the other newspapers in the state in adopting corporate-style management. In 1964 it was the first of the family papers to "go public" (selling shares on the stock exchange). It was the first to modernize its management and the first to have a publisher who is not a member of the family (in 1980, when Otis Chandler became chairman of the board and left the publisher's job to a professional journalist).

With corporate management came the growth of a media conglomerate. By 1978 the Times-Mirror Company ranked 232 in the Fortune 500, topping any other newspaper company. By then they owned major newspapers in New York, Texas, and Connecticut, as well as three small California papers. Perhaps more important, the *Times* owned seven television stations and had been investing in cable systems since 1969. With 625,000 subscribers, they've become the sixth largest cable system in the country.

If the *Los Angeles Times* was the most changed newspaper in the state, none was immune to change. Each became a part of a larger media network; each came to be ruled by a new generation of family owners and professional journalists. Along the way, each improved in quality and moderated its political bias.

Television and Politics

Newspapers were the crucial communication medium in California politics until the 1960s, when television began to supplant them as a source of news and a means for politicians to reach the voters. Surveys show that two-thirds of the public relies on television for news. Over 95 percent of California households have television sets and over 85 percent of these households can be reached in just four areas: Los Angeles, San Francisco, San Diego, and Sacramento.[44] Television could be a significant competitor to newspapers, providing the public with more information and more points of view, but unfortunately television has not met its potential. That potential has been limited by cross-ownership, whereby many newspapers own television stations. However, it has been more severely limited by the nature of the medium itself and the shallow coverage television gives to political news, especially at the state and local level.

In the 1960s television tried to give state politics serious coverage. Nine of the state's sixty-seven stations had Sacramento bureaus. Today, aside from the Sacramento stations, only San Francisco's KRON has a crew in the state capital. Although most newspapers have several reporters who specialize in politics, television reporters are almost all generalists. Only one broadcast journalist in the whole state, KRON's Rollin Post, specializes in politics. The advent of "happy talk" and "action news" in the 1970s significantly diminished political coverage. "Happy talk" focuses on the lighter side and avoids often dull political news; "action news" plays up immediate, breaking stories. Both try to keep the news entertaining and dramatic, staying away from depth and detail. The focus is on events within the station's viewing area, so that state politics take a backseat. "We don't spend much time covering the Capitol," an editor for San Francisco's KGO said, "because most of what the legislature does doesn't really affect people's lives. Our audience doesn't look for political stories. Most of them don't even vote."[45]

Television news editors have decided that their viewers aren't much interested in political news, so they don't spend much time on it. A study of television coverage of the 1974 California election found only 2 percent of news time spent on campaigns.[46] Another study revealed that 60 percent of news time went to commercials, banter, weather, sports, and "cute" items; 25 percent was spent on stories about fires and murders; 6 percent for economics and business; and 10 percent for politics, mostly national and international stories.[47] Television news of state and local government comes mostly from the newspapers or wire services with occasional film of meetings or press conferences. The orientation is entirely visual, focusing on events and personalities and ignoring or oversimplifying complex issues like the state budget.

Yet, given its size and diversity, California is the ultimate media state, and television is the medium most capable of bringing it together. "There's only one way you can reach hundreds of thousands or millions of people, and that's through TV," observed the old media-master Ronald Reagan.[48] But the unenterprising nature of television news reporting has driven politicians to staging events to get attention. Announcements of candidacies or major programs are often made by flying around the state, stopping for press conferences in all the major media markets—minimally San Francisco, Los Angeles, and Sacramento. Television has made Los Angeles, where the stations reach 50 percent of the state's voters, a specially desirable venue for coverage. As a result, candidates for statewide office who are from Southern California start with an advantage, and those from Northern California spend most of their campaign time in the South. But the visual orientation of television news has another impact on the candidates. Assemblyman Tom Hayden, who is more issue-oriented than most, points out that "The candidate who is interested in issues . . . eventually has to give up. There is a tremendous pressure on candidates to do stunts to get coverage. You have to be a media freak."[49]

Candidates and issue-advocates who want coverage are driven to a sort of "political theater" to gain attention. One TV producer says, "If it's interesting, we cover it. If it isn't, we don't. It is up to the candidates to make themselves interesting and to do something newsworthy. It is not the media's responsibility to go after them and draw them out."[50] That's an attitude considerably different from newspaper journalists!

But if television hasn't given newspapers much competition for news coverage of state politics, it has distinctly weakened the power of the newspapers as king-makers. The Chandlers, Hearsts, and McClatchys can no longer create or destroy candidates because television gives political aspirants a way around the print media. They can reach the voters by cleverly staged, visual media events or, even more effectively, by buying television time. An unknown candidate with enough money can suddenly become a gubernatorial contender, as Assemblyman Ken Maddy demonstrated in 1978 when he spent $250,000 on an early television blitz, tripling his ratings in the public opinion polls. "It's funny," one advertising man said, "but politicians now think of the state in terms of television markets rather than counties or Senate districts as they used to."[51] But by 1982, 60-second television spots cost $15,000 in Los Angeles and $8,000 in San Francisco, giving the advantage to candidates with lots of money. Television advertising is too expensive and wasteful for most candidates for local or legislative office because in most areas it reaches voters well beyond their districts. But for statewide candidates, it has become essential. Mary Ellen Leary, a perceptive observer of the 1974 gubernatorial campaign, concluded that "television dominated the candidate's entire campaign effort," which consisted mostly of dreaming up ways of making news to get free coverage and raising money to pay for television ads."[52]

The combination of television's superficial news coverage, political theater, and advertising tends to make politics on TV very personality oriented, thus reinforcing one of the fundamental characteristics of California politics. The 30-second ads or 60-second news reports do not allow time for analysis or depth; they give the viewer a glimpse of a politician, usually in action. Some politicians like this. A member of Jerry Brown's staff said "a perception comes through better on TV than in print. Print can summarize Jerry's stand on something, but who's going to read it? TV lets the personality through. That's what people make up their minds on."[53]

Television has changed politics, making it even more personality-oriented, but it has also had an impact on newspapers. "Television is forcing newspapers to go one step further in journalism," C. K. McClatchy says. "Any paper that hasn't moved that step yet is going to have to right soon."[54] Television has taken away the monopoly newspapers once had on breaking stories because the electronic media can easily scoop the slower print media. But the print media can do some things TV can't (or won't) do. As a consequence, newspapers have shifted their emphasis to more in-depth stories with more interpretation and analysis rather than just reporting events.

This changing role for newspapers has kept them important in politics. They provide such coverage of complex issues as there is; they do the investigative reporting. They still pay attention to state and local government. On their editorial pages they unleash opinions that are muted in the pseudo-objectivity pretended by television news. Additionally, television relies on newspapers and wire services for political stories; the newspapers therefore still, if now indirectly, shape what Californians know about politics. Because newspaper readers are more affluent and better educated than average, the newspapers influence the opinion leaders and those most likely to vote. The competition of television news and campaign advertising has made the newspapers work harder to gain an audience and encouraged them to provide more information and analysis to show they are really different from television and to hold an audience. It's also freed candidates from the tyranny of the newspaper king-makers.

Nevertheless, a new medium on the horizon has the older media worried. It's cable television and it could change the whole configuration just described. As of 1980, California had 284 cable systems serving 1.8 million subscribers. So far, cable has competed with the other media mainly as entertainment, but the technology is being adapted to shopping, reading newspapers, campaigns, and even voting. The impact cable may have on the other media is indicated by a study of Woodland, California, which revealed that cable decreased use of every other available medium: use of traditional television fell by 36 percent, radio by 25 percent, movies by 17 percent, newspapers by 8 percent, and magazines by 6 percent.[55] An experimental cable-information system being developed by Knight-Ridder, owners of the *San Jose Mercury News*, found an even more dramatic drop-off: 45 percent of the households were watching less regular TV and 33 percent were spending less time reading newspapers.[56] California's major newspapers are well aware of this potential and every one has invested in cable systems. Because such systems are franchised by city and county government and regulated by state law, cable is sure to be a political issue in the future.

Reporting California Politics

The role of the media in California politics has changed. Their style has also changed. Still their influence remains great. Contemporary coverage of state politics is undoubtedly better than it once was, although there are still criticisms.

The great newspapers and their electronic competitors vary considerably in their commitment of resources to the subject. Eighteen California newspapers, ten television stations, and nine radio stations maintain news bureaus in Washington to cover the doings of our representatives there. Most employ only one or two correspondents, though the *Los Angeles Times*, which focuses on national news, employs twenty-five reporters plus editors. The press corps in the state capital number over 200, but only about 50 are involved in covering state politics on a daily basis. Most newspapers have only one or two correspondents in Sacramento, but the *Los Angeles Times* has ten and the Associated Press has nine. Only the local newspapers have more. Only one television station outside Sacramento has a bureau there.

Reporting state politics was once a chummy affair known as the "saloon beat." Coverage was an insider's game and publishers played the news to suit themselves. Revelations about the lobbying empire of Artie Samish, for example, were left to a national magazine, because the state newspapers ignored it. The new generation of publishers, editors, and reporters has proven more aggressive and objective. As a consequence, relations with public officials are somewhat less cordial. The legislature, which once allowed reporters free run of their chambers and provided them with desks, no longer does so.

Within the press corps the *Los Angeles Times* is probably the most important single influence. One veteran calls it "a model," with a "high level of state capitol coverage "[57] The Associated Press wire service, however, supplies 250 news operations around the state, and the *Sacramento Bee, Sacramento Union,* and *San Jose Mercury* are also widely read in Sacramento and "wield tremendous power."[58]

Nevertheless, an editor for the *Los Angeles Times* admits that "although critically important to the populace, state government has never been considered sexy enough to merit a lot of attention in the news, certainly not the attention it deserves."[59] Reporting on the governor is often limited to press conferences and speeches. Coverage of the doings of the rest of the executive branch—the bureaucracy—is so weak that one reporter called it "a capitol offense."[60] Reporting on the state supreme court is extremely limited; indeed no reporters are assigned to the beat full time. What coverage the court's decisions do get is superficial, largely due to lack of expertise. Anthony Lewis, a *New York Times* columnist specializing in the courts, blamed that lack of expertise for misconceptions that created the controversy about Chief Justice Rose Bird and the alleged suppression of politically sensitive judicial decisions.[61] These problems are caused not only by reporters' lack of expertise but also by editorial decisions that assign too few reporters to such important beats.

One Sacramento reporter accuses his colleagues of being "too shallow," accepting the "stage shows put on by politicians," and being too easily "used."[62] Others have said the press is too personality oriented, giving readers information more about the politicians than what the politicians do. They also tend to "pack journalism," gravitating to events like press conferences and legislative hearings, so that everybody is covering the same stories. It's not always their fault. Some reporters tell of having stories rejected by their editors because the *Los Angeles Times,* the leader of the pack, didn't cover it.

Election coverage, however, has improved considerably. Whereas most newspapers once gave highly biased play to favored candidates, they are now more balanced. Greater resources are committed to covering campaigns, including more reporters as well as use of public opinion polls and computer analysis of campaign finance and voting patterns. The *Sacramento Bee* and the *Los Angeles Times* have, for the past decade, devoted the greatest resources and provided the most extensive coverage of campaigns, but the San Jose and San Diego papers have been catching up recently.

Television coverage of campaigns, on the other hand, is poor. TV stations rarely send reporters out to follow candidates. They wait for the contenders to come to town or stage dramatic events. Because of federal "equal time" regulations, television stations are cautious about covering one candidate for fear all the others will demand access. The dullness of most political events also keeps television away. The Los Angeles stations, for example, refused to televise a debate between 1982 senatorial candidates Pete Wilson and Jerry Brown. "There's more money in the programs that can have commercials," said a League of Women Voters spokesperson.[63]

Television news, along with candidate advertising and other campaign techniques, has lessened the power of the newspapers by giving candidates a way to reach the voters directly, but the press still has the power to confer credibility, provide evaluations of the candidates, and create a sense of drama and significance that can stimulate or depress voter interest and turnout.

Of course, the newspapers still express their own preferences through their endorsements, but this, too, has changed. Endorsements were once at the whim of the publishers—the Chandlers, McClatchys, and Copleys—but new management has changed the system at most newspapers. Now candidates are usually interviewed by an editorial board consisting of the publisher, editors, and often editorial page writers and political reporters. The boards vote on endorsements, so participation is broader than it once was. Still, when push comes to shove, the publisher has the vote that counts most. Only one of these newspapers, the *San Jose Mercury*, has radically changed past endorsement preferences, though the *Los Angeles Times* no longer states its choice for governor, United States senator, or president. The McClatchy papers remain the most liberal in the state, the *San Francisco Chronicle* and the San Diego papers among the most conservative. (See the rankings in Table 4-1.) But, whereas in the past all but two of these papers virtually always endorsed Republicans, all of them are now less predictable.

The impact of endorsements is greatest in cities like San Jose and San Diego, where the newspapers have a monopoly, but on the whole, the influence of endorsements is probably less than it has ever been. The candidates have other means of reaching voters, and the newspapers are less forceful about their endorsements and no longer back them up with biased news coverage. Several papers now humbly call their endorsements "recommendations," and most now publish them on the editorial page, rather than the front page. Because less than one-third of their readers read the editorial page,[64] that's a substantial limitation. Endorsements in majoi races—for president or governor, for example—probably have little impact because voters know more about them and generally make up their minds before newspaper endorsements are published. But in primary elections with a large field of candidates, close races, nonpartisan local elections, obscure judicial contests, and ballot measures, newspaper endorsements can make the margin of difference. They also give candidates legitimacy and credibility, which can help them win support and money elsewhere.

Changing Media

From the crusading frontier journalism of James McClatchy to the cool professionalism of media mogul C. K. McClatchy, from the brash and brutal boosterism of Harrison Gray Otis to the corporate suavity of Otis Chandler, the media and their power have changed in California. Superficially, that change was wrought by a new generation of family owners, professional editors, and eager reporters.

But the new-style publishers, editors, and reporters reflect deeper changes in California. As the state's population became more affluent and better educated, the newspapers had to change. Competition from television was an added stimulant. The great individual empires of Hearst and Chandler—though not yet of McClatchy—have also been absorbed by larger corporations. Two-thirds of the newspapers in California are now owned by corporate media conglomerates with varied interests. The power of individuals and families has been assumed by corporate executives, and the newspapers they publish are different than they used to be, usually better because they're more professional.

The combination of these factors has changed the media and restrained their exercise of political power. But that power is still there; it's just more subtly used. Greater fairness on the news page and calm, well-reasoned editorials only enhance the credibility and thus the power of the press. And Californians, even more than citizens of other states, still depend on the press for information and opinion.

Notes

[1]Robert Gottlieb and Irene Wolt, *Thinking Big* (New York: Putnam's, 1977), p. 82.
[2]George Mowry, *The California Progressives* (Chicago: Quadrangle, 1963), p. 126.
[3]David Halberstam, *The Powers That Be* (New York: Dell, 1979), p. 148.
[4]"The Bee through 100 Years," *Sacramento Bee*, February 3, 1958, p. 55. Most of the history of the McClatchy family and their newspapers is drawn from this source.
[5]C. K. McClatchy, *Private Thinks* (New York: Scribner's, 1936), p. 92
[6]Ibid., pp. 38–39.
[7]"The Bee through 100 Years," p. 99.
[8]*Sacramento Bee*, October 18, 1980; *San Francisco Chronicle*, October 18, 1980.
[9]*Sacramento Bee*, April 2, 1979.

[10]Richard Reinhardt, "Joe Ridder's San Jose, *San Francisco*, November 1965, p. 68.

[11]Larry Remer, "Chandler v. Copley for the Readers of San Diego," *California Journal* 9, no. 9 (September 1978): 301.

[12]*More* magazine as cited in the *Bay Guardian*, May 11, 1974.

[13]W. A. Swanberg, *Citizen Hearst* (New York: Bantam, 1961), p. 630.

[14]Halberstam, p. 282.

[15]Richard Reinhardt, "Doesn't *Everybody* Read the *Chronicle?*" *Columbia Journalism Review*, January-February 1982, p. 27.

[16]Michael Hobson, "The World of Scott Newhall," *feed/back*, Fall 1975, p. 37.

[17]*More* magazine as cited in the *Bay Guardian*, May 11, 1974.

[18]Halberstam, p. 136.

[19]Stephen Birmingham, *California Rich* (New York: Simon and Schuster, 1980), p. 258–59.

[20]*Sacramento Bee*, April 2, 1979.

[21]Bill Bryan, "Valley Vision: McClatchy's Cable Cabal," *New West*, December 22, 1980, p. 119.

[22]Mary Ellen Leary, *Phantom Politics: Campaigning in California* (Washington, D.C.: Public Affairs Press, 1977), p. 73.

[23]Art Nauman, "Capitol Offense," *feed/back*, Winter 1981, pp. 21–25.

[24]*Sacramento Bee*, April 1–5, 1979. Henry Teichert, head of a Sacramento construction company, ranked first.

[25]Gil Bailey, "The Sudden Expansion of the Washington Press Corps," *California Journal* 9, no. 9 (September 1978): 304.

[26]Kenneth Rystrom, "Rating the Newspapers as Political Persuaders," *California Journal* 10, no. 8 (August 1979): 287–288; and "Voter Response to Newspaper Endorsements," *California Journal* 12, no. 10 (October 1981): 366–367.

[27]*Sacramento Bee*, April 2, 1979.

[28]Interview with authors, Leo Rennert, Washington, D.C., April 1981.

[29]Chuck Buxton and Harold Kruger, "Fort McClatchy," *feed/back*, Spring 1978, p. 24. See also Patti Reichenbach Zeff, "The New Expansionism of the McClatchy Empire," *California Journal* 11, no. 11 (November 1980): 442.

[30]"Precede," *feed/back*, Summer 1980, p. 1.

[31]Buxton and Kruger, op. cit., *feed/back*, p. 27.

[32]"Precede," *feed/back*, Winter 1981, p. 2.

[33]*Wall Street Journal*, September 29, 1980.

[34]Bryan, "Valley Vision," p. 119.

[35]Ben H. Bagdikian, "The Chronicle Chronicles," *San Francisco*, May 1982, p. 64.

[36]Mary Ellen Leary, "Higher Grades for Bay Area Newspapers," *California Journal* 12, no. 4 (April 1981): 133–136.

[37]Lindsay Chaney and Michael Cieply, *The Hearsts: Family and Empire, the Later Years* (New York: Simon and Schuster, 1981), pp. 374–75.

[38]Larry Remer, "Chandler v. Copley for the Readers of San Diego," *California Journal* 9, no. 9 (September 1978): 301.

[39]Joseph P. Lyford, "Something New for Oakland," *Columbia Journalism Review*, January-February 1981, p. 45.

[40]"The World's Oldest Surfer," *Time*, August 13, 1979, p. 60.

[41]Interview with authors, Leo Rennert, Washington, D.C., April 1981.

[42]Rian Malan, "Paper Giant," *California*, October 1982, p. 156.

[43]Ibid.

[44]Leary, *Phantom Politics*, p. 78.

[45]Dorothy A. Kupcha, "The TV Boycott of State Capitol News," *California Journal* 11, no. 3 (March 1980): 101.

[46]Mary Ellen Leary, "The Browning of Campaign Coverage," *Columbia Journalism Review*, July 1976, p. 14.

[47]*Los Angeles Times*, September 16, 1979, Section V, p. 5.

[48]*Los Angeles Times*, May 13, 1976, Section II, p. 7.

[49]Michele Willens, "Promises, Promises," *California Journal* 9, no. 4 (April 1978): 106.

[50]Leary, *Phantom Politics*, pp. 147–48.

[51]*San Francisco Chronicle*, April 16, 1978.

[52]Leary, *Phantom Politics*, p. 172.

[53]Leary, *Phantom Politics*, p. 130.

[54]Leary, *Phantom Politics*, p. 74.

[55]Stewart J. Kaplan, "The Impact of Cable Television Services on the Use of Competing Media," *Journal of Broadcasting*, Spring 1978, pp. 155–65.

[56]*San Jose Mercury*, November 29, 1982.

[57]Lou Cannon, *Reporting* (Sacramento: California Journal Press, 1977), p. 203.

[58]Hal Rubin and Pat Washburn Rubin, "The Fourth Estate," *California Journal* 11, no. 1 (January 1980): 20.

[59]Tony Quinn, "Failure of the Media to Cover the State Campaigns," *California Journal* 11, no. 12 (December 1980): 468.

[60]Art Nauman, "Capitol Offense," *feed/back*, Winter 1981, pp. 21–25.

[61]Anthony Lewis, Preface to Preble Stolz's *Judging Judges* (New York: Free Press, 1981), p. xvii.

[62]Art Nauman, "Capitol Offense," *feed/back*, Winter 1981, pp. 21–25.

[63]*San Jose Mercury*, October 6, 1982.

[64]*Los Angeles Times*, March 18, 1976, Section I, p. 1.

5
THE EXECUTIVE BRANCH

Coping with a Split Personality

California does not have a traditional executive branch—it has executive *branches*. As commonly used, the term "executive branch" suggests cohesion and cooperation, but in California the elected leaders holding this set of offices are like a group of independent corporate chiefs rather than a closely knit, interdependent team working together under shared assumptions and goals.

Most states have constitutional provisions that encourage selection of the governor and lieutenant governor (and, in some cases, all executive branch members) from the same party ticket. California elections occur by office rather than party, allowing for the possibility that members of both parties will serve in the executive branch.

To make matters even more complicated, California's executive branch has an unusually large number of elected offices. In addition to the governor and lieutenant governor, the executive branch includes an attorney general, secretary of state, controller, treasurer, superintendent of public instruction, and four members of the Board of Equalization. Although most states elect lieutenant governors, secretaries of state, and treasurers, only eighteen elect education department heads, ten elect controllers, and only two elect the equivalent to California's Board of Equalization.

If there's a modern-day example of the "rugged individualism" mentality that characterized the state's gold rush, that theme is alive and well in the executive branch of California state government. In 1982 the voters adhered to this tradition by splitting their tickets to elect Republican George "Duke" Deukmejian to the governorship and Democrat Leo McCarthy to the lieutenant governorship. Because of the voters' choices, the executive branch began another 4 year stint of competition instead of cooperation.

The Jerry and Mike Show—Gubernatorial Infighting at Its Best

In 1978 Californians went to the polls to do what they do every 4 years: elect the members of the state's executive branch. Predictably enough, the voters were inconsistent in the expression of their partisanship. Although most of those elected to the executive branch were Democrats, not all were. Such results are routine in California, where the electorate tends to choose candidates by personality rather than political party. Not since 1946 had Californians chosen an executive branch in which all six of the most important partisan offices (governor, lieutenant governor, attorney general, secretary of state, controller, and treasurer) were won by the same party.

But something else did happen in 1978 that represented an unusual wrinkle even in California. As the voters were reelecting Democrat Jerry Brown to the governorship by a comfortable 1.3 million vote margin, Republican Mike Curb ousted incumbent Democratic Lieutenant Governor Mervyn Dymally by 550,000 votes. For the first time since 1894, Californians chose a governor and lieutenant governor from two different parties.

The 1978 split decision was little more than a precursor to 1982. In a reversal of public sentiment, Republican George Deukmejian squeaked out a gubernatorial victory over Democrat Tom Bradley by 53,000 votes (out of 7.7 million cast), and Democrat Leo McCarthy defeated Republican Carol Hallett for the lieutenant governorship by 600,000 votes. Prior to the election, both McCarthy and Hallett were confident that Californians would not tolerate another split in the state's highest two offices. Said McCarthy, "There's a 90 percent chance . . . that the governor and lieutenant governor will come from the same party." Echoing McCarthy, Hallett acknowledged, "It's possible candidates from different parties will be elected again, but I doubt it will happen."[1] So much for expert opinion. Although the Deukmejian-McCarthy administration awaits public judgment, the Brown-Curb affair has taken its place in history. It is to that torrid period in California politics that we now turn.

THE BROWN-DYMALLY MARRIAGE—AND DIVORCE

Although Democrats Jerry Brown and Mervyn Dymally emerged from the 1974 election as governor and lieutenant governor, the two politicians had little in common. Brown sought the top spot as a reformer, someone who offered new politics and spirit for the state. As secretary of state from 1971 to 1974, he had taken a once dormant office and given it new life. Young and energetic, Jerry Brown was viewed by most seasoned politicians as an "outsider." His clashes with the legislature were so confrontational that the two houses actually deleted funds for Brown's Los Angeles office in Century City, forcing him into more austere quarters. Fiercely independent, Brown steered his own course in the executive branch.

Dymally, on the other hand, was cut from different political cloth. A protégé of Jesse Unruh, he was elected to the Assembly in 1962. When the state's reapportionment map in 1966 awarded fourteen seats to Los Angeles County in place of one, Dymally was one of the chief beneficiaries as the state's first black in the upper house. He was very popular with his colleagues and gained a reputation as an individual who could work with different factions. Ultimately, Dymally was elected Senate majority leader.

The differences in political bases of power echoed the different personality traits of Brown and Dymally. Veteran political observer Ed Salzman was among the first to notice the chasms dividing the two leaders: "Brown is ascetic, introverted, philosophical . . . , with name identification that helped him win one office after another. . . . Dymally is an old-fashioned glad-handing politician, a black version of Pat Brown. He fought his way through the political thicket . . . to emerge as head of the nearest thing California has to a political machine."[2] Antiestablishment versus establishment, reformer versus power broker, philosopher versus scrapper—the bottom line was that little other than electoral fate held Brown and Dymally together.

By 1978 the Brown-Dymally "relationship" had worn thin as the two camps bickered both in private political circles and in public alike. Moreover, the voters' assessments of the two leaders were quite different in the political party primary contests. Whereas Brown emerged with 78 percent of the vote, Dymally managed only 55 percent in the quest for his renomination. In addition, Dymally had to fend off allegations that he used his political influence improperly for personal gain. Although the charges were never proven, the bad press was not exactly a boon to Dymally's campaign.

Given the many strains in their personal and political relationships, Brown and Dymally ran entirely separate campaigns in 1978. The result was a split decision: Brown handily defeated Republican Attorney General Evelle Younger, but Dymally lost to Republican Mike Curb. And thus began a new, even more volatile era in the executive branch's top two positions.

THE BROWN-CURB ADMINISTRATION: PETTY POLITICS IN ACTION

Most people view Californians as "laid back" types who value ambiance more than ambition. These perceptions have been applied to the state's governors as well. Historically, Governor Earl Warren (1943–53) was universally praised as a thoughtful man. His successor, Goodwin J. "Goody" Knight (1953–58), represented the grandfather stereotype, white hair and all. Edmund G. "Pat" Brown (1959–67) had a handshake for all and would "politic" with anyone from capitol elevator operators to state Democratic party leaders. Even Ronald Reagan (1967–75), though more partisan than his predecessors, had a folksy image (jelly bean jar, cowboy attire, etc.) that enhanced his popularity as a "down to earth" person first, politician second. Then along came Edmund G. "Jerry" Brown, Jr. and a new breed of California governor.

Casting aside all previous images of prudence, minimal partisanship, and public access, Brown carved out his own distinct gubernatorial personality. In the process he developed an unusual relationship with the public in which most people either hated or adored him. Always on the edge of controversy (if not in the middle of it!), Brown took the state in a new direction after his election in 1974. When Jerry Brown sought reelection in 1978, he ran on a record that emphasized reconsideration of previous policies, innovation, and, for the most part, liberal state budgets. In addition, he presented an image of an antiestablishment politician with an unusual lifestyle.

Jerry Brown—"A Breed Apart."   In his first term as governor Brown rewrote "the script" on the style and politics of the office. Elected at the age of 36, Brown did virtually everything different from his predecessors. After the state built a new $1.3 million governor's mansion in the waning months of the Reagan administration, Brown refused to live in what he called the "Taj Mahal." Instead he rented an apartment near his office. When he traveled by car, he used a Plymouth from the state motor pool rather than a costly limousine; he also flew on commercial jets instead of expensive state-owned aircraft. Brown's style emphasized basic pragmatism over lush comfort. He seemed to go out of his way to shun "the establishment."

Politically, Brown's first term also was unique. Repeatedly, he argued that government had limitations: "The answer in government always seems to be to add more—I think that's wrong."[3] By questioning growth for growth's sake, the young governor seemed intent on charting his own independent course. Yet, if Jerry Brown publicly advocated a "go slow" approach to government, his actions often indicated otherwise.

Between 1975 and 1978 Brown and the Democrat-controlled legislature nudged the state to the left in a number of policy areas. His appointees to the Public Utility Commission focused on consumerism instead of profit margins. His appointees to the Agriculture Labor Relations Board—a creation of his own administration—stressed farmworkers' rights over farm production. His judicial appointments included more blacks, Asians, Hispanics, and women than any previous administration. During his first term Brown's budgets almost doubled from $9.5 million to $16.3 million. Even when controlled for inflation, state expenditures went up by 43 percent during the 4 year period, including massive infusions for education, welfare, and other social services.[4] Some argued the huge increases were partial compensation for a previously frugal Reagan administration; others countered that Brown had a liberal philosophy, regardless of what his public rhetoric might suggest.

The different interpretations notwithstanding, one fact remains clear: Jerry Brown established his own unique style. Based on that style and his record, he was reelected in 1978 by a comfortable margin of 1,350,000 votes. This was the personality and political style with which his new lieutenant governor, Republican Mike Curb, would have to work after his 1978 election.

Mike Curb: From Promoter to Politician. Mike Curb's road to political success had nothing in common with that of Jerry Brown. Whereas Brown had been raised in a political family, Curb was the son of an FBI agent. Brown came to high public office via law school and previous election victories; Curb, a college dropout, used a successful business career as his political ladder. If Brown was shy and almost introverted, Curb was an outspoken young man with great drive.

Curb's rise in the business world was nothing short of spectacular. By the age of 24, he was the head of MGM records. Using business contacts to his advantage, Curb quickly hitched his wagon to Ronald Reagan's fast-rising star. In 1976, when most state Republicans backed President Ford for a full term, Curb supported Reagan's national ambitions and, unlike Governor Brown, became a staunch supporter of Proposition 13 in 1978.

Although Curb and Brown were polar extremes in most cases, they shared certain qualities as well. In his role as governor, Brown had repeated run-ins with a legislature dominated by his own party. Curb encountered similar controversy within Republican circles. Some party leaders criticized Curb for "attaining public office by walking over the backs of his fellow Republicans," while others praised him for "a special kind of loyalty to [Republican] candidates, going around the state, trooping around to elect them."[5]

After a rough primary battle against Assemblyman Mike Antonovich in 1978, Curb emerged as the Republican nominee for lieutenant governor. Five months later Curb defeated Democratic Lieutenant Governor Mervyn Dymally in his first try at elected office. With the Brown-Curb tandem now in place, Californians were in for 4 years of rocky politics.

From Statesmanship to "One-Up-Manship." On the face of it, one would think that a governor reelected by more than a million votes would be in a position of strength. Not so in the case of Jerry Brown who, in the course of his second term, encountered three obstacles: (1) a negative image as a perennial presidential candidate, (2) poor relations with his legislature, and (3) endless infighting with his new lieutenant governor, Mike Curb. The first two elements only heightened the importance of the third.

As a late entry in the 1976 presidential primaries, Brown did quite well by winning five of six contests. Although the nomination went to Jimmy Carter, Brown placed himself in the national limelight. Only 38 years old at the time, Brown's future appeared to be limitless. Yet critics condemned Brown for his travels around the country when, in their minds, he should have minded the store at home.

Brown's image of less than complete dedication to the job—although temporarily improved by his 1978 victory—continued into his second term. The legislature, dominated by Democrats in both houses, seemed to possess more contempt than allegiance for the governor. In fact, many legislators expressed outrage at what they described as unstable executive leadership. The then Speaker of the Assembly Leo McCarthy put the matter into perspective in 1980 when he said, legislators "don't take [Brown] seriously at this point in his career and that's really unfortunate."[6] Assembly Majority Leader Howard Berman expressed even stronger sentiment in noting that a number of legislators felt "estranged" from the governor.[7] As a result, Brown's relationship with the legislature—never on solid ground, anyway—deteriorated during his second term. In a state where gubernatorial vetoes were rarely overturned, Brown's vetoes lost their punch.[8] Although the governor encountered only one setback between 1975 and 1977 (over the hot issue of capital punishment), he suffered five veto overrides in 1978, five more in 1979, and two in 1980. Clearly, these results indicated that the legislature was not about to be pushed around by the governor.

Brown's weak standing within his own party not only made him vulnerable, but also increased the possibilities for his Republican lieutenant governor, Curb. The state constitution gives the lieutenant governor all of the governor's powers when the latter is out of state, and Curb wasted little time in exploiting the opportunities that lay before him. In March 1979, when Brown went to Washington to testify before Congress, Curb took the unprecedented step of appointing a judge to the state appeals court. Upon hearing the news of Curb's frisky activity, Brown rushed back and, as governor, rescinded the acting governor's nomination. The following day Brown filled every existing judicial vacancy, lest Curb do an encore the next time Brown left the state. Yet the damage was done and, at least in some people's eyes, the situation represented an embarrassment for Brown.[9]

Down but not out, Curb waited for his next opportunity to exercise gubernatorial authority. In May 1979, when Brown again was in Washington, Acting Governor Curb signed an executive order allowing oil refineries to increase gasoline lead content—a direct contradiction to Brown's public position. In order to ensure certification of the new rule before Brown returned to California, Curb and his entourage raced from San Francisco to Sacramento at speeds exceeding 90 miles per hour so that the document would be recorded with the secretary of state ahead of Brown's arrival. Alas, Curb's fast-moving automobile lost the race to Brown's faster DC-10 jet, which entered California air space a full 2 minutes before Curb reached the secretary of state's office.[10] Just as Cinderella's carriage became a pumpkin at the stroke of midnight, so Mike Curb lost all his gubernatorial power with Brown's return. At the end of it all, both antagonists were defended by their partisan supporters, while a bewildered public tried to untangle the California version of a Keystone Kops movie.

From the examples just noted, it might appear that Mike Curb was serious about exercising power and authority wherever possible. The lieutenant governor, however, seemed rather selective about the areas in which he chose to assert himself. The requirements of his own office dictated that Curb be a member of several boards and commissions in the state. As his 4 year term neared an end, records showed that the lieutenant governor was present at fifteen of twenty-seven University of California Board of Regents meetings, five of twenty-three California State University Trustee meetings, and only two of forty-two State Land Commission meetings.[11] These figures indicated that Curb would involve himself where he thought the most political benefit would accrue, and low press coverage meetings such as these did not provide the lieutenant governor much of a forum.

FROM JERRY AND MIKE TO THE "DUKE" AND LEO SHOW

The petty bickering of the Brown-Curb administration yielded two noteworthy results. First, with respect to the principals, both emerged from their volatile relationship as losing candidates in subsequent elections. In his 1982 race for the United States Senate, Brown lost the general election to Republican San Diego Mayor Pete Wilson by 500,000 votes. For Curb, the end came earlier as he failed to survive a Republican primary gubernatorial battle with Attorney General Deukmejian.

The second result centered on the electorate's ability to repeat political history. After subjecting themselves to a governor and lieutenant governor from two different political parties, the voters gave themselves a dose of the same medicine in 1982. This time Republican Deukmejian and Democrat McCarthy ascended to the top spots in the executive branch, thus setting the stage for 4 more years of partisan feuding. Apparently the electorate was not as bothered by the split ticket as were political analysts. The voters' behavior underscored a recurring theme in California politics: personalities are far more important than political party labels.

Executive Branch Offices—Decoding Who Does What

Imagine a state where the governor is clearly the supreme authority over all significant policymaking matters; a state where virtually all other important offices of power are determined by gubernatorial appointment; a state where, because of direct hierarchical relationships, the governor would be positioned to accept praise or blame for the actions of his administration.

Imagination, of course, is fantasy; likewise, such political linkage is virtually opposite of that which exists in California. Although the state's governorship is reputed to be relatively "strong" insofar as the powers and opportunities within the office,[12] California's chief executive must share and, in some cases, yield responsibility in major policy areas. Because each officeholder is elected independently, struggles for expanded power and authority abound throughout the executive branch on a regular basis. Rather than work as a preselected team, executive branch members survive by political instinct and individual creativity. Thus, a crisis such as the state's fiscal dilemma is likely to get a different analysis and proposed solution from each officeholder related to the issue.

To be sure, the governor is the dominant authority but not the *only* independent authority. In California, thanks to the Progressive legacy, executive powers are shared among several elected officials. Given this awkward division of responsibility, let's look at all the offices in the executive branch—both for their powers and lack of power where we otherwise might expect it.

THE GOVERNOR

Governor Jerry Brown once wanted to discuss a policy issue with his secretary of agriculture, Rose Bird.

"Get Rose Bird on the phone," Brown said.
"Yes, Governor," an aide replied.
"Well, where's Rose?" Brown asked later.
"She doesn't want to talk to you," the aide sheepishly said.[13]

This exchange tells us quite a bit about the California governor. As the state's highest political official, he could not command the attention of his own appointee. Although the governor is the state's most powerful individual, much of his or her clout is more perceptual than real. We naturally compare the governor of the state with the president of the nation. Yet the fact remains that the governor's powers over state affairs are, for the most part, more limited than the president's powers regarding national matters.

For the record, the governor oversees a budget exceeding $30 billion, three dozen departments, numerous boards and commissions, and about 240,000 state employees, more than 95 percent of whom are protected by civil service. Many of the state's most important boards and commissions decide issues outside of the governor's control, even though their members may owe their original selection to the governor. How, then, do we evaluate the role of the governor in California? Gubernatorial authority falls into three categories: independent, shared, and informal.

Independent Power. Most of the governor's independent authority centers on finance, some appointments, and vetoes. In these three areas the governor is not bound by others, although a number of the appointments overlap with the "shared" category mentioned earlier.

Finance is a double-edged sword for the governor. Working with his director of finance, the governor must prepare a balanced state budget, or at least provide one that ends the fiscal year (June 30) in the black. This means that the governor manages finance in two respects: he or she determines which areas require expenditures and specifies the means to guarantee adequate tax revenues for those areas. It's a tricky matter for the most skilled politician, who is perpetually besieged by pressure from interests in and out of government. The problem is that although everyone has a spending program, few are willing to provide any means of paying the bills. Unlike lobbyists, legislators, or casual political observers, the governor cannot sit back and "hope" things will work out. Invariably, the governor is in the middle of the state's financial destiny.

The constitution requires the governor to propose a state budget to the legislature within the first 10 days of each calendar year. This document, which is the size of a telephone book, generally culminates 6 months of work by the governor's staff. In a budget message the governor must indicate expected sources of income along with expenditure categories.

The constitution also provides that the legislature pass and send a budget to the governor by June 15, for implementation by July 1. Acting independently, the legislature may alter, ignore, and add components different from those presented by the governor. But make no mistake about it: the governor's budget is a priority-setting document to which the legislature must react.

California's bruising battle over the 1983–84 budget illustrates how the governor can dominate the legislature in fiscal matters. A budget failed to emerge by the new fiscal year because of several clashes between conservative Republican Governor Deukmejian and the liberal Democratic majority in the legislature. Deukmejian demanded a budget so that he could approve, veto, or scale down various appropriations for the coming fiscal year. Aware of the governor's power, the legislature's Democratic leadership stalled the budget for three weeks past the July 1 constitutional deadline, hoping to extract "no cut" or minimal reduction agreements from the governor in key policy areas. But Deukmejian would not deal on the Democrats' terms and, ultimately, they relented. Once given the appropriate figures, Governor Deukmejian used the item veto to lop $1 billion from the 1983–84 budget.

Actually, the governor's veto powers are divided into two types: general and item. General vetoes apply to any bills passed by the legislature. In these instances, the governor rejects the bill and usually encloses a message conveying the reasons. Item vetoes are used for appropriations measures, most of which are related to the massive state budget. With this executive tool the governor can sign a measure but reduce the amount of money allocated by the legislature. In the process the governor forces the relevant administrative agencies to scale down their programs in proportion to his or her cuts.

Both general and item vetoes must be exercised within 12 days. They are considered independent gubernatorial powers because the legislature rarely manages to muster the absolute two-thirds votes in each house to overcome the governor's negation.

Despite his reputation as a "maverick" governor, Jerry Brown employed the veto about as often as his predecessor, Ronald Reagan. Reagan vetoed 7.2 percent of the bills reaching his desk and Brown exercised his prerogative 7.4 percent of the time. These similar statistics notwithstanding, the two leaders suffered different post-veto fates—Brown was overridden thirteen times compared to Reagan's single override defeat. Ironically, Brown spent all 8 years with a Democrat-controlled legislature; Reagan enjoyed slim Republican majorities for only 2 of his 8 years.

Personality, more than partisanship, seems to account for relationships between executive and legislative branches. If this is the case, Governor Deukmejian, a former legislator, may attempt to rely on his past connections to offset the difficulties of a Republican governor working with a Democratic legislature. In 1983 Deukmejian demonstrated his political acumen by persuading the legislature to end the fiscal year with a $900 million deficit, something that the Democratic leadership had previously opposed.

Shared Power. Aside from the appointees to his or her own staff, the governor must share responsibility for almost all other executive branch appointments with another branch of state government or, in some cases, another part of the executive branch. In many instances, scrutiny is symbolic; in other cases, the governor's appointees may be rejected by another authority. For example, although the governor's nominees for cabinet and department head positions must be placed before the Senate, confirmation tends to be automatic. Even then, however, the Senate has been known to have "second thoughts." Such an occurrence happened in 1983 when Governor Deukmejian nominated Carol Hallett as his state parks director.

As the former Republican Assembly minority leader, Hallett had made her share of Democratic enemies in the legislature. This antagonism certainly didn't help her cause. More obvious was the deep-seated hostility that developed between Governor Deukmejian and the legislature's Democrats, making it rather convenient for the Senate majority to have little interest in the Hallett nomination. When the confirmation vote was taken, the Democrats abstained and left Hallett several votes short of approval. Although Senate President Pro-Tem David Roberti simply explained that Hallett had "absolutely no qualifications to be director of parks," Governor Deukmejian denounced the effort as "petty partisan politics."[14] But Deukmejian's influence ended there because, in this case, the Senate majority held the upper hand.

Legislative scrutiny carries over to gubernatorial appointments outside the executive branch as well. Of the more than one hundred state boards and commissions, some of the most controversial were created during the Jerry Brown administration, and his appointees did not always engender the legislature's trust. Consider Brown's activities regarding the newly created Agricultural Labor Relations Board. After the legislature passed the California Agricultural Labor Act of 1975, which created the board to oversee farm labor practices, key members soon opposed the board's makeup (appointed by the governor, confirmed by the legislature) and "prolabor" stance.[15] Thus, in 1976 when the ALRB ran out of money halfway into the year, the legislature refused further funding and forced the entire agency to shut down until the next fiscal year. The result was considerable disarray in both the state capital and the agricultural community. A less important but equally dramatic legislative furor occurred in 1979 when Governor Brown attempted to fill a vacancy in the usually uncontroversial State Arts Council. The only problem was that Brown nominated Jane Fonda, known not only for her acting career but also for her adamant position against the war in Vietnam. Taking exception with Fonda for her foreign policy stance, the Senate refused to confirm her appointment.

In another widely discussed area, judicial appointments, the governor ostensibly has wide latitude in filling vacancies and newly created judgeships. Jerry Brown made more than eight hundred such appointments during his two terms, more than any other predecessor. Even here, though, the governor's power can be checked either by the Commission on Judicial Appointments (for Supreme Court and Appellate Court nominees) or by the voters in subsequent elections. Although Brown saw almost all of his higher level appointees approved, a number of his Superior and Municipal Court appointees were rejected by the voters and replaced by another candidate when they came up for ratification.

In 1983 Governor Deukmejian assumed office as an opponent to several boards and commissions that were either established or nurtured during the Brown administration. In most cases Deukmejian proposed deep cuts;[16] in some instances he sought to shift key agency responsibilities out of the shared powers category and into the governor's hands. One such proposal centered on the future of the California Coastal Commission. Passed by the voters in 1972 against strong developer opposition, this agency was designed to control development and guarantee public access to the coast. Deukmejian proposed massive cuts in the agency's budget (29 percent) and staff (22 percent). But these ideas were not as controversial as his plan to place the commission's planning and research office under the jurisdiction of the Air Resources Board. In doing so, the governor would have direct control of the agency's most critical function: land-use planning. Although Deukmejian defended his proposal as an effort to eliminate unnecessary duplication, critics argued the agency's loss of independence would violate "sound management practice" regarding the coast.[17] For the time being, the legislature agreed with them and the governor's hope to consolidate power was unfulfilled.

Informal Power. Personal prestige can either enhance or diminish the governor's clout depending on how the individual stands with two important groups: the public and the legislature. When the governor is popular, he or she has considerable "informal power."

Few governors have wielded informal power as successfully as Ronald Reagan. Swept into office by a million votes in 1966, Reagan could do nothing wrong in the public's eyes during his first term. His broad-based popularity caused the Democratic majority in the legislature to think twice before opposing Reagan. During the course of his 8 year run, Reagan proposed the largest tax increase in the state's history—not an easy task for a conservative Republican. Yet, the public begrudged him little. Reagan took hard positions on welfare, student protests, and "big government" issues that most Californians supported. When he left office in 1975, Reagan departed with as much prestige and informal power as he brought with him in 1967. Because of his immense popularity, the legislature had difficulty checking any major Reagan initiative.

Jerry Brown's informal power had a much more uneven pattern than that of Ronald Reagan. Praised by some as a political magician and ridiculed by others as "Governor Moonbeam," Brown rarely managed to enjoy widespread prestige with either the public or legislature. Compared with other California governors, Jerry Brown's appointments were disproportionately skewed toward women, blacks, Hispanics, Asians, and native Americans; he was the first governor to appoint openly gay attorneys to the bench. There is no question that his actions endeared Brown to some sectors of society; at the same time, Brown was so antiestablishment in rhetoric that he offended much of the California mainstream as well as his own party's legislative leaders. Brown's attitudes toward nuclear power, capital punishment, and higher education had similar cross-cutting effects. As a result, many of Brown's efforts were thwarted by the legislature. At times, he took on the appearance of an ineffective governor.

All things considered, Brown was able to make effective use of his informal power only during the first year of his administration. Seizing upon his brief honeymoon with the legislature and public acceptance of his "new spirit," Brown prodded the legislature into passing the Agricultural Labor Relations Act, establishing a permanent California Coastal Commission, and placing public members on boards and commissions within the Department of Consumer Affairs and State Bar. But the governor's initiative was curbed by a legislature that quickly grew weary of his antiestablishment stance and the public who, by 1976, began to wonder about Brown's values. Yet, somehow Brown managed to keep just enough of the public's trust. Although he campaigned hard against the tax-cutting Proposition 13 in 1978, he was elected to a second term. His low point came in 1981 when, caught between the demands of the agricultural community and concerns of environmentalists, Brown could not come to terms with the Mediterranean fruit fly crisis. His refusal to order the spraying of malathion (an insecticide)—until forced to do so by the federal government—weakened Jerry Brown's image and informal power.

Five weeks into a new administration, Governor Deukmejian attempted to exert his own brand of informal power. Deadlocked with the state senate over a budget bill that would defer half or more of California's $1.5 billion deficit into the next fiscal year, Deukmejian appealed for public support in a statewide televised address: "If you agree [with the proposal], please call, write or send a telegram to your state senator," the governor implored.[18] Within a week, Deukmejian and the Senate reached agreement. Moreover, in March 1983, a month after the governor's speech, a *Los Angeles Times* poll found that 58 percent of those interviewed endorsed his budget plan. As one columnist concluded, Deukmejian "obviously is still in a honeymoon period with the electorate."[19] The big question for the new governor, however, was whether he would be able to sustain that honeymoon over the course of his 4 year term.

The Governor's Powers in Perspective.   The combinations of independent, shared, and informal power available to a governor vary with public support, legislative cooperation, and the officeholder's perception of the job. Each administration weaves its own distinct pattern out of California's political cloth. Once, in a candid moment, Jerry Brown offered his "canoe theory" of gubernatorial politics: "You paddle a little on the left side, then you paddle on the right side, and you keep going right down the middle."[20] Yet State Treasurer Jesse Unruh, formerly Speaker of the Assembly, nominee for governor, and well-known authority on power, offered another view, "Any governor can do something about damn near anything if he's prepared to pay the price for it."[21]

Although all governors seem to command independent and shared power, the crucial factor centers on one's ability to gather and hold informal power. To the extent that the governor can hold the public trust, the governor can maximize control of state affairs. To the extent that he or she fails to keep the public's faith, the governor loses informal power, which has adverse effects on the gubernatorial independent and shared power as well.

LIEUTENANT GOVERNOR

The lieutenant governor's office represents the epitome of symbolism over substance. Elected at the same time as the other executive branch members, the lieutenant governor is almost an officeholder without an office! True enough, he or she becomes acting governor when the governor is out of the state or disabled. Moreover, if the governor permanently vacates the office, the lieutenant governor is constitutionally next in line for the job. Lieutenant governors shouldn't hold their breath for the possibility, however; the last time

this sequence of events occurred was in 1953 when Goodwin J. Knight succeeded Governor Earl Warren, who became chief justice of the United States
Supreme Court. Other than being chairman of several advisory committees—the most important of which is the Commission on Economic Development—the lieutenant governor has little power or public visibility.

Aside from a few executive responsibilities, the lieutenant governor is connected with the legislature. He or she is president of the Senate, technically its
official presiding officer. Once again, although the title is lofty, the job descrip-
tion is not. The only role in the Senate is to cast tie-breaking votes. Inasmuch
as twenty-one votes are required for basic legislation, the lieutenant governor
votes only in the case of a twenty–twenty stalemate, an event that never
occurred during the Brown-Curb administration. Hence, there is little motivation for the lieutenant governor to sit in the Senate chambers.

Despite the empty opportunities within the lieutenant governor's office,
incumbents take it seriously. When Lieutenant Governor Mike Curb attempted to use his office as a stepping-stone to the Republican gubernatorial
nomination, he claimed that being acting governor for more than two hundred
days in Governor Brown's absence gave him the necessary "on the job" training
for the state's highest office. In fact, his position had not provided him with
such opportunities. When Governor Brown left the state, he did his best to see
that the acting governor had as little as possible to "act on." Governor Deukmejian has not traveled out of state nearly as often as his predecessor, thus
leaving Lieutenant Governor McCarthy little opportunity to perform functions
remotely related to the chief executive's responsibilities.

ATTORNEY GENERAL

Although the lieutenant governor is next in line for the governorship, the
attorney general prevails as the second most powerful member of the executive
branch. The clout stems from the officeholder being the state's chief legal
representative and the office's visibility to the public.

The attorney general functions as the state's "top cop" through responsibility
for state and local law enforcement. Elected to head the Department of Justice,
this individual serves as legal counsel to most important state agencies, renders
opinions (interpretations) on existing and proposed laws, and represents the
state in crucial court cases. This rather potent combination of tasks places the
attorney general in the limelight; in the process, he or she has numerous
opportunities to garner public prestige and, hence, a dose of "informal power."

Increasingly, those who have sought the position have become aware not only of the important influence the attorney general commands within the executive branch but, because of visibility, its utility as a stepping-stone to higher elected positions in the state. Earl Warren, Edmund G. "Pat" Brown, and most recently, George Deukmejian have used this statewide office to capture the governor's chair. Thus, the office is important both for its built-in powers and ambitious politicians who hold it.

In the past, veteran law enforcement officers, especially nonpartisan district attorneys, were elected to the position where they kept a partisan low profile. George Deukmejian (1979–83), however, had a partisan legislative background as part of his career. Republican Deukmejian came under heavy fire when, as attorney general, he joined a private lawsuit that challenged the constitutionality of the state's new collective bargaining act, a key accomplishment of the Jerry Brown administration.[22]

In the 1982 general elections Democrat John Van de Kamp, the Los Angeles County District Attorney, won the attorney general's post. The selection of a former D.A. prompted some observers to believe that the office would return to its former low-profile, nonpartisan environment. But in 1983 Van de Kamp showed his independence by refusing to represent the state (and two agencies under Governor Deukmejian) in a court case about several wild and scenic rivers under federal protection. The governor wanted the designations removed so that the state could build dams and allow logging. Van de Kamp claimed the suit was "harmful to the public interest" and refused to represent the governor.[23] In both the Deukmejian and Van de Kamp instances, we have further evidence of the friction that can occur within the executive branch.

THE MONEY OFFICES

In their zeal to prevent excessive power in any one office, the framers of the state's executive branch placed "money responsibilities" in three different elected positions—the controller, treasurer, and the Board of Equalization. Like the offices discussed earlier, each position has a 4 year term. More important, this awkward arrangement has fueled petty jealousies, overlapping jurisdictions, and conflicting information. At times the failure of these executives to agree on basic financial policies has had the humor of a political "who's on first" routine. At more serious moments in the state's history, such as the surplus during the middle and late 1970s, the inability of the money office-holders to agree on the state's financial health jeopardized the credibility of the state government. After all, the voters mused, if "they" don't know how much excess exists, we must have quite a bit. Hence, hilarity became disaster with the passage of Proposition 13 in 1978 and the subsequent weak financial picture during the early 1980s.

Controller.   As one of the state's watchdogs over finances, the controller's responsibilities include oversight of state and local taxing and spending, withdrawals from the state treasury, and collection of various taxes. By virtue of election, the controller also serves as an ex officio member of several boards and commissions, including the Board of Equalization, the Franchise Tax Board, and the State Lands Commission. The last of these has attained new prominence in the 1980s with renewed interest in offshore oil drilling. The State Lands Commission oversees tideland oil lands leases, an important environmental and economic concern for energy-thirsty California.

Past Controllers Thomas Kuchel (1951–55) and Alan Cranston (1959–67) used their offices as stepping-stones for election to the United States Senate. Current Controller Ken Cory, first elected in 1974 and reelected in 1978 and 1982, has also been mentioned as a possible candidate for higher office. His frequent comments about the state's budget crisis in 1983 gave Cory high visibility in California politics.

Treasurer.   Whereas the controller oversees the collection of state funds, the treasurer keeps custody of them. As part of the office's responsibility, the treasurer issues quarterly reports to the legislature on how much money the state has and how any reserves have been invested. Historically viewed as a "dead" office, the treasurer's position has assumed slightly increased importance during the past few years under the leadership of Jesse Unruh. First elected in 1974 (reelected in 1978 and 1982), Unruh opened up the bond borrowing process by permitting savings and loans to compete with banks for state business. Nevertheless, the office remains among the most powerless of the many offices within the executive branch.

Board of Equalization.   Unlike the other executive branch offices, the state Board of Equalization has five members, four of whom are elected from separate districts of equal population. The state controller serves as the fifth member, proof once again of the overlapping jurisdictions found within the executive branch. In the late 1880s, the board had responsibility for a number of tax-related areas, including the collection of property taxes and liquor taxes. These powers have since been removed from the board's jurisdiction. Today, the board's duties are more limited in scope. Most of its functions center on the collection of the sales tax, gasoline tax, and highway user taxes. Ironically, the board does not keep the money; in fact, funds are sent to the treasurer.

The Cumbersome Process of Managing Tax Dollars. Given the many money agencies in California, it is amazing that the state functions with any efficiency at all. Of course, the miscalculations from 1978 into the early 1980s indicate that considerable slack persists. Ironically, these are not the only money agencies in the state. Although the Board of Equalization receives sales tax receipts, personal income taxes are sent to another agency altogether—the State Franchise Tax Board! Over the years a number of efforts have surfaced within the legislature to merge some of these offices, but special interests have successfully repelled any serious modifications. No initiative has ever threatened to eliminate any of these offices, partly because the voters wish to elect as many individuals as possible to the executive branch. All good intentions notwithstanding, the plural executive extracts a cost in the name of inefficiency. Nowhere is this more clearly demonstrated than in the management of money matters.

SECRETARY OF STATE

Historically, the secretary of state has held a "clerical" reputation for keeping the official records of the legislature and all executive departments; certifying signatures for initiatives, referenda, and recall petitions; publishing sample ballots; and giving official notification of election results. Even though today's computers tabulate outcomes within hours of the election's end, the secretary of state announces the "official" results a few weeks after the election.

For nearly six decades the secretary of state's office was controlled by the Jordan family. Frank C. Jordan was elected in 1910 and every 4 years thereafter until his death in 1940. In 1942 Frank M. Jordan, his son, won the office and was reelected until his death in 1968. Both father and son ran the office in the same low-key way.

When Jerry Brown was elected to this "dead" office in 1970, he gave the position a fresh, lively, and highly changed look. Brown dusted off and enforced a number of old, previously ignored statutes regarding campaign finance records. In 1974 Secretary of State Brown helped draft Proposition 9, the Fair Political Practices Initiative designed to create an independent commission on campaign contributions, expenditures, and lobby activities. The public passed the initiative by a 70 to 30 percent margin, and Jerry Brown had his first taste of informal power. Given his new visibility, Brown used the little-known secretary of state's office as a launching pad for the governorship in 1974.

The current secretary of state, March Fong Eu, has shown that the Jordans are not alone in the ability to win the office repeatedly. First elected in 1974, the first statewide officeholder of Asian descent has been reelected in 1978 and 1982 by lopsided margins. Though not as vocal as her immediate predecessor, she has drawn the secretary of state's office into several frays regarding initiative qualifications, candidate ballot descriptions, and campaign reporting laws.

THE SUPERINTENDENT OF PUBLIC INSTRUCTION

The superintendent of public instruction is an office with two built-in liabilities—a nonpartisan electoral base and shared policymaking responsibilities. The first dilemma imposes a burden on the public, most of whom have little information about educational issues and various ways of dealing with them. Without party affiliation to guide them, voters are particularly unclear about the candidates' positions. Little wonder, then, that 3 weeks before the 1982 election, 22 percent of the voters were undecided on who to choose for the job.[24]

The second dilemma places the superintendent of public instruction in a position with little political footing. Although the office is an elected position, his or her policy options and funding levels are largely shaped (and limited) by the governor-appointed Board of Education and the education committees in the legislature. When push comes to shove, the superintendent of public instruction has precious little independence.

The 1982 election results reveal much about the problems connected with the state's highest education office. Wilson Riles, elected first in 1970 and reelected in 1974 and 1978, sought an unprecedented fourth term. Although he was known as an innovator, the last 8 years of Riles' administration saw California students doing poorly on nationwide tests. During the same period the state legislature drastically reduced its appropriations for education. Although Riles could not control the appropriations levels, critics maintained that he could influence the direction of education resources—no matter how precious they might be.

Several candidates opposed Riles in his bid for another term. Unable to secure a majority in the June primary, he was forced into a November run-off election. His opponent was William Honig, superintendent of education for a school district in Marin County. That the district contained only three schools was not widely known. Yet Riles, not Honig, was the issue. The real concern of the public was that student performance had dropped and the public perceived that the superintendent of public instruction was at fault. Given this growing sentiment, Honig ousted Riles by a convincing margin.

The Bureaucracy

Elected officials may appear to hold the reins of power in California, but bureaucrats throughout the state provide the muscle for changing political goals into policy realities. Like the population it serves, California's public bureaucracy mirrors the largesse of the state; it is huge, complex, and ever changing both in scope and functions. Most of us confront (or are confronted by) the bureaucracy on a routine basis. Students attending institutions of higher public education, drivers who are stopped by the California Highway Patrol, and self-employed individuals who submit quarterly income estimates and tax payments to the Franchise Tax Board are but three examples of the numerous ways in which Californians deal with the state bureaucracy.

More than 240,000 people actually work for the state of California. Except for the 90,000 workers in the University of California and California State University systems who are hired and fired by their own tenure arrangements, more than 95 percent of the state's bureaucrats obtain their positions by scoring high on competitive civil service examinations. If the credibility of a state's bureaucracy depends upon its independence from political manipulation, the relative isolation of California bureaucrats from patronagelike appointments and dismissals gives the state high standing. On the other hand, such isolation sometimes works against the efforts of a newly elected administration to be innovative and pursue new priorities.

Bureaucrats are supposed to carry out general policy directives as organized by the elected and bureaucratic hierarchies above them. Most of the time the executive, legislative, and judicial branches are the starting points for such policymaking. Although they sketch out the broad plan, however, these institutions give the bureaucrats responsibility for working out the "details." Sometimes the bureaucracy itself may exercise power to determine its own objectives and, hence, make as well as implement policy goals. Such occurrences are rare except in the most technical of policy areas. For the most part the public bureaucracy exists to serve—to carry out assigned tasks.

Most bureaucrats are permanent state employees, but many agency heads are selected by the governor or the governor's appointments secretary. As part of the appointment process these individuals usually must be confirmed by the Senate prior to their assumption of office. Moreover, if the governor should become displeased with their performance, then agency heads must resign upon the governor's demand. Thus, if the civil servants within an agency only "follow the rules," the rules are usually determined by political appointees. To this extent a new agency head can drastically affect the direction of the agency in question—a further indication that bureaucracy is not as "neutral" as it's cracked up to be.

The changing management of the Air Resources Board (ARB) shows how a new gubernatorial administration can nudge bureaucrats in a new direction. Although the ARB was created during the Reagan administration, it kept a low profile by restricting its work to enforcement of the state's motor vehicle standards. After Governor Jerry Brown appointed Tom Quinn as the new ARB head in 1975, Quinn began an aggressive campaign to clean up the environment and punish those responsible for its pollution. Within 3 months, he ordered Chrysler Corporation to recall 70 percent of its California-manufactured cars and fined the auto company $328,000 for violations of the state's emissions standards. Quinn also took on industrial polluters like oil refineries, power plants, and factories, threatening to shut them down unless they complied with state standards. When evidence existed that a regional air pollution agency in Southern California was soft on polluters, the state ARB assumed responsibility for its functions until the local agency complied with state standards. As Jerry Brown's ARB chief, Tom Quinn did much to alter the priorities of his agency. His actions serve well to remind us that the "neutral" bureaucracy is guided by political leaders and goals.[25]

ADMINISTRATIVE ORGANIZATION STYLES—
RONALD REAGAN AND JERRY BROWN COMPARED

Elected officials come and go from office dependent upon the public will or the officials' own changing priorities. Bureaucrats, especially those protected by civil service, are permanent fixtures of government; to this extent, the bureaucracy goes on regardless of who runs the executive branch positions. These facts notwithstanding, every new governor attempts to synchronize his or her own objectives and the bureaucracy into a single driving force. Through organization (or reorganization) of the state's top administrative agencies and programs, the governor gives an early indication as to the administration's goals and the cabinet officials who will help reach those goals.

Between World War II and Ronald Reagan's governorship, the state's chief executives were fairly content to let the bureaucracy take care of itself. New agencies were created from time to time, but the underlying value of state politics was to let the bureaucrats do their work. Ronald Reagan changed this relationship in the sense that he became the first chief executive to reorganize the state's bureaucracy extensively. In an attempt to eliminate duplication and bring coherence to the bureaucracy, the Reagan administration placed most agencies, commissions, and boards under four "superagencies": Business and Transportation, Resources, Health and Welfare, and Agriculture and Services. Each agency head became part of the governor's cabinet along with the director of finance.

When Jerry Brown assumed the governorship, he modified the superagency constellation established by Reagan. Under Brown, the four superagencies consisted of Business and Transportation, Resources, Health and Welfare, and State and Consumer Services. These four agency heads joined the director of finance in Brown's cabinet. However, Brown also gave cabinet status to the heads of the Air Resources Board (Quinn) and the secretary of agriculture (Rose Bird). The elevation of the last two department chiefs to cabinet level status served notice of Brown's determination to solve the state's lingering pollution problems and the recurring battles between farmers and farmworkers in California's multibillion-dollar agriculture industry.

The Executive Branch, California Style

California's executive branch is a fascinating component of state government and politics. Lacking cohesion, party discipline, and any single sense of purpose, executive branch members muddle through in pursuit of their mandated tasks. If there is any single notion holding these offices together, it lies with the fact that the office titles and job descriptions rarely match up. For the most part, elected executive branch positions are held by leaders with uncertain amounts of power.

True enough, the governor, attorney general, and, perhaps, the controller do exercise authority in varying degrees. Apart from these offices, the remaining positions could easily be appointive, in which case the governor's power might be strengthened. Conversely, positions like the superintendent of public instruction could fall under civil service, thus taking politics out of education to the maximum possible extent. Short of these changes, many of the elective offices in the executive branch (particularly controller, treasurer, and the Board of Equalization) could be consolidated to eliminate their overlapping responsibilities. But the "coulds" in California politics rarely become reality. The state seems to be built on a subliminal theme that equates democracy with numerous executive branch elections. As a result, accountability often replaces efficiency as the state's number one political necessity

Even the bureaucracy, most of which is independent in an official sense, is not impervious to political winds or direction. Civil servants carry out their functions without the fear of removal. Yet the tenor of their jobs changes with each administration. The state's bureaucracy is an extension—albeit indirect— of the governor's powers. Much the same can be said for employees in the Departments of Education and Justice, whose emphases change with the elections of the superintendent of public instruction and attorney general. In the meantime, the executive branch exists as a less than integrated governmental unit.

Notes

[1]"State's No. 2 Race Is Being Run in Shadow of No. 1," *San Jose Mercury*, October 11, 1982.

[2]Ed Salzman, "What Would Dymally Be Like as Governor of California," *California Journal* 7, no. 3 (March 1976): 77.

[3]Quoted in John C. Bollens and G. Robert Williams, *Jerry Brown in A Plain Brown Wrapper* (Pacific Palisades, Calif.: Palisades Publishers, 1978), p. 111.

[4]California Legislature, "Analysis of the Budget Bill," February 24, 1982, p. A-8.

[5]"Curb Strives For Credibility in Governor's Race," *San Jose Mercury*, May 25, 1982.

[6]"Brown's Veto Punch Has Lost Its Sting," *Los Angeles Times*, March 24, 1980.

[7]Ibid.

[8]Between 1946 and 1974, not a single gubernatorial veto was overturned by the legislature. Governor Reagan had one such setback in 1974. These records represent a considerable departure from the Jerry Brown era.

[9]Assembly Speaker McCarthy referred to the appointment as an "embarrassment" to Brown, but the governor's executive assistant, Gray Davis, claimed that Curb was staging a "political tug-of-war." See "In Defiant Move, Curb Appoints Appellate Judge," *Los Angeles Times*, March 29, 1979.

[10]"Curb Again Defies Brown," *Los Angeles Times*, May 17, 1979.

[11]"Curb Strives For Credibility in Governor's Race," *San Jose Mercury*, May 25, 1982.

[12]In a comparative study of state executives, Joseph A. Schlesinger ranks formal power of the California governor near the top. However, the study does not take into consideration the multitude of other elected offices within the state's executive branch which, by their presence, cast long shadows on the governor's authority. See "The Politics of the Executive," in Herbert Jacob and Kenneth N. Vines, eds., *Politics In The American States*, 2nd ed. (Boston: Little, Brown, 1971), pp. 210–237.

[13]Hal Rubin and Pat Washburn Rubin, "California's Power Elite," *California Journal* 11, no. 1 (January 1980): 15.

[14]"Deukmejian Loses First Appointment Battle," *San Jose Mercury*, April 29, 1983.

[15]Bernard L. Hyink, Seyom Brown, Ernest W. Thacker, and Steven D. Brown, *Issues in California Politics and Government* (New York: Crowell, 1977), p. 92.

[16]Some of Deukmejian's more controversial proposed agency cuts included: State Public Defender (49 percent); California Energy Commission (63 percent); Agricultural Labor Relations Board (26 percent); Air Resources Board (10 percent). See *San Jose Mercury*, January 24, 1983.

[17]"Deukmejian Disabling Coastal Commission, Critics Say," *San Jose Mercury*, March 21, 1983.

[18]"Deukmejian Takes His Budget Fight To The People," *San Jose Mercury*, February 10, 1983.

[19]"Most Support Governor's Handling of Budget Crisis," *Los Angeles Times*, March 8, 1983.

[20]"Governor Energetic But Inconsistent," *Los Angeles Times*, November 9, 1979.

[21]Ibid.

[22]Tom Quinn, "Deukmejian's Clash with Brown and Even His Own Deputies," *California Journal* 11, no. 2 (February 1980): 51.

[23]"Attorney General Bows Out of State Case," *San Jose Mercury*, March 22, 1983.

[24]"Honig Tops Riles in Funds," *San Jose Mercury*, October 28, 1982.

[25]For an excellent account of Quinn's reign of the ARB, see Carla Lazzareschi, "The Pressure Tactics of Smog Boss Tom Quinn," *California Journal* 8, no. 7 (July 1977): 224–26.

6
THE LEGISLATURE

The Struggle for Power

"Next to the governor, the [Assembly] Speaker is considered California state government's most powerful political figure. . . . [T]he Speaker can name committee members and make or break committee chairmen. . . . He is the boss, the most powerful legislator in Sacramento. . . ."[1] So concludes the *Los Angeles Times*, but the California Constitution barely touches on this important post: "Each house shall choose its officers and adopt rules for its proceedings."[2] In fact, the framers of the constitution devoted more attention to freight regulation and nonprofit golf courses than to leadership in the legislature.

Reading the constitution actually reveals little about how the legislature works. Even close scrutiny of the legislature's rules and the process by which a bill becomes law is not enough. To understand the legislature, we must examine its players and teams, its power struggles, and the rewards at stake. It is essential to look beyond the formal organization to the highly volatile political process that actually moves the legislature.

Fortunately, the smoke-filled, backroom legislative politics of years past have given way to a political body open to public inspection. The titanic 1980 battle for the Assembly speakership and a parallel leadership struggle in the Senate exposed the internal politics of the legislature as never before. The contenders each spent millions of dollars to win those positions. The clashes were over not only titles, but also who would control the legislative process and its support units and thus shape the laws and policies for California.

The Battle for the Assembly Speakership, 1979–80

Through much of 1979 and 1980, the Assembly speakership was subject to a bitter power struggle. A series of political events and challenges left Speaker Leo McCarthy, the capable and highly regarded leader of 5 years, standing on political quicksand. For a year, three powerful Democrats—McCarthy, Howard Berman, and Willie Brown—fought for this position. Yet the prize would have been worth next to nothing had it not been for the changes brought about by a former Speaker, Jesse Unruh.

Prior to Unruh's rise to the speakership (1961–68), lobbyists and interest groups enjoyed a direct relationship with legislators. Unruh changed that relationship by placing himself between lobbyists and legislators. His ability to make the speakership a magnet for lobbyists' money, a funnel for monetary assistance to other Assembly members, and a source of rich committee appointments and devastating removals permanently increased the value of the speakership: the office became hot political property. Without these fundamental changes, the McCarthy-Berman-Brown dispute would have been little more than a petty squabble for a titular office among equally petty egos. But if the egos were petty, the value of the office was not—and the contenders knew it.

THE CONTENDERS

Leo McCarthy.   A popular liberal Democrat during most of his reign, Leo McCarthy defeated Willie Brown for the speakership in 1974. Having solid backing from the Democratic majority, McCarthy had every intention of continuing in the post until 1982, when he would most likely run either for the governorship or United States Senate. But McCarthy was bucking tradition. Although the speakership provided rich resources and power, the office's high visibility actually hindered the efforts of former Speakers Jesse Unruh and Bob Moretti to attain statewide offices. When the dust settled after his fight with Berman, McCarthy ultimately sought and secured nomination to a lesser office, lieutenant governor.

Howard Berman.   First elected to the Assembly in 1972, Howard Berman became McCarthy's chief assistant just 2 years later as majority leader, in part as reward for helping McCarthy beat Brown. A crafty politician and a wizard on apportionment, Berman was a leader in his own right. In Southern California he was known as half of the "Waxman-Berman machine," a rather powerful alliance between Assemblyman Henry Waxman and himself. Together they secured elections of several Democratic candidates to the Assembly, State Senate, and Congress—the latter being where Waxman moved in 1974. With "an unbeatable base among liberals, labor, Jews and Democratic leaders,"[3] Berman viewed himself in good position to wrestle the speakership from McCarthy in 1979.

Willie Brown.   As a protégé of former Speakers Unruh and Bob Moretti, Willie Brown was all but knighted "Speaker-in-waiting" prior to his last-minute derailment by McCarthy and the anti-Moretti faction. In his fight with McCarthy in 1974, Brown first attempted to gather a Democratic majority, the traditional way for the party in power to select a new Speaker. Failing that, he committed the "unforgivable sin" of soliciting Republican votes—a move that cost him dearly. After McCarthy secured the speakership, he sent Brown packing to political no-man's land. Stripped of his key committee positions and lavish office, Brown was *persona non grata* in the early years of the McCarthy-run Assembly. Eventually, the hard-working Brown earned his way into McCarthy's good graces and replaced Berman as majority floor leader. If there was ever an instance of political rehabilitation, Willie Brown represented such a phenomenon.

These three leaders—McCarthy, Berman, and Brown—had friendships and disaffections that went back 15 years. Over this period old alliances ended and new alliances developed. Ironically, when the speakership tussle ended in 1980, Berman, the previously trusted ally, was *out*, while Brown, the former foe, was *in*. Such are the dynamics of California politics.

ORIGINS OF THE BERMAN CHALLENGE

Personalities, not political philosophies, are crucial to understanding California politics. This is not to say that conservative Republicans and liberal Democrats are indistinguishable, but in California they sometimes get along better than like-minded individuals of the same political party. The McCarthy-Berman clash demonstrates this point clearly enough. Politically, both were liberal Democrats with comparable voting records on the big issues. McCarthy had appreciated Berman's skills early in his legislative career and made him majority leader before Berman's freshman term was over. In fact, the two were without a public dispute on legislative bills, appointments, and political strategy until Berman's "Christmas Rebellion" of 1979.[4]

Two serious issues led Berman to turn against McCarthy: the Speaker's use of campaign money and his reluctance to apprise Berman of his future plans. Ever since the days of Jesse Unruh, the speakership has been the Assembly's most potent fund-raising agent. As such, the Speaker divides over a million dollars among legislative allies every election year. For the legislator locked in a close race, a donation of $50,000 or more from the Speaker is often the difference between victory and defeat. Berman suspected that McCarthy jeopardized the Speaker's fund raising and donating because of his own need to raise money for a United States Senate or governorship campaign in 1982. Berman reached this conclusion after McCarthy held a fund-raising dinner on December 1, 1979 that raised $500,000. Although McCarthy eventually agreed to pass out the money among needy Democratic candidates, it was only after some not-so-gentle public prodding by Berman, who accused the Speaker of keeping the money for himself.

Berman fumed as McCarthy charted one uncertain political course after another with activities that seemed to interfere with the legislature's agenda. Although he was supposedly the most trusted of McCarthy's aides, Berman was left without a hint as to what higher office McCarthy would seek and when he would resign the speakership. Undoubtedly, McCarthy didn't know the answer to these questions as the 1982 Democratic primary races remained unsettled. But McCarthy's uncertainty was little consolation to Berman, who worried that the upcoming 1980 election strategy was in jeopardy with McCarthy concentrating on the 1982 race. Given this combination of events, Berman moved to replace McCarthy.

CAUGHT BETWEEN A ROCK AND A HARD PLACE

By the end of December 1979, Berman announced that twenty-six of the Assembly's fifty Democrats supported him for Speaker. Because party majorities had always settled speakership contests in the past, he urged McCarthy to bow to the will of the party's majority and step down. But there was a catch. McCarthy was reelected to a 2 year term in December 1978. According to tradition, the post was his until December 1980 unless Berman could muster a forty-one–vote majority on the Assembly floor, and McCarthy intended to stand by that tradition. On January 7, 1980, Berman took his case to the floor. The motion to remove McCarthy received twenty-seven Democratic votes, a net gain of one, but still far short of the majority as Republicans refused to take part one way or the other. The next day Berman again called for a vote on McCarthy, with the results standing pat at twenty-seven to twenty-three for Berman. Moreover, he vowed to call a vote every day to show that McCarthy was continuing as Speaker without a majority of his own party's support.

For his part McCarthy used his power as Speaker to retaliate. On January 9, he dumped Berman from his majority leader post and replaced him with Willie Brown. Within days, all Berman supporters holding committee chairmanships were also removed from their positions. Such decisions were solely the prerogative of the Speaker. As McCarthy supporter Lou Papan noted, "loyalty to the Speaker is expected from the chairmen of committees because, after all, he does appoint them. In this case, there are some whose judgment he has come to doubt."[5]

By the end of January, Assembly Democrats were tiring of the stalemate. Many felt the dispute had interfered with the legislature's work; they also began to fear voter repercussions as Assembly Republicans attempted to capitalize on Democratic divisiveness. Because the Berman forces had not been able to secure more than twenty-seven votes, they decided to wait until the following December when, once again, a simple party majority would elect the Speaker. For the moment McCarthy had beaten back the challenge. Meanwhile both sides turned their attention to the upcoming Democratic primary in hopes of breaking the political logjam.

To the delight of Assembly Republicans, Democrats McCarthy and Berman spent the first 6 months of the 1980 election campaign using their political ammunition on each other. By the June primary each leader raised more than $1 million for nine key Assembly races—some of which took dead aim at incumbents. In Southern California, incumbent McCarthy loyalist Jack Fenton lost to Berman-backed Mathew Martinez in the 59th district. Meanwhile, in the Central Valley, incumbent Berman ally Carmen Perino was defeated by McCarthy candidate Pat Johnston in the 26th district. The final score was five to four in favor of Berman, not enough to cause any immediate change in leadership.

The battle then moved to the pivotal November general elections, the last stop before the speakership vote in December. Again, each side put $1 million into the campaign war chests of their allies. In the fight against Republicans, Berman supporters won six seats, while the McCarthy team won but two. After the election McCarthy announced that he would not be a candidate for reelection. To this Berman responded, "I think it's mine to lose at this point."[6] Little did he realize the full implications of his statement.

ENTER WILLIE BROWN AND THE REPUBLICANS

Traditionally, the dominant party in the Assembly selects the Speaker in a meeting behind closed doors. Whoever emerges with a majority in the caucus gets unanimous party support on the floor, thereby ensuring the necessary forty-one–vote majority. True to tradition Berman vowed that he would not turn to the Republicans as leverage against McCarthy. Equally true to tradition the Republicans chose to remain on the sidelines and benefit from the intraparty Democratic strife. As minority leader Carol Hallett stated in January 1980, "We fully intend to continue with the [neutral] role we have chosen from the beginning—spectators at a somewhat entertaining event."[7] Yet what was true in January 1980 changed dramatically before the year's end.

After the November general election Berman enjoyed a decisive margin (twenty-six to eighteen) over McCarthy, with three Democrats still undecided. When McCarthy dropped out, Berman began to "count his chickens" and make plans for his speakership. In light of these events Berman's ascendance seemed a certainty for several reasons:

He had excellent credentials; colleagues considered him competent and industrious.

The Waxman-Berman machine had become the envy of Democratic circles; it could deliver.

Berman's brother Michael was considered the state's leading reapportionment expert; if the legislature remained in Democratic hands after the 1980 elections and census of the state's population, then the apportionment formula put into place for the next 10 years would doubtlessly favor Democrats.

After being on the short end of apportionment plans in the 1960s and 1970s, Republicans were concerned for good reason. Slowly they began to reassess their "neutral" position.

McCarthy backers also had good reasons to fear a Berman speakership. His clever use of mailers and money in the primary and general elections worried McCarthy incumbents that they "would be next." As McCarthy supporter Doug Bosco noted, "Most people feared that a cold, ruthless machine would suddenly grip the state with Howard at the head of it and everyone else in the face of it."[8] Meanwhile Berman did little to assuage such fears, perhaps because of his own bitterness or perhaps because of his perceived need to protect the rear flank. When Berman offered seven of the Assembly's twenty-two chairmanships to McCarthy backers, they considered the move a slap in the face rather than an effort at reconciliation. As a result McCarthy supporters did not cave in. Instead they searched for another Speaker candidate. Ultimately Willie Brown emerged as the point man for these forces.

Here is another case where events, the political climate, and perhaps, a little luck charted a new course in the Democratic leadership struggle. When asked in January 1980 if he had any aspirations to be Speaker, Willie Brown joked, "Speaker? I want to be President and beyond that, Pope, and I'm not even Catholic."[9] But what was a laughing matter in January became a serious issue in November.

Dismayed by the possibility of Berman's leadership, McCarthy loyalists turned to Brown as a new alternative—an ironic twist given the McCarthy-

Brown battle of 1974. When Brown declared his candidacy in early November, Berman claimed twenty-eight of the forty-seven Democratic votes. But by the end of the month, Berman and Brown were stalemated at twenty-three votes each, with the forty-seventh member, Tom Hannigan, refusing to vote because of disgust and reluctance "to make any commitment that makes me a part of this ongoing craziness."[10] In addition to Hannigan's neutrality, four Berman supporters—Richard Alatorre, Art Torres, Waddie Deddeh, and Bruce Young—switched to Brown within a week's time.

Aside from knotting the contest, these defections were noteworthy for two reasons. First, the four Assemblymen all came from Southern California, thus giving Brown a nearly even distribution of regional support (thirteen Northern Democrats, ten Southern Democrats), hence demonstrating his statewide appeal. Berman remained more of a regional candidate, with seventeen of twenty-three votes coming from Southern California. Second, the Alatorre-Torres switch sent ripples through the Hispanic community and, more specifically, United Farm Workers leader Cesar Chavez. A strong Berman proponent because of the latter's long close association with organized labor, Chavez accused Alatorre and Torres of sacrificing the Chicano cause to seek personal gains.

Meanwhile, with the Democratic majority seemingly fixed in concrete, Brown did the unthinkable—he entered into negotiations with minority leader Hallett for the Republicans' thirty-three votes. In late November Hallett pledged enough votes to secure Brown's election in exchange for

- Five or six new Republican committee chairmanships
- Vice-chairmanships for Republicans on all other Democrat-chaired committees
- An equal amount of funding for reapportionment research
- New Assembly rules that would remove the Speaker's independent power to assign bills to committee and place that responsibility in the hands of the Assembly Rules Committee.[11]

Of all the demands, the last one had the most far-reaching implications. For more than 20 years the Speaker had been powerful in part because of his or her sole decision of where to send new bills—to friendly or unfriendly committees. If denied this option, the Speaker's powers would be reduced greatly. Still Brown consented to all of Hallett's terms and the agreement was sealed.

On December 1, 1980 the year-long battle for the speakership came to an end. Predictably enough, the Democratic caucus remained tied at twenty-three

TABLE 6-1   Vote for Speaker by Party and Region*, 1980

| | Brown | | Berman | |
	Democrat	Republican	Democrat	Republican
North	13	11	6	1†
South	10	17	17	0
Subtotal	23	28	23	1
Total		51		24

*Southern California counties include: Imperial, San Diego, Riverside, Orange, Los Angeles, San Bernardino, Ventura, Santa Barbara, and Kern. All remaining counties are part of Northern California.

†The lone Republican Berman supporter, Jean Moorhead (Sacramento), felt sufficiently ostracized by the Republican party leadership that she switched to the Democratic party after Brown's election.

each for Brown and Berman. Brown then took the issue to the Assembly floor where, with Republican help, he defeated Berman by a vote of fifty-one to twenty-four (see Table 6-1).

In winning the speakership, Brown became the first black to secure a top position in either house of the legislature. He also defeated Berman in both parts of the state, by a margin of twenty-four to seven in northern districts, and by an advantage of twenty-seven to seventeen in southern districts, thus crossing regional lines in the process. But it also showed the inability of the state's Democratic Assembly members to accept internal discipline. With the majority of his support coming from the minority party, it remained to be seen how long Brown could govern both as the Democratic Speaker and keep major promises to the Republican minority.

BROWN'S REIGN AS SPEAKER

The day Willie Brown was elected Speaker, he announced at a news conference two things he would *not* do as Speaker that had been accepted practices of his predecessors:

• He would not use the Speaker's office to raise political campaign funds for candidates to the Assembly.

• He would not shape legislation to fit his own particular political viewpoints.[12]

His public goals notwithstanding, Brown quickly adapted himself to the traditional powers of the speakership. At the end of his first year as Speaker, he had raised $1,300,000 as the first part of a $2,500,00 kitty to elect Democratic candidates in the 1982 primary and general elections.[13] Brown also used the speakership to influence non-Assembly races. For example, he contributed a $50,000 loan to Art Torres in a successful 1982 primary fight to oust Democratic State Senate incumbent Alex Garcia.

Inside the Assembly Brown freely exercised the Speaker's prerogative of naming new chairmen to crucial committees. In virtually every case the departing chairman was a Berman backer, while the new chairman was in Brown's camp.[14] If such changes were rude awakenings to the departed, they were well within the long-established traditions of the Speaker's power.

With respect to his Republican backers, Brown gave in on minor issues but broke with the Republicans on major questions. For example, he created six Republican chairmanships (for mostly minor committees), named Republican vice-chairmen, and approved the necessary changes giving the Rules Committee power to assign bills to other committees. But because the Rules Committee was dominated by Brown backers, the change was more cosmetic than anything else.

It was on the reapportionment issue, however, that Brown separated himself most from Republicans and protected Democrats wherever possible. He put the Elections and Reapportionment Committee in the hands of new ally Richard Alatorre. As the committee came closer to adopting a reapportionment plan highly favorable to Democrats, Republicans accused Brown of backing out of a preelection agreement. For his part the Speaker claimed that he had made no reapportionment commitments to the Republicans. In Brown's words, "I have always deferred to political realities. One reality is that there is a majority of Democrats in the Assembly, and any reapportionment plan is going to reflect that."[15] Thus, Brown assured all Democrats—Brown and Berman supporters alike—that their seats would be protected in 1982 to the best of his abilities. With this move, Brown took a long step toward unifying Democrats in the Assembly.

By the end of Brown's first year in office, he had rid himself of his Republican crutch and solidified his popularity among Democratic colleagues. Given the deep divisions of a year earlier, Brown's accomplishments were nothing short of remarkable. As one Republican foe grudgingly admitted, "I've been waiting all year for Willie's waterloo. He was so strung out with his pledges here, his little deals there, the only question seemed to be when his house of cards would tumble. But I'm not waiting now. Take this any way you want: Willie Brown is one amazing man."[16]

As for Howard Berman, the Southern California lawmaker picked up his marbles to play in a new game. In 1982 he, along with supporters Mel Levine and Mathew Martinez, sought seats in the newly apportioned United States House of Representatives. With Berman gone and the Republicans under control, Brown was now truly in charge of his own as well as the Democrats' destiny in the Assembly.

Changes in the Senate—The Sleeping Giant Awakens

On November 10, 1980 David Roberti called Senate President Pro-Tem James Mills and told him that he wanted Mills's job. As the Senate's majority leader with a political base in Los Angeles, Roberti enjoyed substantial respect among his colleagues. But now he sought more than respect: he wanted the Senate's most powerful position. Roberti informed Mills that he controlled eighteen of the Senate's twenty-three Democratic votes, along with two Republicans. This combination left Roberti just one vote short of the twenty-one votes necessary to replace Mills.[17]

Mills initially responded with unabated anger. He labelled Roberti's vote count claims as those of "a liar" and "an incompetent," and said that he would never support Roberti for the job, even if Mills lost his own majority.[18] Mills had lived through such threats before, always surviving in the face of adversity. Throughout most of his 10 years as President Pro-Tem, Mills had been dogged by Fresno Democrat George Zenovich, who tried unsuccessfully on a half dozen occasions to replace him. But Mills defeated Zenovich every time. Yet Mills forgot that as the times change, so do the politicians. The Democratic Senate composition of 1980 was a far different body than it was in 1971.

INCREASED PARTISANSHIP—CAUSES AND CONSEQUENCES

In his decade at the helm of the upper house, Mills ran the Senate much like a social country club. Indeed the very nature of the Senate's leadership organization encouraged a legislative body of individualists. Whereas the Assembly Speaker served alone at the pinnacle of power, a five-member Rules Committee was (and remains) the collective basis of Senate leadership. By virtue of his position, the President Pro-Tem assumed the chairmanship of the Rules Committee. During the Mills regime—as in the past regimes—this suggested an atmosphere of collegiality rather than any power struggle.

Until 1980 the Senate remained a legislative institution with a "chummy, clubby atmosphere where friendships often meant more than party and political alliances were frequently based on issues and other pragmatic considerations rather than partisanship."[19] In addition, Mills had an unwritten rule that no Senate member was supposed to campaign—or assist the campaign—against another, regardless of party. Without warning, this rule was broken in 1980 when Democratic Senator Albert Rodda, a 20 year veteran, was defeated by unknown Republican John Doolittle.

Once an aide to conservative Republican Senator H. L. Richardson, Doolittle received substantial assistance from the Richardson organization. As a master of mass-mailing techniques, Richardson was able to raise a huge war chest for Doolittle as well as other Republican legislative candidates. His Computer Caging Corporation assembled, recorded, and reported thousands of campaign contributions. These, in turn, were funneled to a half dozen Richardson-headed political committees. Two such committees—the Law and Order Campaign Committee and Gun Owners of California—donated $60,000 of Doolittle's $80,000 campaign budget, much of it at the last minute. Meanwhile Rodda, with $17,000 of his $82,000 campaign fund in the bank on election day, was caught by surprise. The result was even more shattering for Rodda's Democratic colleagues, who viewed the Rodda-Doolittle contest as a turning point in Senate traditions.[20]

Given the 1980 election results, Roberti and a number of other Senate Democrats wanted a more partisan leader to keep the GOP from making further inroads into a shrinking (twenty-three to seventeen) Democratic majority. Moreover, inasmuch as fourteen of the twenty seats in the 1982 election were held by Democratic incumbents, Democrats knew that their task would be difficult under any conditions, let alone the new problems posed by Richardson. Meanwhile Roberti became the favorite of two previously divided groups in the Senate: liberals and "outsiders" with moderate political orientations. With that combination, his coalition was formed.[21]

On the surface, Roberti's problem paralleled that of Howard Berman—both had to deal with leaders who no longer enjoyed majority support within their own party. But the similarity ended there. Unlike the partisan Assembly, the Senate had a reputation for electing presidents pro-tem from bipartisan coalitions, thus freeing Roberti to court Republicans without fear of Democratic recrimination. He solicited just enough Republican support to show Mills the futility of any resistance.

By the end of November 1980 Mills decided to go quietly. He indicated that he wanted to avoid duplicating the turmoil that had plagued the Assembly. He did. On December 1, 1980 the Democratic caucus voted twenty-two to zero for Roberti in a closed-door session; only Mills chose not to vote.

Although only chairman of the Rules Committee by virtue of his election to the president pro-tem office, Roberti managed to get allies elected to prominent committee positions, thus consolidating his new leadership position. Liberal Democrat Barry Keene was elected to the Rules Committee to replace potential Roberti foe Bob Presley, and John Garamendi was chosen as majority floor leader. By 1981 Roberti was securely established as the Senate's most important leader.

It was in the area of increased partisanship, however, that Roberti made his biggest splash. Under his regime the president pro-tem's staff grew from thirteen to twenty-nine members. According to one observer, the increased staff size reflected Roberti's intent to make his office "a center of policy and political activity . . . like the Speaker's office in the Assembly."[22]

Although overshadowed by the flamboyant Assembly Speaker Willie Brown, Roberti has had a major impact on the internal organization of the Senate. In the fund-raising area he emerged as the antithesis of his predecessor. Whereas Mills never gave out more than $50,000 to all candidates combined in any single election year, Roberti raised $578,000 in 1981 alone. After spending $227,000 in that year, he began 1982 with a surplus of $350,000 for Senate candidates. (Roberti himself was not up for reelection in 1982.) Moreover, Roberti promised and raised a 1982 war chest of $1 million. He demonstrated his sincerity by the attention he gave to the 1982 primary in which Assemblyman Art Torres challenged Democratic Senator Alex Garcia. By the primary's end, Roberti had contributed $125,000 to Garcia in a losing cause!

It remained to be seen to what extent Roberti would mold the Senate into a well-organized machine. Fragmented leadership in the Rules Committee still made it more desirable for lobbyists and other legislative advocates to deal with Brown in the Assembly. For these structural reasons Roberti's long-term goals to centralize power seemed more theoretical than probable. Yet one thing was for sure: the Senate's partisan consciousness had reached levels never before attained in its past. For this reason alone, the Roberti look would have a long-term impact in the Senate.

The Making of a Professional Legislature

There is an old saying that goes, "the more things change, the more they stay the same." Although such a theme may be true for many political phenomena, it has not been the case with the California legislature. The story of the legislature's evolution is every bit as remarkable as the development of California from a series of missions and large ranchos to a multifaceted urban, industrial giant. In fact, these changes have come hand in hand.

At the end of the nineteenth century the legislature basically consisted of a part-time, agriculture-oriented body subservient to the will of the Southern Pacific Railroad. One hundred years later this institution stands as a full-time assemblage, with a broad-based composition and a staff of more than 2200 professionals to assist them. Other changes have occurred as well. Whereas the legislature was once the bastion of white males, today it houses sizable delegations of blacks and Hispanics, along with smaller contingents of women and Asians. Although these groups still do not mirror the state's population in a proportional sense, many of their members have assumed key positions of leadership and influence.

En route to its maturity the legislature underwent changes induced by the Progressives, fell in and out of the clutches of power interest groups, became dominated by key lobbyists, and succumbed to the problems of party factionalism. Today this body has strong centralized leadership in the hands of the Assembly Speaker and, to a lesser extent, the Senate President Pro-Tem. It enjoys the reputation of being among the most professional of all fifty state legislatures. This is not to suggest that the California legislature has emerged as the perfect lawmaking institution. To the contrary, today it contains residues of all the aforementioned forces as part of its complicated makeup.

EARLY DEVELOPMENT AND DIRECTION

The California legislature did not begin exactly in the form of a fine-tuned, smooth-working organization of elected leaders. In fact, it was known as "the legislature of a thousand drinks."[23] The body was so disorganized in 1850 that virtually no official business was enacted due to failure of a quorum. Nevertheless, the absence of numbers did not prevent the legislature from considerable unofficial business. Evidence suggests that those present were available for favor and influence. After temporary locations in San Jose, Vallejo, and Benicia, the legislature settled on Sacramento as the state capital in 1854.

Other changes occurred as well. When first organized in 1849, the legislature consisted of sixteen Senators and thirty-six Assemblymen, with a full half of each house representing the mining areas of Sacramento and San Joaquin Counties. At first, members were elected annually in the Assembly and every 2 years in the Senate. But things changed as the state's political system matured. By the time of the second constitutional convention in 1879, the Senate had grown to forty members and the Assembly enlarged to eighty. Also the Senate's terms were fixed at 4 years (half elected every 2 years), and the Assembly's terms were set at 2 years. This election format remains the same today.

The nature of electoral districts has also changed over time. Until 1926 members in both houses were elected in districts carved out by population. However, politicians quickly learned that the South was growing at a rate much faster than the North, fueling Northern California fears that control of the state would ultimately fall into Southern hands. Thus in 1926 the state's voters passed a constitutional amendment known as the "federal plan," with the Assembly chosen by population and the Senate chosen by territory—basically one Senator per county with a few exceptions. This method, an attempt to give Northern rural interests permanent veto power over Southern urban interests, prevailed until the United States Supreme Court issued a series of reapportionment decisions in the 1960s providing that all legislatures be chosen by the concept of "one man, one vote."[24]

In the earliest days of the state legislature the leadership positions seemed more ceremonial than anything else. The Assembly speakership, coveted as a crucial position of power today, was almost routinely passed from one member to another with the onset of each legislative session. This casual attitude about power persisted for the better part of a half century. Beginning in 1915, the speakership was no longer considered merely an honor. Those in control attempted to keep power as long as their party held a majority, and intraparty rumblings were kept to a minimum.

The Southern Pacific's Early Hold on the Legislature.   When the United States Congress passed the Pacific Railroad Bill in 1862, it also directed California's destiny for the next 50 years. The nation gained a transcontinental railroad by 1869, but California succumbed to the economic and political clout of the Southern Pacific Railroad. By the early 1880s the railroad enjoyed a virtual monopoly over the state's transportation network, holding 85 percent of the rail lines.[25] Ten million acres in federal land grants made the Southern Pacific the state's biggest landowner. The results of its domination were predictable enough. Practically all of the state suffered at the railroad's hands. Cities were pitted against each other for the Southern Pacific's favor, merchants were forced into excessive competition with one another, and newspapers—given the value of railroad-related advertising—maintained a silent posture on the entire matter.[26]

The Southern Pacific's economic clout became the basis for its political successes. By the 1880s both major political parties in California were under the railroad's political control. Moreover, the railroad's ability to make policy favorable to its needs (or stop laws inimical to its interest) extended to the legislature itself. In fact, the Southern Pacific Political Bureau, led by Chief Counsel Williams F. Herrin, because the *de facto* legislature in the state on questions relevant to its needs. So frightened were officeholders in both the Assembly and the Senate that "scarcely a vote was cast in either house that did not show some aspect of Southern Pacific ownership, petty vengeance, or legislative blackmail."[27]

The impact of railroad political dominance of California was devastating to the legislative process. As public awareness of the railroad's clout grew, would-be reformers spoke out in opposition, not only to the railroad, but to the institutions purportedly designed to reflect all public interests. Almost like dominoes, the legislature, governorship, political parties, and even the Railroad Commission (a regulatory agency created to control the railroad) fell from the public's grace. Moreover, distrust of the legislature because of interest group manipulation became a permanent pillar of the state's political culture. When the railroad's domination ended in the early 1920s, other vested interests took its place as private sources of power affecting the public legislative process.

The Progressive Revolution. The Southern Pacific Political Bureau thought that it had a lock on the political process because of its control of both major political parties and their legislators. What the Southern Pacific did not count on, however, was an attack from outside the existing political order.

The assault began with a group of dissidents who shared a common theme— hatred for the Southern Pacific and all the corruption related to its control of politics. They also resented the railroad for its complete control over their economic lives. Fully aware that established institutions were suspect, the antiestablishment movement coalesced around the Progressive philosophy. Their general objective was to remove special interests from politics. Specifically, however, they wanted to rid California of the Southern Pacific's stranglehold. Political outsiders, a few reformist newspapers, the struggling small business class, and abused farmers formed the Progressive alliance.

The Progressives first succeeded with the election of Hiram Johnson, an avowed antirailroad candidate, to the governorship in 1910. From there, they soon elected majorities to the legislature both by dumping railroad-sponsored incumbents and by making converts among those holding office. But their ability to keep the Progressive philosophy as a viable alternative was short-lived. The career of C. C. Young ably demonstrates the point. In 1913 Young was elected Speaker of the Assembly as a Republican. In 1915 he was reelected

Speaker as a Progressive. Then things changed, and in 1917 Young was reelected as a Republican. Indeed by 1920 the Progressive philosophy had earned its place in history more as a short-lived movement than as a permanent political party.

By the 1920s the legislature was again in the hands of conservative Republicans promoting the objectives of different private interests. Although the railroad was no longer the force it had once been, its reduced power was due less to an aggressive legislature and more to industrialization and new, competing modes of transportation. All of this suggested that the legislature remained a body available to manipulation from without. The players changed, but the rules stayed the same. Instead of domination by a single interest—the Southern Pacific—the state legislature was conquered through "the triumph of many interests."[28]

THE RISE OF STRONG LEADERSHIP: SOME CAUSES

Between 1920 and 1965 this nation underwent dramatic political change. Government, viewed in benevolent, passive, and limited terms in the early 1900s, became a moving force in the distribution of values, goods, and policies. Politics in California reflected all these changes and more.

Seemingly overnight, California became the number-one state in agriculture, automobile production, defense industries, and a host of other areas. By 1963 California was the most populous state in the Union with one of the largest budgets. Everything about California, except for the organization of the state legislature, suggested it had joined the "big time." Here was a body that continued to meet on a part-time basis as late as 1966. Until that time the legislature formulated the state budget every 2 years, and spent no more than 120 days in session every other year to make general laws. Here was also a state that, by virtue of the "federal plan" adopted in 1926, permitted twenty-one Senators from the smallest counties to represent less than 10 percent of the population. Meanwhile, Los Angeles County, with 35 percent of the state's population, had only one State Senator in Sacramento. These traditions felt the strains of modernization as California struggled to come to terms with its new position.

The Impact of Reynolds v. Sims.   When the United States Supreme Court handed down its reapportionment decisions in the 1960s, the one of greatest importance to California was *Reynolds* v. *Sims*. Simply stated, this decision ordered the upper houses, such as the State Senate in California, to organize their districts by population. As a result of the court-ordered apportionment changes in 1965, about half of the Senate's forty seats shifted from rural northern to southern and urban areas. Because of the consolidation of old districts in some localities and the creation of new districts in others, the 1966 elections produced twenty-two new Senators and thirty-three first-term Assemblymen. Yet the new legislature reflected more than mere numerical changes.

Reapportionment in California opened new vistas to both legislative organization and leadership. Political scientist Alvin Sokolow found characteristics in the new members distinctly different from those of past members: "This group was younger, better educated, and had a larger percentage of attorneys and other professionals than those in previous years. . . . Proportionately, fewer of them . . . could be classified as moderates, and they tended to increase liberal-conservative polarizations in both the Senate and Assembly." In addition, representatives of racial minorities, particularly blacks and Asians, increased the legislature's diversity.[29] As a result, freshmen of both parties— along with a few veterans—sought a greater amount of party organization and discipline than the legislature had ever experienced. These developments led to a pronounced centralization of power in the Assembly and, to a more modest extent, in the Senate.

The Creation of a Full-Time Legislature.   Until 1966 part-time legislators received $6,000 annually for their services. But in that year the public passed a ballot proposition that did two things: it made the legislature a full-time body and increased basic salaries to $16,000 annually in the hope that better-qualified people able to make full-time commitments would seek election. Since then their salaries have increased considerably. Basic salaries today are almost twice those of 1966.

Realistically, the typical California legislator of the 1980s earns between $40,000 and $50,000 a year. Although the base salary in 1983 was $28,110, their total compensation included a *per diem* (daily) allowance of $62 for every day the legislature convenes. Assembly members and Senators also benefit from perks like leased cars, gasoline, credit cards, and a liberal pension plan. Although this may seem quite a bit by some standards, it really isn't when we consider that this body considers between 3,000 and 4,000 bills per year as well as a budget in excess of $30 billion. If these individuals were corporate executives with similar responsibilities, they would be grossly underpaid.

The increased compensation and full-time status of the legislature have led to some interesting changes in its composition. Table 6-2 illustrates some fundamental gains for women and racial minorities. Also, dramatic changes

TABLE 6-2   Profile of the California Legislature, 1965–80

Senate			Assembly	
1965	1980		1965	1980
		Sex		
33	37	Men	79	71
0	2	Women	1	9
		Minorities		
0	3	Hispanic	1	3
0	2	Black	4	6
0	0	Asian	1	2
		Age		
33	30	Youngest	29	26
70	70	Oldest	66	67
51	52	Average	46	45
8.1	6.8	*Years in Office*	6.7	5.1
		Occupation		
2	12	Full-time legislator	4	26
16	13	Attorney	30	18
16	9	Business/farming	28	24
		Education		
3	0	High school only	6	6
14	13	Bachelor's degree	29	25
19	25	Advanced/profession degree	34	44
		Former offices		
12	23	Assembly	—	—
11	5	Local government	17	29

Source: California Journal 12, no. 1 (January 1981): 4. © 1981 by The California Center. Reprinted with permission.

took place with respect to education levels and occupations engaged in prior to entering the legislature. With a more professional and better-educated legislature, its members quickly accepted the contention that strong organization would promote more efficient work loads, enhanced expertise, and more meaningful legislation. These changes fell right into line with the growth of leadership power.

The Supporting Cast.   California ranks among the most professional of the fifty state legislatures. This reputation stems partly from the caliber of those elected to office, especially since the legislature became a full-time body with better pay in 1966. However, there are other reasons for the legislature's professionalism. Unlike some state legislatures that must function with little assistance, the California state legislature has provided itself with numerous sources of support, including the Legislative Analyst, the Legislative Counsel, the Auditor General, and committee consultants.

The Legislative Analyst is the legislature's most important budgetary reference office. With a staff of 120, many of whom are accountants and fiscal experts, the chief task of the Analyst is to dissect the governor's budget (and its implications) upon its presentation to the legislature. Notoriously nonpartisan in behavior, the Legislative Analyst enjoys great prestige with the legislature. When A. Alan Post became the state's first Legislative Analyst in 1949, he served in that capacity until his retirement in 1977—all this with absolutely no job security because the legislature could replace him at any time. Nevertheless, Post worked under both Republican and Democratic leadership. Upon his retirement, he was replaced by William Hamm, formerly of the U.S. Office of Management and Budget, who remains today in the Legislative Analyst's office.

When a legislator introduces a bill, he or she does so with the assistance of the Legislative Counsel, the legislature's chief attorney. This office drafts a bill in its proper form. It also includes a digest covering whatever changes the proposal may have for existing laws as well as the anticipated constitutionality of the new bill in question. No small enterprise, the Legislative Counsel employs about three hundred people, about 25 percent of whom are attorneys. In addition to the normal eight to five daily grind, staff members work whenever the legislature works, leading to schedules that may begin early in the morning and end early in the morning!

Because the legislature appropriates billions of dollars every year, it has an agency to oversee the use of its funds. The Auditor General, a certified public accountant, examines the programs to which monies are committed both for their efficiency and utility. Teams of evaluators are sent throughout the state on periodic bases for onsite inspection and analysis. As with the Legislative Analyst, this office gives the legislature an independent counterweight to the governor and his or her Department of Finance. Approximately 160 people work in the Auditor General's office.

Much of the legislature's activity occurs through the committee system, a complicated apparatus that greatly expanded with the legislature's professionalism in 1966. Committee consultants are an unusual hybrid in the legislature: they are both subject experts in their particular committee areas (i.e., judiciary, transportation, industrial relations) and political animals who know how to cater to the committee's whims. Each legislative committee has at least one consultant; some of the "juice" committees (so named for their ability to attract major campaign contributions) have two or more consultants. Those committees with the most full-time consultants are the Assembly Ways and Means Committee and Senate Finance Committee, each containing more than a half dozen professional staffers.

Generally chosen by the committee chair, consultants perform many functions. They scrutinize each bill that comes before the committee by analyzing the benefits and drawbacks as well as the bill's proponents and opponents. As the consultant makes these evaluations, the subject expertise and political acumen of the consultant become part of the legislative process. As one account notes, "the opinion of consultants tends to enter directly into the deliberative process and often becomes public policy simply because legislators are too busy or too lazy to make their own objective studies."[30] Consultants, then, offer legislators a shortcut to the tedious lawmaking routine.

One step removed from committee consultants, another group in the legislature has little more than strictly political responsibilities. Although these staffers are technically assigned to research bills, their loyalties start and end with the house leadership. One 1980 study of the Assembly alone shows sixty-seven consultants employed by the two party leaderships. Of the thirty-seven Democrats, twenty-two worked in the Democratic consultant's office, five in the caucus chairman's office, five in the caucus secretary's office, three as employees for the floor leader, and two serving as Democratic whips. For the Assembly Republicans, some thirty consultants were divided into similar positions.

Increases in staff support have generated controversy among the legislature's observers. One legislator, a former staffer himself 10 years ago, has lamented, "the staff is bigger and brighter today, but the product is no different and no better."[31] In response one consultant noted, "we are a professional staff, helping members pass their legislation, publicizing it when it passes and assisting other staff . . . in making their offices function more properly."[32] Although the debate on this issue remains inconclusive, one fact is certain: staffers provide a good deal of information, help, and clout in the legislative process.

Viewed in their entirety, the legislative analyst, the legislative counsel, the auditor general, and committee staffers are the glue of California's legislative machinery. Without these capable personnel the state would be in another league, doubtlessly inferior to the body it is today.

The Legislative Process

With as many as 4000 bills introduced each year, the legislature divides most of its responsibilities into committee work. During the 1983–84 two-year session, the Assembly had twenty-three committees, all chaired by Democrats. The upper house was organized into twenty committees; Democrats chaired eighteen, and Republicans were given charge of two insignificant assignments.

With Democrats enjoying numerical advantages in both houses (forty-eight to thirty-two in the Assembly; twenty-six to fourteen in the Senate), they had majorities on all committees. Nevertheless, their numbers were not great enough to guarantee smooth operation of the legislative process, because some of the most controversial bills required Republican help for passage.

The legislature asserts its powers in three main ways. First, either or both houses may issue opinions, officially known as resolutions. These do not have the impact of law but, instead, reflect the legislature's (or a single chamber's) feelings about a given matter in which they have interest but no jurisdiction.

Second, the legislature may pass a law. In routine matters absolute majorities (forty-one in the Assembly, twenty-one in the Senate) are required for passage. Where appropriations, urgency measures (those that take place immediately), and veto overrides are at issue, absolute two-thirds majorities must prevail in both houses (fifty-four in the Assembly, twenty-seven in the Senate) for the bill to be made law.

Third, proposed constitutional amendments and bond issues originate in the legislature. Proposed constitutional amendments require absolute two-thirds majorities, while absolute majorities are needed for bond issues. Unlike routine bills, which go to the governor for approval or veto, these legislative efforts are submitted to the voters for their adoption or rejection at the next general election. Although the legislature functions in all these respects, lawmaking consumes the vast majority of the members' time and energy. With this in mind, we turn our attention to the perils of getting a bill through the legislature.

THE OFFICIAL VERSION

Any bill may begin in either the Assembly or the Senate. The introductory phase is simple enough: the sponsoring legislator merely hands a bill to the clerk of the chamber, at which point it is recorded and given a number. Although it may seem cumbersome, a bill receives three readings before it emerges from one house and moves to the other. In the process all interested parties usually have the opportunity to speak out at one or more points along the way.

The "first reading" is little more than acknowledgment of the bill's submission. After the bill is titled and numbered, either the Assembly Speaker or the Senate Rules Committee dispatches the bill to an appropriate committee.

Committee consideration is the most important state in a bill's life. If the bill is sent to a "friendly" committee, its chances are better than if it were put in the hands of a "hostile" committee. Thus, the biases of the house leadership can indicate much about a bill's future. Committees meet regularly to deliberate the bills before them. Their activities include hearings, debate, proposed amendments, and, ultimately, a vote on the bill's future. More than half of all bills submitted each year die in committee. Moreover, even if a committee is ambivalent about a bill and releases it without recommendation, the bill will probably die on the house floor. If a committee majority approves the bill, a "do pass" is recorded. Still very much alive, the bill is sent to the full house for consideration.

When a bill is given the green light by committee, it is then put on the Assembly or Senate calendar. There the bill receives a "second reading." At this point committee-suggested amendments are entertained, as well as those from any other legislator of the house in which the bill is being considered. The most serious debate occurs at this juncture because those forces that may have been defeated in committee now have the opportunity for a final assault. Many a bill has been changed dramatically during the second reading because of last-minute alliances and renewed political pressures. After all the proposed changes are voted up or down, the bill is then sent out for reprinting and, hopefully, final action in the house of its original introduction.

The "third reading" occurs when the bill is considered in its final form. Now the talk centers on the merits of the bill as a whole. If the bill's sponsor anticipates a close vote, he or she may ask the leadership to wait until enough of the "right" members arrive. Even if the bill is defeated, the sponsor may ask the leadership for "reconsideration" at another time. In both instances, the leaderships usually extend these courtesies to a legislator. Debate on the bill ends when a majority expresses itself accordingly. If the bill passes with the necessary votes, it is then sent to the other house where the process begins anew.

Should the two houses pass different versions of the same bill, the matter is then referred to conference committee. The Speaker appoints three members in the Assembly, and the Rules Committee selects the same number in the Senate. The conference committee must iron out all differences so that, in the end, the two houses approve identical versions. If the conference committee cannot agree, a new committee may be selected or, in some cases, the bill may be shelved indefinitely. Likewise, unless both houses accept the conference committee version without alteration, the bill is also dead.

Assuming that the bill emerges from both houses in identical fashion, it is then sent to the governor. If the governor signs the bill or takes no action within a 12-day period, the bill becomes law. If the governor vetoes the bill, the legislature can exercise its right to override the veto at the end of its legislative session. At that point the bill becomes law only if it secures absolute two-thirds majorities in both houses, a rare phenomenon (see Figure 6-1).

FIGURE 6-1   California's Legislative Process

INITIAL STEPS BY AUTHOR

IDEA
Sources of bills: legislators, legislative committees, governor, state and local governmental agencies, business firms, lobbyists, citizens.

▶ DRAFTING
Formal copy of bill and "layman's digest" prepared by Legislative Counsel.

▶ INTRODUCTION
Bill submitted by senator or Assembly member. Numbered and read for first time. Assigned to committee by Assembly or Senate Rules Committee. Printed.

ACTION IN HOUSE OF ORIGIN

COMMITTEE
Testimony taken from author, proponents and opponents. Typical actions: Do pass; amend and do pass; no action; hold in committee (kill); amend and re-refer to same committee; refer to another committee; send to interim study.
  Appropriation bills, if approved by policy committee, are referred to Finance Committee in the Senate and to Ways and Means Committee in the Assembly.

▶ SECOND READING
Bills given do-pass recommendations are read a second time and placed on file for debate.

▶ FLOOR DEBATE AND VOTE
Bills are read a third time and debated. A roll-call vote follows. For ordinary bills, 21 votes are needed in the Senate and 41 in the Assembly. For urgency bills and appropriation measures, 27 and 54 votes are required. If these numbers are not reached, the bill is defeated. Any member may seek reconsideration and a second vote. If passed or passed with amendments, the bill is sent to the second house.

DISPOSITION IN SECOND HOUSE

READING
Bill is read for the first time and referred to committee by the Assembly or Senate Rules Committee.

▶ COMMITTEE
Procedures and possible actions are identical to those in the first house.

▶ SECOND READING
If cleared by committee, the bill is read a second time and placed on the daily file (agenda) for debate and vote.

▶ FLOOR DEBATE AND VOTE
The procedure is identical to the first house. If a bill is passed without having been amended in the second house, it is sent to the governor's desk. (Resolutions are sent to the secretary of state's office.) If amended in the second house and passed, the measure returns to the house of origin for consideration of amendments.

RESOLUTION OF TWO-HOUSE DIFFERENCES (IF NECESSARY)

CONCURRENCE
The house of origin decides whether to accept the second-house amendments. If the amendments are approved, the bill is sent to the governor. If the amendments are rejected, the bill is placed in the hands of a two-house conference committee composed of three senators and three Assembly members.

▶ CONFERENCE
If the conferees fail to present a report, the bill dies. If the conferees present a recommendation for compromise, both houses vote on the report. If the report is adopted by both, the bill goes to the governor. If either house rejects the report, a second (and even a third) conference committee can be formed.

ROLE OF THE GOVERNOR

SIGN OR VETO?
Within 12 days after receiving a bill, the governor can sign it into law, allow it to become law without his signature or veto it. A vetoed bill returns to the house of origin for possible vote on overriding the veto. It requires a two-thirds majority of both houses to override.
  Urgency measures become effective immediately after signing. Others usually take effect the following January 1st.

Source: California Journal (February 1983). © 1983 by The California Center. Reprinted with permission.

THE UNOFFICIAL VERSION

It would be nice to say that bills are judged by their merits—the good ones winning and the bad ones losing. But there is no guaranteed coexistence between politics and merits. The merits of a bill are defined by the clout behind it. Those who build political alliances to their advantage are likely to enjoy the most clout. As a contrast to the "official version" of the legislative process, let's examine the "unofficial version" that gives so much color to what otherwise might be viewed as simple black or white solutions to political issues.

The Importance of Leadership Contacts. Much of a legislator's success depends upon his or her relationship to the Assembly Speaker or the Senate Rules Committee. Inasmuch as these forces determine committee assignments and the routes bills travel, their support is essential for any hope of legislative success. It is a rarity when a bill passes in spite of the leadership's opposition.

If a legislator is well connected with the leadership, his or her horizons expand greatly. Such a situation was chronicled in 1981 when Assemblyman Richard Alatorre, a last-minute convert in Willie Brown's speakership victory over Howard Berman, was given the chairmanship of the Elections and Reapportionment Committee. With this single connection Alatorre became the most important person in the Assembly for determining the compositions of Assembly districts via reapportionment.

Strong leadership serves a function other than the political: it reduces the slack in the legislative process. Under Brown and Roberti, the divisions of labor have been made clear. Brown has organized his priorities in the Assembly, and Roberti and the Rules Committee have brought tighter partisan organization to the once free-wheeling Senate. As a result the legislature today works well, although deep suspicions between the two houses not only continue, but sometimes interfere with a bill's future.

Logrolling. A few years ago the late Assemblyman Edwin Z'berg sat in conference with a new staffer. Z'berg, then the legislature's leading environmentalist, was informed by his secretary that two members of the California Real Estate Association were waiting to see him about a bill pending in the Assembly. Z'berg rarely found common ground with the realtors, but he asked his secretary to show them in. Shocked, the staffer asked the Assemblyman for an explanation. Z'berg merely smiled as the realtors filed into his office.

In the following 10 minutes the realtors asked Z'berg to support a bill in which he had little interest and even less praise. But Z'berg listened and told the lobbyists that he would give the matter some thought. Responding with "that's all we can ask," the realtors left the Assemblyman's office.

The door had barely closed before the confused staffer quizzed Z'berg. "Why did you talk with them? What will you do?" the staffer asked. The veteran legislator answered that many colleagues were seeking his support on the issue, that the Real Estate Association had helped him on his legislation in the past, and that he could give his vote "without too much pain." Such is the definition of *logrolling*: legislators help one another as well as opponents for past support or hope of future support. Z'berg was paying a debt.

Logrolling is as much a part of the legislative agenda as the daily call for a quorum. With so many diverse interests at work, this bargaining tool is a key informal ingredient for getting things done. Often legislators seem to cast votes totally foreign to their public positions or past political behavior. Often they do so because of logrolling.

Many purists criticize logrolling as a devious way to cut political deals. Others argue that the legislative process is so complex that laws cannot be made without compromise. Regardless of its acceptability, logrolling is a mainstay in the informal operation of the legislature.

The Flow of Money. "Money is the mother's milk of politics," former Assembly Speaker Jesse Unruh once said. Unruh underscored the importance of his words by using money to consolidate the powers of his office. Not only did the speakership continue as the source of agenda setting and committee assignments, but the office became the major legislative position for fund raising. In fact, until Senate President Pro-Tem Roberti began his fund-raising activities in 1981, the speakership was the state's major fund-raising and spend-ing source for legislators. If one had good relations with the Speaker, he or she could expect election help in the form of campaign contributions. With Rober-ti's involvement in fund raising, similar results have occurred in the Senate. The 1982 Torres-Garcia battle is the best, but not only, example of the extent to which house leaderships become involved in individual campaigns.

Lobbyists have also come to recognize the importance of directing money to the right legislative leaders. In 1981, for example, Assemblyman Tom Bane, a member of the Finance, Insurance, and Commerce Committee, introduced and secured passage of a bill that allowed state-chartered lending institutions to issue home mortgages with unrestricted annual interest rate variations. Coin-cidentally, Bane also received about $50,000 from the savings and loan and banking industries in campaign donations.[33]

Nevertheless, money is not always omniscient in the legislative process. Sometimes a bill is too controversial for all the pressure points to be soothed. Such was the case in 1981 when a wealthy state developer and Democratic contributor, Nathan Shapell, promoted a bill that would allow development of large parcels (one of them his) without environmental impact reports and guarantees. Shapell seemed to have his bases covered, having given $9,000 to Assembly Majority Leader Mike Roos, the bill's sponsor, $7,000 to Willie Brown, and $5,000 to David Roberti. The bill was touted by promoters as a way of ending California's housing shortages, rather than circumventing environmental guarantees.[34] Passed in the Assembly and Senate, it was sent to the governor's desk. But the story had a surprise ending. Jerry Brown, who also had received campaign contributions from Shapell ($2,200), vetoed the bill, thus negating a carefully orchestrated effort.

Taken together, leadership connections and money reveal much about lawmaking. To be sure, the correlations are far from perfect. There are times when. leadership clout is insufficient to get a bill passed; there are also times when vast sums of money do not generate the desired legislative results. Nevertheless, these need to be recognized as unofficial components of the legislative process.

Today's Legislature—Leadership in Transition

The California legislature appears to be better organized and more efficient today than in recent memory. Democratic Assembly Speaker Willie Brown, initially victorious only because of Republican votes, has consolidated his power to the point where he enjoys widespread Democratic support. His party once again has a smooth-working operation in the lower house, with clear distinctions between the Democrats and Republicans. The virtue of this division is that the voters now have a better handle on whom to blame or praise for the Assembly's work.

The Senate has changed incredibly. Partisanship, once a forbidden word, has not only been introduced but is thriving. Democratic Senate President Pro-Tem David Roberti, in the wake of his successful revolution against James Mills, has moved to separate the Senate's political parties by the distribution of new committee assignments (in cooperation with the Rules Committee) and his fund-raising abilities. If the Assembly was once a legislative organization without parallel, the new Senate has mounted a formidable challenge to that claim.

Yet the legislature remains plagued with problems—some as old as the institution itself, others relatively new. One problem centers on the tough vote requirements for the most important legislative items. The fact that absolute two-thirds requirements are necessary for budgets, urgency matters, and veto overrides places two-party politics in a double bind: either one party must have an overwhelming majority in both houses or bipartisan arrangements must be made. Short of either option, important issues may remain unresolved. We saw such an instance in July 1983 when, despite majorities in both houses, Democrats were unable to get a budget to Republican Governor Deukmejian until 3 weeks into the 1983–84 fiscal year. The Republican minority in the legislature was large enough to force the Democrats to back down on virtually every major point (except education) before the budget received their support and passage.

A more contemporary problem has arisen concerning the ways members are nominated or recruited for nomination. In those states with strong political parties, nominations often are arranged or at least guided by party leaders. Not so in California with its "free for all" environment. Given this power vacuum, the state has developed a novel source of legislative recruitment—the legislature! In 1960 one former legislative staffer was elected to the legislature. By 1980 about 25 percent of the legislature's members had prior staff or committee consultant experience. The benefits of these power positions are enormous. With knowledge of fund-raising techniques, access to mailing lists, and awareness of the public mood, these individuals have tremendous advantages over challengers without similar legislative backgrounds. Some argue that these experiences make staffer-turned-legislators into better public officials. Others counter that the arrangement creates an inbreeding network that is unhealthy for the state's political process. Placed in perspective, some of California's legislative problems remain questions without resolution in the 1980s.

Overall the legislature of the 1980s faces tasks without recent parallel. Living in the shadow cast by Proposition 13 and other tax-cutting measures, both house leaderships are being tested for their abilities to cope with increased demands at a time of reduced resources. So far, they have managed but with greater difficulty each year. In the meantime Assembly Speaker Brown and Senate President Pro-Tem Roberti have not only put their own houses in order but have formed a solid alliance against the Deukmejian administration. Yet the cost of their opposition may change as the decade and its politics progress.

Notes

[1] "Speaker of Assembly: From the Power Flow the Political Funds," *Los Angeles Times*, October 3, 1978.

[2] Article IV, Section 7(a).

[3]Susan Littwin, "Bagel Boroughs," *California Journal* 7, no. 9 (September 1976): 300.

[4]"McCarthy vs. Berman," *Los Angeles Times*, January 6, 1980.

[5]"Anti-McCarthy Letter," *Los Angeles Times*, January 10, 1980.

[6]"Berman Victory May Benefit Governor Brown," *Los Angeles Times*, November 9, 1980.

[7]"Berman Ahead in Second Vote," *Los Angeles Times*, January 9, 1980.

[8]"Brown Elected," *Los Angeles Times*, January 2, 1980.

[9]"Berman Fights Back," *Los Angeles Times*, January 10, 1980.

[10]"Brown Claims Votes," *Los Angeles Times*, December 3, 1980.

[11]"Brown Elected," *Los Angeles Times*, December 2, 1980 and Daniel Blackburn, "How Brown Solidified Speakership," *California Journal* 13, no. 1 (January 1982): 6.

[12]"Neutral Speakership," *San Jose Mercury*, December 3, 1980.

[13]"Campaign Funds," *Los Angeles Times*, February 4, 1982.

[14]Consider the fates of the following chairs who were Berman supporters:

- Lawrence Kapiloff (Water, Parks and Wildlife) was replaced by Norm Waters, a Brown supporter.
- Walter Ingalls (Transportation), was replaced by Bruce Young, a last-minute Brown convert.
- Richard Robinson (Economic Development and Planning) was replaced by a Republican.
- Teresa Hughes (Housing and Community Development) was replaced by a less conspicuous Berman supporter, Mike Costa.

In addition to these changes, the all important Elections and Reapportionment Committee—pivotal in a reapportionment year—was taken from Marilyn Ryan, a Republican and tacit Berman suporter, and given to Richard Alatorre.

[15]Blackburn, "How Brown Solidifed Speakership," p. 6.

[16]Ibid.

[17]"Mills' Reign Ends," *Los Angeles Times*, November 25, 1980.

[18]"Mills Won't Quit," *Los Angeles Times*, November 14, 1980.

[19]Vic Pollard, "Senate's New Era," *California Journal* 12, no. 2 (February 1981): 43.

[20]This was not the first time Richardson committees had contributed massive amounts to Republican candidates; rather, it was the first time that Richardson openly confronted a Democratic incumbent. Other Richardson recipients prior to the 1980 Rodda-Doolittle contest were

- Ed Davis, Republican State Senate candidate ($32,000) in 1980.
- Dan O'Keefe, Republican State Senate candidate ($86,000) in a 1980 special election.
- Ollie Speraw, Republican State Senate candidate ($33,000) in a 1979 special election.

In addition, Richardson committees have given sizable amounts to a number of Republican Assembly incumbents and candidates. See *Los Angeles Times*, November 24, 1980.

[21]"Mills' Reign Ends."

[22]"Senate's First Year Under Roberti," *San Francisco Chronicle*, January 2, 1982.

[23]See George E. Mowry, *The California Progressives* (Chicago: Quadrangle Books, 1963), p. 12.

[24]In *Baker* v. *Carr* (369 U.S. 196), the United States Supreme Court held in a 1962 decision that the distribution of seats (and district sizes) in state legislatures was subject to federal court scrutiny because of the equal protection clause in the Fourteenth Amendment. In the 1964 case of *Reynolds* v. *Sims* (377 U.S. 533), the Court decided that both state legislative houses had to reflect a representation formula where district populations were substantially equal in population.

[25]Mowry, *California Progressives*, p. 10.

[26]Oscar Lewis, "The Monopoly of the Big Four," in N. Ray Gilmore and Gladys Gilmore, eds., *Readings in California History* (New York: Crowell, 1966), pp. 249–50.

[27]*Fresno Republican*, August 23, 1911, quoted in Mowry, *California Progressives*, p. 63.

[28]L. Harmon Zeigler and Henrik van Dalen use this classification for California in "Interest Groups in State Politics," in Herbert Jacob and Kenneth N. Vines, eds., *Politics in the American States*, 3rd ed. (Boston: Little, Brown, 1976), pp. 105–06.

[29]Alvin D. Sokolow, "The First Session," *National Civic Review* 57, no. 5 (May 1968): 244.

[30]"67 Assembly Aides Doing Partisan Work for Bosses," *Los Angeles Times*, June 30, 1980.

[31]Daniel J. Blackburn, "Staff Power," *California Journal* 12, no. 5 (May 1981): 171–72.

[32]Assemblyman Sain Farr (D–Carmel), quoted in A. G. Block and Robert S. Fairbanks, "The Legislature's Staff—No. 1 Growth Industry in the Capitol," *California Journal* 14, no. 6 (June 1983): 219.

[33]"The 'Juice Committees' in Capitol," *Los Angeles Times*, December 2, 1981.

[34]"Governor Brown Weighs Touchy Bill Backed by Key Contributor," *Los Angeles Times*, September 25, 1981.

7
JUDICIAL POLITICS

The Perils of Rose Bird

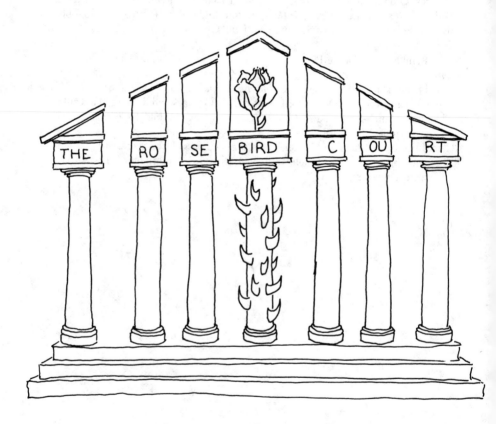

Courts are political institutions: Judges get their jobs through the political process, their decisions are choices between alternative policies, they depend on other branches of government for the implementation of their decisions, and they sometimes fall prey to the pressure of organized interests and public opinion. They play a crucial, if sometimes obscure, part in the shaping of public policy and the political process.

California's Supreme Court has long been a national trendsetter and a leader in what is called "judicial activism," but the stormy career of Rose Elizabeth Bird as chief justice of the court has heightened awareness that the courts are political and raised questions about just how political they should be. Her career provides a primer in judicial as well as California politics.

The Appointment

As Governor Ronald Reagan's second term came to an end in 1974, he hoped Donald Wright, Chief Justice of California's Supreme Court, would retire so he could choose Wright's successor. Reagan had appointed Wright to the position in the first place, although he was disappointed when Wright turned out to be more liberal than expected. He must have been even more disappointed when Wright delayed his retirement until 1977 when Jerry Brown, a liberal Democrat, was governor.

Brown chose Rose Bird, an old friend and political ally, whom he had known when she was a public defender in Santa Clara County. When Brown became governor, he appointed Bird Secretary of the Agriculture and Services Agency, an extremely sensitive position in a state where farming is a major industry. In that position Bird presided over the establishment of the controversial Agricultural Labor Relations Board, a mechanism for implementing unionization of farmworkers.

157

The choice of Bird broke several traditions in the way governors make such appointments. Governors almost always appoint members of their own parties (Bird and Brown were both Democrats) and graduates of top law schools (Bird went to the University of California's Boalt Hall). But unlike most other members of the high court, Bird had no previous judicial experience; at 40, she was 20 years younger than the average appointee; and she was the first woman ever to serve on California's Supreme Court.

The governor appoints members of the state's highest courts and also makes appointments to fill vacancies in lower courts. Jerry Brown used this power to appoint people like Rose Bird who weren't from the legal "establishment"— they were younger and more likely to have served as public defenders or public interest attorneys and they were also members of groups that had rarely been represented on the bench before, including women, blacks, Hispanics, Asians, and gays. By 1983 Brown had appointed over half of the 1400 judges in the state, including five members of the Supreme Court, among them a black, a woman, and an Hispanic (see Table 7-1). Brown was giving the aging, white, male-dominated courts new points of view and making them more representative of the state's diverse population. To do this, he had to ignore men already on the bench, denying them hoped-for promotions. One flamboyant critic accused him of using a "3-B formula: blacks, browns, and broads," at the expense of qualified white male judges, causing them to become "demoralized, frustrated."[1] Another critic alleged that sex and race were Brown's "only criterion, with little concern for experience or ability. It's clear they have appointed unqualified and barely qualified minority members over well qualified male judges."[2] Brown's defenders thought otherwise.

THE COURT SYSTEM

Whether Brown's appointments were constructive or destructive, there's little doubt that the hundreds of men and women he made judges during his two terms in office will be the most lasting impression he made on the state, especially because so many were so young. California's judges preside over justice courts in the state's few remaining rural areas, municipal courts in urban areas, superior courts in every county, district appellate courts, and the Supreme Court itself (see Table 7-2).

Most cases are tried in municipal or superior courts presided over by a single judge. Municipal courts and justice courts in rural areas try misdemeanors (minor crimes) and civil suits (contract or other noncriminal disputes) involving amounts less than $15,000. More serious crimes (felonies), divorces, and probate and civil suits involving more than $15,000 are heard in superior courts.

TABLE 7-1   Judicial Appointments by California Governors

	Male	Female	White	Black	Hispanic	Asian
Jerry	84.8%	15.2%	76%	11%	9%	4%
Brown	646	134	669	96	80	35
Ronald	97.4%	2.6%	93.1%	2.6%	3.3%	1.5%
Reagan	478	13	457	13	16	5
Edmund G.	97.7%	2.3%	93%	3%	2.5%	1.5%
Brown, Sr.	390	9	372	12	10	6

Source for appointments of Edmund G. Brown, Sr. and Ronald Reagan: San Francisco Examiner, July 8, 1979.

Decisions of justice and municipal courts may be appealed to superior courts whose decisions, in turn, may be appealed to district courts of appeal. There are district appellate courts in San Francisco, Los Angeles, Sacramento, Fresno, San Diego, and San Bernardino. Cases appealed to these courts are heard by panels of three judges. The court of last resort, to which the decisions of the district courts of appeal may be appealed, is the California Supreme Court. However, if issues pertaining to federal laws or the United States Constitution are raised, further appeal may be made to the United States Supreme Court.

THE APPOINTMENT PROCESS

The governor appoints almost all of these judges, but not entirely on his own. Potential nominees are first screened by the state bar association (a professional organization for attorneys) through its Commission on Judicial Nominees Evaluation. This review was started when Jerry Brown's father was

TABLE 7-2   California Court System

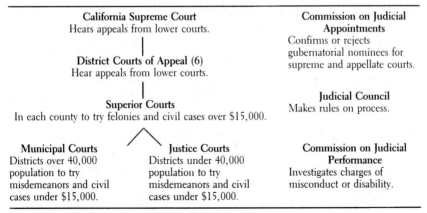

California Supreme Court
Hears appeals from lower courts.

|

District Courts of Appeal (6)
Hear appeals from lower courts.

|

Superior Courts
In each county to try felonies and civil cases over $15,000.

Municipal Courts
Districts over 40,000
population to try
misdemeanors and civil
cases under $15,000.

Justice Courts
Districts under 40,000
population to try
misdemeanors and civil
cases under $15,000.

Commission on Judicial Appointments
Confirms or rejects gubernatorial nominees for supreme and appellate courts.

Judicial Council
Makes rules on process.

Commission on Judicial Performance
Investigates charges of misconduct or disability.

governor and is carried out by a group of eighteen lawyers and seven laypersons appointed by the board of governors of the bar association. The governor submits names of those being considered for appointment. Confidential questionnaires are sent to about a hundred judges, lawyers, and others who have worked with the potential nominee. They are then evaluated on their "intellect, temperament, trial experience, willingness to work, ability to make decisions, objectivity, humor, courage," and other attributes.[3] Although the governor may nominate someone who does not win the approval of the Commission on Judicial Nominees Evaluation, neither Ronald Reagan nor Jerry Brown ever did.

Nominees for appellate and Supreme Court justices must go through another, more difficult process, however. Once screened by the bar association, their names are submitted to the Commission on Judicial Appointments, which is made up of the chief justice of the Supreme Court, the senior presiding judge of the courts of appeal, and the Attorney General, an independently elected official. The commission, which was created by an initiative amendment to the state constitution in 1934, has the power to reject a gubernatorial nominee, though it has done so only twice, in 1939 and 1982.

THE BIRD APPOINTMENT

When Rose Bird's name was submitted to the commission in 1977, its members include Matthew Tobriner, the senior member of the Supreme Court and the acting chief justice, a liberal who had been appointed by Jerry Brown's father; Parker Wood, an elderly conservative and the senior judge of the courts of appeal; and Evelle Younger, the Republican attorney general and the leading contender for the Republican nomination to run for governor against Jerry Brown.

The commission's decision on Rose Bird was more controversial than usual because opposition to Bird's appointment was more vehement and better organized than usual. Her opponents were mostly Jerry Brown's opponents: agribusiness, conservatives, and Republicans. They expressed a legitimate concern about her lack of judicial experience, which consisted entirely of clerking for a justice of Nevada's Supreme Court. They alleged that her career as a public defender would bias her decisions in favor of defendants in criminal cases. She was also expected, on the basis of her performance as secretary of agriculture, to be antibusiness. These concerns were heightened by Bird's relative youth, which meant she was likely to exercise these biases on the court for a very long time.

Bird's youth and inexperience also caused discontent within the legal profession and some resentment because she did not get to the high court in the traditional way by proving herself and maturing in the lower courts. Her selection also meant that many prominent and senior judges and attorneys had been denied promotion. But these reservations were not made public. Bird had, after all, been judged qualified by the bar association, and some of her opponents from within the legal profession probably did not want to be associated with the more outspoken, partisan opposition.

Bird's defenders pointed to approval of her qualifications by the Commission on Judicial Nominees Evaluation and the inappropriateness of rejecting an otherwise qualified nominee because of the way she might decide a case. They also argued that Bird's experience as an administrator would be useful in the heavily administrative post of chief justice.

When the hearings closed, Tobriner cast his vote in favor of Bird. Appellate Justice Wood, perhaps expressing the gut-feeling of the old guard of the legal profession, voted against her appointment. Evelle Younger was in a difficult position. As attorney general, he was the chief law enforcement officer in the state. He could hardly vote against Bird for obviously "political" reasons and she had been judged qualified. On the other hand, he hoped to run for governor against the man who was appointing Bird, and twenty-six of thirty-seven Republican members of the state legislature had signed a letter urging him to vote against Bird. In the end Younger voted for confirmation, perhaps because to have done otherwise would have appeared too overtly political or because there really were no solid grounds on which to reject Bird. Perhaps he was also concerned about losing women's votes in the coming election.

JUDICIAL ACTIVISM

Opposition to Bird's appointment was intense in part because she was young, female, and inexperienced. But there was more to it than that. At the same time Bird's appointment was going through the process, so was that of Wiley Manuel, the state's first black Supreme Court justice. Manuel's appointment by Brown was unopposed, partly because he had some experience on the bench but largely because he was seen as a moderate, while Bird was known to be a liberal.

The controversy was intense because Bird's appointment took place at a time of heightened consciousness about the political nature of the judiciary—in California and elsewhere. The courts have always been political in the sense that they exercise power and make choices between alternative courses of action, thus shaping public policy. In the past this has generally been done in a restrained and conservative way. This restraint, along with the formal, ritualistic procedures of the courts, created an image of propriety and objectivity that gave them a mythic stature above politics. Of course, nothing could have been further from the truth. The restraint merely gave the courts a safe, conservative bias. Reluctant to overturn decisions made by the electorate, the legislature, or the executive, the courts tended to uphold the status quo.

But in recent decades the courts have been faced with increasingly difficult choices, and, increasingly, they've shown a willingness to intervene, perhaps because other institutions have failed to solve the problems. The United States Supreme Court under Chief Justice Earl Warren, a former California governor, expanded civil rights, broadened the rights of defendants in criminal cases, and mandated the reapportionment of state legislatures.

The California court has been equally active, sometimes taking the lead over its federal counterpart. When voters overturned a fair housing act in 1964, the state Supreme Court ruled their decision unconstitutional and upheld the housing legislation. In 1970 Los Angeles was ordered to desegregate its schools. In 1971 the court ruled the system of financing schools unconstitutional. In 1972 they decided the death penalty violated the state constitution because it was "cruel or unusual punishment." The liberal, activist court of the 1970s expanded the rights of minorities, workers, consumers, and defendants—in most cases going beyond the United States Supreme Court by using the state constitution as grounds. Those who took offense at these decisions suddenly saw the courts as the political entities they have always been and set out to moderate their rulings by political means. In addition to being criticized for her own shortcomings and for her association with Jerry Brown, Rose Bird also became the target of increasing antagonism toward an activist court, which she had done nothing to create, but whose liberal activism it was feared she would extend.

The Chief Justice at Work

Like the six associate justices on the California Supreme Court, the chief justice casts one vote when cases are decided. What sets the chief justice apart is the administrative power of the office. The chief justice has responsibilities for his or her own staff and the staff of the court. The chief handles the Supreme Court's relations with the outside world, regulating the flow of information to the press and the public. Procedures for hearing cases, deliberating, and reaching decisions are controlled substantially by the chief justice, who also oversees the entire state court system as chair of the Judicial Council. The council is mostly composed of other judges appointed by the chief, including three appellate court justices, five superior court judges, three municipal court judges, and two justice court judges. Four additional members are attorneys, chosen by the board of governors of the state bar association, and each house of the legislature annually delegates one of its members to sit on the council.

Despite her administrative experience before appointment to the court, Rose Bird's handling of all of these powers has been controversial. One scholar of the courts says, "she has not been diffident about shaking up the Court's hoary administrative procedures and, along with them, the old-boy network that managed much of the Court's work."[4] Another said she had "destroyed staff morale . . . , alienated the trial bench . . . , lost the confidence of the press . . . , [and] forfeited whatever capacity a chief justice might have for leadership."[5] Nobody denies she's made an impression.

Either because of lack of sophistication or fear of the press, Bird's management of the Court's communications with the outside world at the beginning of her term isolated her and her associates. She rarely gave interviews, issued few press releases, refused requests for information, and gave little or no warning about the announcement of opinions. After much criticism, Bird systematized announcement of decisions and began to pay more attention to relations with the press.

Inside the court Bird isolated herself and deviated from tradition by surrounding herself with an entirely new staff unfamiliar with the operations of the court and loyal only to Bird. In the past the court staff has thought of itself as a "family," with long-standing staff members moving from justice to justice as the membership of the court changed. Justices brought in some of their own people, but most used the knowledgeable permanent staff.[6] Bird did not and though it was surely unintentional, her practice alienated and demoralized the permanent staff. It also left her without experienced advisors in her own office.

On the other hand, Bird made an effort to streamline the court's proceedings, keeping track of cases by computer, compiling a list of unwritten rules followed by the court, starting meetings earlier, reducing formality, taking care to distribute the work load of justices equally, and trying to get cases decided earlier. She also followed the lead of her governor in trying to be a model of frugality. She got rid of the chief justice's limousine and stays in motels rather than fancy hotels when traveling.

Bird used her powers as chair of the Judicial Council to tighten up the meeting schedule, halt the practice of meeting at expensive resorts, and stimulate earlier and more thorough discussion of proposals than before, when the council tended to "adopt rules first and ask questions later."[7] The composition of the council also changed under Bird. She used her appointment powers, as her mentor used his, to appoint more women and minorities to the council and its advisory committees.

As with her court staff, Bird changed the staffing of the council. Her determination to run the council herself brought about the resignation of a respected senior civil servant as head of the council's administrative staff. She replaced him with one of her own, offending the other members of the Judicial Council by failing to consult them. After this exercise in patronage Bird imposed a merit system for recruitment of council employees.

An administrative power that infringes more significantly on the actual decisions of the court is the chief justice's power to appoint temporary judges when vacancies occur because of illness, retirement, or disqualification. Especially on the Supreme Court, when the chief chooses a temporary replacement, she may be influencing the outcome of a case. Bird has made over two hundred such temporary appointments, usually choosing liberals. She appoints some favorites repeatedly.

By selection of temporary justices, the chief may "pack" the court. On close cases one vote may make the difference. The four-to-three vote upholding the controversial Democratic plan for legislative reapportionment (overturned by the voters in the 1982 election) included a temporary justice in the narrow majority. Bird's appointments have voted her way 80 percent of the time. This is not unusual, however; appointees of Donald Wright, her predecessor as chief justice, voted as he did 75 percent of the time.[8]

In addition to these appointive powers, the chief makes assignments to the appellate courts. At all levels Bird used her powers to advance women and minority judges and sometimes to punish those whom she perceived as having crossed her in the past.

The Supreme Court at Work

The real work of the chief justice and the court is making decisions on hundreds of specific cases each year. The work load is heavy, and because it is the highest court, no one else can make the decisions; there can be no delegation. Nor does the court have as much control as the other branches of government as to which issues it must decide. The court itself initiates no cases. Somebody else—an aggrieved citizen, an ambitious attorney, or a special interest—decides to raise the issue and go through the appellate process. The court can choose which cases it wishes to hear, but because it cannot initiate, it also cannot control the precise content of a case, which may or may not be the ideal set of circumstances on which to test a point of law.

Thousands of cases are appealed to the Supreme Court each year; only about two hundred can be heard and decided. The process begins with the filing of petitions for hearing. Each Wednesday morning the justices hold a conference to consider about eighty such requests. Petitioners must argue that some point of law in their case is significant enough to merit reconsideration. Research assistants of individual justices prepare summaries of the case called conference memos, which are circulated to members of the court. On the basis of these digests the justices determine which cases the court will hear.

Once a hearing is granted, cases are assigned to a justice to write a "calendar" memo providing more detail than the conference memo and usually pointing toward a decision. Usually the same justice (or more likely his or her staff) writes both the conference and calendar memos, but if the author of the conference memo opposed hearing the case, the chief justice assigns the case to a justice who voted to grant a hearing. With the calendar memo as background, oral arguments are heard. Attorneys representing the two sides in the case appear before the court, argue the case, and respond to sometimes highly pointed questions from the justices. These arguments supplement written briefs.

Following the oral argument is a "post-hearing conference." The justice who prepared the calendar memo states the case, there is discussion, and a vote is taken in order of seniority. The chief justice casts the final vote, sometimes dramatically. If the majority sides with the author of the calendar memo, he or she writes the opinion of the court. It is, however, the prerogative of the chief justice to assign the writing when voting with the majority.

A draft of the majority opinion is circulated to one justice at a time. Each justice may choose to concur with the opinion, suggest changes, or write a dissenting opinion. Other dissenters may concur with the first, ask for modifications, or write their own dissent. The process of circulating opinions takes weeks and often months as each justice deliberates and signs or writes an opinion, and then passes the whole growing pile of paper (known as the "box") back through all the other justices. As the box circulates, opinions and even votes may change. Nothing is final until every justice signs either an opinion or a dissent. Only then is the ruling filed and announced.

The whole process is slow and collegial—a group effort requiring trust and honesty. The author of the original conference and calendar memos must put the case reasonably fairly and accurately. The justices must respect one another's rights to mull over the arguments as the opinions circulate.

Collegiality—a spirit of cooperation, trust, and respect for disagreement—
was a strong tradition on the California Supreme Court, at least until the
1970s. Under the leadership of Chief Justice Phil Gibson and his successor,
Roger J. Traynor, the thoughtful, often ground-breaking decisions of the court
gave it a reputation as the finest in the country. But in the 1970s it began to
function less well. Some of Governor Reagan's appointees injected a distinctly
uncollegial ideological element into the proceedings of the court. Preble Stolz,
the leading scholar of the court, observes that "the downhill direction was
established well before Bird's appointment."[9] Her own abrasive style and
tendency to isolate herself only hastened the decline of the collegial process.

The court also became far more activist and controversial in the 1970s. Its
decisions on desegregation, school finance, civil rights, the death penalty, and
the rights of defendants, among others, brought the court more and more
attention and more and more enemies. In other words, the court was already
controversial and, according to Stolz, in decline when Bird was appointed.

The court Bird joined was already divided. Two justices—Mathew Tobriner
and Stanley Mosk—were Democrats and liberals appointed by Jerry Brown's
father. Tobriner was the senior member of the court; as acting chief justice, he
had chaired the Commission on Judicial Appointments when it confirmed
Rose Bird as chief, with his support. He would become her only ally on the
court. Mosk was next in seniority, a younger man, allegedly embittered at not
having been promoted to chief justice, and thus not favorably disposed toward
Rose Bird. Mosk supposedly murmured "Somebody's sitting in my chair" when
Bird first arrived.

There were two justices even newer than Bird. Wiley Manuel was appointed
at the same time as Bird. He was a political moderate and the first black to serve
on the court. The other appointee of Jerry Brown was Frank Newman, a
Berkeley law professor who had been one of Rose Bird's teachers. Appointed a
few months after Bird and Manuel, Newman was a liberal with no experience
on the bench. But his appointment, like Manuel's, was uncontroversial. Unlike the Chief, he was male, older, and a part of the accepted legal community
as it defined itself.

Finally, there were two justices, Frank Richardson and William Clark, who
were Republicans and conservatives appointed by Ronald Reagan. Richardson
was an old pro, seemingly content to go his own way. Clark, a combative and
ideological conservative, had been a confidant of Governor Reagan. Long a
source of conflict on the court, he would become Bird's arch-nemesis.

At the time of his appointment to the court, the state bar's Commission on
Judicial Nominees Evaluation concluded that Clark, who became an attorney

without completing law school and whose practice consisted mostly of minor contract work, had "not demonstrated that he has . . . experience and capacity to handle complicated or difficult matters with that degree of skill which should be expected of Supreme Court justices."[10] Chief Justice Donald Wright, as a member of the Commission on Judicial Appointments, voted against Clark's confirmation. After working with Clark for years, Wright said "There's nothing but a vagueness there on how he thinks."[11] In a 1983 study of the court, journalist Betty Medsgar alleged that Clark spied on the court for Reagan, let people outside the court influence and perhaps even write his opinions, leaked information to reporters, and was incompetent to discuss legal concepts.[12]

Voting patterns on the court reflected these ideological orientations: four liberals, a moderate, and two conservatives. But these ideologies had shades of meaning and by no means predicted the outcome of every case, each of which had individual merits and points of law on which judgments had to be made, irrespective of ideology.

Rose Bird has been seen as the most liberal member of the court, but one study of voting records showed that Associate Justice Newman voted "more consistently for defendants, workers, consumers and plaintiffs in negligence cases" than Bird or anyone else.[13] Tobriner's record was almost as liberal, however, and Bird came close. In the very controversial area of the rights of the accused (defendants), Bird built up a particularly strong record in their favor, meaning that she was a stickler for following the rules of evidence and interrogations as well as court procedure, and when she suspected that these rules had been violated, she ruled in favor of the defendants and against the prosecution. "The active protection of civil liberties," Bird declared, "has historically been the highest calling of those who have sat on the bench,"[14] and it is, indeed, on these issues that she has been most active.

Stanley Mosk shared this orientation, but he split with his liberal colleagues on the issue of affirmative action, writing the opinion in the Bakke case and leading the battle against so-called reverse discrimination. Wiley Manuel was also somewhat liberal on issues pertaining to the rights of the accused, but he voted the same as Bird only about half the time.[15] Clark and Richardson, the conservatives, often found themselves a losing minority on the court.

Bird, then, was not in the least outside the mainstream of legal thinking on the court. Yet she became the primary target of criticism. As chief justice, however, she did not control the outcome of decisions, nor was she a leader that any of the others would follow. Getting her off the court would not even have changed the outcome of most decisions. But the controversy that arose during her appointment hearings never subsided. There was criticism of the quality of her written opinions and some of her administrative actions, but most of the antagonism to Rose Bird was because of who she was, not what she did. As chief, she was the most visible member of the court. As a liberal and a woman, lacking in judicial experience, she was seen as vulnerable. Finally, she became a focal point because she was to face the voters in November 1978. Like a duck on a conveyor belt in a shooting gallery, she was inching toward election day.

Judicial Elections

Unlike their peers in the federal courts and some states, California's judges must face the electorate. Municipal and superior court judges serve 6 year terms. Vacancies due to death or calculated retirement usually occur between terms, and the governor appoints a replacement who faces the voters when the term expires. But opposing candidates may challenge the incumbents and sometimes succeed at attaining a judgeship without benefit of appointment. Most lower court judges, however, gain office by appointment and are easily reelected, often without challenge.

The voting for appellate and Supreme Court justices is a little different. Since 1934 they have been required to face the voters for approval or rejection without opponents on the ballot. New appointees are submitted to the voters at the next general election. If they win, they serve out the term of the justice they were appointed to replace, then run again for a standard 12 year term.

Historically, these elections have been little more than formalities. Incumbents always won with majorities of over 85 percent. But in 1966 a campaign was organized against justices who had voted to invalidate the 1964 initiative repeal of the Fair Housing Act and the "no" vote went up from its previous average of 11 percent to a record high of 25 percent.[16] As the court became more liberal and activist, the voters did not. They elected Ronald Reagan governor in 1966 and 1970, and their mistrust of government grew following the prolonged Watergate scandal. By 1974, 25 percent was the average "no" vote and more municipal and superior court judges faced challengers. By 1980, one-third of the municipal and superior court judges up for election were defeated or forced into a runoff[17] (if no candidate receives more than 50 percent in the primary, the top two contenders go to a runoff in November). Women and minority judges are more likely to face challengers and more likely to lose when they do.[18]

In November 1978 the voters were asked: "Shall Rose Elizabeth Bird be elected to the office [of chief justice] for the term prescribed by law?" Associate

Justices Frank Richardson, Frank Newman, and Wiley Manuel were also on the ballot. Racism, sexism, electoral drift to the right, concern about the liberal activism of the court and increasing dislike of Jerry Brown added up to a treacherous situation for Rose Bird to face the voters. As she somewhat bitterly pointed out, by 1978 "some of the special interests [had] perceived that in fact if you're able to pour enough money into a judicial race you may in fact be able to influence that [race]."[19]

Three such interests emerged to oppose Bird's confirmation. The Republican Party's Central Committee recommended rejection but did little campaigning. A second group, the No on Bird Committee, was formed by supporters of Assemblyman Ken Maddy, an unsuccessful candidate for the Republican gubernatorial nomination, and funded by agribusiness interests who were out to get Bird because of her record in agricultural labor relations. But the most formidable threat was posed by State Senator H. L. Richardson's Law and Order Committee, which announced that it would spend a million dollars to defeat Bird. Richardson, a conservative Republican from Southern California and no relation to Justice Richardson, is the state's master of direct-mail fund raising. In addition to the Law and Order Committee, he controls Gun Owners of California, an antigun control group. Both organizations are capable of raising hundreds of thousands of dollars in an election year through the sophisticated use of computerized mailing lists, making Richardson one of the most powerful individuals in California.

Neither these nor any other organized groups opposed the other justices on the November ballot, despite the fact that they were Brown appointees with liberal voting records. Not surprisingly, a leader of the National Women's Political Caucus said, "We find it very difficult to believe that this attack would have been levied if a man had been appointed with the exact same qualifications, the exact same integrity, honesty and temperament."[20]

Despite the announced opposition, not much happened until *New West* magazine published an article condemning Bird for a seemingly antifeminist vote in the brutal Caudillo rape case.[21] A four-vote majority of the court, including Bird and an ad hoc justice she had appointed, ruled that rape did not constitute "great bodily injury." There was never any question that the defendant, Caudillo, was guilty of rape. But under recent legislation, if rape constituted "great bodily injury," he could have been given a much heavier sentence. The majority ruled that rape, though a serious crime deserving heavy punishment, was not in itself great bodily injury and that this term had been intended to apply to something that went beyond a specific crime like rape. The issue was legislative intent—what the lawmakers meant by their law—

and the court majority ruled that they did not intend this application. Without dealing with the complex legal arguments in the case, the author of the *New West* article sensationalized Bird's opinion, playing to those who already thought she was soft on crime. Bird's opponents readily accepted the issue that had been handed them, but feminist groups, which could have been outraged, stayed loyal to Bird.

In September two more actions by the court gave further impetus to the campaign. First, they refused to sanction a delay in the desegregation of the Los Angeles schools. Although this was a minor decision on a case that had been decided years before Bird was on the court, she was unfairly blamed by her opponents. Later the same month the court upheld the constitutionality of Proposition 13, the overwhelmingly popular June initiative that drastically reduced property taxes. But Bird dissented, arguing that the part of the proposition that resulted in neighbors paying widely different taxes based on when they bought their homes violated the equal protection clause of the United States Constitution.

Bird's opponents played on these hot issues throughout the campaign, saying she was soft on crime, in favor of busing, and willing to overturn the voters' wishes on Proposition 13. H. L. Richardson's group planned a heavy television campaign using these issues, but the spots they prepared were so lurid that only a couple of television stations in the state would run them. They had to rely on a mail campaign instead. In the end they spent far less than the million dollars Richardson had boasted he would raise, but they did spend an unprecedented total of $301,452, mostly for mailing.[22]

The campaign in favor of the confirmation actually did better, raising $341,452,[23] mostly from the legal profession, but also from organized labor, women's groups, and other supporters of Jerry Brown. Bird herself kept a low profile in the campaign, giving only a few speeches and interviews (which were nevertheless big news when she gave them). Just how to campaign is a problem for judicial candidates, because they normally attempt to hold themselves above politics and have little experience as campaigners. But women's groups worked hard to keep the state's highest female officeholder in power, and the opposition of Senator Richardson rallied the legal and Democratic establishments to Bird. All the leading newspapers in the state also endorsed Bird. Her defense became a defense of the courts.

Then the *Los Angeles Times*, in a front page election day story that also made the front page of every other major newspaper in the state, reported that the Supreme Court was withholding a controversial decision (*People* v. *Tanner*) overturning the "use-a-gun–go-to-prison" law until after the election.[24] The use-a-gun–go-to-prison law was a popular anticrime measure mandating imprisonment for anyone using a gun when committing a crime. Overturning such a law would be politically dangerous. Suppressing such a controversial decision until after the election, however, would have been unethical, if not illegal. Associate Justice William Clark, an antagonist of Bird's, had spoken with reporters. So had Justices Mosk and Tobriner. All later denied talking about the specific case in question, which would have been highly inappropriate. In these conversations the justices did not deny that the case had been decided. Through extremely ambiguous questioning, the reporters believed that they had confirmed that a decision had been made and was being withheld, so they ran their story.

Despite the news story, Rose Bird won confirmation on that election day. Her 51.7 percent margin of victory was, however, the narrowest in the history of California's judicial confirmation elections. Other justices on the ballot did better: Frank Richardson won 72.5 percent approval, Frank Newman got 65.3 percent, and Wiley Manuel won 61.5 percent. Most of the "no" vote on all three judges must be accounted for by the general antagonism to the courts and their perceived liberal activism. That Bird did worse than her colleagues suggests that other factors were at work in her case, however. Preble Stolz blames "partisanship" and "hostility to Governor Brown," but discounts the possibility that being a woman hurt—in fact, he thinks it "may have helped."[25] Others disagreed, but gender was only one of Bird's problems. Her association with Jerry Brown, her inexperience, her liberal record, and her sometimes abrasive personality also hurt. With all these negatives, of which none of the other justices on the ballot had more than one, Bird faced the voters as their confidence in government was at its nadir.

Judges on Trial

The election was over, but the trials and tribulations of Rose Bird and the Supreme Court were not. News stories on the alleged suppression of controversial decisions continued. The board of governors of the state bar association, the State Senate, and the Judicial Council demanded an investigation. Rose Bird, without consulting her colleagues on the court (which surely displeased them), called for an investigation by the Commission on Judicial Performance. On December 1, 1978 the Commission announced that it would hold hearings on alleged improprieties by the Supreme Court.

The Commission on Judicial Performance was created by constitutional amendment in 1960 and consists of five judges appointed by the Supreme

Court, two lawyers chosen by the state bar association, and two citizens nominated by the governor and approved by the State Senate. Its job is to look into allegations of misconduct and mental or physical disability. If charges are confirmed, the commission may recommend censure, removal from office, or mandatory retirement; the Supreme Court makes the final decision. When charges are brought against a member of the Supreme Court itself, a special tribunal of seven members of the appellate bench drawn by a lot decides.

Although over 300 complaints are filed with the commission each year, only about 25 percent are found worthy of investigation and action is taken on less than 10 percent, with only two or three actually requiring action by the Supreme Court. Since it was established, the commission has helped remove six judges and censured ten others. A municipal court judge who chased an attorney around his chambers with a battery-powered dildo was the first to be recommended for removal from office. In 1977, 82-year old Associate Justice Marshall McComb was removed for senility. More often, investigation of misconduct results in semi-voluntary retirement—73 judges have resigned or retired in such circumstances.

The commission's unprecedented investigation of the conduct of the California Supreme Court began in June 1979 in a law school auditorium in San Francisco. Unlike previous investigations, this one was public. Television cameras and reporters were there to bring to the public its first and most extensive look into the inner workings of one of its most powerful institutions. One by one, members of the court staff and justices themselves gave testimony, revealing much about themselves and their working relationships.

The basic task of the commission was to determine whether announcement of the *Tanner* decision had been put off until after the election and whether anyone associated with the court had violated confidence in speaking to the press. In *Tanner*, a trial court judge had ruled that the use-a-gun–go-to-prison law was unconstitutional because it limited judicial discretion in sentencing. Tanner's crime was a rather mild-mannered robbery—he stole $40, using an unloaded gun and telling his victim how to set off the alarm and call the police. In light of these facts, the judge wanted to put him on probation rather than imposing the mandatory sentence. The Supreme Court upheld his ruling, but on slightly different grounds—they didn't rule the use-a-gun–go-to-prison law unconstitutional, but they said it conflicted with another statute giving judges discretion in special circumstances and that one or the other of the statutes would have to be repealed.

Justice Tobriner drafted the majority opinion and it slowly circulated among the other justices. Clark added a dissent. Bird wrote a separate opinion concur-

ring with the majority but on slightly different grounds. The arguments continued to circulate. The votes were clear in July, but the decision was not
announced until December—a month after the election, a year after the case
was first heard, and well beyond the court's 200 day average for deciding cases.
The issue before the commission was whether the delay was caused by legitimate legal disagreements or political considerations.

The justices and their assistants tried to explain why the process took so long,
but they failed to gain much sympathy. Their testimony revealed not only
procedural delay, but deep and bitter personal antagonisms that also slowed
things down. The principal rivals were Bird and Clark. Among many things
that may have delayed the announcement of the *Tanner* decision was their fight
over a footnote Clark had inserted. Bird interpreted it as an unwarranted attack
on her and she may have been correct. A staunch ideological conservative,
Clark seemed willing to use his position to embarrass his liberal chief. Their
personal relationship paralleled their ideological disagreements. Bird said it was
"cool but correct" and Clark called it "unfortunate."[26] He claimed she even
snubbed his staff on elevators and denied them her old carpets when she
remodeled her office. Bird's testimony in her own defense revealed her resentment of Clark as well as her rigidity and suspiciousness. Preble Stolz harshly
concluded that "Bird showed herself to be temperamentally ill-suited to be
Chief Justice."[27]

Then in July, before testimony from all the justices had been heard, the
public hearings of the Commission on Judicial Performance came to an abrupt
end. Justice Mosk refused to testify in public. Hearings concluded behind
closed doors and on November 5, 1979 the commission reported the results of
its investigation: no charges of wrongdoing would be filed. But did that mean
"not guilty" or "insufficient evidence"? The commission didn't say, but the
implication was that the announcement of the *Tanner* decision had not been
intentionally delayed.

The critics and public opinion were less generous in their judgments. The
justices were condemned as "peevish adolescents indulging in snits, refusing to
speak to each other for weeks, sending aides back and forth with spite messages," and desperately trying not "to let Dorothy see who is pumping the
Wizard of Oz machine behind the screen."[28] Bird, Clark, Tobriner, and Mosk
came off especially badly. Manuel, Newman, and Richardson fared better, but
only because they seemed not to be part of the problem, not because they
contributed to a solution.

Betty Medsgar, who interviewed members of the Commission on Judicial
Performance and somehow got access to testimony that has never been made

public, condemned the commission for its terse report, claiming that they had
allowed Bird and Tobriner to be "framed." Medsgar asserts that secret testimony clearly shows Justice William Clark to be the culprit in the case. It was
Clark himself, Medsgar alleges, who delayed the announcement of *Tanner* in
order to accuse Bird and her allies of that very impropriety. Clark was also the
one who stirred up rumors about delay among politicians and the press.[29]

Continuing Controversy

The trials and tribulations of Rose Bird and the California Supreme Court
continued. They constantly faced controversial issues and their decisions, simi-
larly, remained controversial. In 1979 the court upheld a 1977 initiative that
reestablished the death penalty. Liberals Newman and Mosk voted with the
majority, but Bird and Tobriner dissented. Bird declared that the penalty was
"arbitrarily and discriminatorily inflicted upon the poor, who are unable to
retain competent counsel"[30]—a statement that affirmed her opponents' views
about her sympathy for defendants. In 1981 the court made a controversial
decision in favor of state funding of abortions for those qualifying for state
medical assistance. The following year Bird, Mosk, and Newman voted against
putting Proposition 9, a sweeping law-and-order initiative, on the June ballot
because it lacked the required number of signatures and perhaps because the
twelve-point initiative dealt with more than one issue, in violation of a constitutional requirement that initiatives be limited to one subject. Proposition 9,
which overturned several previous court rulings such as those limiting the use
of improperly obtained evidence, nevertheless was allowed on the ballot by the
court majority and won overwhelming approval by the voters.

Also in 1982, the court voted four to three to approve the Democratic
apportionment plan for the state legislature and congressional delegation. The
Republican party, however, put the plan to the voters through the initiative
process and it was rejected in the June election. In December, the legislature,
still dominated by Democrats, approved another pro-Democratic scheme. Republicans countered by a 1983 initiative that would have put their own pro-
Republican plan into effect, but the court refused to allow it to go before the
voters on the grounds that the state constitution prohibited reapportionment
more than once every ten years. Justice Frank Richardson, the only Republican
on the court, cast the sole dissenting vote.

In these cases and others Chief Justice Bird stuck to her liberal, activist
orientation. She was equally unwavering in her administrative practices, continuing to appoint ad hoc justices who agreed with her and to advance women
and minorities. She defended her earlier abrupt actions by citing a bout with

cancer early in her term: "Because I didn't know how much time I had, I moved quickly."[31] But good health didn't seem to change her behavior. She shocked Santa Clara County by blocking the appointment of a respected local appellate judge—and an old friend of Jerry Brown's—to preside over a new district appellate court for reasons that seemed purely and personally vindictive. Bird and her staff gave offense when they failed to attend the retirement dinner of a respected member of the Supreme Court rescarch staff. And she ramrodded her choice for clerk of the court through on a narrow four-to-three vote, when such choices are traditionally unanimous.

Bird was not the only controversial member of the high court. Associate Justice Stanley Mosk seemed to be moving away from his past liberalism, voting in favor of the death penalty and switching his vote on the *Tanner* case, thus reversing the court's earlier position and upholding the use-a-gun–go-to-prison law. He continued to speak out against affirmative action, proposing a constitutional amendment limiting preferential treatment for minorities. Civil rights organizations were so infuriated by this that they called for an investigation by the Commission on Judicial Performance. The commission, however, ruled Mosk's activities acceptable.

In 1981 Justices Tobriner and Manuel retired, and William Clark resigned to join the Reagan administration. Governor Brown chose Otto Kaus and Allen Broussard, both moderates with judicial experience, to replace Manuel and Clark. Broussard is black and more liberal than Kaus, but both were confirmed without a hitch. Brown's choice of Cruz Reynoso as a replacement for Tobriner was more controversial. He had experience as an appellate justice, but he is Hispanic and a liberal. One of his colleagues on the appellate bench had, in fact, labelled him "a professional Mexican rather than a lawyer."[32] A favorite ad hoc appointee of Rose Bird's, he usually voted as she did. During the hearings of the Commission on Judicial Appointments, Attorney General George Deukmejian, a leading contender for the Republican nomination for governor at the time, grilled Reynoso on his positions on various issues, declared that Reynoso too frequently sided with defendants in criminal cases, and voted against confirmation. But Reynoso won the votes of Rose Bird and the other member of the Commission and was confirmed.

Kaus, Broussard, and Reynoso all faced the electorate for confirmation in November 1982, along with conservative Justice Frank Richardson, who was up for his first full 12 year term. Interestingly, all four voted to put a controversial law-and-order initiative on the June ballot—only the justices not up for a vote that year voted against doing so. After the electorate approved Proposition 8, Richardson, Kaus, and Reynoso voted with the court majority in ruling it constitutional.

Two days after Reynoso's appointment, H. L. Richardson's Law and Order Committee announced a campaign to defeat him. John Feliz, the committee's spokesman, denied that race was an issue (they had also denied that gender had been an issue in Rose Bird's case) and insisted that their concern was with Reynoso's qualifications. Feliz admitted wider political implications, however: "The campaign that will have to be waged on [Reynoso's] behalf will drag down Jerry Brown, Tom Bradley, John van de Kamp and every other liberal candidate who tries to protect him."[33] A month later, pleased by the court's ruling keeping the Gann initiative on the ballot, Feliz exclaimed "The Supreme Court has yielded to the will of the people. They should."[34] In addition to Senator Richardson's group, a new, more establishment-oriented Republican group opposed Brown's three new appointees; their slogan was "vote no on Jerry's judges." Governor Brown was more of an issue in 1982 than he had been in 1978. In fact, when voters were told which judges he had appointed, a public opinion poll showed the vote against them increasing considerably.

Nevertheless, all four justices survived the election. Frank Richardson, the lone Reagan appointee, won 75 percent approval. The Brown appointees did less well. Broussard got 56 percent, Kaus got 55 percent, and Reynoso won only 52 percent. In fact, all 36 appellate judges on the ballot won voter approval and no superior or municipal court judges suffered defeat in the November 1982 election, which may suggest that public antagonism toward the courts was tapering off.

All this did little to divert pressure from Rose Bird, who has been under almost constant threat of recall since 1978. A Progressive reform intended as a way to get rid of corrupt officeholders, recall allows voters to kick out an elected official by first petitioning for a recall election and then voting for removal from office. To recall a statewide official, like the chief justice, petitioners need the signatures of a number equivalent to 12 percent of those who voted in the preceding general election. Based on the 1980 voter turnout, it would take 731,244 signatures to get a recall of Rose Bird on the ballot—a formidable task, but one that could be accomplished with sufficient resources and commitment.

Four attempts to recall Chief Justice Bird were launched in the four years following her confirmation election. In 1982 Bird prepared to defend herself by organizing the Committee to Conserve the Courts, which raised $68,000 in contributions from lawyers, but all four recall efforts failed for insufficient signatures and lack of energy. After Bird sided with a majority of the court to stop a vote on the Republicans' 1983 reapportionment initiative, there was talk of launching yet another recall. If that's not enough, the chief justice must face the voters again in 1986 to attempt to win a full 12 year term—the

1978 election was for the remainder of her predecessor's term. With Cruz Reynoso attempting to win a full term on the same ballot, the 1986 election seems likely to be hard fought.

But elections and recall weren't the only political pressures on the court. The controversy produced a plethora—possibly a Pandora's Box—of proposals to reform the organization of the courts. The Republican party and the Law and Order Committee demanded 8 year terms instead of 12 year terms for appellate and Supreme Court justices, as well as contested elections. The State Senate has approved a proposed constitutional amendment requiring Senate confirmation of judicial appointments. The Commission on Judicial Performance put forth reforms to make itself more independent. Senator Ken Maddy, a Republican associated with the 1978 No on Bird Committee, proposed taking away the power of the chief justice to appoint members of the Judicial Council, allowing judges to appoint their own representatives. Maddy admitted "We're not really talking about the need for a change. We're talking about . . . a slap in the face to Rose Bird."[35]

The only positive note was the changed composition of the court itself. Clark, Bird's greatest antagonist, was gone. Betty Medsgar reports that tensions on the court "dissolved" when Clark left for Washington.[36] In addition to Kaus, Broussard, and Reynoso, Governor Brown appointed Joseph Grodin to the court when Frank Newman resigned in December of 1982. Grodin, a former labor lawyer and appellate justice, was pushed by Bird and is a friend of Kaus. The accommodating, professional style of both Grodin and Kaus is expected to ease relations on the high court, now dominated by five Brown appointees. Republican Governor George Deukmejian will alter that if he gets a chance, but it's unlikely because most of the Brown appointees are young enough to serve beyond Deukmejian's term in office.

Politics and the Courts

The precipitous decline in the prestige of the California Supreme Court and the saga of Rose Bird have at least been instructive. We've learned how little we knew about the courts and how poorly we understand them; we've learned that their role in our political system may be changing; and, as a consequence, the debate about what their role should be has intensified.

Until all this happened the press and the public paid little attention to the courts, so much of what seemed to be revelations shouldn't have been. But the media devote scant resources to covering the courts. At the time of the Bird controversy, only one major newspaper in the state had a reporter working full time on the Supreme Court. Newspapers usually just report decisions without explaining how they were reached or putting them in political context. The original stories about the *Tanner* case were extremely unsophisticated about the case and the process. Anthony Lewis blames them for the mess that followed the 1978 election, saying the stories showed "how much damage a newspaper can do to a fragile institution when it writes without understanding or sensitivity in especially sensitive circumstances."[36] That meant that the recent controversies could not be seen in their historical context, particularly with regard to the traditional activism of the California Supreme Court.

But some responsible observers feel the Bird court went too far. "Nothing is sacred anymore," a judge declared. "The Court doesn't pay attention to precedents. It's difficult for trial judges to know what the law is. They change it every ten minutes." The Bird court represents "the highest point of judicial activism we've ever reached," a law professor observed.[37]

Chief Justice Bird condemns her opponents for "attempting to impose a new rule of law on the judiciary—the rule of extortion and the law of the jungle." The pressures, she thinks, are an effort to destroy "judicial independence."[38] She attributes the apparent increased activism of the court to the fact that it is dealing with issues that other branches of government have failed to solve. And with more lawyers than any other state (72,000), Californians seem especially prone to make use of the courts. But a legislator responds, "we may be chided by the courts for not acting, but it's not their position to act for us, which is what they've done."[39] If the other branches have failed to act—on issues like segregation, civil rights, abortion, tax law, and housing discrimination—the courts might have avoided controversy and left them to act by the exercise of judicial restraint. The California Supreme Court chose activism instead. Their activism drew opposition and press coverage and, increasingly, the justices came to be seen as the politicians they were.

This change has been called the "politicization of the courts," but they've always been political. We're just more aware of it now because there's been more conflict within the courts than in the past and much of it has been made public. That's in large part due to the fact that the courts are more representative of the society than they once were. Judges are no longer all white males with similar educational and life experiences and moderate politics. Different perspectives and life experiences can engender mistrust and conflict. Differing political viewpoints can have the same effect.

There's nothing wrong with conflict when it represents legitimate differences in a society, but when conflict is mishandled, it can be bad for institutions like the courts. The judiciary needs to be trusted in order for its decisions to be obeyed. It needs to be seen as fair and above the pettier aspects of politics. But when the judiciary is inconsistent, deeply divided, or even scratching at one another's eyes, it loses credibility and thus power. This problem will be resolved, however, if the new majority on the court works well together.

A larger question is the role of courts in a democracy. Should judges make decisions based on their own consciences and points of law, or should the courts follow public opinion? Chief Justice Bird has repeatedly asserted the need to make decisions based on what she believes to be the true meaning of the law, even when these decisions are unpopular. Senator Richardson believes she should follow public opinion. In a way both are correct. The framers of our judicial system intended the courts to be somewhat independent of politics so that they could make decisions under less pressure and, when necessary, constrain public opinion. In this sense Rose Bird is right. On the other hand, the California Constitution sought to avoid a completely independent judiciary by making these offices appointive and providing for votes of confidence. In this sense Senator Richardson's concern for public opinion was taken into account. Rose Bird is right to make decisions she believes in; Senator Richardson is right to challenge her. That's judicial politics.

Notes

[1]Gale Cook, "Judging the Bench Brown Built," *San Francisco Examiner*, July 8, 1979.
[2]*Los Angeles Times*, May 1, 1978.
[3]Garvin F. Shellenberger, "Evaluating Candidates for the California Bench," *California State Bar Journal*, October 1980, p. 432.
[4]Peter Schrag, "California's Highest Court on Trial," *The Nation*, December 8, 1979, p. 582.
[5]Preble Stolz, *Judging Judges* (New York: Free Press, 1981), p. 115.
[6]Ibid., pp. 109–110; see Stolz for a general discussion about the court as "family."
[7]Ralph J. Gampell, "A Defense of Chief Justice Rose Bird," *California Journal* 11, no. 8 (August 1980): 324.
[8]*San Jose Mercury*, February 14, 1982.
[9]Stolz, *Judging Judges*, p. 75.
[10]Betty Medsgar, *Framed* (New York: Pilgrim), p. 24.
[11]Ibid., p. 50.
[12]Ibid., pp. 44–51.
[13]Kenneth Kahn, "The Bird Court: How Liberal Is It?" *California Journal* 12, no. 2 (February 1981): 69–70.
[14]Ibid., p. 70.

[15]Ed Salzman, "Reviewing the Record of a Beleaguered Chief Justice," *California Journal* 9, no. 8 (August 1978): 253.

[16]Preble Stolz, "Voting for Justice: Electing Judges in California," *California Data Brief* 2, no. 4 (1978): 2; and Kit and Preble Stolz, "Are the Voters Forcing Judges to Act Like Politicians?" *California Journal* 9, no. 9 (September 1978): 296.

[17]Dena Cochran, "Why So Many Judges Are Going Down to Defeat," *California Journal* 11, no. 9 (September 1980): 359.

[18]*Los Angeles Times*, April 16, 1978; and Cochran, "Why So Many Judges," p. 359.

[19]Steven Pressman, "State of the California Judiciary: Damaged but Still Leading the League," *California Journal* 11, no. 7 (July 1980): 359.

[20]*Los Angeles Times*, October 20, 1978.

[21]Jonathan Kirsch, "Rose Bird and the Politics of Rape," *New West*, July 31, 1978, pp. 28–31.

[22]Stolz, *Judging Judges*, p. 47.

[23]Ibid.

[24]*Los Angeles Times*, November 7, 1978.

[25]Stolz, *Judging Judges*, p. 119.

[26]Jonathan Kirsch, "Courting Disaster," *New West*, July 30, 1979, p. 90.

[27]Stolz, *Judging Judges*, p. 292.

[28]Guy Wright and Edward Lascher, quoted in Stolz, *Judging Judges*, pp. 398–99.

[29]Medsgar, *Framed*, pp. 154–55, 204.

[30]*San Jose Mercury*, April 28, 1982.

[31]Medsgar, *Framed*, p. 64.

[32]*San Jose Mercury*, January 23, 1982.

[33]Ibid.

[34]*San Jose Mercury*, March 12, 1982.

[35]*San Jose Mercury*, April 28, 1982.

[36]Anthony Lewis's preface to Stolz's *Judging Judges*, p. xvii.

[37]Kang, "Brown's Court Legacy," *California Journal* 13, no. 9 (September 1982): 311.

[38]Ibid.

[39]Pressman, "State of the California Judiciary: Damaged, but Still Leading the League," p. 56.

8
THE LOCAL CONNECTION

Grassroots Challenges to Elite Control of City Government

The 1960s and 1970s were decades of struggle in cities throughout California. In San Francisco, San Diego, Oakland, Los Angeles, Sacramento, Santa Cruz, Chico, Stockton, Santa Monica, San Jose, and elsewhere, community groups organized to battle old-guard elites. Some fought for minority rights; others demanded better neighborhood services, environmental protections, or rent control. In many of these cities the conflict centered on the system of representation, as the out-groups demanded a stronger voice. All of these issues were fought in the context of state politics because in California, as in other states, local government is created, given its powers, and strictly regulated by state government.

San Jose was one of the state's urban battlegrounds. Although it is a Northern California city just 50 miles south of San Francisco, San Jose looks more like San Diego or Los Angeles. Single-family housing, shopping centers, and low-rise electronics factories sprawl California's fourth largest city (population 630,000) over 160 square miles of Silicon Valley. The affluence hides the fact that over one third of the city's population is black or brown and poverty persists. In other words, San Jose is typically Californian.

The grassroots challenges mounted in San Jose and other California cities changed policies, governmental institutions, and informal power structures in these communities, but it remains to be seen whether the changes are temporary or long term.

Minority Discontents: Death and Life in San Jose

It was 4:30 A.M. when John Henry Smith, a black, 37 year old IBM research chemist made a U-turn against a traffic signal. Police officer Rocklin Wooley, young and white, was watching and pulled Smith over. Later Wooley testified that Smith jumped angrily out of his car, grabbed a tire iron, and tried to attack him. Two off-duty police officers came to Wooley's assistance.

What happened after that was never quite clear. The policemen sprayed mace on Smith and set their dog on him. He ran across the street screaming, but the dog was set on him again. He was subdued and brought back to the patrol car. By then, Smith must have been frightened out of his mind. He panicked and ran away again. Officer Wooley pulled out his gun and fired, killing Smith.

The 1971 slaying added another episode to the history of conflict between San Jose's mostly white police force and its substantial black and Hispanic population. Similar incidents had set off days of rioting in the Watts district of Los Angeles in 1965 and in the Hunter's Point section of San Francisco in 1966. Repeated confrontations between minority citizens and police built up to a grim tension in which minor incidents escalated to violence, with each side blaming the other.

Two days after the shooting the city's police chief declared, "It's regrettable [Officer Wooley] had to take the man's life, but Smith was "under the influence of something." The chief's allegation couldn't be verified at the time and was subsequently disproven by an autopsy. "If John Henry Smith were a white man," a black leader lamented, "he would be living today."[1]

An outraged minority community organized to vent their anger in protest. Two meetings of over 150 people produced a committee that demanded the prosecution of Rocklin Wooley and the firing of the police chief for "prejudicial remarks" made prior to any investigation.[2] The committee then turned its attention to the city council.

Cities are responsible for police protection, except in unincorporated areas, and city councils are the legislative bodies responsible for city government. The angry citizens thought they were going to the right place: San Jose's city hall. Reflecting the bland new city it governs, the city hall with its turquoise panelling and smokey-mirrored windows, looks more like a recycled Holiday Inn than what most people would imagine as a seat of government. An angry crowd of 300 marched past the marble statue of Christopher Columbus and up the sweeping spiral staircase to the city council chambers. There they packed into the theater-style seating, rumbling angrily and waving a few signs.

On a long, raised dais facing the crowd were the city council and administrators, all in a row. In 1971 there were six men and a woman on the council. One of the men, the mayor, was Japanese; another was Chicano. Both had been appointed to vacancies on the city council by a white power structure that hoped the appointments would assuage minority concerns. The council members slumped in their big leather chairs and listened dejectedly as the angry crowd demanded action. "The community will not wait," a leader proclaimed, but expected immediate action against "systematic genocide against blacks, Chicanos and poor whites."[3]

Although some members of the city council made statements of sympathy, they did nothing. Nor did they act the following week when 600 angry citizens jammed the council chambers. No council member would even make a motion to meet the crowd's demands to suspend the policemen, fire the police chief, and create a citizen committee to investigate. Instead the mayor and the council said they did not have the power to meet the community's demands. The power to fire was the city manager's, not theirs. The power to investigate and prosecute was the district attorney's, not theirs. The skeptical audience was advised to trust the system and to be patient. For weeks this scenario was repeated. Eventually, the protest lost energy and the issue seemed to die.

But over the years the repercussions of the Smith case continued to be felt. His family sued the city and was conceded a settlement. Patrolman Wooley was fired, and tried and acquitted of manslaughter. A blue ribbon committee set up by the city council to review police practices made recommendations for improving training and community relations, some of which were adopted. Some years later the police chief was pushed to resign. And over the years relations between the police and the minority community did slowly improve.

The Duties and Structure of Local Government

Discouraged by the city council's unresponsiveness, the leaders of the protest decided that the problem was one of representation. Until the minority neighborhoods had council members directly accountable to them, nothing, they thought, would change. Thus, as a result of the shooting of John Henry Smith, the movement to change the method of electing San Jose's city council began. That meant changing the city charter—the local equivalent of the state or federal constitution.

CHARTERS

All local governments—cities, counties, school districts, and other special districts—are created by the state and given their powers and structures of government by charter or by general law. Cities and counties differ a bit, however, in how they come to exist, what they do, and how they do it.

The state of California is divided into fifty-eight counties, which function in large part as administrative units of the state. They operate the jails, courts, and the rest of the criminal justice system through which state laws are enforced. They conduct elections. They are the agents of the state welfare system and parts of the taxing system. They also provide minimal police and fire protection in unincorporated, usually rural, areas.

Counties are created by the state, and all are given the same "general law" charter, which provides for an elected five-member board of supervisors as the central governing body. The board may hire a chief administrator, usually called the county executive, but counties also have elected sheriffs, tax assessors, district attorneys, and other administrators. California's eleven most urbanized counties are "home rule" rather than general law counties. This distinction simply means that the state gives them more options for organizing their governmental institutions. They could, for example, have eleven-member boards of supervisors, or they could choose to elect the county executive or choose not to elect the tax assessor.

Cities come into being in a different way and have somewhat different responsibilities. As an area develops, the population may come to need and want more local government services. Septic tanks need to be replaced by a more efficient sewage system. The minimal police and fire services provided to rural areas by counties need to be supplemented. Parks, swimming pools, and libraries are needed as vacant lots are paved over, old swimming holes filled in, and small book collections overextended. In order to provide these services, the community must "incorporate," gaining recognition from the state. California's oldest cities, like San Jose, San Francisco, and Los Angeles, were granted their charters when California became a state in 1850. Newer cities got their charters when residents signed petitions, won county approval, held an election, and voted to incorporate. In 1964 the state created special agencies called Local Agency Formation Commissions (LAFCOs) in each county to oversee this process and try to make sure an area is viable and sensible as a city.

When the process is completed, the city gets its charter, which defines its form of government. Cities with fewer than 3,500 people operate under "general law," which is technically not a charter, but provides each with the same form and powers of government. General law cities are virtually all ruled by a five-member city council, which, in turn, hires an administrator called a city manager to actually run the city. The city manager hires and fires other city administrators, like the police chief. The manager also makes up the budget and proposes other policies like land-use plans for the city council's approval.

Cities with populations over 3,500 may opt to become "charter" or "home rule" cities, gaining greater flexibility in defining their own structures of government. Usually this opportunity is used to expand the number of council members from the general law standard of five to as many as fifteen, as in Los Angeles. It may also provide for an elected executive, a mayor, and give that official all or some of the powers of the city manager. California's general law system is so flexible, however, that only 80 of the state's 433 municipalities have opted to become "charter cities." These tend to be the state's largest cities.

When an area becomes a city by going through the process of incorporation and gaining a charter, it assumes responsibility for police and fire protection, sewage and garbage disposal, parks and recreation, streets and traffic management, libraries, and land-use planning. The county still provides the area with its criminal justice system (other than police), elections, tax collection, welfare, public health, and sometimes transit systems.

STRUCTURES OF GOVERNMENT

Most of the institutional arrangements of local governments in California were created at the turn of this century by the Progressive reformers. They amended the state constitution to make all local elections nonpartisan, forcing voters to choose candidates without benefit of party labels. They also switched the dates of local elections in most cities so that they would be separate from state and national elections on the theory that this would weaken the power of the machines in this area. Both nonpartisan and isolated elections were justified on the theory that "there is no Democratic or Republican way to pave a street," so any influence of partisan politics should be purged from the business of local government. These reforms also had the effect of significantly lowering voter turnout, because fewer people hear about and are interested in local elections. Those who voted tended to be more affluent and better educated. They were also more likely to vote conservatively, and local government became more conservative under this system.

The Progressives also changed the way city council members were chosen. The old way was by wards or districts, with each member representing a specific area of the city. The reformers thought the wards were the building blocks of machines and also argued that district representation was too narrow and failed to take into account the needs of the city as a whole. They introduced at-large elections through which the whole city elected all members of the council.

In addition to nonpartisan, isolated, at-large elections, the Progressives took executive power away from boss-dominated mayors and gave it to city managers who were supposed to be businesslike, professional administrators appointed by the city council. Under this system, which became very popular, mayors served only to preside over meetings and cut ribbons—or they were eliminated entirely.

A NEW REFORM MOVEMENT IN SAN JOSE

San Jose adopted all these reforms in a major electoral confrontation between the reformers and old machine in 1916, but over the years some changes
have been made. Following the reform, members of the city council took turns
performing the ceremonial duties as mayor, but in 1967 the city began directly
electing the mayor. Though that official still lacked power to veto, hire, or fire,
direct elections made the mayor a more influential political leader. A few years
later, in 1974, the city shifted its elections to concur with state and national
elections, cutting costs and nearly quadrupling voter turnout.

This modified council-manager form of government was judged inadequate
by the coalition protesting John Henry Smith's death in 1971. They felt that
unresponsiveness was built into the system. Council members elected at-large
didn't have to pay attention to any one part of town as long as they could keep
the majority happy. In San Jose that majority was white and middle class, not
poor and black or brown. Between 1950 and 1975, 74 percent of the city
council members had lived in just two neighborhoods.[4] Most had been
businessmen or attorneys. Only two were minority persons and both got on the
council initially not by being elected but by being appointed to fill a temporary
vacancy. No minority person had been directly elected to the city council since
at-large elections were instituted in 1916; the white vote simply swamped the
minority vote.

The city council added to the frustration of the protestors by seeming to pass
the buck to the city manager. But in San Jose's form of government the
manager, not the city council, had direct power over the city workers, including the police department. The manager did not act, and because he was
appointed by the council, not elected by the people, the crowd had no direct
influence over him.

Reform structures of government, like those of San Jose, made it hard for
political machines, but they also made it hard for frustrated minorities to be
heard. The system was designed to respond to a consensual majority; other
points of view had no outlet and posed no political threat to politicians who
could keep the majority happy. Federal courts have ruled at-large election
systems unconstitutional in some southern cities because they intentionally and
systematically denied blacks representation.

To the mostly Hispanic protesters in San Jose, at-large elections had the
same effect—denying them the representation their numbers deserved. They
fixed on the idea of changing from at-large to district elections as an essential
first step in attaining the changes they wanted. Although minorities made up
almost a third of San Jose's 1970 population of 450,000, they had little electoral

influence because of low turnout and at-large elections. Shifting to district elections would ensure them of at least one and perhaps two or three representatives who would be directly accountable to them. It would also be easier for other grassroots candidates to be elected in smaller districts—San Jose had grown so large that candidates without a lot of campaign money and the support of the staunchly conservative and pro-growth *San Jose Mercury* and *News* stood little chance of winning. But a candidate who was running in a district election would need to reach fewer voters and could rely more on volunteers and less on costly advertising and newspaper support. District elections, its supporters dreamed, would not only bring minority representation, but would challenge the old elite throughout the city!

Other Cities

The movement for district elections was not unique to San Jose. Half the largest cities in the United States use the system. The courts recently imposed them on Dallas, Houston, and some other southern cities. And 22 cities in California elect council members by district, a small minority of the state's 434 cities, but a significant one because it includes most of its largest cities.

LOS ANGELES

Los Angeles, California's largest city with almost 3 million people, has used district elections except for a brief interlude during the heyday of the Progressives. Since 1924 Los Angeles has been governed by a fifteen-member city council and a "weak-mayor" form of government (see Figure 8-1). There is no city manager as in San Jose; instead Los Angeles has a directly elected mayor who does not sit on the council but is the central figure in Los Angeles city politics. But the power of the mayor—and of the city council—is substantially diluted by the delegation of responsibility for sixteen departments, including police and fire, to independent commissions whose members are appointed by the mayor and approved by the city council to serve 5 year terms. Managers of the departments are mostly hired by the commissioners rather than the mayor or council. Most city workers are under civil service. This massive delegation of power substantially weakens the mayor and the council, although they still play an important role in selecting commissioners and in the budgetary process. The mayor's power is further enhanced by high public visibility and by his or her own staff.

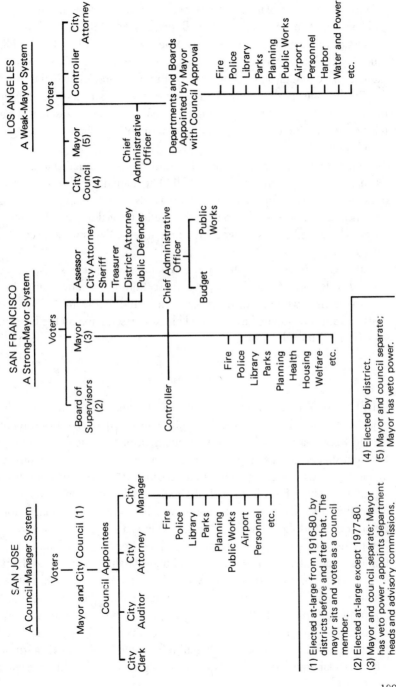

FIGURE 8-1 Forms of City Government

SAN JOSE
A Council-Manager System

Voters

Mayor and City Council (1)

Council Appointees

City Clerk — City Auditor — City Attorney — City Manager

Fire
Police
Library
Parks
Planning
Public Works
Airport
Personnel
etc.

SAN FRANCISCO
A Strong-Mayor System

Voters

Board of Supervisors (2) — Mayor (3)

Assessor
City Attorney
Sheriff
Treasurer
District Attorney
Public Defender

Controller

Chief Administrative Officer

Budget — Public Works

Fire
Police
Library
Parks
Planning
Health
Housing
Welfare
etc.

LOS ANGELES
A Weak-Mayor System

Voters

City Council (4) — Controller — City Attorney

Mayor (5)

Chief Administrative Officer

Departments and Boards Appointed by Mayor with Council Approval

Fire
Police
Library
Parks
Planning
Public Works
Airport
Personnel
Harbor
Water and Power
etc.

(1) Elected at-large from 1916-80, by districts before and after that. The mayor sits and votes as a council member.

(2) Elected at-large except 1977-80.

(3) Mayor and council separate; Mayor has veto power, appoints department heads and advisory commissions.

(4) Elected by district.

(5) Mayor and council separate; Mayor has veto power.

189

While San Jose's bland, contemporary city hall reflects the city's recent, rapid growth, Los Angeles's city hall suggests the Midwest cities so many Angelenos migrated from in the first decades of this century. The building, a squat skyscraper, is classically vigorous American architecture. It would look more in place in Chicago or Kansas City. But if San Jose's city hall is unintimidating, this one speaks authority. The entry court is large, stark, and formal, marked by ceramics representing the city's major industries. Inside is a massive rotunda. Along the endless corridors are information telephones like the ones in airports.

With its marble pillars and beamed ceiling, the city council chamber is more like a church than a public meeting hall. The audience sits in pews, straining necks to see what's going on. The council sits in a V-shape, not facing the audience as in San Jose, but facing the president of the council, whom they select. The chamber was designed at a time when citizens were spectators, not participants.

Although Hispanics are unrepresented on Los Angeles's district-elected council, it is otherwise a reasonable cross-section of the community. In 1982 there were eight white men, three black men, and four women. District elections and able organizing have ensured black representation on the Los Angeles City Council for a long time.

SAN FRANCISCO

Unlike any other local government in California, San Francisco is both a city and a county. By the turn of the century these two units of government had identical boundaries, so by a 1911 amendment of the state constitution, they were consolidated. Los Angeles County, by contrast, has eighty-one cities, including the City of Los Angeles itself. Because of the consolidation, the local legislative body, which is elected at-large, is called the board of supervisors rather than the city council. In contrast to San Jose's city manager form of government and Los Angeles's weak-mayor system, San Francisco uses a "strong-mayor" system (see Figure 8-1). The directly elected mayor of San Francisco has extensive appointment and budgetary power as well as the power to veto actions of the board of supervisors. San Francisco's chief executive thus operates more like a governor or the president than the purely ceremonial mayor of San Jose or the relatively weak executive in Los Angeles.

Just as the architecture of the Los Angeles and San Jose city halls reflects those cities, so San Francisco's city hall reflects the cosmopolitan spirit of that city. An elaborately baroque, domed structure, it is more European than

American and suggests a benevolent monarchy rather than the authoritarian stolidity of Los Angeles's city hall or the unpretentious democracy of San Jose's. The supervisors' chambers are reached by a broad, marble staircase, the kind you expect to see the Prince and the Princess of Wales descending. The chambers themselves are a bit like a fine men's club—dark wood panelling covers the walls, and the seating, as in Los Angeles, is in pews. The supervisors are in rows facing one another with their chosen president at the center, alone on a raised platform.

To many San Franciscans, their city government seemed like a not-so-benign monarchy or a gentlemen's club. Although one black and one Hispanic were on the board in 1970, they were not perceived as representing the city's large minority population. Adding to this discontent were emerging neighborhood and environmental movements, which were critical of high-rise development in downtown San Francisco and which saw the board as dominated by downtown interests. These factions were frustrated by their failure to win direct representation themselves and their inability to oust incumbents loyal to downtown interests. Given the members' high name familarity, newspaper support, and an incumbent's ability to raise money, seven elections had seen thirty-one of thirty-six incumbents reelected.[5]

In 1971 a coalition of groups interested in changing this started a petition to put district elections on the ballot. They didn't get enough people to sign their petition the first time, but in 1973 they did, only to see their proposal defeated by a two-to-one vote. But they continued their work, slowly building a strong, broad coalition of Hispanics, blacks, Asians, gays, liberals, environmentalists, neighborhood groups, and labor unions. They put district elections back on the ballot in 1976. Spending only $25,000 (one-fifth of which was from unions), the coalition recruited 3,800 volunteers and distributed over 400,000 pieces of literature.[6]

The opposition included ten of the city's eleven incumbent supervisors, the newspapers, the chamber of commerce, and downtown businesses. They spent twice as much money, but with contributors like Pacific Telephone, Southern Pacific, Wells Fargo, the Bank of America, and Bechtel, they could afford it. This time, though, the establishment lost. The voters approved district elections 52 to 48 percent. The diehard conservative opposition did not give up, however. The following year they attempted to repeal district elections and to recall liberal Mayor George Moscone, who had been elected by much the same coalition that voted for district elections. Their efforts failed, however, and the grassroots coalition that supported districting and Moscone seemed to be in the driver's seat for the moment.

Most California cities use at-large elections to select city council members. A few, like Los Angeles, San Bernardino, Riverside, and Bakersfield, have stuck with district elections. Others have recently returned to districting after half a century of at-large elections. In 1971 both Sacramento and Stockton switched back to district elections. In Sacramento the change was brought about by an emergent coalition of liberal Democrats, which had already succeeded in electing two minority persons to the city council. In Stockton the move was more exclusively supported by black and Hispanic voters. Minority representation increased from zero to three of nine when districting was introduced.

Oakland and San Diego used a compromise system in which council candidates were nominated by district and the top two choices of district voters then ran at-large. But the system virtually guaranteed that the more conservative candidates would win the at-large runoff. In Oakland, where the population was half black, no blacks served on the city's council for decades. Hispanic, neighborhood, and other nonestablishment candidates in San Diego were also unsuccessful. As a consequence efforts in both these cities to change the system to pure district elections got under way in the 1970s. Vehemently opposed by the conservative establishments of both cities, the reform was twice defeated by the voters of San Diego, but won approval in Oakland in 1980.

Neighborhood Discontents: Controlling Growth

Meanwhile, back in San Jose, a handful of mostly young, minority, liberal activists determined to challenge the city's conservative white power structure by putting district elections on the ballot through the initiative process. To amend a city charter, signatures numbering 15 percent of the votes cast in the city for all candidates in the preceding gubernatorial election are required— about 17,000 valid signatures in this case. The proposal then goes to the voters and a majority must approve the change.

That same year, 1972, the city council appointed a group of attorneys, business leaders, and moderate community activitists to review the entire city charter. This group eventually recommended major changes, including a San Francisco-style strong mayor and nomination of council members by districts with runoffs at-large. The city council voted to put these measures as well as the initiative districting proposal on the ballot. The petition circulators, who were just 2,000 signatures short of their goal, stopped gathering signatures.

Then the big gun opposition emerged. A committee of the old guard, including six former mayors, pressured the council into removing the proposals from the ballot. The districting advocates tried to pull their petition drive together again, but by the time the dust settled, the deadline for filing their petition had arrived and they were a few hundred signatures short.

The districting movement seemed to have been crushed in 1972, but some of the activists kept the idea alive, and the next few years brought changes that made a resurrection possible. Like many California cities, San Jose had grown rapidly—from 90,000 in 1950 to 450,000 in 1970 and over 600,000 in 1980. The growth brought new people and new problems. And the new people were not beholden to the old guard, whom they'd never even heard of. Change was in the wind.

THE POLITICS OF GROWTH

Besides the provision of basic services like police, fire protection, sewage, and traffic control, the greatest power cities have is the control of land use. Through their planning powers, cities determine how and where they will grow. In expanding cities like San Jose, city councils make dozens of decisions about growth every week. Until well into the 1970s, San Jose's city councils cheerfully allowed as much growth as possible wherever their friends the developers wanted it. The power structure of the city was based on growth and profit. Builders and developers met regularly with city officials in an informal group called the Book-of-the-Month Club, which also served as a campaign organization when the city needed voter approval of bonds for municipal improvements required for growth.

The boosters of the Book-of-the-Month Club had their way with city government from the 1940s to the 1970s, when growth caught up with them. The people for whom the boosters had built a new city rebelled. They complained that their neighborhoods had inadequate police and fire protection or lacked parks and libraries or suffered from traffic congestion. These services were responsibilities of city government, but they had frequently been deferred to facilitate immediate growth.

The issue that brought the debate about growth to the forefront of San Jose politics was overcrowded schools. School districts are separate units of local government, created by the state and run by locally elected school boards. But school districts in the new parts of San Jose had been unable to build schools rapidly enough to keep up with the growth the city government allowed. In 1973 a group of parents, angered by overcrowded classrooms and split sessions, got an initiative on the ballot to forbid new growth where schools were overcrowded. The measure passed, despite the opposition of the old guard, the

builders, and the newspapers. At the same time the voters elected two controlled growth candidates for city council, shifting the majority away from its
historic pro-growth orientation.

The initiative was the first indication of a new majority that might question
not only growth, but other policies of San Jose's old guard. But this new
majority was white and middle class and not, as yet, well-organized, and it had
virtually no contact with the minority, Eastside and downtown activists who
had supported district elections. In 1974 these forces came together to support
mayoral candidate Janet Gray Hayes, a mild liberal whose winning slogan was
"Let's make San Jose better before we make it bigger." Her campaign, with its
strong grassroots base, narrowly defeated the old-guard candidate, and it also
initiated the process of coalition building between the minority community and
the emerging neighborhood movement.

THE NEIGHBORHOOD MOVEMENT

The problems of growth caused neighborhood after neighborhood to organize to fight for more police patrols, a local park, or a stop sign—the kinds of
small things cities do that make our lives more bearable. Old neighborhoods
organized because of neglect or lost services—fewer cops because the force had
to be spread over a larger area, or heavy commuter traffic on neighborhood
streets because major road construction had been deferred. New neighborhoods
organized because their schools were overcrowded or because they had no
parks. The neighborhood movement was given further impetus by a city planning program based on public participation by "planning areas." The process
helped the movement toward district elections by bringing people together,
often for the first time, and building district identities. It also generated leaders
and established a system of contacts between them.

By its peak in 1978 there were 118 neighborhood and homeowner groups in
San Jose—about one for every 5,000 residents, a high density for such a new
city. At least half of these groups were well established, with dues-paying
members, newsletters, and the ability to mobilize, at least on issues of immediate local interest.

REVIVING DISTRICTING

Then, in 1976, as these trends were accelerating, there was another shooting
like that of John Henry Smith. Police were called to break up a family hassle.
When a young Chicano reached into his car, the officers thought he was going

for a gun. They shot and killed him. Weeks of marches on city hall and weeks of frustration at the apparent inaction of the city council followed. Later that year the protests resulted in a new police chief, but when nothing had happened by March, some of the protesters, mostly the same sort of people who had been involved in the earlier districting movement, got together to chart their strategy. Some wanted to launch an initiative for a police review board, but though that got to the heart of the problem, it was thought to be too controversial and so was deferred. The other option, which was adopted, was to revive district elections.

Instead of rushing to the streets with petitions, this time the tiny band of district election supporters began by seeking endorsements of the concept by key groups and individuals. Several neighborhood groups readily gave their support. So did the Central Labor Council, representing 100,000 workers in all the AFL-CIO unions in the county. Theirs was a key endorsement because they had not supported districting the first time around and because they had money and credibility. The neighborhood and labor endorsements came more easily this time not only because the attitudes of these groups had changed, but also because several districting activists were by this time accepted and respected members of these groups. This mounting support, along with the tenacious advocacy of the activists and the consistent evidence of the popularity of districting in public opinion polls, also produced tentative endorsements of the reform by all four successful council candidates in 1976.

When one of these candidates, a realtor and born-again Christian, spent over $65,000 to win a council seat, people were reminded of how much money counted in at-large elections. In a growing city like San Jose, those who stood to benefit most from who was on the city council were builders, developers, realtors, and other growth-oriented businesses. These interests had funded increasingly lavish campaigns in San Jose, and though their candidates sometimes lost, they were never totally isolated because they also invested in the campaigns of control-growth candidates just to keep doors open. In the minds of many neighborhood activists, these control-growth candidates eventually sold out to the people who could pay for their next campaign.

Thus the argument that district elections would cut campaign costs and lessen the influence of the building industry was raised, a theme that appealed to neighborhood, homeowner, and environmental groups. For minority and labor groups, however, the chief advantage was still better representation through improved opportunities for their people to get elected. For some in both camps, it was also a chance to confront the city's old-guard elite and make the system more responsive to the grassroots.

CHARTER REVISION TACTICS: INSIDERS AND OUTSIDERS

As a consequence of this organizing activity—plus the mayor's desire for greater power, the city council's wish for better pay, and the city manager's dream of loosening up the civil service system—the mayor and council appointed a new charter revision committee to study and recommend change. Unlike the first districting endeavor, the activists this time had good contacts in city hall and managed to get several supporters and allies appointed to the committee. Although the city council directed the committee to study the powers of the mayor, the civil service system, and council salaries, the committee quickly and unanimously agreed to put districting first and began holding public hearings and taking expert testimony.

While some districting activists worked with the charter revision committee, others formed a group called Citizens for Responsive Government (CRG). There was constant tension within CRG between political insiders who wanted to work for districting through the charter revision committee and more radical activists who preferred a San Francisco-style initiative. The insiders argued that the committee route was easier and would lead to a broader coalition, avoiding antagonizing the city council and some other community leaders whose support for districting was tepid at best, but whose opposition could be formidable. Those who preferred an initiative reminded the others of the city council's treachery in 1972 and argued that the initiative process was an essential grass-roots organizing tool. A decision was made to pursue both strategies, simultaneously, hoping the council would put the proposal on the ballot, but prepared to launch an initiative campaign if necessary or to use it as a threat to make sure the council put a plan CRG liked on the ballot.

But first they had to come up with a plan, and cutting a city into districts is no mean feat. Traditional boundaries must be respected and genuine community striven for if the fundamental goals of district representation are to be met. The Charter Review Committee and CRG devised four different schemes of six, eight, ten, and fourteen districts. Public hearings and private discussions expressed support for the ten- and fourteen-district plans because the smaller districts (with populations of 55,000 and 39,000, respectively) better reflected communities of interest. Because of concern that a city council of fourteen members would be too large, the Charter Review Committee and CRG agreed on the ten-district plan as a compromise.

The next step was getting the city council to put the plan on the ballot. That decision was to be made at a council meeting on May 16, 1978, which began with a report from the Charter Review Committee citing "a high degree of

frustration in the neighborhoods" due to the lack of council attention.[7] Districting, the Committee declared, would increase accountability, cut campaign
costs, and broaden representation.

To ensure victory at the council hearing, CRG had organized a letter writing
campaign in April, followed by lobbying sessions with council members. Then
they orchestrated a broad coalition of forty-eight groups to speak at the hearing,
a process that also helped publicize the cause. At the hearing speakers from
unions; homeowner, neighborhood, and renter groups; minority organizations;
the National Women's Political Caucus (NWPC); the Campaign for Economic
Democracy (CED); and others paraded to the speaker's podium in an impressive display of the breadth and depth of support for districting.

The opposition that night was weak and ill-organized. A former mayor, the
most powerful attorney in town, denounced the plan. Also opposed were one or
two minions of the old guard and the shrewdest and most able lobbyist-
developer in the city. But the most vigorous criticism came from the city
manager, who claimed districting made for narrow-minded parochialism.

The objections came too late, however. Before the meeting the districting
coalition had counted on the support of three council members, and expected
two to lean in favor and two to be opposed. In the end six voted to put district
elections on the ballot.

The Campaign for District Elections

The campaign was launched that night. The supporters had put together the
coalition they needed: a broad cross-section of grassroots groups plus most of
the city council and several other elected officials. Thus the campaign in San
Jose would not be quite the same confrontation it had been in San Francisco.
Over the summer a new steering committee of about two dozen activists from
key sectors of the coalition was organized.

Their simple campaign strategy was based on the resources available: plenty
of people and little money. They continued seeking endorsements of community leaders and organizations, maintaining a bandwagon effect: "Everybody's
for district elections." They sought maximum free publicity with press releases,
free speech messages on radio, and a carefully selected and well-trained speakers bureau scheduled for as many public meetings as possible. But the major
way they planned to reach voters was through hundreds of volunteers walking
door to door. To give the campaign visibility, the city was blanketed with small
signs along the streets and on supporters' lawns.

It was as cheap a campaign as possible—the bare minimum. But still there were expenses. The biggest was printing campaign literature and signs. The campaign manager and volunteer coordinator had to be paid, and although the office space was donated, operating expenses, like telephones, had to be met. Fund raising was difficult because the campaign couldn't count on the big contributions most candidates get. Even liberal donors were stingy about giving to an issue campaign with no candidate star-power.

Nevertheless, the coalition came up with the $13,753 needed for their bare-bones campaign. Most of it came in the form of small contributions (under $50) from community activists and the fund-raising events. Candidates for various offices gave $1,000. The National Women's Political Caucus, a feminist group that saw districting as a chance to elect more women, gave $360 and many volunteers. The San Jose chapter of the Campaign for Economic Democracy (CED) came through with $1,155. The San Jose CED had actively supported districting since 1977 and also threw much of its volunteer energy into the campaign, as the local chapters in San Francisco, Oakland, and San Diego did in the districting campaigns in their cities. But the biggest organizational donor was labor unions. They came up with $2,716, about 20 percent of the total raised, and also supplied several of the most active campaigners.

Meanwhile two opposition groups appeared. One was made up of the city's old guard. They spent little money, but did most of the public speaking against districting. The other opposition group existed only to funnel money from builders and developers to an advertising agency. Virtually all the money for "Citizens Against Unfair Representation" came from out-of-town corporate developers. The districting coalition cheerfully pointed out that the only individual named in the documents of this "citizens" group did not even live in San Jose. Altogether, the group spent twice as much as the other side, with $10,000 coming from the Builders Association alone. Their money went for signs, mailings, and newspaper and radio advertisements.

The organized opposition was mostly a feeble front for the builders, but if the city manager had had his way, it would have been more formidable. He wrote to the city's most powerful business leaders, urging them to oppose districting actively. But they showed little interest, and before the city manager could mobilize them, he found himself in a fight for his job. Four of the seven council members turned against him and his managed-growth policies. Dubbed the "Gang of Four," the group included the Chicano councilman who was running for mayor against incumbent Janet Gray Hayes. They briefly gained control and ran roughshod over the mayor and city manager, ultimately firing the latter. The Gang of Four disintegrated when one of them resigned after a second drunken escapade with the police. Hayes and her allies regained control, but the fiasco added to public cynicism about the council, and the districting campaign was able to take advantage of the anti-city hall mood.

The city manager's effort to mobilize the city's business elite did succeed, however, in producing "the march on the *Mercury News*."[8] A group of businessmen met with the publisher to lobby for newspaper opposition to districting. Although historically unabashedly conservative and probusiness, the newspapers had recently gone through a change in ownership that brought in a new, professional, more liberal management, and the old guard feared they would be soft on districting. Already the new management had provided more objective coverage of districting on the news pages than the city's elite liked. The editorial pages were different, however, and the newspaper went along with the old guard.

With the addition of the chamber of commerce and the Small Businessmen's Association to the opposition, the lines were drawn and the debate proceeded. The arguments of the antidistricting campaign centered on the threat of boss politics, disenfranchisement, parochialism, and inefficiency. They reminded voters that districts once were called wards and had been an integral part of machine politics in San Jose and other cities. They also pointed out that the existing at-large system allowed each voter to choose all members of the council: "I want the whole damn bunch responsible for my neighborhood," a powerful old attorney declared. "I don't want just one."[9]

Most effectively, they claimed district representatives would care about only their own districts, not the whole city. "That's not my district, I couldn't care less," was the attitude they said would dominate. It was even possible, they suggested, that some districts would gang up on others to force them to take things they didn't want.[10] With this threat and an increase in the size of the council from seven to eleven, "chaos and indecisiveness" were sure to follow,[11] making the council a debating society and, worse, increasing the size and cost of government just after the voters had said they wanted less by slashing taxes with Proposition 13 in June. The new system, they said, would cost a million dollars a year.

The supporters of district elections scoffed at the boss politics argument, pointing out that with nonpartisan elections, a civil service system, and weak political parties, "it couldn't happen here." To the argument that district elections permitted voters only one council representative rather than all of them, the proponents pointed out that some neighborhoods had never had even one representative, while others had five or six. Districting ensured each area at least one attentive council member, and because each area got one, it was fair.

All neighborhoods would be represented, and citizens would have better access to their representatives. At-large elections, audiences were reminded, had been instituted when San Jose's population was only 30,000. But in 1978, with 550,000 constituents, a council member had to represent more people than a member of Congress. They couldn't possibly know the finite details of the needs for stop signs and library books in every part of the sprawling, 160 square mile city. Districting would reduce this scale, producing more knowledgeable, accessible, and accountable representation. The cost, they claimed, would be only about $200,000 a year, and this would be an investment in good government, which could produce savings in the long run. Districting would also decrease the cost of campaigns. Grassroots candidates would have a real chance and the power of the pro-growth elite would be broken. With districts drawn to represent real communities of interest, this reduction in campaign costs would give minorities, women, working people, and neighborhood activists opportunities to be elected that they would never have under the at-large system.

Election day arrived, and when the votes were counted, districting had won a narrow victory: 52 percent voted yes and 48 percent voted no, almost exactly the same margin as in San Francisco. The strongest support came from the minority and traditionally liberal precincts, as well as from recently developed areas that had never been represented and from precincts targeted by the proponents' volunteers. Negative votes came from white, conservative, affluent precincts, especially those that had been overrepresented before. "Today the people of San Jose reclaimed control of City Hall," the victors declared. "Big money isn't running this town anymore."[12]

The Impact of District Elections

A rare congruence of minority, labor, feminist, and neighborhood interests put district elections back in the charters of San Jose, San Francisco, Stockton, Sacramento, and Oakland, though the movement failed twice in San Diego. To some extent they were successful in redistributing power, but the struggle did not end with these victories. The economic elites of these cities continued to exercise great power, and certain events beyond the control of the insurgent grassroots minimized what they could do once they got control of city hall.

CHANGES IN REPRESENTATION BUT PERHAPS NOT IN POWER

The new system has survived and thrived in Sacramento, where the city manager conceded that the new council was a "much younger and more diversified council than ever before. Because of their average age and their district obligations, they're more vigorous. These people will stand alongside any of our other councils."[13] In Stockton minority representation increased, but "district chauvinism" and racial tension are problems, and some analysts observed "a backlash against district elections," which may mean the "gains may not be sustained."[14]

If backlash threatened in Stockton, it struck repeatedly in San Francisco. The first election of supervisors by district returned six former at-large incumbents, but increased the number of women supervisors and added a black supervisor as well as Harvey Milk, an out-of-the-closet gay. Eugene Lee, a leading authority on local politics, judged the victors in "congruence" with their districts, meaning they were sociologically and ideologically like the people they represented, and the board of supervisors was thus more representative of the city.[15] The second election by district, in 1979, further broadened that representation, resulting in a board of five men, one of whom was gay, and six women, two of whom were black. Perhaps the only disappointment was that no Hispanic was elected. The cost of campaigns was also cut from the at-large average of $100,000 to a district average of $30,000.[16]

In operation the districted board paid more attention to the small scale needs of neighborhoods, although the *San Francisco Bay Guardian*, a gadfly weekly, pointed out that "a comparison of voting records of the at-large and district-elected Boards . . . found the district Board only marginally more progressive and representative of neighborhood interests." A majority was still "more favorable to downtown than to the neighborhoods," and the initiatives of the mayor were almost always approved. Still there were enough "progressives" on the board to constitute a threat and to push through some liberal legislation like building height limits and rent control.[17] Eugene Lee believed "neighborhood groups gained in power,"[18] and another social scientist felt the district supervisors were effective "advocates for their bailiwicks," dealing well with an increased "volume and variety of constituency service."[19]

But there were deep ideological divisions and personality clashes that led to bitter infighting. Although these differences probably merely represented differences within the city itself, they were seen as a sign that districting wasn't working. The city's business interests, though still getting much of what they wanted, felt there were too many liberals on the board and that neighborhood matters were getting too much attention. Attacking "eleven little fiefdoms,"[20] they put the system back on the ballot by initiative in August 1980, relying on a low voter turnout to bring their side victory. Only 35 percent of the voters showed up, and the repeal squeaked through by 50.57 percent. As in preceding campaigns, the big business-funded antidistrict forces outspent their opponents two to one. The loyal advocates of districting reluctantly pulled themselves together, circulated petitions, and put districting back on the November ballot. By then, however, the disillusioned San Francisco voters had had enough. They rejected another change

In San Jose, where the political system is less entrenched and divisions are not as old or as deep as in San Francisco, the transition was less tumultuous. The districted city council elected in 1980 included four men and six women (one black and one Hispanic). They were younger than previous councils and the ideological range was broader—from a Kennedy liberal to a born-again Christian conservative. Several were neighborhood activists who could never have been elected at-large. They were also highly representative of their districts, making the council as a whole more representative of the city.

Campaign costs were cut substantially, with winning campaigns averaging $25,800. Although more grassroots campaigns evolved, the local builders' group endorsed eight of ten successful candidates and gave over $38,000. A local journalist argued that builders *gained* influence with districting because it was cheaper to "buy a council member." And a developer who had actively opposed district elections confidently observed that "the builders will land on their feet regardless of what happens."[21] Nevertheless, the builders and developers contributed only 14.7 percent of the total campaign funds, less than they had under the at-large system, and small contributors (less than $100) gave $68,000, 26.4 percent of the total spent by the successful candidates.

To the builders' satisfaction, the new council was not notably more anti-growth than its predecessors. District representatives did, however, work to achieve compromises on new developments that would keep them from harming existing neighborhoods. Minor neighborhood problems were taken more seriously, and the council as a whole was a little more liberal, supporting policies like rent control. On police-community relations, the issue that had given impetus to the district movement in the first place, the council showed little interest beyond getting more cops into their districts. But improved training and recruitment, policy changes, and a new police chief had largely resolved the problems of the 1960s and 1970s.

What happened in San Francisco and San Jose raises questions about whether the struggle was worth the effort. The districting movement had to fight an old, entrenched power structure every inch of the way in San Francisco and, ultimately, they lost. In San Jose, a new city with a less cogent power structure and greater political opportunity,[22] there was greater consensus on districting and the movement was able to bring change from within the political system. In both cases some of the goals of district elections were attained. The districted councils were more representative and the cost of campaigns was cut.

Attention to the little things that make neighborhoods livable was greater. Renters, environmentalists, and minority groups also made gains.

But those who hoped to redistribute power and change public policy by altering the electoral system were disappointed. The substantial clout of the economic elite was still felt. Downtown interests and the chamber of commerce still got most of what they wanted in San Francisco, and the builders did nicely in San Jose. These interests have the sustaining force of money: profit motivates their involvement in local politics and it also finances their political activity. They also have concern about jobs and the economic well-being of the community on their side.

WHAT'S LEFT TO GOVERN: LIMITS ON LOCAL AUTONOMY

The winners in the districting movement—and, indeed, anyone involved in local politics—faced another serious problem, in addition to the persistent power of business interests and community elites. The autonomy of local government, its power to make decisions for itself and carry them out, has been whittled away by intergovernmental mandates and regulations and budgetary limits.

Intergovernmental Mandates and Regulations. More and more of what cities and counties do is constrained by higher levels of government. As creations of the states, local governments have always operated within the confines of what states allow them to do. But in recent years the states have mandated expenditures about which local government has little choice. In California this is particularly true of counties, where as little as 20 percent of the budget may be spent at the discretion of local officials. The rest, most of which comes from the state or federal governments in the first place, must be spent for programs like welfare, health, and operation of the courts. Local government must also invest staff time to meet such requirements as planning and environmental reviews. Although the federal government has no direct constitutional control of cities and counties, it also imposes programs by threatening to withhold grants and other funds if local governments fail to comply with welfare eligibility, environmental quality, fair housing, or other stipulations.

Budgetary Limits. An even more serious constraint on local autonomy is the money available to provide services. In 1978 California voters approved Proposition 13 (see Chapters 9 and 10), which slashed property taxes, the major source of funding for local government. Before Proposition 13, school districts got over half their funds from property taxes, counties got over a third, and cities got about a quarter of the spending from this source. Proposition 13 cut local revenues from property taxes by about 50 percent, but it also made it impossible for local governments to raise the tax. Financing of local governments became uncertain as cities and counties lost control of their major source of funds.

As a consequence local governments turned more and more to state and federal aid. At first the state government used its surplus to "bail out" local government. But the surplus ran out and the bail out was reduced. The state has also leaned toward allocating what funds it does have to school districts, leaving cities and counties to fend for themselves. Cities actually came out of the crisis better than counties and school districts because they were less dependent on property taxes than school districts and had fewer mandated programs (especially social services) than counties. Cities also have more alternative sources of income. San Jose, for example, has a tax on gas and electric utilities, which produces 14 percent of its annual revenues. The state constitution also includes a one cent sales tax that is collected by the state but returned to the local jurisdictions where sales occur. Counties get some of this, but because most commercial enterprises are located in cities, the bulk goes to them. That tax is now a major revenue source for cities, producing 22 percent of San Jose's income.

While these limits on local government revenues were making their mark, other sources of state and federal aid were also reduced. The Reagan administration began cutting various federal grants, and the state began tightening its own budget. Local government found itself caught in a pincer movement. On one side, state and federal regulations imposed costly service requirements, and on the other, revenue limits made them impossible to pay for. With less and less money, local government had to reduce or eliminate services and lay off workers.

Local Opportunity, State Constraints

California, with its weak political parties, absence of machines, amorphous power structures, initiative process, and traditional openness, provides great opportunities for grassroots community groups, especially at the local level. The victories of the district election supporters may have been limited by the continued influence of economic elites and by budget constraints, but they were still substantial. They altered the system of representation, providing electoral opportunities for candidates without money and establishment connections. Neighborhood and women candidates were highly successful; minority and gay candidates did well where these populations were concentrated in limited areas. New voices were heard. Issues that were "never allowed to surface when propertied interests were dominant," including police review boards, rent control, equal pay, and neighborhood traffic control, "suddenly [got] an airing."[23] Similar changes in the system of representation and on other issues were fought out in dozens of other California cities.

Substantial as these opportunities are, they are almost entirely structured by government at the state level. What cities may or may not do is granted and may be taken away by the state. Nothing illustrates that point better than the impact of Proposition 13 on cities. Just as the newly elected district representatives took office, they found themselves scrapping over what to cut, not how to improve their neighborhoods. California's state political system provides the openness and opportunity, but it also imposes limits on what can be done in local politics.

Notes

[1] *San Jose Mercury*, September 21, 1971. The history of San Jose's district election movement presented in this chapter relies heavily on newspaper coverage, but is also based on 10 years of participant observation by one of the authors.

[2] *San Jose Mercury*, September 24, 1981.

[3] *San Jose Mercury*, September 28, 1971.

[4] Jack Corr and Fred Keeley, "San Jose City Charter, A Bicentennial Proposal," 1976, p. 17.

[5] Eugene C. Lee and Jonathan Rothman, "San Francisco's District System Alters Electoral Politics," *National Civic Review* 67, no. 4 (April 1978): 173.

[6] *San Francisco Chronicle*, November 4, 1976.

[7] *San Jose Mercury*, May 15, 1978.

[8] Philip Troustine and Terry Christensen, *Movers and Shakers* (New York: St. Martin's Press, 1982), pp. 126–27.

[9] *San Jose Mercury*, October 15, 1978.

[10] Ibid.

[11] Ballot Argument, Santa Clara Registrar of Voters, November 1978.

[12] *San Jose Mercury*, November 5, 1978.

[13] *Sacramento Bee*, January 21, 1973.

[14] Rufus B. Browning, Dale Rogers Marshall, and David H. Tabb, "Blacks and Hispanics in California City Politics: Changes in Representation," *Public Affairs Report* 20, no. 3, June 1979, p. 6.

[15] Lee and Rothman, "San Francisco's District System," p. 176.

[16] Ibid., pp. 174–75.

[17] *San Francisco Bay Guardian*, August 14, 1980.

[18]Lee and Rothman, "San Francisco's District System," p. 177.

[19]Howard E. Hamilton, "Choosing a Representation System: More than Meets the Eye." *National Civic Review* 69, no. 9 (September 1980): 432.

[20]Campaign literature.

[21]*San Jose Mercury*, October 15, 1978.

[22]See Trounstine and Christensen's *Movers and Shakers* for a detailed analysis of San Jose's power structure in contrast with those of other older cities like San Francisco.

[23]"California Variants." *The Economist*, December 6, 1980, p. 33.

9
TAX POLICY

Citizen Politics in Action

During the late 1970s distrust of elected officials as managers of the public purse became a national affliction. Wherever government systems permitted tax cutbacks by initiatives or referenda, the voters responded en masse. In those states where the public's voice was limited to pressure politics, legislatures felt the wrath of countless tax reduction groups. Commonly described as the "taxpayers' revolt," the antitax movement reached its zenith in 1978, when smoldering resentment against government waste, welfare fraud, controversial education techniques, and massive inner-city assistance burst into political flames. Predictably, California stood at the forefront of the antitax issue.[1]

If some citizens had problems relating increased taxes to big government, their difficulty disappeared by 1978. Double-digit inflation had pushed the small income gains of most wage earners into considerably higher tax brackets, forcing them into the unenviable position of paying more state income taxes and enduring a lower standard of living. Similar disasters confronted homeowners, who watched soaring property values command new taxes that exceeded their sense of fairness. Faced with the choice of less government or higher taxes, polls showed the voters preferred the former over the latter! And the easiest way of expressing the public's antitax feeling seemed to come by cutting property taxes. Unlike income taxes, which are withheld from each paycheck, or sales taxes, which are charged on a "pay-as-you-go" basis, property taxes are collected from property owners as one large bill every year. Hence they are particularly irksome.

Like many states, California allows local governments to employ the property tax as a major source of revenue. Historically, these taxes have been used to finance fire and police departments, school districts, local welfare assistance, and a variety of special services ranging from cemetery care to sewage disposal. In 1978 alone, local governments were scheduled to collect $11.5 billion in property tax revenues. The tax amounted to 27 percent of all city revenues, 40 percent of all county revenues, 47 percent of all school district revenues, and 90 percent of the revenues collected by fire districts.[2]

As the combination of government growth and inflation squeezed the state's homeowners, the property tax grew disproportionately large and unpopular. One national study found that while California property taxes were 89 percent of the national average in 1942, they had become 142 percent of the national average by 1976. Local governments played the numbers game of lowering property tax rates slightly every year, although the actual dollar amounts collected skyrocketed as a result of the higher assessed value of properties. Thus, the stage was set for revolt in California.

When the voters took it upon themselves to reduce property taxes in 1978, California's relief was offset by new challenges. Suddenly, other forms of taxation became fair game for the state's tax-cutting crusaders. Yet these "benefits" were not without some "costs." As tax reductions went into effect at the state and local levels, many of California's programs were curtailed or eliminated completely. A new mentality tarnished the Golden State. If the public wanted to be "number one" in education, highways, welfare, and other areas during the 1960s, being in "the middle" was good enough in the 1980s. Thus, changes in tax policy had ripple effects on virtually every aspect of California politics.

Howard Jarvis and the Crusade for Proposition 13

California's lawmakers attempted to quell public anger before the *tax* issue become an *election* issue. In 1977 it became clear that the state treasury would enjoy a surplus for the foreseeable future. Governor Brown and the state legislature, however, couldn't come to terms on a formula for distributing state surplus monies to the citizen.

Meanwhile, as elected state officials fumbled about, a seasoned political activist, Howard Jarvis, promoted a citizen-sponsored initiative providing much more extensive tax relief than any plan contemplated by either the governor or legislature. In December 1977 Jarvis and his Sacramento-based ally, Paul Gann, collected 1,200,000 voter signatures (more than double the amount required by law) to qualify a property tax relief initiative for the June 1978 election. The secretary of state subsequently numbered the proposed law as Proposition 13.

Under its provisions the Jarvis-Gann initiative limited all property taxes to one percent of the market value retroactive to the 1975–76 fiscal year.

Homeowners, apartment building owners, and businesses of all sizes would qualify for permanent local property tax reductions averaging 57 percent. In the future, county assessors would be permitted to raise property values for cost-of-living purposes by no more than 2 percent during any single year. (For example, a house worth $100,000 one year could be raised in value to $102,000 the next year, with one percent tax adjusted accordingly.) *Only* when property was resold could the tax assessor reappraise the house or business at current market value. For the overwhelming majority of society who remained in stable positions of home residence or business ownership, enactment of this initiative would not only reduce but virtually freeze property taxes. If passed, Proposition 13 would have the mammoth effect of slashing all California property taxes by $7 billion.

HOWARD JARVIS—A "CITIZEN POLITICIAN" AT WORK

When Ronald Reagan ran for the California governorship in 1966 in his first try at any elected office, he campaigned with the slogan of "citizen politician." In other words, Reagan ran as an outsider, an ordinary person who was fed up with "Big Government." In a state where personalities are far more important than political parties, such handles are routine. But Reagan did not own the rights to the "citizen politician" theme. In many ways Howard Jarvis projected the same mentality—a simple person who, as Peter Finch screamed in the movie *Network*, was "mad as hell and not going to take it anymore." And with that theme California had another antiestablishment hero in the making.

Who was Howard Jarvis? In California politics he was long considered by many as a gadfly for conservative causes. After retiring as a wealthy newspaper publisher and manufacturer in 1962, Jarvis lost handily in his bid to win the Republican nomination to the United States Senate. He suffered the same fate in 1972 when seeking the Republican nomination to the state's elected tax agency, the Board of Equalization. In 1977 Jarvis ran for mayor of Los Angeles but finished far down the list of candidates.

Poor showings at the polls concerned Jarvis very little. He used his candidacies as an ongoing forum to hammer away at excessive taxation and big governments. For 15 years Jarvis pursued his objective with little public fanfare. However, by 1978 his own values and those of the public seemed to grow closer together. Given the change in public sentiment, Jarvis resorted to the initiative process because "the people are fed up with politicians and their promises."[3]

As public resentment toward government officials grew, many who previously ridiculed Jarvis for his unconventional behavior paid tribute to him in

1978. A number of conservative political leaders spoke of Jarvis as a future candidate for office. One Republican gubernatorial candidate actually promised a state appointment to Jarvis if elected, but the candidate failed to win his party's nomination.

Again and again, Jarvis canvassed the state to relate his own tax miseries to those of the general public. Describing himself as "a rugged bastard who's had his head kicked in a thousand times by the government,"[4] Howard Jarvis became a household word in California. Serving as the paid director of the Apartment Association of Los Angeles, the 75 year old activist offered a permanent tax relief plan that would give help to all and promised that California would be the starting point for a nationwide wave of taxpayer revolts. "I'm not interested in my own taxes," Jarvis said at one point. "I'm not gonna be here much longer to pay taxes. What I'm concerned about is the thousands of people—both elderly people in drastic situations and the young people who have no way to build anything for themselves. These people need help."[5] Apparently, millions of Californians had similar concerns.

THE LEGISLATURE'S ALTERNATIVE—TOO LITTLE, TOO LATE

While Proposition 13 gathered steam, the state government remained paralyzed over the tax relief issue. Throughout 1977 Governor Brown insisted on his "circuit breaker" approach, a method whereby low-income individuals would get the lion's share of tax reduction benefits. Although Brown's proposal received token consideration in the Assembly, it was ridiculed altogether in the Senate. More than a half dozen tax relief measures were scuttled that year, as a fragmented legislature demonstrated an inability to reach any consensus.

Only the fear that the Jarvis-Gann initiative might succeed convinced Brown to relent and motivated a divided legislature in the 1978 election year. After considerable haggling, the embattled legislators finally produced their own tax reduction proposal in March 1978 for the upcoming June election. Known as Proposition 8, the legislature's referendum would reduce property taxes on all owner-occupied homes by approximately 32 percent. Apartment building owners, businesses, and corporate interests would continue to pay property taxes at the current rates, thus providing what became known as a "split assessment roll" (one assessment rate for businesses, a lower assessment rate for homeowners). Whereas Proposition 13 offered no direct relief to renters, Proposition 8 gave the state's renters a tax credit of $75 per taxpayer. If passed, Proposition 8 would cut residential property taxes by $1.4 billion, a mere one-fifth of the savings guaranteed by Proposition 13.

Yet for millions of beleaguered and would-be homeowners in California, the call of Proposition 13 offered a quick fix to bring housing costs back to "the good old days." Table 9-1 illustrates the increased burden suffered by new homeowners between 1973 and 1978. With property taxes factored in as part of the average monthly house cost, the typical payment escalated from 28.4 percent of a family's income for a home purchased in 1973 to 43.0 percent for a new purchase in 1978. The differential between home costs and income, less than three to one in 1973, ballooned to almost four to one by 1978, resulting in unaffordable payments. Passage of Proposition 13 promised that the typical income percentage used for new home payments would decline from 43.0 percent to 36.4 percent.

THE VOTERS DECIDE: BUY NOW, PAY LATER

As the voters contemplated the two tax-cutting alterations, various organizations and political personalities lined up on either side of the question. A citizens group headed by Jarvis called the United Organization of Taxpayers actively promoted the initiative along with dozens of homeowner associations across the state. Most of the half dozen candidates for the Republican gubernatorial nomination expressed support for the proposition. Given a sizable surplus in Sacramento, they seemed to agree with Jarvis that the $7 billion in tax reductions would cut out only some of the fat in government. Thousands of bumper stickers expressed support for the Jarvis measure with the slogan: "Save the American dream: Vote for Proposition 13."

Despite considerable grassroots support for Proposition 13, the list of well-known opponents to the measure (and proponents of Proposition 8) was much more substantial and diverse than the collection of those favoring the initiative.

TABLE 9-1   California Incomes, Housing Prices, and Mortgage Burden

	Year of home purchase					
	1973	1974	1975	1976	1977	1978
Average household income	$16,120	$17,608	$18,832	$20,309	$21,902	$23,575
Average price of new home	$44,200	$50,900	$55,500	$69,500	$77,500	$89,600
Average new home mortgage rate	8.5%	9.7%	9.3%	9.3%	9.3%	9.8%
House payment burden (including property taxes)*	28.4%	32.5%	32.2%	37.4%	38.7%	43.0%
Post-Jarvis burden*	23.6%	27.4%	27.1%	31.4%	32.5%	36.4%

*Percentage as related to income.

Source: Los Angeles Times, August 27, 1978. Copyright © 1978 by Los Angeles Times. Reprinted with permission.

Governor Brown and a lopsided majority of the legislature criticized the Jarvis measure as an attempt to dismantle state and local governments. Virtually all local government units took issue with Proposition 13 for the projected extensive cuts the initiative would make in the local tax base. Outside the public sector, major newspapers, organized labor, and a majority of leaders in the corporate world also joined the fight against the Jarvis initiative. The state's leading financial institutions, insurance companies, and utilities raised more than $1 million to oppose Proposition 13, even though the business sector would receive two-thirds of the projected tax savings. Before the campaign was over, the "No on 13" committees outspent the "Yes on 13" committees by a margin of two to one. Thus, on paper the opponents seemed to be in a position to defeat the Jarvis tax relief measure.

During the early course of the tax relief battle, public opinion remained indecisive on the Jarvis proposal. In March 1978 a *Los Angeles Times* survey found that 35 percent of those interviewed favored Proposition 13, 27 percent opposed it, and 38 percent remained undecided. By late May, however, public opinion had shifted decisively in the direction of the proposed change with 52 percent in favor, 35 percent against, and 13 percent undecided.

The breaking point came in mid-May, when the Los Angeles County tax assessor mailed updated tax assessments to the county's 1.7 million property owners. Because Los Angeles County contains 35 percent of the state's population, voter sentiment there was particularly crucial to the upcoming election. Fuming over property tax hikes of 100 percent and more, thousands of residents converged on the assessor's office in protest. But unlike most instances when the public might have to swallow its disgust, on this occasion it had an opportunity to act.

On June 6, 1978 California voters went to the polls in record numbers. Although nominations to six statewide offices and a dozen other state propositions awaited public response, all of these matters took a backseat to the tax relief question. The results were convincing. While Proposition 8 lost by 53 to 47 percent, Proposition 13 carried by a near two-to-one majority of 65 to 35 percent. Basking in the success of his electoral triumph, Jarvis summarized the passage of Proposition 13 as the will of the people when he stated, "Tonight was a victory against money, the politicians, [and] the government."[6]

Passage of Proposition 13 brought substantial and immediate property tax relief to California. In addition to property tax cuts of $7 billion, 100,000 jobs were eliminated from state and local governments. Program cutbacks and loss of services were minimal as the state used its $6 billion surplus to "bail out" local governments and special districts. Yet by 1982 the cushion was gone.

Depleted of its surplus as a result of annual rescue efforts to local governments, the state treasury was $700 million in the red, leaving California with the undesirable choice of drastically reduced services or major tax hikes in the 1982–83 fiscal year.

The property tax issue in California illustrates the power of citizen politics under the most difficult circumstances imaginable. The Proposition 13 coalition was ridiculed by leaders in the public and private sectors alike, condemned by the press, and badly outspent. Yet, the initiative became law. Why? First, a substantial portion of the California electorate lost confidence in their state and local officials as thoughtful spenders of the taxpayers' money. Thus, the voters wanted to teach government leaders a lesson on who really controls the public purse. Second, the voters saw the Jarvis initiative as a way of cutting taxes now. Jarvis presented them with a simple solution to the tax burden and the voters bought it. Third, the governor and legislature allowed the tax problem to remain unsolved for too long. Tired of waiting for political leaders to get their act together, the public assumed the policymaking role.

Where California Gets Its Money—Past and Present

A number of questions revolve around government taxation. How much money is needed? Who should pay for the services provided? Why does government tax some more or less than others? These are tough questions to answer mostly because of the difficulty in securing agreement over what should or should not be financed by government. Taxation works only to the extent that lawmakers convince the public of its need. In other words, we are addressing a perennially controversial issue, one whose importance is likely to vary with collective public sentiment, changes in the economy, and society's concerns.

During the state's 135 year history, elected officials and the public have asked and answered the preceding questions repeatedly. California's tax formulas have changed with the public mood, the state's problems, and—to an increasing extent—the nation's economy. On occasion the perceptions of taxpayers and lawmakers have differed widely, leading to revolts such as that described with Proposition 13. In fact, as California has grown and changed, its taxation methods and emphases have been altered as well.

In the early years the state government relied mainly on the *property tax* as its income source. Both the 1849 and 1879 state constitutions also directed that property taxes be collected by local governments as their principal source of revenue. Meanwhile the Progressive philosophy, which opposed big business, flourished in California, and the state legislature enacted new taxes on banks, insurance companies, corporations, and all public utilities. As a result of these changes, local governments enjoyed a new level of financial independence, and the state developed a more diversified tax base to support its own activities. This division of tax responsibilities continued without major alteration until the onset of the Great Depression in 1929, when both governments—state and local—found that their depleted treasuries were unable to meet mounting public problems.

Hard economic times led the state to pursue new tax sources. Thus, in 1933, California enacted a *sales tax* initially set at 2.5 percent. The tax originally was created to guarantee consistent state support for public education and permanent assistance for local governments that were not generating enough reserves from property taxes. By the late 1970s the state sales tax gradually had climbed to 6 percent, with an additional 0.5 percent permitted for levy in certain counties with state-approved public transportation districts. The 0.5 percent provision was first established in 1960 with the creation of BART (Bay Area Rapid Transit District), a three-county cooperative effort in and around San Francisco. Since then a number of counties throughout California have added the extra 0.5 percent, thereby making the 0.5 percent sales tax applicable to about half the state's population.[7]

Of the basic 6 percent statewide sales tax, not all of the money remains in Sacramento's coffers. Under the most recent formula effected with Senate Bill 90 in 1972, the state receives 4.75 percent, cities and counties keep 1 percent, and an additional 0.25 percent remains in county hands for transportation. The latter 0.25 percent should not be confused with the special 0.50 percent made available for transit district taxes. Thus, although over $9.5 billion was collected in sales taxes in 1981–82, the state was able to keep slightly under $8 billion.

A second major state tax was developed during the Great Depression to finance California through rough times. In 1935 the state adopted the *personal income tax* on a graduated scale. Those with relatively low incomes were taxed for 1 percent of their adjusted income, and those with greater earning power ($250,000 and over) paid as much as 15 percent. Over the years the number of percentage brackets were first reduced to six, and then slowly expanded to eleven. Today the personal income tax obligation varies between 1 and 11 percent. Despite the increased brackets, the personal income tax in California pales next to its federal equivalent, where the maximum tax obligation can be as high as 50 percent. Compared with other states, however, California's personal income tax takes more money on a per capita basis than most of its counterparts, particularly at the higher income levels.[8]

Bank and general corporation taxes constitute California's third largest source of revenue. As with the sales and personal income taxes, these percentage assessments have also increased over the years. When first passed in 1929, bank and corporation taxes were set at 4 percent. After a temporary decline to 2 percent in 1933 and 1934, these taxes were gradually increased to higher flat rates. In 1959 the tax was changed from 4 percent to 5.5 percent. Since that year, several increases have been passed by the legislature, with the last series of changes taking place between 1980 and 1982. In 1979, responding to the projected long-term income losses in the wake of Proposition 13, the legislature raised bank and corporation taxes from the prevailing 9 percent rate to 9.6 percent. One year later in 1980 the tax was increased to 11.6 percent.

Sales, personal income, and bank and corporation taxes are the three mainstays of California's state revenues. For the 1981–82 fiscal year these taxes accounted for 89.3 percent of the state's income. The remaining sources of taxation are derived from an unusual combination of industries and what some refer to as "sin" activities. With respect to the former category, a special tax is levied on insurance companies doing business in California. Generally, the rate is 2.35 percent of the total premiums paid in the state, with a lower assessment rate for life insurance policies. Translated into budget dollars, the insurance tax amounted to $517 million or 2.5 percent of the state budget in 1981–82. The primary "sin" taxes are cigarette taxes ($202 million or 1.0 percent), liquor taxes ($147 million or 0.7 percent), and horse-racing taxes ($128 million or 0.6 percent). Although these taxes have widespread impact on consumers, their rates are considered low relative to other states. Together they amounted to only 2.3 percent of the general fund revenues for 1981–82.

The remaining taxes flowing into the state's general fund come from a variety of areas. These include motor vehicle fuel taxes (raised from 7 cents to 9 cents per gallon as of 1983), energy use surcharges, and various permit fees. Together this potpourri of miscellaneous taxes comes to about 3.7 percent of the state's revenues.

Before proceeding further, we should put California's income and tax policies into perspective. By almost any definition imaginable, California is a wealthy state with a high tax burden. Comparative state data assembled by the Council of State Governments showed that in 1978 California's per capita income of $8,927 ranked second behind Nevada ($9,439) when considering the forty-eight contiguous states. Examination of state tax obligations in 1979 revealed that California's per capita tax contributions of $720 ranked third behind Delaware ($845) and Minnesota ($772).[9] To be sure, these data are rough and do not consider a number of variables (such as additional local tax obligations, breakdown of tax types, and so on). Nevertheless, the state's income and taxes seem to be fairly compatible. Compatible or not, however, a number of Californians have taken action to lessen the tax burden. As we will see, Proposition 13 in 1978 was only the first of a several salvos to hit the state's treasury over the next few years.

TAX POLICIES IN THE 1980S: THE REVOLT GOES ON

Rather than satisfy Californians after its passage in 1978, Proposition 13's success seemed to spur them on to bigger and better things. After the legislature passed a revised budget in July 1978, it allocated $5 billion of the $6 billion surplus to cities, counties, special districts, and school districts. Thus, even after the "bail-out" distribution, the state was left with a $1 billion cushion. But thanks to a healthy economy and increased taxes from higher personal incomes, the state seemed to thrive in spite of Proposition 13. In May 1979 Richard Silberman, the state director of finance, revised earlier predictions and declared that the state would end the 1978–79 fiscal year with a $2.7 billion surplus. To tax reduction advocates Jarvis and Gann, these figures indicated that further trimming was in order. As Jarvis complained in 1979, "the fat is still there. The state legislature has spent $4 billion to $5 billion so that local governments will not have to cut away the fat."[10]

Inasmuch as the state "bail out" left local governments about $2 billion short of the previous year's revenues, they set about to reduce some services and charge for others. In the area of reductions cities closed parks, school districts ended free summer school, and local governments across the state eliminated almost all proposed capital projects. Meanwhile local governments increased or imposed new fees on various services in order to close the gap between revenues and expenditures. Consider a small sample of the numerous fee increases put into place immediately after Proposition 13's passage:

- Arcadia raised the admission tax at Santa Anita Racetrack.
- Garden Grove increased the cost of city-sponsored swimming lessons from $1 to $8.50.
- Culver City hiked the utility users tax from 8 percent to 14 percent.
- Inglewood enacted a fire service fee, street maintenance assessments, and a 10 percent tax on drinks sold at bars.
- Oakland adopted a 5 percent tax on entertainment events and boosted a residential property transfer tax by 50 percent.

- Sacramento doubled the zoo admission price to $1.50 and increased build-
  ing permit fees by 31 percent.

Dozens of local governments adopted various plans to compensate at least
partially for revenue losses. In a *Los Angeles Times* random survey of 110 cities,
counties, and other local government units, about half enacted new user levies
within a month of Proposition 13's passage.[11] Some of the increases were of a
serious nature, others were not. These events notwithstanding, tax reduction
proponents continued their efforts at minimizing the tax obligation at all levels
of government.

Proposition 4 (1979).   Fortified with news of the state government's continuing surplus in 1979, tax reduction leaders sought new means to curb
government spending. Paul Gann, coauthor of Proposition 13, organized a
new initiative drive to freeze state and local government appropriations at the
1978–79 levels, with built-in provisions for population increases and inflation.
Dubbed "the spirit of 13," the proposed constitutional amendment easily qualified for a November 1979 election.

This time state leaders seemed to be more in touch with the voter's mood.
Given their weakened credibility by opposing Proposition 13 the year before,
most public officials either remained neutral or supported what became known
as Proposition 4. In the "politics makes strange bedfellows" tradition, Assembly
Speaker Leo McCarthy—a staunch Proposition 13 opponent—wrote one of
the ballot arguments favoring the initiative. In McCarthy's words, "No government should have an unrestricted right to spend the taxpayers' money. . . .
Government should be subject to fiscal discipline no less than the citizens it
represents."[12]

Opponents to Proposition 4 claimed that its passage would nail the coffin on
California's economy and prevent any chance of recovery from the slashes
brought about by Proposition 13. Because the initiative prevented local governments from counting taxes from new industries or businesses as part of their
new tax base, opponents argued that Proposition 4's enactment would discourage growth.

Whatever the merits of the various arguments, the Proposition 4 battle was a
one-sided affair. While initiative supporters raised almost $1.5 million, oppo-
nents collected about $10,000! When the 1979 initiative was put to the voters
for their reaction, the measure passed by a 74 to 26 percent landslide.

Yet, for Gann and his supporters, their initiative election victory may have
been hollow. A study conducted by the Department of Finance 3 years after

Proposition 4's passage indicated that state spending for the 1982–83 fiscal year would be $1.7 billion *below* the limit established by the Gann formula.[13] For the time being, at least, Proposition 4 did not seem to be a budget-cutting measure.

Proposition 9 (1980). When Paul Gann led the fight to qualify Proposition 4 for the ballot, his former ally Howard Jarvis shied away from the effort. Jarvis argued that the initiative had too many contingency provisions to cut government growth seriously. To an extent Jarvis had a point. With continued population growth and substantial inflation in the early 1980s, the potential savings from Proposition 4 remained unclear. Most analysts agreed that only when these two factors subsided would Proposition 4 get its true test. Thus, unsatisfied with the Gann initiative, Jarvis designed a new tax-cutting measure that would provide immediate, tangible reductions. The seed was sown for what ultimately became known as Proposition 9 in 1980.

The new Jarvis effort took aim at California's personal income taxes. If enacted, the proposed constitutional amendment would cut the income tax in half, regardless of the taxpayer's bracket. Coupled with ongoing tax credits and deductions that would remain untouched, the proposition would actually reduce personal income tax obligations by 54 percent. For 1980–81, Legislative Analyst William Hamm estimated that the state treasury would suffer a loss of $4.9 billion, or about 25 percent of the state budget. In subsequent years the figure would hover between $4 and $5 billion. With a surplus in the $1 billion range, Hamm argued that the 1980–81 budget would be balanced only with drastic cuts in expenditures.

Fearful that Jarvis would equal his 1978 success, Governor Brown ordered all state departments to prepare 1980–81 budgets containing 30 percent cuts. He argued against the initiative on the grounds that Proposition 9 was a gimmick for the rich and that, if passed, would award 55 percent of the savings to only 10 percent of the state's taxpayers. This, along with substantial state cuts in health, education, and welfare programs, would create severe problems for the poor and middle classes.

Jarvis and his backers remained unimpressed. After gathering 800,000 signatures (250,000 more than necessary) to place Proposition 9 on the ballot, the well-known antitax crusader launched his new campaign. Declared Jarvis, "We are convinced the surplus in California is going to be bigger than it ever was. . . . [N]one of these disasters happened that they said would [after Proposition 13 passed]. . . . They're going to say this will destroy the state. We have a $3 billion bigger budget than we did last year."[14]

Jarvis's figures on budget increases were correct. But he failed to acknowl-edge that as part of the "bail-out" effort, the 1978–79 budget spent $1.1 billion more than the state collected; in 1979–80 the state spent another $1.5 billion more than it received. These deficits, combined with increases in the "bail-out" funds, all but wiped out the once $6 billion surplus. Unbalanced budgets like these ultimately led to California's fiscal crisis of 1983.

When the votes were counted, the Jarvis balloon finally popped. Organized labor, public employee organizations, the state Parent-Teacher Association, and senior citizen groups mounted a formidable campaign against the tax-cutting initiative. Given a deteriorating economy and uncertainties over the long-term impact of Proposition 13, Californians defeated Proposition 9 by a decisive 61 to 39 percent margin. Once again, though, the tax issue was the election's major drawing card. About 500,000 more people cast votes on this issue than they did for the presidential candidates from all the political parties combined, proving that taxation remained high on the public agenda. The only difference this time was that the voters were unwilling to take another tax-cutting step—at least for the moment.

Propositions 5 and 6 (1982). In 1980, the same year in which the voters defeated Howard Jarvis's Proposition 9, the state budget climbed 14.1 percent. Even when controlled for inflation, real expenditures increased by 5.4 percent. During the 1980–81 fiscal year, California's state budget rose again, this time by 13.9 percent, or 4.8 percent when controlled for inflation. A curious para-dox plagued California. Although opponents warned that the state could not live with Proposition 9's cuts, the state's coffers bulged. What most observers failed to recognize, however, was that these gains would be short-lived.

Indeed the 1980–81 fiscal year represented an unfortunate turnaround for California's (and the nation's) economy. Between January 1980 and December 1981, unemployment in California rose from 6.1 percent to 8.9 percent. Other problems troubled the state as well: dramatic reductions in corporate profits (down 8.2 percent) and housing starts (down 13.8 percent). Predictably, the state budget reflected these changes beginning in 1981. With less money flow-ing in, the 1981–82 budget increased by only 4.4 percent, or an actual 4.0 percent decrease in real dollars when controlled for inflation.

The sudden shift in the state's financial condition caused great concern among California's leading economists and political leaders. But for those who noted the apparently large budget increases of 1979–80 and 1980–81 in spite of Propositions 13 and 4, such alarm seemed little more than a California version of the boy who cried "wolf" one too many times. Turning to other traditional sources of revenue, the tax reduction forces focused on California's inheritance and gift taxes.

A long history of antagonism has surrounded the inheritance tax concept. Opponents have argued that taxing estates represents a "double tax"; taxes are first paid when the money is earned and paid again after one's death. Proponents have countered that the inheritance tax serves as a painless way of equalizing wealth and accruing badly needed revenues. As inflation increased during the 1970s and the sizes of estates grew proportionately, division over this issue intensified.

In 1982 Propositions 5 and 6 were placed on the June ballot. Both propositions were written to abolish the state's inheritance and gift taxes, a financial package that would cost the state treasury about $500 million per year.[15] Given the financial setbacks described earlier, passage of this initiative would cut deeply into California's revenue sources. Governor Brown said as much in April 1982 and urged voter rejection of Propositions 5 and 6 because "we can't afford tax cuts this year" as the state faced a potential deficit in 1982–83 of $1.4 billion.[16]

Anticipating the implications of outright inheritance and gift tax elimination, the legislature attempted to defuse the issue with a 1981 law that reduced the inheritance tax by 27 percent. It was hoped that this change—coupled with the claim that 50 percent of the inheritance tax repeal benefits would go to 6 percent of the population—would discourage voter approval of Propositions 5 and 6.

Despite the legislature's effort and the governor's warning, the voters remained hungry for tax reduction. In the June 1982 election both propositions passed by nearly two-to-one margins, thus further cutting into the state's shrinking treasury.

Proposition 7 (1982).   Inflation presents at least two serious problems for the typical wage earner. First, it tends to erode purchasing power; moreover, annual cost-of-living increases tend to lag behind increased costs brought about by inflation. Second, when salaries do increase in response to the inflationary cycle, those with higher incomes find themselves in higher tax brackets. Thus, as a result of "bracket creep," one's new income tax liability may offset the benefits of any wage increases in an inflationary year. In fact, on some occasions, the combination of income increase and bracket creep can lead to a net income loss if the higher taxes are more than the wage addition.

During the late 1970s and early 1980s, California and the nation were wracked by double-digit inflation. As a result of bracket creep on a mass scale,

California's personal income tax payers discovered a larger and larger percentage of their paychecks going to the state treasury in the form of higher withholding schedules. To cite a case in point, during the 1977–78 fiscal year, Californians paid $4.7 billion in personal income taxes. During the next 12 months, the Consumer Price Index (the nation's most respected inflation indicator) rose 9.2 percent. Meanwhile, during the 1978–79 fiscal year in California, personal income taxes jumped from $4.7 to $5.8 billion, or a 23 percent increase. In other words, because of bracket creep, taxes were rising faster than inflation.

Even with the smashing victory of Proposition 9 in 1978, the voters sensed that they were not getting their money's worth in real tax relief. And they were right, partially because of bracket creep and partially because Proposition 9's lower local property taxes reduced an important itemized area from state income tax obligations. Yet the reasons for this phenomenon were not as important as the continued public outcry for meaningful and permanent tax relief.

Attempting to alleviate the public's anxiety, state legislators tried to do something about the spiraling personal income tax and bracket creep. In 1978, A.B. 3802 (Kapiloff–Dem.) provided that the state's eleven income tax brackets be indexed annually by the amount of inflation exceeding 3 percent. Therefore, if inflation rose at an annual rate of, say, 10 percent, then the tax brackets would be adjusted upward by 7 percent. In 1979, A.B. 276 (Bergeson–Rep.) established *complete* indexing but for only the 1980 and 1981 income years. (Governor Brown vetoed subsequent legislative efforts to make complete indexing permanent.) Beginning in 1982, the state was scheduled to resume its partial indexing formula.

Given the scheduled termination of A.B. 276 in 1982, an initiative drive was organized to continue full income indexing on an annual basis. As with previous tax-cutting measures, Howard Jarvis was a prime sponsor of this effort. The initiative ultimately was placed on the ballot as Proposition 7.

Assessing the financial impact of Proposition 7, the state's legislative analyst calculated that full income indexing would reduce the state's collections by $230 million in 1982–83, $450 million in 1983–84, and larger amounts thereafter. Proponents of the measure argued that the proposition represented California's only hope to cope with inflation. Failure to pass the initiative, they contended, would result in a net tax hike if the state reverted to its 3 percent plus formula. Opponents countered that a continuation of full indexing was regressive because 75 percent of the extra benefits from Proposition 7 would go to the state's wealthiest 25 percent. Moreover, they pointed out that a substantial portion of the reduction from full indexing would be illusory, inasmuch as lower state income taxes would mean lower deductions and, hence, higher federal income taxes.

When the June 1982 election dust settled, Proposition 7 joined Propositions 5 and 6 in the winner's circle. By a sweeping margin of 63 to 37 percent, the electorate voted to continue complete indexing. This outcome represented yet another blow to California's battered state treasury.

California's Tax Sources in Perspective

Two observations become clear when assessing the state tax picture in California. One of these points is obvious; the other, more subtle. First, the state has developed a diversified base of revenue raising, although, as we will see, some of that diversity has been lost in recent years. By relying on a variety of tax sources, the state government has enlarged as its population has grown. In 1942 the state had a population of 7,441,000 people. (Los Angeles County has about that many today!) Total state revenues for the 1942 fiscal year amounted to $388 million.[17] Given a current population of 23 million people and a 1984–85 budget in the $30 billion range, much has changed over a brief 40 year period. Modernization, expanded public services, bureaucratic growth, and, of course, inflation have made previous budgets pale when they are compared with their successors. These changes parallel the growth of the nation as well as those of other industrialized states. Nonetheless, they remain stunning in magnitude.

Money and population nowithstanding, a second, less publicized development has emerged with California's tax-collecting efforts. Over the years some taxes have remained relatively constant with respect to their percentage of the tax base. Others have changed markedly. Figure 9–1 illustrates the consistency of the bank and corporation taxes (ranging between 8.6 and 15.7 percent) and the sales taxes (ranging between 28.5 and 39 percent). Yet dramatic changes have occurred to the extent to which the personal income tax has grown as a revenue source relative to other tax sources. Whereas the tax accounted for less than 10 percent of all state revenues before 1957, it quickly grew to more than 35 percent by 1982. Meanwhile the inheritance tax, which at one time amounted to as much as 4 percent of the state's annual revenues, was eliminated in 1982. Also, fuel taxes, comprising 18.3 percent of all revenues in 1942, had dwindled to less than 4 percent by 1982.[18]

When these developments are considered together, the changing revenue collection pattern in California suggests a dramatic tax burden shift over a comparatively short period of time. Indeed one of the critical issues facing Californians during the 1980s will center on the degree to which they are willing to pay higher personal income taxes to keep the state afloat while other tax sources remain less utilized.

FIGURE 9-1   California's Tax Burden, 1942–82

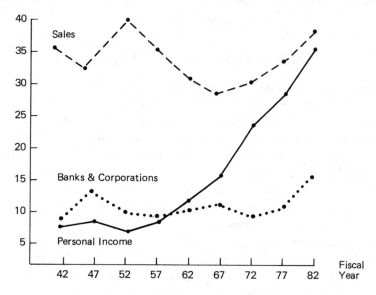

DWINDLING FEDERAL ASSISTANCE—ANOTHER DOOR SHUT

As the 1980s wore on and the federal government's reduced expenditures took shape, California was not left unscarred. Embarking on his "new federalism," President Reagan promised to get the federal government out of areas that in the days before President Franklin D. Roosevelt had been reserved for state activity alone. Thus began a deliberate effort to shift basic social welfare responsibilities from the federal government to the states, so that the latter faced the unpleasant choice of reducing services or finding new monies to replace lost federal revenues. For fiscal 1983 the president's proposed budget reduced federal contributions to ongoing federal and state programs in California by $1.5 to $2.0 billion. Some of the leading reductions included the following areas:

- *Food stamps:* $129.6 million less than the previous year.
- *Medi-Cal:* $240 million in federal reductions.
- *Medicare:* $250 million less in federal benefits.
- *Job-training programs:* $42 million less in federal contributions.
- *Aid to families with dependent children:* $400–550 million less in federal funds.

- *Social services and child welfare:* $87 million less than granted in 1982.
- *Child nutrition:* $26 million less than in 1982.
- *Education:* $131 million less for a variety of programs.[19]

Although the Reagan administration did not eliminate these programs per se, it did cut down the funds for them, leaving the states to either pick up the slack or accept the reductions. In California the choice was obvious. Faced with a state budget already in the red and limited local government revenue-raising abilities via Proposition 13, the state bit the bullet. The result was a state government able to provide even less than previously anticipated.

The wide range of funding cuts initiated by the Reagan administration was actually the second half of a double-barrel federal blast at California's treasury. Until October 1980 the state had enjoyed income from a popular program known as *Revenue Sharing.* Unlike other federal grant-in-aid programs, Revenue Sharing issued annual grants to states and local governments for use in virtually any area. State governments received one-third of these funds annually (approximately $2.3 billion), and local governments were awarded two-thirds of the funds (about $4.6 billion). For a number of states and communities with limited revenue-raising abilities, federal revenue sharing had become the difference between balanced and unbalanced budgets. But when the State and Local Government Assistance Act was extended by Congress in 1980 for another 3 years, the portion of direct state aid was eliminated. For California the loss amounted to about $276 million that would no longer be flowing into the state's general fund from Washington.

IMPACTS ON CALIFORNIA SPENDING: THE BROAD PICTURE

California has a history of being generous to schools, welfare recipients, and local government assistance programs. Yet few political propositions are cast in concrete. As the times change, the voters change, too. When California passed Proposition 13 in 1978, the state and its electorate charted a new course for spending patterns as well as revenues.

Given a sizable state surplus and a robust economy during the end of the 1970s, California presented a much healthier picture than actually existed. From 1978 on, the state government spent more monies than it collected from its various revenue sources. Observers knew that it would be only a matter of time before the well ran dry. The 1982–83 fiscal year became the watershed year. For the first time since the Great Depression, the budget declined in current as well as constant dollars.

Of the ten major state spending areas designated in Table 9-2, 1982–83 funding commitments were reduced in six categories, increased in three, and unchanged in one. The state's share of Medi-Cal—a program caring for one out of every eight Californians—was reduced by 9 percent. State expenditures on welfare programs were cut by 5 percent, and another 280,000 people receiving state welfare support were placed under county jurisdictions and funding responsibilities.

Funding for the two major university systems (University of California and California State Universities) remained virtually unchanged in the face of increasing enrollments. Meanwhile the state raised UC fees by $200 per year and CSU fees by $100. In other areas the state legislature reduced its own operating expenses by 4 percent, and salaries of 230,000 state employees were frozen at current levels. All of these commitments suggested policies ranging from nearly identical funding to slight cuts from the 1981–82 fiscal year, although the preceding year's 7.4 percent inflation rate meant that the same dollar would not go as far in 1982–83 as they did the year before.

But the biggest losers in the 1982–83 budget were the state's cities. Having appropriated $166 million in 1981–82 for general relief, the state halved the figure to $83 million in 1982–83. This change, coupled with reductions in state funding for local assistance, community colleges, and programs for the elderly and disabled, left the local governments in the most precarious position since the passage of Proposition 13. Moreover, with a two-thirds vote required in order to raise property taxes for added local revenues, it was not likely that the cities would be able to offset their depleting state funds.

TABLE 9-2   State Budget: A Comparison

	1981-82 ($, in millions)	1982-83	Change (%)
State operations	2,520	2,480	−2
Legislature	98.8	94.4	−4
Medi-Cal	2,670	2,430	−9
Welfare	2,570	2,440	−5
Schools	7,230	7,420	+3
Universities	1,100	1,140	+4
State universities	960	960	0
Community colleges	1,070	1,060	−1
Cities	166	83	−50
Counties	2,080	2,260	+9
Total state budget	25,400	25,200	−1

Source: Legislative Analyst.

Clearly, the 1982–83 state budget was the creation of all the tax changes adopted between 1978 and 1982. Yet reaction to the document was far from unanimous. Predictably, evaluations of the budget went hand in hand with the political persuasions of the evaluators. Democratic State Senator Diane Watson, whose district has a disproportionately poor, black population lamented: "We're sacrificing our poor, our handicapped, our senior citizens, our children to balance the budget."[20] At the other end of the political spectrum, Proposition 13 proponent William Campbell, a State Senator from an affluent district, noted that the state was finally synchronizing itself with the voters' attitude on less government spending: "This year, ladies and gentlemen, we bit the bullet. You check the bullet, there are teeth marks on it."[21] But the question remained, what political indigestion would the electorate suffer as a result of its new diet?

Taxation, California Style: Some Final Thoughts

California's tax policies have grown, shifted, and sputtered during the state's evolution. Yet the most dramatic changes in the tax arena are of comparatively recent vintage. Between the Great Depression and 1978 the state developed new taxes both to meet commitments for increased services and to cope with an exploding population. During this 50 year period, the state government embarked on a massive water network, thousands of miles of highways, a three-tiered higher education system, aggressive agriculture support, a string of social welfare programs for the destitute and underprivileged, and numerous other policy decisions designed to meet the state's current and future needs. All of these endeavors cost money, and the growth changes in tax patterns reflected the state's willingness to bear those costs.

In recent years California's elected policymakers and voters apparently have reconsidered their tax policies. And with this rethinking has come concurrent reductions not only in tax obligation but in state and local commitments as well. This reversal has not been unique to California; a number of states lowered their priorities to match incomes during the late 1970s.

By the mid-1980s most state governments opted for tax increases to cope with troubled economies and needy sectors of society. Between 1980 and 1983 the state tax surplus for the fifty states, $6.5 billion, evaporated to a near break-even figure of $291 million. To prepare for a worsening crunch, thirty-four states enacted permanent tax increases in 1983 to compensate for unbalanced budgets.[22]

California seemed on the verge of a major tax increase in 1983. Focusing on a $1.5 billion deficit and education woes, the legislature's Democratic majority proposed a one cent increase in the sales tax. But Republican Governor Deukmejian resisted any major changes other than $466 million in "loophole closures" and general belt-tightening measures. Given the voters' recent behavior at the polls, Deukmejian's posture was probably more in touch with the public pulse than the proposals put forth by the legislature's Democratic majority.

What may be said of the tax revolt in California? Have the state's leaders and voters acted with prudence or callous disregard for the public good? Although there are no simple answers to these questions, three propositions deserve final consideration. First, in a state that makes great use of the initiative and referendum, the major tax policy changes of the late 1970s and 1980s have been carved out by the voters, not the legislature. The legislature has moved toward tax policy alterations only when its members felt that ballot initiatives were excessive, or that perhaps as a result of public antipathy, their jobs were in jeopardy. Such was the case in 1978 with a belated referendum, Proposition 8, designed to reduce the threat of Proposition 13. Similar defensive actions were carried out in 1980 (indexing) and 1982 (inheritance taxes). All of these cases share a common theme—the legislature's inability or unwillingness to move except under the public's "initiative gun."

Second, the combination of the legislature's immobility and the public's activism has done more than simply *reduce* the tax burden for Californians—it has led to a *relative shift* in the tax burden as well. While sales taxes and bank and general corporation taxes have remained basically unchanged, the weight of the personal income tax has grown heavy on the taxpayer's back. Reduction in federal funding has only exacerbated the revenue-raising dilemma. Given this shift, it is little wonder that the public has cut and slashed tax obligations wherever it could control its own destiny.

Third, despite many good intentions regarding the changes effected between 1978 and 1982, the jury is still out in terms of the overall benefits that tax cuts have or have not brought to the state. Clearly, one cumulative result from the tax policy shifts has been for more dollars to remain in people's pockets, although the benefits have hardly been across the board. Equally important, the state has had to pare back funding for virtually all state and local government programs. Is this trade-off acceptable to Californians? In his book *The Responsible Electorate*, V. O. Key wrote that "voters are not fools. . . . [T]he electorate behaves about as rationally and responsibly as we should expect. . . ."[23] By contrast, political activist Howard Jarvis once evaluated the public's sophistication by claiming that "people who decide elections don't read."[24] How do we reconcile these perceptions? The answer may not be clear until the budget cuts of the eighties filter down to the public originally responsible for them.

Notes

[1] A national CBS-*New York Times* poll conducted in 1978 found that "Californians [as well as other states] strongly favored cutting back services instead of adding new taxes to make up for lost revenue from property taxes. In California, the finding was 61 percent to 25; elsewhere, 61 percent to 19." See *New York Times*, June 28, 1978.

[2] "Ballot Proposition Analysis," *California Journal* (May 1978): 6.

[3] *Los Angeles Times*, January 16, 1978.

[4] "Maniac or Messiah," *Time*, June 19, 1978, p. 19.

[5] *Los Angeles Times*, January 23, 1978.

[6] "Sound and Fury over Taxes," *Time*, June 19, 1978, p. 13.

[7] As of 1981, the following districts imposed the ½ percent "Transit District Transactions" tax:

Bay Area Rapid Transit District (San Francisco, Alameda, and Contra Costa Counties)

Los Angeles County Transit District

Santa Clara County Transit District

Santa Cruz Metropolitan Transit District

The number of people in these counties constituted 48.5 percent of the state's population. Source: California State Board of Equalization, *Annual Report* 1980–81 (Sacramento, 1981), p. 54.

[8] For a detailed comparative study of state and local tax obligations, see Stephen E. Lile, "Family Tax Burdens Among the States," *State Government* XLVIV, no. 1 (Winter 1976): 9–17.

[9] See The Council of State Governments, *The Book of the States* 1980–1981: 23 (Lexington, Mass.: The Council of State Governments), pp. 343, 350.

[10] Quoted in *The Christian Science Monitor*, June 13, 1979, p. 85.

[11] *Los Angeles Times*, July 3, 1978.

[12] Secretary of State, *Ballot Proposition Arguments*, 1979 Special Elections, p. 7.

[13] Report of the Legislative Analyst, *Analysis of the Budget Bill of the State of California for the Fiscal Year July 1, 1982 to June 30, 1983* (State of California), February 1982, B-2.

[14] *Los Angeles Times*, February 10, 1980.

[15] Although essentially the same in their objectives, the propositions contained slight differences. Proposition 5 had a retroactive clause (January 1, 1981); Proposition 6 forbade any future attempts by the legislature to reenact these taxes. The secretary of state's office therefore ruled that the proposition with the most votes would become operative. Proposition 6 carried by a 64 to 36 percent margin; Proposition 5 won 62 to 38 percent.

[16]*Los Angeles Times*, April 21, 1982.

[17]California used a biennial budget until the constitution was amended in 1966. Thus, between July 1, 1941 and June 30, 1943 the state budget was actually $776 million.

[18]In 1981, S.B. 215 (Foran–Dem.) increased motor fuel taxes from 7 to 9 cents per gallon, along with fees for drivers' licenses and automobile registration. The fuel tax increase did not go into effect until January 1, 1983.

[19]*Los Angeles Times*, February 8, 1982.

[20]*Los Angeles Times*, June 4, 1982.

[21]Ibid.

[22]See "Budgets: A Nationwide Struggle," *Los Angeles Times*, July 7, 1983.

[23]V. O. Key, *The Responsible Electorate* (Cambridge, Mass.: Belknap Press, 1966), p. 7.

[24]*Los Angeles Times*, February 10, 1980.

10
EDUCATION POLICY

The Politics Behind
"Why Johnny Can't Read"

Public education in California has a history as the state's most serious and expensive commitment. When California voters approved a new sales tax in 1933, they did so as part of a constitutional amendment that placed public education at the top of all policy priorities. Public education would be granted "a superior right" to state revenues, the amendment declared. In 1983, 50 years later, Governor George Deukmejian assumed office with a strict "no new taxes" pledge, regardless of the state's problems. Yet Democrats and Republicans in the legislature were of a single mind in forcing the governor to accept new taxes (Deukmejian called them "loophole" closures) so that an additional $500 million could be pumped into the state's number-one priority: a troubled education system.

Education is big business in California. One of every five residents is engaged full time in K–12 education, as a student, teacher, or support staff employee. So many children attend public schools that California's elementary and secondary students exceed the total populations of thirty states.[1] These figures suggest a huge financial commitment as well. Prior to the last-minute scuffle for additional monies in 1983, the Legislative Analyst's Office estimated that over $13.5 billion would be spent on California's 4.2 million students during fiscal 1983–84, or about $3200 per student.[2] But despite the state's historical commitment and the appearance of massive funding, education policy is at a crossroads in the mid-1980s.

Several issues have converged to raise serious questions about contemporary education in California. The most prominent concern centers on the best way to fund the state's 1044 separate school districts, a matter that has been argued for more than 15 years through the courts as *Serrano* v. *Priest*. This single case touches on a variety of issues including equality of opportunity, state versus local autonomy, taxation, and the problems related to redistribution of wealth.

Even as the leading government agencies have attempted to resolve *Serrano*, other problems have surfaced in California's public education system. In recent years students have scored poorly on national tests, classroom sizes have increased, and high school dropout rates have set new records. These problems have persisted even as state funding has grown steadily. How do we explain these developments? To what extent are they the results of poorly conceived programs, administrative failures, inadequate teachers, or financial commitments that have not kept up with inflation? Inasmuch as education policy is a cornerstone of state government, these questions must be addressed as part of our understanding of California politics.

The Struggle over Educational Finance: *Serrano* v. *Priest*

In 1968 John Serrano, acting on behalf of his son, Andrew, filed a class action suit over California's long-standing method of education funding. Little did Serrano know that the repercussions from this single case would shake the foundations of school finance not only throughout California but across the country. Serrano argued that the state's system of school finance discriminated against students who lived in low wealth districts with poor property tax bases. At that time 55.7 percent of California educational revenues came from local property taxes.[3] State Treasurer Ivy Baker Priest was named defendant because her office had the responsibility for sending state aid to local school districts.

THE ISSUE

Serrano brought suit because of the state's inattention to the funding disparities that existed from district to district. For its part the state of California was not concerned with equal funding as part of its education policy objective. Rather, the state distributed funds in such a way that all school districts would be guaranteed a minimum level of support. To this extent, state assistance only reinforced the inequities that existed at the local levels.

Prior to 1972, when the State Supreme Court issued its first decision on the *Serrano* case, each school district obtained local education finance from a set tax rate on assessed property values. The problem with this system, according to Serrano, was that the property tax base varied significantly from district to district. For example, in 1969–70 the wealthiest elementary school district in the state had almost 10,000 times more assessed valuation per pupil than the poorest district.[4] Low wealth districts were forced to establish high tax rates to guarantee moderate revenues, while high wealth districts could produce

TABLE 10-1   Comparison of School District Tax Rates and Expenditure
Levels in Selected Counties: 1968–69

County	ADA*	Assessed value per ADA* ($)	Tax rate ($)	Expenditure per ADA ($)
Alameda				
Emery Unified	586	100,187	2.57	2,223
Newark Unified	8,638	6,048	5.65	616
Fresno				
Colinga Unified	2,640	33,244	2.17	963
Clovis Unified	8,144	6,480	4.28	565
Kern				
Rio Bravo Elementary	121	136,271	1.05	1,545
Lamont Elementary	1,847	5,971	3.06	533
Los Angeles				
Beverly Hills Unified	5,542	50,885	2.38	1,232
Baldwin Park Unified	13,108	3,706	5.48	577

*Average daily attendance.
Source: Legislative Analyst, *Public School Finance, Part V, Current Issues in Educational Finance* (1970), p. 8. Reprinted in *Serrano v. Priest* (487 P.2d 1241, 1252).

equivalent revenues at a much lower rate. The differences were dramatic. As Table 10-1 illustrates, Beverly Hills generated over twice the expenditure levels of nearby Baldwin Park with less than half the tax rate. Consequently, the money available for one's education was to a large degree a function of where one lived. Unresolved was the larger question of whether the differences in funding levels related to any differences in educational quality. In Serrano's eyes, the answer was "yes."

Serrano's selection of State Treasurer Priest as the respondent in his suit was more than a symbolic gesture. The plaintiff argued that in addition to school district expenditure levels unjustifiably based on local wealth considerations, the state was at fault because it permitted heavy reliance on local property taxes and did not use its funds to equalize the disparities. In fact, the suit argued that the state formula actually widened the expenditure gap between poor and wealthy districts.

State funds for education were divided into two categories: basic and equalization aid. "Basic aid" consisted of a set amount ($125) that was allocated to each student regardless of a district's need. Thus, students in Beverly Hills received as much basic aid as their significantly poorer counterparts in Baldwin Park. "Equalization aid," although generally apportioned in varying amounts, had the primary function of bringing the poorest districts up to state minimums. Regardless of the type of aid, the bottom line was simple: the state had no desire to equalize the vast differences created at the local levels. The constitutionality of this attitude became a focal concern in the *Serrano v. Priest* case.

WINDING THROUGH THE COURTS

Serrano v. Priest has had an unusually complicated judicial history. There have been a number of court trials, two major State Supreme Court decisions, and subsequent questions still in litigation. In 1983, 15 years after the original filing date, a Los Angeles Superior Court judge held that the state had achieved "significant parity" and, therefore, compliance with earlier Supreme Court decisions. Yet pointing to wide differences in Los Angeles County alone ($1,792 per pupil in the Paramount School District vs. $2,772 in Beverly Hills), Serrano advocates promised a series of appeals up the judicial ladder.[5]

When John Serrano first filed suit claiming that the state's financing system was fundamentally unfair and unequal, the defendants countered that the case had no legal standing. They contended that questions about variations in money-raising abilities and tax rates were irrelevant, because no law or constitutional provision pertained to such differences. The original trial court agreed with this position and dismissed the case. But Serrano appealed to the California Supreme Court. In October 1971 the state's highest court reversed the trial court's dismissal and ordered that the case be heard on the facts. Citing the "equal protection clause" of the Fourteenth Amendment in the United States Constitution, the court's six-to-one opinion declared:

> We have determined that this funding scheme invidiously discriminates against the poor because it makes the quality of a child's education a function of the wealth of his parents and neighbors. Recognizing as we must that the right to an education in our public schools is a fundamental interest which cannot be conditioned on wealth, we can discern no compelling state purpose necessitating the present method of financing.[6]

The Supreme Court's decision held for the first time that education is a fundamental right that cannot be conditioned on wealth. Moreover, education is an indispensable necessity for two important reasons: "First, education is a major determinant of an individual's chances for economic and social success in our competitive society; second, education is a unique influence on a child's development as a citizen and his participation in political and community life."[7] After determining that the state's needs were not served by the present educational finance system, the high court took its action. Two and a half years later a Los Angeles County Superior Court found for Serrano.

On April 10, 1974, Los Angeles County Superior Court Judge Bernard Jefferson declared that the state's financing system for public education was in violation of both the Fourteenth Amendment and the California Constitution's "equal protection of the laws" provision. Judge Jefferson noted that although there is no constitutional requirement for a particular level of financial support, the California Constitution requires that expenditure levels not be based on wealth considerations. To achieve equality, he ordered per pupil expenditures apart from categorical–special needs programs be reduced to "insignificant differences, which mean amounts considerably less than $100 per pupil within a maximum period of six years."[8]

Once again the decision was appealed, although this time by the defendants. But this time the State Supreme Court was not interested. On December 30, 1976 the justices upheld the judgment of the trial court in what became known as *Serrano II* (18 cal 3d 728). The Supreme Court concluded that the trial court had "properly determined on findings supported by substantial evidence that . . . the financing system before it was invalid as denying equal protection of the laws as guaranteed by the California Constitution [and that the court's factual determinations were supported by] no less than 299 findings of fact, none of which is challenged by defendants as lacking in substantial support."[9] Although the decision would be challenged again as too lenient, for the time being the issue was settled. Faced with the unpleasant choice of cutting assistance to the wealthiest districts or providing massive funds for the poorest, the legislature could no longer escape responsibility to remedy a school finance system repeatedly declared unfair and constitutional.

LEGISLATIVE EFFORTS TO COMPLY WITH SERRANO

If the efforts to solve the problems of educational finance seemed to be frustrated by a judicial "hall of mirrors," resolution was just as elusive in the legislature. Caught between the Supreme Court's order for equal finance and a shortage of funds, the legislature inched its way toward compromise. In fact, it took three pieces of legislation—S.B. 90 (1972), A.B. 65 (1977), and S.B. 154 (1978)—before the legislature managed to silence critics in and out of the judiciary. Even then its efforts remained without challenge only until 1980, when *Serrano* allies attacked the legislature's final plan as too little, too late.

Senate Bill 90 (1972). Initially, the legislature modified the school finance system by passing Senate Bill 90, known as the "Property Tax Relief Act of

1972." This measure increased the state contribution from approximately 30 percent to 44 percent of the total cost and decreased local contributions to the 50 percent level. But more than money was at stake. Responding to the equal finance issue, the new law contained a provision that would gradually limit taxes raised by school districts unless the voters there elected to do so. Education critic Kenneth Karst noted that the combination of more state money and local spending limits was designed to bring wealthy and poor districts closer together, "provided that the voters of wealthier districts approve no [tax rate] overrides."[10]

Even with the override disclaimer, S.B. 90 faced criticism almost as soon as it was put in place. *Serrano* allies argued that under the legislature's gradual plan, the "time limit anticipated for the revenue limits of high-spending districts to coverage with the revenues guaranteed low wealth districts was 20 years. . . . Property wealth, in other words, would continue to influence school district spending levels for many years. . . ."[11] Recognition of these defects led Judge Jefferson to invalidate S.B. 90 and the state's school finance system in 1974. The legislature had to begin again.

Assembly Bill 65 (1977). In 1977, after the State Supreme Court upheld the Jefferson decision in *Serrano II*, the legislature passed another school finance equalization scheme. A.B. 65 attempted to equalize the financial burden in several ways. First, it increased the ability of low wealth school districts to raise revenue, but slowed down the same ability for wealthy districts. Second, A.B. 65 provided special incentives for low wealth districts to raise tax rates; if, after their efforts, the districts failed to raise enough, the state would contribute the necessary money to raise district funds to an established minimum. Finally, the new law included a requirement that excess monies raised by high wealth districts would go to the state "for redistribution to low wealth districts as equalization aid."[12] Equalization experts hoped that the new law would finally bring the state's diverse districts to within the $100 window provided by *Serrano*.

Many of the equalization features of A.B. 65 were to take effect on July 1, 1978, for the 1978–79 school year. But a crushing blow struck local district revenue sources when California voters approved Proposition 13 on June 6, 1978. With property taxes cut by 57 percent, California's education system was hit hard. Proposition 13 cost the schools approximately $2.8 billion in lost local revenues.[13] In addition, with property taxes in high wealth areas now cut back drastically, the hope for redistributing revenues from high to low wealth districts was shattered.

Senate Bill 154 (1978).   The fiscal year in California runs from July 1 to the next June 30. Thus, when the voters cut property taxes by a total of $7 billion on June 6, the legislature had about 3 weeks to respond to a variety of local needs. Education was foremost among them. In an attempt to keep local services functioning, the legislature passed S.B. 154, generally known as the "bail-out" bill. Various versions of the "bail out" have been passed each year since 1978, although the original $4.5 billion was reduced to less than half by 1982–83.

Under the education portion of S.B. 154, the state attempted to equalize expenditure disparities to the extent that financial limitations permitted. Low wealth districts received 91 percent of what their total revenues would have been prior to Proposition 13, while high wealth districts were limited to 85 percent of expected revenues. With the clamp on local fund raising, the state now assumed 58 percent of the K–12 education bill. Yet the *Serrano* plaintiffs were not satisfied. The legislature's aid formula, they argued, enabled wealthy districts "to continue their historic spending advantage over poor districts."[14] The battle over education finance continued.

SERRANO II

On June 23, 1980, the Western Center on Law and Poverty petitioned on behalf of the *Serrano* plantiffs, seeking enforcement of the California State Supreme Court's judgment in *Serrano II*. The Western Center lawyers claimed that only 37 percent of the state's students and 27 percent of the school districts fell within the $100 per pupil range. The Beverly Hills–Baldwin Park comparison, cited in 1968, was rekindled in *Serrano II*. For example, in 1982, the plaintiffs argued, Beverly Hills outspent Baldwin Park by a margin of $2858 to $1842 per student for all educational services.[15] With California now funding 64 percent of all K–12 education costs, the slightest hint of noncompliance suggested the possible reallocation of billions of dollars up and down the state. The legislature's efforts notwithstanding, *Serrano* allies contended that California had not complied with the Supreme Court's order.

The state of California countered that its funding formula had placed the overwhelming majority of students within the court-ordered equalization plan. The state's claim was based on two critical assumptions. First, they argued that the $100 range issued in 1974 was at least $200 in 1982 if adjusted for inflation. Because all other indexes and tax formulas accounted for inflation, the $100 figure deserved adjustment as well. Second, the defendants contended that there were two ways to approach the funding issue. One way, base revenues, represented the primary reason for state money—to promote basic education services. The state opted for this criterion because all districts receive base revenues. Another way, total revenues, included a variety of programs for such categories as declining enrollment, home-to-school transportation, meals for the needy, and a dozen other special areas. The state argued that this was an inappropriate way to measure compliance. According to this logic, in 1982, 93.6 percent of all school children were in school districts with expenditures within the $100 band;[16] all of which demonstrated the state's sincere effort to carry out the court's order. Thus, with the plaintiffs and defendants at odds over definitions, the compliance question had two parts: whether it had been carried out and which terms were correct?

On April 28, 1983 Superior Court Judge Lester Olson ruled that the state was justified in its use of the inflation adjustment concept. The judge also agreed that the base revenue approach represented the correct means for measuring compliance of the *Serrano II* judgment. Given these determinations, the rest was a foregone conclusion: "All of the evidence points to an effort on the part of the Superintendent of Public Instruction and the Legislature to comply with the letter and the spirit of *Serrano II*, while coping with all of the other monumental-fiscal problems in California," Judge Olson wrote.[17] Although new State Superintendent of Public Instruction Bill Honig was pleased, *Serrano* advocates promised an appeal. As one chapter of the education finance saga closed, another was about to begin.

The Cost of Education: What We Pay, What We Get

The equality question in educational finance is first cousin to the state's general financial commitment to the entire education issue. Does the state spend enough for education? Do the taxpayers get their "money's worth"? Finally, what criteria do we use to answer these and other questions related to the costs and benefits derived from public education?

The *Serrano* plaintiffs argued that the amount spent on a child's education is a key determinant of the education quality received by a child; in other words, dollars make a difference in helping a student learn. Although this proposition may have some intuitive appeal, the available evidence is far from clear. A few education scholars have suggested that the schooling-achievement relationship is insignificant compared to the influence of the student's home environment or social class. Studies by James Coleman in the late 1960s and Christopher Jencks in the early 1970s indicated that school inputs had only a marginal impact upon students.[18] But the *Serrano* case produced different results.

When the State Supreme Court in *Serrano I* sent the case back to superior court for trial on the merits, experts provided volumes of testimony on the schooling-achievement question. After considering all of the evidence, Judge Jefferson concluded "that a school district's per pupil expenditure level does play a significant role in determining whether pupils are receiving a low-quality or a high-quality educational program as measured by the pupil test-score results on the standardized achievement tests."[19] Regardless of any other issues, this concept was accepted as the centerpiece of all future discussions. The question was not over whether money improved educational achievement, but whether it was provided in a fair and constitutional manner.

ELEMENTARY AND SECONDARY SCHOOLS

About 89 percent of the children in California attend public schools. Of the remaining 11 percent who opt for other alternatives, the largest share—two-thirds—select Catholic schools; the others go to other parochial schools or secular private schools. Nevertheless, with nine out of every ten children in the public sector, education funding receives considerable government attention at the state and local levels.

Californians have long prided themselves on their generous funding for education and the quality of instruction. During the 1982–83 fiscal year, the legislature allocated $8.2 billion for elementary and secondary schools, or 73 percent of all the monies spent in education. In fact, for a number of years, K–12 education has received more money than any other item in the state budget. But numbers alone don't always tell the whole story. And in California the perceptions of generous funding and quality instruction are no longer accurate.

Two important pieces of information, per pupil expenditures and the percentage of per capita income, point to a pronounced change in the state's policy toward education. In 1968, when John Serrano filed his original lawsuit, California ranked 23rd among the states in per-pupil expenditures.[20] National Education Association figures show that by 1981 California had dropped to 35th place.[21] These data point to a downward commitment at least in relation to other states. In the past few years the state's gentle caution has become outright resistance. During the early 1980s constant dollar expenditures (allocation amounts controlled for inflation) decreased markedly. Table 10-2 indicates that between 1974–75 and 1983–84 inflation-adjusted expenditures rose by a respectable 9.4 percent. However, between 1980–81 and 1983–84 expenditures have declined by an astonishing 7.5 percent or $114 per pupil.

TABLE 10-2   K-12 Total Education Revenues (All Sources): 1974–83

Year	Total funding		1972–73 dollars	
	Per ADA ($)	Change (%)	Per ADA ($)	Change (%)
1974–75	1530	8.8	1290	−0.6
1975–76	1650	7.8	1287	−0.2
1976–77	1834	11.2	1342	4.3
1977–78	2045	11.5	1397	4.1
1978–79	2207	7.9	1398	0.1
1979–80	2611	18.3	1525	9.1
1980–81	2784	6.6	1497	−1.8
1981–82 (estimated)	3013	8.2	1504	0.5
1982–83 (estimated)	3110	3.2	1460	−2.9
1983–84 (budgeted)	3204	3.0	1411	−3.4
Cumulative change	1674	109.4	121	9.4

Source: *Financial Transactions of School Districts*, Reprinted in *Analysis of the Budget Bill: For the Fiscal Year July 1, 1983 to June 30, 1984*, Report of the Legislative Analyst, p. 1276, Table 4.

Perhaps this helps to explain why, despite the state's precarious fiscal position, the legislature rebelled against Governor Deukmejian's modest funding increases for the 1983–84 budget.

Another statistical measurement underscores the state's diminishing commitment to educational finance. The percentage of a state's per capita personal income spent for education is one of the most widely used means of calculating the adequacy of educational expenditures. The advantage of this measure is that it takes into consideration the state's ability to finance education. Figure 10-1 compares California's position in per capita income with the percentage of income used for education between 1970 and 1982. During this period per capita income in the state remained among the highest in the nation, ranking 5th in 1982. But although income remained strong, the percentage of personal income earmarked for public education took a nose dive. In 1982 the state hit rock bottom—50th of 50 states in the percentage of personal income spent on public schools. Whereas 6 percent of all personal income went to education in 1973, the commitment slipped to 3.7 percent by 1982.[22] This statistic is as telling as any about the willingness of Californians to fund education. In the words of a recent California State Department of Education report, "the 'school revenue as a percent of personal income' statistic measures a state's commitment of its income to education and that commitment is at an all time low."[23]

Viewed in their entirety, these data point to some inescapable conclusions about the nature of education as a public policy in California: Despite an ability to increase its financial commitment, California underfunds its public schools, and the degree of underfunding is increasing.

FIGURE 10-1   The Financial Condition of California Public Schooling
Expressed in Rank Order

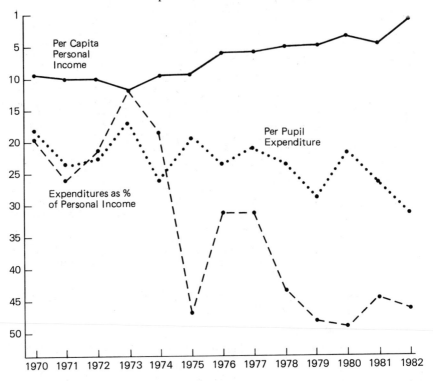

POSTSECONDARY EDUCATION

California's state-supported system of postsecondary education serves almost
2 million students at 136 campuses, making it the largest in the nation. Higher
public education consists of three separate parts: the University of California
(UC), the California State University (CSU), and the California Community
Colleges. Each part of the system has a distinct function. According to the
state's master plan for higher education, the University of California selects
first-time freshmen from the upper one-eighth of all California public high
school graduates, and the State University selects students from the top one-
third. Community colleges have an "open door" policy to all high school
graduates and others who are at least 18 years old.

State support for postsecondary education is something of a mixed bag. On
the one hand, the Census Bureau ranks California 41st among the states in
percentage of personal income spent on higher education,[24] a record only

slightly better than the K–12 commitment. On the other hand, California is one of the last states with an official "no tuition" policy in its higher education system. Although UC and CSU charge students incidental fees for noneducation-related expenses, the state's fiscal crisis of 1983 led to sizable fee increases as a means of putting higher education a bit more on a "pay-as-you-go" basis.

University of California.   With 9 campuses, 5 research hospitals, and more than 150 research centers, the University of California is more than the flagship of higher education in California; it is rated among the best in the country. Known as the state's research institution, the university leads all other public and private higher education institutions in scholarly awards. The library at Berkeley ranks second only to Harvard, with the library at Los Angeles ranked third.[25] The nine-campus system employs almost 100,000 people, including 6,500 professors, and has about 140,000 students. Of its $4 billion education and research budget in 1982–83, approximately $1 billion was allocated by the state, with the rest coming from the federal government and private donations. Two related problems have plagued the UC system in recent years. Funding has become a concern as the state has struggled with a mounting revenue deficit. Between 1981 and 1983 the state increased the UC budget by 11 percent, substantially less than almost every comparable higher education institution in the country. Funding for 1983–84 was actually 2 percent less than the 1982–83 year. As a result, problems ranging from deteriorated buildings to depressed faculty salaries threatened the university's standing in the academic community. Because of funding woes, a second problem, the possibility of tuition, has threatened to increase student costs substantially. Governor Deukmejian's cuts in the legislature's UC authorizations for 1983–84 virtually assumed that incidental fees would be increased by $150 this year. With fees already at $1,200 in 1982–83 and rising faster than the national average, the impact of the proposed change remained uncertain.

California State University.   The California State University, a 19 campus system, is another 4-year institution of higher learning. When the postsecondary system was first established in the early 1960s, CSU was designed primarily as a teaching institution, and UC was given research responsibilities. That distinction remains, although in recent years a number of professors at CSU have assumed research roles along with their teaching responsibilities.

Some 300,000 students attend the CSU schools. The budget for 1982–83 was set at $952 million for a staff of 35,000, including 18,000 professors. Although 1983–84 funding increased by 4.8 percent, the CSU trustees turned to fee hikes for additional funds. Student fees, which averaged about $500, were increased by about $200 to compensate for the governor's education reductions.

Community Colleges. California's 2-year community college system is without parallel. The system consists of 107 colleges and enrolls over one million students. The next closest state is Illinois, which has approximately 300,000 students and 50 colleges.[26] The community college network is the workhorse of the three higher education institutions in California. According to the California Postsecondary Education Commission, community colleges enroll 42 percent of all high school graduates, or 70 percent of those going to college.[27] In particular, community colleges attract a far greater percentage of part-time and minority students than the UC and CSU system.

Until now the community college system in California has been the only tuition-free institution of its kind in the country. That distinction first was threatened in 1982 when the legislature refused to fund selected avocational, recreational, and personal development courses, as a way of holding the line on the state's $1.1 billion contribution. In early 1983 Governor Deukmejian proposed to ease the state's financial pressures by charging fees of $100 per year for full-time students and $50 for those attending part time. Although this represented a significant increase over the $11 in annual fees paid by students in 1982, it still compares quite favorably to the national average among community colleges of $552 per student.[28] The likelihood of a fee increase grew greatly, as Deukmejian vetoed $230 million from the 1983–84 community college budget. The Postsecondary Education Commission predicted that such an increase could force as many as 100,000 students to drop out of the state's community colleges.[29]

STRETCHING THE DOLLAR TO THE BREAKING POINT

California's reputation for generous education funding is no longer consistent with its behavior. Although the state has the ability to pay, it lacks the commitment to fund as it once did. No doubt the tax revolt of 1978 has been partially responsible for the state's cutback in education aid. Also, the deep recession and lagging state revenues of the early 1980s led to funding reductions almost across the board. But these events tell only part of the story.

The simple fact is that values sometimes change for reasons beyond the purse of economy. Whereas public education was a high priority for the public and the legislature in the 1960s, that priority lost a good deal of support during the

1970s and early 1980s. Why? The next section assesses the problems of getting a quality education and the public's growing resentment of its cost and product.

The Question of Quality Education

For the past decade Californians have registered a significant and consistent decline of confidence in the state's public school systems. Although public attention once centered on the equality of finance issue, interest has shifted to how and what students are learning. It is clear that many parents are upset over reports that not only Johnny, but also his teacher, can't read.

One indication of public dissatisfaction with the schools comes from public opinion polls. The information in Table 10-3 shows that public confidence in 1981 was about half the strength as in 1973; conversely, negative opinions doubled during the same period. A second indicator is the decreased number of candidates running for seats on the local school boards. According to the California School Boards Association, one-third of the 150 Bay Area school board elections scheduled for November 3, 1982 were cancelled because "only enough candidates filed to fill the available seats."[30] These two factors, disenchantment with the product and disinterest in the system, go a long way toward explaining the public's basic dissatisfaction with public education in the 1980s. They also set the stage for the defeat of Superintendent of Public Instruction Wilson Riles and the election of successor Bill Honig in 1982.

Three controversial issues confront California's public education in the 1980s. They are the concern with a return to "basics," questions over student

TABLE 10-3   Confidence in the
California Public Schools

	1973	1975	1981
A lot	23%	15%	12%
Some	51%	45%	39%
Not much	25%	38%	47%
No opinion	1%	2%	2%
Confidence Index*	90	40	30

*Based on the ratio of positive to negative opinions (disregarding the "some" category).

Source: Current Opinion, August 1975, p. 80; and California Opinion Index, October 1981, p. 4. Reprinted from Hans Weiler, "Education, Public Confidence, and the Legitimacy of the Modern State: Do We Have A Crisis?" Phi Delta Kappan 64, no. 1 (September 1982): 10.

competency, and the fear of a deterioration in teacher preparedness. Admittedly, an overlap holds these issues together much like the links in a chain fence. Nevertheless, each has caused public concern with different aspects of the education system.

With voter support for California's public education system eroding rapidly, many citizens found an outlet for their frustration in the 1982 race for state superintendent of public instruction. Fairly or not, voter attitudes toward this election symbolized their feelings about the condition of education.

In California the state superintendent is the titular head of the Department of Education. As with other elements in the state's executive branch, election for the position takes place every 4 years. Unlike the other offices, however, this election takes place on a nonpartisan basis. Although granted few formal powers in the California Education Code,[31] the superintendent has become a powerful voice for education in California. Wilson Riles, superintendent between 1971 and 1983, was particularly adept at using his office to organize the state's various education factions into an effective lobbying force in Sacramento.

Riles had the unenviable task of presiding over a department that was practically crumbling before his eyes. The superintendent doesn't fund education; the legislature does. Yet the superintendent has responsibility for formulating policy with the funds—no matter how inadequate—given to him or her. Despite poor legislative support, Riles was able to keep the department intact for most of the 1970s. Still resentment increased.

In 1982, with public confidence in the schools at a new low, the time seemed ripe to mount a challenge to Riles. His strongest opponent was Bill Honig, a former teacher and superintendent of a small school district in Marin County. Although other candidates were better known, Honig struck a responsive chord with the public by attacking Riles on the issues on which he was most vulnerable: academic and disciplinary standards in high schools. According to education Professor James Guthrie, "when high school scores were going down, Wilson was defensive about the whole thing. Academic standards were going to hell, and he was absolutely silent about it."[32]

Honig exploited Riles' weakness by accusing him of "presiding over the worst deterioration of a state public school system in the U.S."[33] Repeatedly, he blamed Riles for the declining test scores of California students and promised to return the schools to an emphasis on academic, "traditional" courses.

Although an April 1982 public opinion poll showed Honig with only 2 percent of the vote, he continued to hammer away at the discontent theme. "This dissatisfaction with the schools is there, so if I can get across that message, I'll win," he said.[34] By the June primary Honig emerged from the pack of eight challengers to collect 25 percent of the vote. Because the 41 percent captured by Riles was less than a majority, the two candidates squared off in a November showdown. Honig won decisively, 56 to 44 percent. With his victory he set out to fulfill his campaign promise.

STUDENT COMPETENCY

For years prior to the 1982 election the public sensed decay in California's K–12 education. Ironically, the data were not always compatible with this perception. Test results from the California Assessment Program indicated that scores for students in grades 3, 6, and 12 actually had stabilized or increased in the last several years.[35] But this news was not enough to offset the negative publicity surrounding a significant drop in California Scholastic Aptitude Test (SAT) scores.

The SAT, taken by college-bound seniors, is this country's only real national exam. Table 10-4 indicates declines by California students on both the verbal (down 27 points) and math (down 11 points) portions of the test. Closer examination of all the data, however, shows that the drop in California scores closely paralleled the national decline and that, despite the dip, California students generally scored better than the national average. Nevertheless, the drop in California test scores signaled to the public that something was wrong with the schools.

TABLE 10-4   Average SAT Scores of College-Bound Seniors, California and the Nation, 1973–82

SAT Score	1973	1974	1975	1976	1977	1978	1979	1980	1981	1982
Verbal										
California	452	450	435	430	427	427	428	424	426	425
Nation	445	444	434	431	429	429	427	424	424	426
Difference	7	6	1	−1	−2	−2	1	0	2	−1
Mathematics										
California	485	484	473	470	470	466	473	472	475	474
Nation	481	481	480	472	470	468	467	466	466	467
Difference	4	4	1	−2	0	−2	6	6	9	7

Source: California Assessment Program, California State Department of Education, *Student Achievement in California Schools: 1981–82 Annual Report* (California State Department of Education, 1982), Table 39, p. 177.

Honig focused on two major defects in the schools: students were not spending sufficient time in school and the courses they took favored electives at the expense of academic work. His concerns were echoed loudly in a 1982 report published by the State Department of Education. The report compared California high school students with their counterparts across the nation and concluded that over a 4 year high school career, California students received about 2½ months less schooling than the national average. Moreover, things only went from bad to worse when the entire California school career, grades kindergarten through twelve, was calculated. According to the report, a typical California student's life "would be 72,000 hours shorter than that of a typical student in the nation; this is the equivalent of one and one-third sixth grade school years. This large discrepancy is the result of shorter instructional days and a shorter school year. California ranks among the ten states with the shortest school year in the nation."[36]

In March 1983 State Superintendent Honig proposed tougher mandatory standards for California schools to remedy the major shortcomings in their educational programs. Among the reforms Honig sought were longer school years, increased achievement testing, and more required courses.[37] At about the same time the State Board of Education, a ten-member policymaking authority appointed by the governor, proposed new advisory minimum course requirements. Current requirements are established by individual school districts in response to district needs and goals. In four of five areas the board's proposals surpassed those of Honig. (See Table 10-5.) According to both plans substantial numbers of present students were not meeting the proposed standards.

TABLE 10-5   High School Course Work,
Years Completed Per Subject Area

Subject area	Average years required in all districts	Mean years completed by seniors	Honig proposed minimum	Student % not meeting	State board proposed minimum	Student % not meeting
English	3.14	3.8	3.0	4	4.0	26
Mathematics	1.30	2.8	2.0	9	3.0	39
Science	1.13	2.1	2.0	34	3.0	70
Social studies	2.78	3.1	3.0	22	3.0	22
Foreign language	0.03	1.5	—	—	2.0	50

Sources: California Assessment Program, California State Department of Education, *Student Achievement in California Schools: 1981–82 Annual Report* (California State Department of Education, 1982), Table 26, p. 164. David Savage, "L.A. Officials Oppose State School Proposal," *Los Angeles Times*, January 31, 1983, Section 2, pp. 1–2.

For the most part the concept of returning to the basics seemed to be accepted as an idea whose time had come. Certainly the legislature thought so. Acting on a bill sponsored by State Senator Gary Hart (Santa Barbara), the legislature opened up its purse and passed new taxes at a time when Governor Deukmejian was opposed to both. The impetus for educational reform had a new momentum unparalleled since the early 1960s. Yet not all concerned jumped on the bandwagon.

Some educators pointed to some undesirable consequences of the reform proposals. Prominent officials in the Los Angeles Unified School District feared the emphasis on academic rigor would practically eliminate vocational courses, thereby hurting those students who did not intend to go on to college. One high school principal said that the new requirements would leave no room in a student's schedule for courses like accounting, shorthand, typing, and auto shop. "We have kids who leave here and go to Harvard University and others who will go to the West Valley Occupational center and into a skilled trade," he said.[38] For the latter category of student, vocational courses would be far more meaningful than algebra or a foreign language.

Others objected to the proposed changes on the grounds that they would disproportionately hurt black and Hispanic students. Presently, 7 percent of white students fail to graduate high school because they don't meet existing course requirements. The rates for blacks and Hispanics are considerably above that at 26 and 18 percent, respectively.[39] Given the significant difference between present minimums and those proposed by Honig and the State Board of Education, the number of minority students who fail to graduate could increase greatly. Should this be the case, they would be at a tremendous disadvantage when entering the job market.

These reservations have done little to stop the move toward reassessment and redesign of the state's education requirements in the mid-1980s. Few debate the call for reform; rather, the bulk of discussion has centered on finding the ingredients for the best formula.

TEACHER PREPAREDNESS

Teachers have been assigned a significant part of the blame in the search for responsibility for the decline in student achievement levels. It is difficult to say just how much of the fault should be placed in teacher's laps. After all, having a shorter school day than districts elsewhere is a handicap totally out of an educator's control. But to many parents, the issue is quality not quantity. The problem, as they see it, is not that their child can't learn, but their child's teacher can't educate.

Although the evidence is incomplete, some data show that teachers do not have the best records of ability or preparedness. Surveys reveal that the teaching profession attracts a disproportionately high percentage of college students with low academic ability as measured by achievement tests, aptitude tests, and grade point averages. Education Professor Michael Kirst, formerly president of the State Board of Education, points out that SAT scores for prospective teachers "have fallen about twice as fast as the average SAT decline [and] a study of students at more than 1,000 colleges covering 19 subject majors showed that potential teachers ranked 17th in math and 14th in English."[40] Even worse is the fact that the teaching field fails to retain those teachers who have high academic ability. Research shows that teachers who excel on the National Teachers Examination are almost twice as likely to leave the profession than others with similar experience.[41]

Those critics who are concerned with the decline in the caliber of teachers have offered two suggestions to reverse the slide. One answer centers on competency testing for those who want to become teachers. The California legislature enacted such a requirement, the California Basic Educational Skills test, in 1982 as a means of ensuring that new teachers would have minimum knowledge in reading, writing, and mathematics. Early results were something of an embarrassment to the education establishment. In January 1983, 35 percent of the prospective teachers taking the test failed, indicating they lacked the academic ability of an average college student.

A second answer lies with the possibility of attracting higher caliber people into the teaching profession through the offer of better pay. Such a change would go a long way toward reversing the economic calamity suffered by teachers in recent years. A comparative study by Michael Kirst and James Guthrie finds that between 1976 and 1981 teachers' salaries increased 39 percent. Meanwhile, production workers' salaries went up 45.5 percent, and per capita income across the nation increased 63.9 percent.[42]

Although sentiment is favorable toward increased teacher salaries, the likelihood of major change is not great. In fact, school districts are hard pressed just to keep the teachers they have on the payroll now. For the 1983–84 school year, 5000 teachers received warning dismissal notices because their schools lacked sufficient funds to pay them. The California Teachers Association predicted that actual dismissals would triple previous levels.[43]

Good teachers are hard to find under any conditions, but in California they seem to be at a premium. One recent study compared the average beginning salaries for math and science teachers, about $12,680, with the starting salaries they might attract from firms in the private sector, perhaps $20,000. The study concluded, "when beginning teachers are paid only $12,000 to $13,000 a year, superintendents and principals are intensely worried; they realize fully that teacher altruism cannot be counted on forever to staff classrooms."[44] Inasmuch as math and science are considered particularly deficient areas of California education, administrators have their hands full improving on the current situation.

California Education in Transition

The condition of California public schools is not disastrous, but it's close. Almost all districts have been forced to cut back services. Teachers are paid inadequate salaries, and working conditions and reduced classroom time have contributed to the substandard education of the state's children. Aside from doing poorly on expenditure measures, California now has the second highest teacher-student ratio in the nation.[45] With all the data in prespective, the only amazement is that test performances have not declined further than they have. But danger signals are everywhere.

In 1983 public education showed its vulnerability on a new scale. The 520 student Emeryville School District gained notoriety when, in March, it became the first local agency since the Great Depression to go bankrupt. Within a month's time, the 32,000 student San Jose Unified School District, eighth largest in the state, announced that it would file for bankruptcy by the end of the fiscal year. Increasingly, California schools are without sufficient funds to make ends meet. Because localities are limited in their ability to raise taxes by the state constitution via Proposition 13, the answer must come from the state government.

Recognizing the state's dual responsibility to meet the *Serrano* mandates and provide a quality education for its students, the legislature and Governor Deukmejian finally acted in 1983. The governor first proposed a $350 million increase for 1983–84 over the 1982–83 year; but the legislature rejected the proposal as an inadequate response for the state's crisis condition. Instead, acting in a rare display of bipartisanship, the legislature provided an extra $500 million in new monies (and taxes) beyond the governor's request. And although Deukmejian publicly opposed the move as too expensive, the legislature prevailed. The extra monies were designed to strengthen high school graduation requirements, increase teachers' starting salaries, lengthen the school day and year, and streamline dismissal procedures for poor teachers.

It is unclear if California's problems will improve with more funds. The weight of the evidence suggests, however, that such a result is entirely possible. But independent of quality instruction, test scores, curriculum, and school day lengths, more funds are necessary to protect school districts like Emeryville and San Jose from inadequate local bases. Moreover, without increased funds the state will be forced to level school expenditures down to meet the *Serrano* mandates, rather than up as the plaintiffs had hoped.

The extra funding for 1983-84 was just that—additional monies to squeak through another year. In the meantime, the long-term problem of permanent funding increases remains unresolved. At issue is whether the state is now ready to increase its role in education. Given the money-raising difficulties at the local level, such a move may be in the offing.

Notes

[1]The conclusions are based on: United States Department of Education, National Center for Education Statistics, *Digest of Education Statistics* (1982), p. 53, Table 45; *The World Almanac and Book of Facts 1983* (New York: Newspaper Enterprise Associates), pp. 202, 207; Report of the Legislative Analyst to the Joint Legislative Budget Committee, *Analysis of the Budget Bill for the Fiscal Year July 1, 1983, to June 30, 1984*, p. 1269 (hereafter referred to as L.A. report).

[2]L.A. report, p. 1276.

[3]*Serrano v. Priest*, 487 P. 2d 1241, 1246 (footnote 2) (hereafter referred to as *Serrano*).

[4]Legislative Analyst, *Public School Finance*, Part V, "Current Issues in Education Finance" (1970), p. 7. Reprinted in *Serrano v. Priest* (487 P. 2d 1241, 1247).

[5]"School Funding System Upheld," *Los Angeles Times*, April 29, 1983.

[6]*Serrano*, 1244, 1266.

[7]*Serrano*, 1255-56.

[8]Trial Brief of Serrano and Gonzales Plaintiffs p. 6 (November 23, 1982), Superior Court of California, Judicial Council Coordination Proceeding No. 1554, Orange County Superior Court No. 37 92 31, Los Angeles No. C 938 254, Los Angeles Superior Court No. CA 000 745 (hereafter referred to as Plaintiff Brief).

[9]Plaintiff Brief, p. 8.

[10]Kenneth Karst, "California: Serrano v. Priest's Inputs and Outputs," *Law and Contemporary Problems* 38, no. 3 (Winter-Spring 1974): 335.

[11]Plaintiff Brief, pp. 12-13.

[12]California State Department of Education, *California Schools Beyond Serrano: A Report on Assembly Bill 65 of 1977* (Sacramento: California State Department of Education, 1979), p. 17.

[13]Ibid., p. iii.

[14]Plaintiff Brief, p. 16.

[15]"Equality in Public School Funding Before Court," *Los Angeles Times*, December 13, 1982.

[16]Trial Brief of Defendant Wilson Riles, p. 3 (November 23, 1982), Superior Court of California, Judicial Council Coordination Proceeding no. 1554, Orange County Superior Court no. 37 92 31, Los Angeles Superior Court no. C 938254, Los Angeles Superior Court CA 000745.

[17]Memorandum of Decision, Superior Court of the State of California, Judicial Council Coordination Proceeding no. 1554 (filed April 28, 1983), p. 7.

[18]See James Coleman, *Equality of Educational Opportunity* (Washington, D.C.: HEW 1966) and Christopher Jencks, *Inequality: A Reassessment of the Effects of Family and Schooling in America* (New York: Basic Books, 1972).

[19]Quoted in Karst, "California." H.E.W., p. 342.

[20]U.S. Department of Health, Education and Welfare, National Center for Educational Statistics, *Digest of Educational Statistics* (Washington, D.C., 1969), p. 56, Table 74.

[21]National Education Association, *Rankings of the States, 1982* (Washington, D.C.: NEA, 1983), Table H-10.

[22]"State Hits Bottom in School Funding," *Los Angeles Times*, September 8, 1982.

[23]California State Department of Education, *Fact Sheet: Public School Revenues* (State of California, revised September 1, 1982), p. 3.

[24]L.A. Report, p. 1480.

[25]"UC: No. 1 in the U.S., But Can It Last?" *Los Angeles Times*, April 21, 1983.

[26]David Breneman and Susan Nelson, *Financing Community Colleges* (Washington, D.C.: Brookings Institution, 1981), pp. 8–10.

[27]California Postsecondary Education Commission, *Postsecondary Education in California: 1981 Information Digest* (State of California, 1982), p. 23.

[28]*State of California Governor's Budget Summary for 1983–84* (State of California, January 10, 1983), pp. A21–A22.

[29]"College Rolls May Fall 100,000," *Los Angeles Times*, July 22, 1983.

[30]David Alcott, "School Boards' Power Diminished, Most Agree," *California School Boards Association Journal* 42, no. 1 (January-February 1983): 32.

[31]*California Education Code*, Sec. 33112 (West, Los Angeles, 1978).

[32]"Riles Faces Most Serious Challenge Yet for Schools Post," *Los Angeles Times*, February 1, 1982.

[33]"Rival Opens Sharp New Attack on Riles," *Los Angeles Times*, March 10, 1982.

[34]"Riles Foe Honig Advocates Return to Education Basics," *Los Angeles Times*, April 21, 1982.

[35]L.A. Report, p. 1281.

[36]California State Department of Education, California Assessment Program, *Student Achievement in California Schools, 1981–82 Annual Report* (Sacramento: California State Department of Education, 1982), pp. 157–58.

[37]"Honig Unveils Plan to Improve Schools," *San Francisco Chronicle*, March 15, 1983.

[38]"L.A. Officials Oppose State School Proposal," *Los Angeles Times*, January 31, 1983.

[39]California State Department of Education, *Statewide Summary of Student Performance on School District Proficiency Assessments, 1981* (Sacramento: California State Department of Education, 1982), p. 7.

[40]Michael Kirst and James Guthrie, "Declining Teacher Quality: Public Schools' Toughest Problem," *California Journal* 14, no. 4 (April 1983): 141.

[41]Ibid., p. 141.

[42]Ibid., p. 143.

[43]"Teacher Layoffs May Rise in '83," *San Francisco Chronicle*, April 5, 1983.

[44]James Guthrie and Ami Zusman, "Looking for 'X'," *California School Boards Association Journal* 41, no. 6 (September 1982): 32–33.

[45]"State Hits Bottom in School Funding," *Los Angeles Times*, September 8, 1982.

11
LAND AND WATER

Roots of Economic Vitality

Land and water are among the most important cornerstones of California's economy and politics. Their interdependence is such that one is seldom discussed without mention of the other. Land and water are the staples of California's burgeoning cities and multifaceted industries. Yet the importance of these ingredients for urban growth, industrial expansion, or anything else doesn't compare with their role in California's agriculture.

California land, especially the state's 500 mile long Central Valley, is as rich as any land in the world. The quality of our land has enabled California to be the nation's number-one state in agriculture. Blessed with warm summers and mild winters, farmers can grow almost anything they want as long as they have enough water. But if rich land is a natural asset in California, plentiful water is not.

The lack of water is particularly pronounced in the areas that need it the most. In fact, California has a history of water shortages largely because most of the state's people and rich farmland do not fall in regions with substantial precipitation or natural waterways. As Carey McWilliams once said, "although it takes less water to irrigate in the northern part of the state, the bulk of the irrigable land is in the southern part. California, therefore, is a state that is upside down, a state in which nature seems to be at cross-purposes with man."[1]

Practically from the beginning of statehood to the present, Californians have struggled to compensate for the land-water mismatch. As early as 1887 the legislature passed the Wright Act, designed to permit establishment of local irrigation districts. But local entities couldn't solve their water needs by themselves. In 1927 the State Department of Public Works produced a State Water Plan, a comprehensive approach for the management of all state waters. This, in turn, became the springboard for two massive programs, the federal government's Central Valley Project and the state-financed State Water Project. The two programs transported water from areas of excess (the North) to areas of need (the South). But by the early 1960s many experts concluded that new demands were beginning to outrun existing supplies. Thus began the battle over the Peripheral Canal.

This chapter starts with a discussion of the Peripheral Canal issue. Far from just a means of moving water, the canal touches on a wide variety of questions including environmentalism, economic growth, and the future of California agriculture. Few issues have divided the state as much as the Peripheral Canal proposal. It is also the issue that most directly connects the future of land and water in California.

The Peripheral Canal Controversy

The proposed Peripheral Canal remains as the only unfinished link of California's State Water Project. At present the state system moves about 2.1 million acre-feet per year from Northern California to Central and Southern California along a 444 mile aqueduct.[2] The federal government's Central Valley Project provides another 4.1 million acre-feet per year along its own aqueduct. The 6.2 million acre-feet provided annually by these two networks represent the largest portion of California's water movement, although the state has also benefited from 5.5 million acre-feet of imported Colorado River water.

In recent years two developments have threatened the stability of California's water policy. Because of increased population and the growth of large farming interests, the state's water needs have grown faster than its ability to meet them. Additionally, when Arizona completes its own mammoth water project in the late 1980s, more than 1,100,000 acre-feet of Colorado River water currently "on loan" to California will revert to Arizona's hands.[3] That's where the Peripheral Canal enters California's land and water picture.

Approximately 40 percent of the state's rain runoff drains into a single source, the San Joaquin Delta. Most of the water comes via two rivers, the Sacramento and the San Joaquin, and their numerous tributaries. After the water meanders through the Delta, it ultimately flows into San Francisco Bay. The Peripheral Canal would channel a portion of the annual flow away from the Delta and into the State Water Project aqueduct. Of the 14 million acre-feet that annually flow into the Delta, the Peripheral Canal is designed to move up to 2.5 million acre-feet around the region in a 42 mile arclike conduit before sending it south. (See Figure 11–1.)

FIGURE 11-1   Proposed Peripheral Canal in the San Joaquin Delta

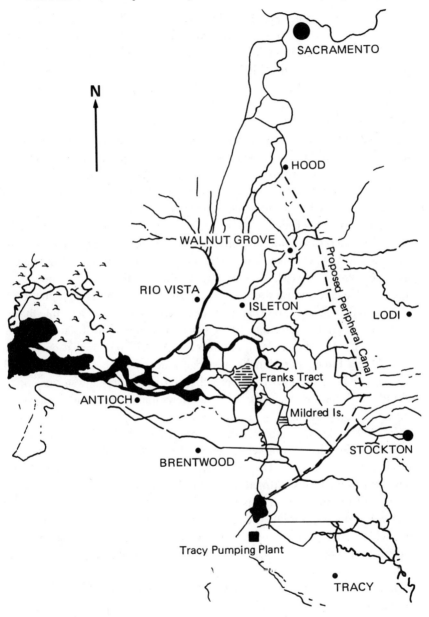

TINKERING WITH OR IMPROVING UPON MOTHER NATURE?

If precipitation were spread evenly throughout California, an average of 22 inches, a more than ample supply, would fall annually. Unfortunately, the state is not organized in such a neat pattern. As it happens, the northern third receives 75 percent of the state's rain, while the southern two-thirds have 80 percent of the need. Beyond the geographical division, agriculture accounts for 85 percent of all the water used in California,[4] hence the inevitable connection between land and water.

Considerable controversy has surrounded the concept of denying the natural flow of water into the Sacramento–San Joaquin Delta region. The Delta is a freshwater environment covering more than 1,100 square miles and 700 miles of waterways. It is a home for numerous waterfowl as well as a spawning ground for salmon, striped bass, sturgeon, American shad, and steelhead.

As a farm area the Delta covers about 780,000 acres. At one time most of this land was under water. But through installation of an intricate system of levees over the past 50 years, about 550,000 acres have been recovered for agricultural use. Delta fruit and vegetable crops are worth more than $250 million annually. The Delta region is extremely sensitive to saltwater intrusion from the San Francisco Bay. Sizable flows of fresh water move through the Delta into the bay to prevent such an event from taking place. This precarious balance is at the center of the Peripheral Canal controversy. As it is, pumps that operate the State Water Project occasionally misjudge water amounts and pull so much fresh water from the low-lying Delta that the freshwater-saltwater balance is disturbed. When that happens, salt water flows into the area and threatens the surrounding farmland.

In 1960 the legislature passed the Burns-Porter Act. The key portion of this legislation provided for the construction of a Delta facility to improve water efficiency in the region. The new Department of Water Resources (DWR), separated from the Department of Public Works in 1956, was instructed to search out various water transportation alternatives. After several years and a number of studies, the DWR determined that the Peripheral Canal would be the best means both to improve efficiency and to move surplus water to other parts of the state. By 1978 the state concluded that the canal was not only desirable for agriculture but necessary to protect fish and wildlife in the Delta region. Otherwise, the fish and wildlife populations would be reduced to 60 percent of the 1968–75 numbers.[5]

Yet others remained unconvinced. Some contended that the $7 billion expenditure was an environmental hazard. Others argued that the canal was little more than a state subsidy to agribusiness. Finally, doubters in the North viewed the canal as Southern California's meal ticket to population growth at Northern California's expense.

SUPPORTERS OF THE CANAL

By the early 1980s virtually every water-using group in the state had taken sides on the Peripheral Canal question. Major supporters fell into four categories: the water districts in Southern California, farmers, the *Los Angeles Times*, and leading state government officials.

Water Districts. The state water agencies are interdependent in the sense that one is linked to another. Of the water agencies promoting the Peripheral Canal, the Kern County Water Agency had the most at stake. As the major water district for farmers, the Kern district alone uses one-half of the water generated by the State Water Project. Legally, however, the agency is entitled to only one-fourth of the state supply.[6]

The extra water for Kern County comes courtesy of the massive Metropolitan Water District of Southern California (MWD). This agency serves 11 million people in six counties. Although authorized to tap one-half of the State Water Project output, the MWD has taken only one-fourth because of the excess Colorado River water that has been available to Southern California. Of course, when Arizona assumes its full share, the MWD will claim its full portion of state water, thus jeopardizing the water supply for Kern County. Together, the Kern and Metropolitan districts have been ardent supporters of the Peripheral Canal.

Farmers. It should surprise no one that farmers are major promoters of the Peripheral Canal. For years the California Farm Bureau has touted the project as a necessity for state agriculture. Water is the key ingredient to healthy production and major farmers in the state are worried that future supplies may not match needs.

During the past 50 years large-scale farming has become commonplace in California. Most of these farms have been served by the federal government's Central Valley Project (CVP). Under the jurisdiction of the U.S. Bureau of Reclamation, the CVP is supposed to provide only enough water to irrigate 160 acres per person. By the late 1970s it had become apparent that the CVP was

serving the biggest names in agribusiness including Southern Pacific Land
Company (109,000 acres), Boston Ranch (24,000 acres), and Standard Oil of
California (11,500 acres). As a reclamation project, federal water was sold to
these buyers at one-third the cost of state water, with electricity available at
one-tenth the commercial rate.[7] In 1980, water delivered to CVP customers
cost $36 per acre-foot, whereas State Water Project water cost $120 per acre-
foot.[8] Because of these facts, CVP policies came under close federal scrutiny
during the early 1980s. Major farm interests worried that they would not have
adequate water supplies if the CVP reverted to the 160 acre rule. Because state
water has no limitation on availability, they lobbied hard for the Peripheral
Canal.

Los Angeles Times. A daily readership of 1,100,000 is more than enough
reason for the *Times* to promote adequate water supplies for Southern California. Readers drink water, and without water the south state cannot grow. But
the *Times'* interest in water would appear to extend beyond the obvious needs of
its constituents.

The *Times* has a history of involvement in water politics. As early as 1905
publisher Harrison Gray Otis spearheaded a drive for a $25 million bond issue
designed to move water from the Owens Valley to Los Angeles. In order to
ensure passage of the bond, Otis, land speculators, and other sympathizers
created an artificial water shortage by secretly dumping thousands of gallons of
water into the city's sewer system.[9] Both indirectly and directly the *Los Angeles
Times* is connected with some of California's richest farmland. Ruth Chandler,
aunt to current publisher Otis Chandler, married James G. Boswell and, upon
his death, became chairman of the board and chief stockholder of the J. G.
Boswell Company. With 147,000 acres, Boswell is the state's largest farm and
seventh largest landowner. As for Chandler and the *Times*, the parent company
(Times-Mirror Company) owns 25 percent of the 272,000 acre Tejon Ranch
Company, of which 25,000 acres are devoted to agriculture.

Government Officials. Regardless of political party or region of residence,
major current and past government officials have endorsed the Peripheral
Canal. These include former governors Edmund G. "Pat" Brown (Dem.),
Ronald Reagan (Rep.), Jerry Brown (Dem.), and current governor George
Deukmejian (Rep.). Pat Brown gave active support to the Burns-Porter Act,
genesis of the Peripheral Canal concept. Preliminary studies of the Peripheral
Canal's feasibility were completed under Ronald Reagan's tenure, and the Jerry

Brown administration solicited public support for a referendum guaranteeing both funds and construction. Major state agencies, notably the Department of Water Resources and Department of Fish and Game, have also supported the Peripheral Canal concept.

OPPONENTS OF THE CANAL

Those against the construction of the Peripheral Canal fall into two categories: strategic and long-term opponents. The strategic opponents have included the California Farm Bureau and major land companies such as J. G. Boswell and Salyer Land Company. Although committed to the canal in principle, these powerful interests temporarily joined with long-term opponents in 1982 against a canal referendum, Proposition 9, because it included environmental safeguards unacceptable to the procanal groups.

The long-term opponents, mainly Northern Californians and environmentalists, have resisted the canal under virtually all conditions. Given their history as adversaries, these elements represent the heart of serious opposition.

Northern Californians.   The question of water divides the north and south portions of the state like no other issue. Ever since the canal was first suggested in the mid-1960s, every prominent legislator in Northern California has worked to prevent its construction. Leo McCarthy, Speaker of the Assembly between 1974 and 1981, consistently spoke out against the canal. Given his powers as Speaker, his objection was significant. The *San Francisco Chronicle* editorialized against the canal on a regular basis, and the McClatchy papers joined the opposition in 1980.

Aside from prominent individuals and organizations, Northern Californians in general were against the canal. A field poll in 1982 showed the north state opposing the canal by a nearly eight-to-one margin.[10] Sentiment was even stronger on Proposition 9, as Northern Californians voted "no" by a ten-to-one margin.

Environmentalists.   Caught between their concern for water quality in the Delta and the warnings by various state agencies, environmentalists have found themselves in a quandry over the Peripheral Canal. The Sierra Club's California Regional Conservation Committees gave a tentative blessing to the canal in 1977. But after farm interests expressed the desire for a canal without environmental protection, the Sierra Club withdrew support and joined the opposition.

A similar reversal took place with the Planning and Conservation League (PCL). Although the league expressed cautious approval of the canal as a means of protecting the Delta, it switched sides when key leaders became convinced that the state would cave in to agricultural interests regardless of the price. Thus, the league concluded in 1979, "until an affirmative program to bring about water conservation is adopted and implemented, PCL will oppose the expansion of the SWP [State Water Project] and the Peripheral Canal in particular."[11]

A third environmental group, Friends of the Earth (FOE), was less equivocal about its position against the canal. Arguing that the state's major problem was not the need for more water but the better management of the water that is available, FOE's chief spokesperson said "what we need is not a canal, but reform."[12]

Viewed as a whole, environmentalists were too uncertain about the canal's negative side effects to support the concept with any conviction. Moreover, the closer the state came to possible construction, the more reluctant the environmental coalition became.

BRINGING THE CANAL ISSUE TO A VOTE—AGAIN AND AGAIN

After the legislature passed the Burns-Porter Act in 1960, the state began to contemplate the Peripheral Canal seriously. Anxious to plan well for both Delta protection and water quality, the experts considered a variety of alternatives before settling on the canal option. In 1961 the state established the Interagency Delta Committee, a select group of federal and state water advisors, to pursue the best means of implementing the Burns-Porter objectives. By 1965 the committee endorsed the canal as the ideal facility for solving California's water problems. Still the state moved slowly in forging a fragile alliance between growers, environmentalists, and Southern California interests.

In 1974 the Department of Water Resources issued an Environmental Impact Report on the Peripheral Canal proposal. Citing the state's multiple needs, the report determined that the canal has "the greatest potential for obtaining desired environmental conditions in the Delta and the least interference with established and projected activities in the Delta, while meeting the water needs . . . of the SWP and CVP."[13] Three years later, a second environmental impact report reached the same conclusion.[14] After 15 years of research, the time seemed right for action on the canal.

Legislative Efforts.   Urged on by a series of positive reports and confronted by the state's worst drought on record, the legislature moved toward approval of the Peripheral Canal. In 1977 the Senate authorized funds for construction by a vote of twenty-eight to seven. The bill contained a provision that ensured protection for the Delta, but it also permitted the flow of water through the canal upon demand rather than only during surplus conditions. With Northern legislators miffed over the latter arrangement, the bill died in the Assembly. Election year politics in 1978 temporarily stalled the canal question, although Governor Brown and opponent Evelle Younger both expressed support for the proposal.

In 1979 new legislation, Senate Bill 200, was proposed to authorize appropriations for the canal. This time the bill encountered opposition from Southern Californians because the legislation's language stated that the first priority of the Peripheral Canal was water quality. Given this shift in emphasis, water users feared that the supply might not be available in consistent or predictable quantities. Thus, the bill died in the Senate Finance Committee by a six-to-five vote.

Sensing they were close to breaking the logjam, canal proponents revived S.B. 200 in 1980. A change in the composition of the Finance Committee also suggested a better future for the bill. In January the committee approved the canal by an eight-to-five vote. Later in the month the full Senate concurred by a vote of twenty-four to twelve. In July 1980 the Assembly approved the measure by a vote of fifty to twenty-eight, and Governor Brown signed the bill into law. But despite the bill's language, some opponents sensed that they had been sold out.

As a means of reassuring environmentalists and wary Northern Californians, the legislature placed a referendum on the November 1980 ballot to write Delta water quality standards into the state constitution. With the blessing of leading conservation and environmental groups, the voters approved the measure, Proposition 8, by a 54 to 46 percent vote. With these new guarantees, however, the state's farmers once again opposed the canal.

Proposition 9 (1982).   As soon as Governor Brown signed S.B. 200 into law, dissenting groups began circulating referendum petitions for repeal of the legislation. The odd coalition consisted of some environmentalists, who would make a last ditch effort to prevent the Peripheral Canal, and farm interests who had become convinced that S.B. 200 and Proposition 8's water standards had made the cost of future water supplies too high. Environmentalists provided the rhetoric, and farmers supplied the clout. Within 90 days of Governor Brown's action, the new alliance submitted to the Secretary of State a referendum petition with 720,000 valid signatures—more than twice the number required. The referendum was placed on the June 1982 ballot as Proposition 9. If passed, the measure would establish the canal as state policy without further delay.

Proposition 9 was supported by organized labor, Los Angeles-based land and energy firms, and the State Department of Water Resources. The opposition was led by major Central Valley farm operations and ecology-minded groups such as the Environmental Defense Fund and the League of Conservation Voters.

The sources of financial assistance told the story as well as anything else. The two leading "yes" contributors were Getty Oil Company, $240,000, and Newhall Land Company, $90,000. Operating Engineers No. 3, a union that would build much of the canal, donated another $24,000. Yet, it was the "no" side that showed the real financial muscle in the Proposition 9 battle. J. G. Boswell Company gave $1,150,000, and Salyer Land Company added another $725,000. Proposition 9 was as much a fight between giant landowners ("yes") and giant farmers ("no") as anything else.

At the end of the $6 million campaign, the "no" side prevailed, 37 to 63 percent. For the time being, the issue was settled. But most observers considered that the Peripheral Canal matter would be raised again. The only question was, when?

Agripolitics without Parallel

California is the third largest state in the nation; only Alaska and Texas are bigger. Yet not all of California belongs to Californians. Of the state's 101 million acres, the federal government owns 45 million acres. State and local governments control another 5 million acres, leaving only about half the land in private hands.

Much of the private land is divided into large parcels, the biggest shares of which are devoted to agriculture and range lands. These huge chunks of real estate have been assembled through a variety of ways. In some cases, like the Tejon Ranch and the Irvine Land Company, the holdings are the outgrowths of massive land grants originally awarded by the Mexican government to early residents. In other cases, modern industries and agribusiness have acquired substantial holdings in California, further recognition of the state's potential for large profits.

Finally, the Southern Pacific Railroad is the most prominent force of all the land giants in California. Originally granted 6.5 million acres by the federal government as partial payment for building the transcontinental railroad, the

Southern Pacific still owns 2 million acres in the state. Because the Southern Pacific leases most of its crop land to other farmers, the corporation does not always play a role in farm matters befitting its huge size.

Agripolitics is big in California. Political actors throughout the state, both in and out of government, take special care to promote the needs of this $14 billion industry. And well they should. California has been the nation's number-one state in agriculture for 35 years. In 1983 the state's farm products were exceeded in value by only eight nations! With these dimensions in mind, let's look at the land, the most active agricultural interests, and some of the issues confronting the farming community in the 1980s.

WHO OWNS THE BREADBASKET?

California produces more than 200 different crops each year and leads all other states in 48 areas. So significant is the state's farm output that California alone supplies 25 percent of the table food and 50 percent of the fresh fruit consumed in the United States. As important as California agriculture is to the nation, it has an even greater impact at home. Agriculture accounts directly or indirectly for one out of every three jobs in the state when processing, distribution, and marketing are taken into account.

The magnitude of the state's farm production is matched by the sizes of its farms. During the early 1970s then U.S. Secretary of Agriculture Earl Butz warned a gathering of family farmers: "Get big or get out."[15] These words long have been taken seriously in California. For some time now farming has been big business in the state. To be sure, small family enterprises still exist, but in decreasing numbers. Meanwhile the size of the "average" farm has grown considerably since the end of World War II. The data in Table 11-1 reveal two interesting facts about the evolution of agriculture in California. First, the number of farms today is almost half the amount that existed 30 years ago, but the sizes of the remaining farms have nearly doubled. In other words, farming increasingly has become an enterprise for big players. Second, the acreage used for farming has decreased by nearly 10 percent, but production per acre has increased. Put another way, farms are now operating with greater efficiency. Perhaps this is why the state has experienced a small resurgence in the number of farms since 1970

Average farm sizes can be misleading in California, where a select few farm and farm holdings dominate the state's agricultural picture. The largest forty-five farms in California control more than 3.7 million acres, or about 11 percent of California's total agricultural land. Viewed even more selectively, the top fifteen farm businesses constitute the state's largest land barons. In some

TABLE 11-1   California: Number of Farms, Land in Farms, and Size of
Farm (1950–82)

Year	Number of farms	Land in farms (000 acres)	Average size of farm (acres)
1950	144,000	37,500	260
1955	124,000	39,000	316
1960	108,000	38,800	359
1965	82,000	37,800	461
1970	64,000	36,600	572
1975	73,000	34,300	470
1980	80,000	33,900	424
1981	83,000	34,000	410

Source: *California Agriculture, 1981* (California State Department of Food and Agriculture, Sacramento, Calif., 1982), p. 14.

cases, these expansive operations spill over into as many as a dozen counties. Table 11-2 catalogs the leading names in state agriculture and the extent of their immense holdings as of 1981. The number-one farm operator, J. G. Boswell Company, is so massive that its 147,000 acres are approximately as large as the combined city limits of San Francisco, Oakland, and San Jose.[16]

Despite the diversity of California's agriculture, ten major farm products account for more than half of the state's $14 billion industry. These include milk and cream ($2 billion), cattle ($1.4 billion), cotton ($1 billion), grapes ($787 million), nursery products ($504 million), hay ($495 million), flowers ($464 million), lettuce ($448 million), eggs ($421 million), and oranges ($409 million).[17] In 1983 the estimated value of these goods amounted to $7.9 billion.

Most of the state's major farm industries flourish in Central and Southern California under the right conditions. Those conditions include vast amounts of imported water, most of which comes from Northern California. As of 1982, J. G. Boswell, for example, grew cotton on 155,000 acres in the water-starved Central Valley between Fresno and Bakersfield. Salyer Land Company used another 55,000 acres nearby for the same purpose. Without imported water, these farm businesses would dry up long before a season's end. Hence, these interests have been among the most active supporters of the Peripheral Canal without any environmental restrictions.

The relationship between water and farmers is a haunting refrain in California agripolitics. As one observer notes, "wherever the canals go, land values escalate. A 54,803 acre water district that was worth $10.6 million in 1966 increased in value to $146 million in 1979 after irrigation water was brought in."[18] Rich land makes rich farm interests as long as the necessary supplies of water are available.

TABLE 11-2   The Fifteen Largest California Farm Operators

Name	Counties	Cropland acres farmed
J. G. Boswell Co.	Fresno, Kern, Kings, Tulare	147,505
Salyer Land Co.	Kings and Tulare	73,141
South Lake Farms, Inc.	Fresno, Kern, Kings, Tulare	58,829
Newhall Land and Farming Co.	Butte, Colusa, Contra Costa, Fresno, Los Angeles, Madera, Merced, San Luis Obispo, Santa Barbara, Santa Clara, Sutter, Ventura	53,976
Westlake Farms, Inc.	Kings	51,735
McCarthy Farming Co.	Colusa, Fresno, Kern, Kings, Madera, Monterey, Santa Barbara, Tulare	45,274
Anderson Farms Co.	Colusa, Fresno, Merced, Solano, Sutter, Yolo	39,867
Superior Farming Co.	Kern, Madera, Riverside	33,576
Heidrick Farms, Inc.	Yolo	30,600
Wolfsen Land and Cattle Co.	Merced, Fresno, Stanislaus	29,083
The Irvine Co.	Imperial and Orange	28,257
La Cuesta Verde Ginning Co., Inc.	Fresno, Kern, Kings, San Luis Obispo	27,415
Tejon Ranch Co.	Kern and Los Angeles	25,495
E. L. Wallace and Sons	Sutter, Solano, Yolo	24,272
Tenneco West, Inc.	Kern, Madera, Merced, Riverside, San Joaquin, Tulare	23,893

Source: *California Journal* 12, no. 6 (June 1981): 222. © 1981 by The California Center. Reprinted with permission.

With increased foreign competition and unpredictable weather, farmers' net profits have been shrinking in recent years. Nevertheless, California farmers have fared quite well relative to the rest of the nation. Between 1979 and 1982, net farm incomes outside California dropped by 39 percent. Inside the state, incomes went down by only 22.8 percent. Given California's recent problems both with drought (1976–78) and excess water (1981–83), these results are all the more astounding.

FARM ORGANIZATIONS—TURNING UP THE VOLUME ON POLITICAL ACTIVITY

Prior to the mid-1960s, farm interests were well represented in Sacramento. The legislature was organized by population in the Assembly and by land in the Senate. In those days the northern and central parts of the state, largely rural, were able to balance the southern and urban interests. With urban interests dominating the Assembly, rural constituents had tight reins on a majority of the Senate. But the United States Supreme Court's reapportionment decisions ended the stalemate. After both houses were structured along population formats in 1965, the Assembly emerged without much change. But, as political scientist Alvin Sokolow notes, a major upheaval took place in the Senate. Long the bastion of farm interests, the Senate's reorganization shifted 15 seats "from rural and northern areas to metropolitan constituencies in Southern California and the San Francisco Bay area, leaving two-thirds of the state's area with four seats [of the forty] and concentrating 14 in Los Angeles County alone."[19] In Sokolow's survey of legislative incumbents at the time many predicted that "agricultural interests were bound to suffer . . . because of the loss of Senate seats by the central valley and other farming areas in the state."[20] Apparently the farming community agreed.

The reapportionment decisions led to a rebirth of political activity for agriculture in California. From this point on, farmers and their numerous organizations assumed an aggressive posture. As a key official in the Department of Food and Agriculture put it, before reapportionment "farmers didn't have to be articulate. Their needs were automatically taken care of. Now farmers must skillfully lobby in order to convince an urban slanted legislature of the viability of their needs."[21] But the farmers' dismay was the farmworkers' delight, because reapportionment promised a Senate that might be more sympathetic to farmworkers' rights.

The California Farm Bureau. We already know that California is a haven for interest group politics. Agriculture is no exception. More than three dozen agricultural organizations maintain lobbyists in the state capital. Some, like the American Dehydrated Onion and Garlic Association, are rather narrow in purpose, whereas others, such as the Western Growers, incorporate a variety of farm concerns. Agriculture representation includes all aspects of the industry, from the California Seed Association to the California Food Producers. Many of these organizations have banded together as members of California's Agricultural Roundtable, an informal group of lobbyists who meet weekly in Sacramento to discuss farm issues of mutual concern.

Although the state has a variety of farm interests at work, the California Farm Bureau Federation easily stands out as the dean of them all. With 98,000 members throughout California the federation has an annual budget in excess of $4 million. Recognizing its members' special needs, the Farm Bureau provides insurance, farm supplies, and endless amounts of information. It has a weekly newsletter, the *Ag Alert*, which publishes current commodity and political news for growers. All of this information points to an organization with a variety of services for its members. But today's Farm Bureau does more. With all the sophistication of big city slickers, it is an interest group that has learned to flex agricultural muscles in an increasingly urban state.

With its own political action committee, Farm PAC, the Farm Bureau ranks with the heavyweights in state politics. In 1982 the organization spent more than $100,000 for the June election, most of which went to the "No on Proposition 9" campaign. Another $200,000 was earmarked for the November legislative and statewide contests. Yet money is only one sign of the Farm Bureau's clout. The organization maintains a staff of seven full-time lobbyists—larger than any other agriculture group—to pursue its farm objectives in Sacramento. And its political team has become adept at stretching influence.

Whereas the Farm Bureau once quietly relied almost exclusively upon Republicans, the organization now spends money and time on Republicans and Democrats. In the words of John Thurman, former chairman of the Assembly Agriculture Committee, agriculture has "learned all Democrats aren't bad and all Republicans aren't good—they work with both sides of the aisle now and make contributions to both parties."[22] Its influence extends all the way up to Democratic Assembly Speaker Willie Brown, a San Franciscan, who has become highly attentive to agriculture largely because several rural Assembly members formed part of the coalition that elected him to the speakership in 1980.[23]

Of all the recent changes in California politics, the California Farm Bureau has to be particularly pleased with the election of George Deukmejian to the governorship. Deukmejian's predecessor, Jerry Brown, saddled farmers with the Agricultural Labor Relations Board, a labor-management agency that, according to Farm Bureau President Henry Voss, has a strong bias toward labor.[24] Brown's attitudes on the Peripheral Canal and conservation also put him at odds with the Farm Bureau. But the Deukmejian administration has played a different tune.

Republican Deukmejian sought the governorship as a solid ally of organized agriculture. Prior to election, he was quoted as saying, "Farmers and ranchers, by their efforts and productivity, have proven to be our friends. As governor, I intend to be their friend."[25] After assuming office, Deukmejian appointed Clare Berryhill—formerly a grower, farm lobbyist, and Republican legislator— to head the state's Department of Food and Agriculture. Berryhill immediately announced a pesticide policy of less state regulation, something of vital importance to growers who equate regulation with unnecessary costs. His action offended environmentalists, conservationists, and other interest groups professing concern with water quality.

Regardless of who's in power, organized farming has become a key force in

California politics. Its recent activities regarding Proposition 9 in 1982 along with other elective contests readily demonstrate agriculture's resurrection. As Farm Bureau lobbyist James Eller says, "Political involvement by farmers and ranchers in the 1980s is as important as making two blades of grass grow where one grew [before]. . . . Farmers must become involved in farming."[26] Given recent election results, the political spadework of organized agriculture has reaped a near-record yield.

The United Farm Workers. The large-scale farm interests in California have witnessed an equally large-scale effort to organize the state's farmworkers. The past decade has meant a lot to the United Farm Workers (UFW) and their long-time leader, Cesar Chavez. As recently as 1972, the union, then unrecognized as a legal bargaining unit, was striking against lettuce growers in the south state and leading secondary boycotts against grape growers in the central and north portions. A decade later the UFW, now the official union for most of the state's farmworkers, was California's second largest campaign contributor in the 1982 general elections, with total donations in the neighborhood of $750,000. In 10 years the union ascended from political shadow to political giant, upsetting the long-standing relationship between farm owners and employees in California's rural environment. And with this evolution, the state's agripolitics map also changed.

Chavez began his effort to organize farmworkers in the 1960s. At first his efforts were simple: to provide a transportation system for farmworkers to the various fields as they worked their way from the south to the north parts of the state over the long harvest season. He had his hands full. Many in the labor pool were Mexican migrants who spoke little English and tended to go back and forth between their country and the United States. Sometimes the problem was one of sheer logistics: locating enough workers to be in the right place at the right time. With an endless labor pool available for tapping by the growers, Chavez knew that careful organization was necessary for the workers to find stable employment. His transportation efforts paid off and the farmworkers developed a great loyalty to Chavez.

Having stabilized the labor pool, Chavez then worked for union recognition. He demanded that his members be paid decent hourly wages instead of piece-by-piece pay. He also called for improved working conditions, a pension system, and English lessons for those who wanted to learn. Major farmers ignored his pleas. In 1966 Chavez organized a boycott against table grapes, a 6 year effort that led to the first contracts between growers and the UFW in 1972. But the union's gains were sporadic and subject to the whims (and desperation) of the growers.

After Jerry Brown won the governorship in 1974, the UFW saw an opportunity for long-term success in the fields. By that time a number of growers were sufficiently weary from the struggle that their ranks were split. Finally in 1975 Brown and the legislature reached agreement on the California Agricultural Relations Act. The new law permitted the state's 240,000 farmworkers to decide on union representation. Within a year's time the UFW won most of the election victories, although an agreement with the Teamsters meant that they would have jurisdiction over workers in packing sheds and other areas away from the fields.

Meanwhile a five-member Agricultural Labor Relations Board (ALRB) was created out of the 1975 legislation to mediate disputes between the workers and growers. Between 1975 and 1982, the membership on the board changed considerably. Still the members appointed by Brown and confirmed by the Senate were consistently disposed toward farm labor and strict control of pesticides use. Both positions rankled organized agriculture.

By 1982 most farmers in the state agreed that almost anyone—Democrat or Republican—would be an improvement over Jerry Brown for California agriculture. Said Don Gordon, chief lobbyist for the Agriculture Council of California, "although we don't know who will replace [Brown] as governor, right now we feel that there is no way to be worse off."[27] Apparently the UFW feared much the same result. After making massive contributions to Democrats in both Senate and Assembly races, Chavez concluded, "I think we have some friends there [in the Legislature] now."[28] He may need them.

Workers in Transition.   In his last year of office Governor Jerry Brown vetoed three bills that the UFW considered harmful to their interests. Brown also used his final days in office to fill three vacancies on the Agricultural Labor Relations Board, thus hoping to perpetuate his prounion policies long after his departure. But nothing lasts forever, especially in politics. Shortly after he took office, Governor Deukmejian presented his proposed budget for the 1983–84 fiscal year. Calling for an end to unnecessary government, Deukmejian asked for the elimination of fifty positions from the Agricultural Labor Relations Board staff, making the personnel reduction the largest cut for any single state agency. Overall, the new governor proposed cutting the agency's $9 million budget by 25 percent. Although Deukmejian defended his changes as part of a general plan to bring the state out of debt, those within the ALRB weren't so sure. In the words of one official, the changes would "absolutely gut our agency and render it almost completely ineffective."[29]

Before the budget battle ended, the legislature gave in to only part of Deukmejian's proposal. The ALRB remained as a viable entity. Nevertheless, with a new General Counsel closely allied with big farmers and the likelihood of a Deukmejian-appointed board majority by 1985, Chavez and the United Farm Workers had been served notice. The patterns of agripolitics were on the move again in the California fields.

Some Lingering Issues in Water and Land Management

The challenges to the management of California's water and land have intensified with the state's development. As urban areas have attracted more people, farmers have been called upon to produce more food. All the while, water supplies have remained fixed, thus pitting farmer against city dweller over water allotments. With 1.6 million gallons of water required to produce enough food for one person in a year's time, something has to give. Farmers cannot provide for growing numbers of people with fixed amounts of water. Perhaps California Farm Bureau spokesman William DuBois put the land-water controversy in perspective when he said, "Farmers grow food. The only way farmers will use less water is if people eat less food. And I don't think many people want to do that."[30] If he is right, the Peripheral Canal or another means of north-to-south water movement may be inevitable. If he is wrong, then farmers, who use 85 percent of the state's water, may be in for a rude awakening when California loses its Colorado River supply to Arizona in the late 1980s.

Although the Peripheral Canal remains at the top of California's land-water agenda, other related problems remain unattended. Among these are the dropping water table, land conservation, and pesticide control.

THE VANISHING WATER TABLE

For years farmers in most parts of the state have been using more water than they receive. How can you use more than you get? Is this agriculture's equivalent to a magician's sleight of hand? Hardly. The excess use of the supply has to do with manipulation of the water table.

The water table is that point beneath the land's surface where supplies of water can be drawn for use. For the farmer, drawing water by well is cheaper than buying water from either the state or federal water projects. And there are virtually no governmental restraints on such efforts.

California has detailed policies on the flow and quality of water, but the state has ignored the question of pumping water below the surface. Without any rules on groundwater management, farmers have pumped water from the ground under the assumption that if they don't, others will. In the words of one state geographer, "You have mass anarchy here [in the Central Valley]. Every individual farmer is looking out for himself. . . . And no farmer is going to stop pumping if everybody else is pumping."[31] The stampede on California's water table today is every bit as frantic and chaotic for farmers as the state's gold rush was to prospectors 135 years ago.

At the end of World War II, the water table in the Central Valley varied between 50 and 100 feet beneath the ground's surface. Concern over depletion and sinking land was part of the rationale behind the state water project's development in the 1960s. Twenty years later the state's farmers are borrowing against California's future at an unprecedented rate. In 1982 the valley's water table averaged 217 feet below the surface. In the San Joaquin Valley alone (the southern half of the Central Valley), farmers were overdrawing water annually by more than 1.5 million acre-feet, prompting concern both in Sacramento and Washington, D.C. A report by the federal government's Council on Environmental Quality concluded that "the San Joaquin's agricultural prosperity rests in part on the very shaky foundation of groundwater overdraft."[32] Others think the foundation may have already crumbled.

One federal expert, a geologist with the United States Geological Survey, believes that massive overdrawing of groundwater in the Central Valley is draining the area such that the land ultimately will become a desert. According to Howard Wilshire, "desertification" has several symptoms: groundwater overdraft; lack of proper drainage, allowing slats to choke the soil; irrigation that leads to unnatural soil erosion; and overgrazing, which removes plant life from the land.[33] Wilshire contends that this process is now at work in the San Joaquin Valley, jeopardizing the future of California agriculture.

The vanishing water table does not bode well for California's tomorrows. Until the state establishes a comprehensive policy that regulates groundwater removal, the problem will only worsen.

LAND CONSERVATION

Conservation of farmland has been a hot and cold issue in California agripolitics. Pressures to change land use from agriculture to urban development have varied with the times. When California's population was growing by leaps and bounds during the 1950s and 1960s, farmers and environmentalist allies feared massive losses of land to urban sprawl. As growth slowed, interest rates skyrocketed, and the economy slumped during the 1970s and 1980s, many of these fears subsided. What troubles farmers most today is that land conservation is subject to change with the economic pressures of the moment. Many feel considerable insecurity over their long-term abilities to hold on to the land.

The only major state land conservation program on the books is the Williamson Act of 1965, an effort to preserve agricultural land by encouraging farmers to contract voluntarily with local governments to keep their land for agricultural use. If a farmer agrees to continue agricultural use for a period of 10 years, the land is taxed at a special low agricultural rate rather than its "highest and best use" potential as previous law had stated.[34] Each year the agreement is automatically extended another year unless the farmer expresses an intention to use the land for other purposes. If the farmer refuses to wait the 10 year period for the Williamson contract to expire, he or she must pay a substantial penalty for immediate release.

Much of the clout behind the Williamson Act was removed in 1978. With the passage of Proposition 13, farmers were given new low tax rates; they no longer had to abide by land-use restrictions unless they were in the middle of ongoing Williamson Act agreements. From 1978 on, increasing numbers of farmers signed intentions to opt out of their Williamson contracts at the end of their 10 year period. Although most continued to farm, nobody knew when and under what circumstances a given farmer or farm business would convert to other use.

Further weakening of the Williamson Act took place in 1981, when the legislature passed a 5 month "window period" (January through May, 1982), permitting landowners to withdraw immediately from their Williamson contracts without penalty. At the end of the allowed time property owners holding 98,500 acres applied to cancel their agreements. Some applications came from remote rural regions, but many came from popular coastal farm areas where developers were pressing hard for new land.[35] These recent events have only made land use more difficult to control in comparison with the past.

The latest attempt to stabilize land conservation occurred in 1982 when the legislature enacted the Farmland Mapping and Monitoring Program. Whereas previous efforts at determining the loss of farm areas to urban and suburban growth were based on sketchy estimates, the new act systematically counts the loss of farm acres to development on an annual basis. Originally the concept had wide support from prominent interests including farm groups (California Farm Bureau, Cattlemen's Association), development and business interests (California Chamber of Commerce, Association of Realtors, Building Industry Association), and environmental groups (Sierra Club, People For Open Space). Since the act's passage, however, supporters have disagreed on how to define and implement the new law. Realtors have advocated a measurement method that indicates a minimal number of land conversions; environmentalists have suggested that such an approach underestimates the loss of prime farmland to urban use.[36] The fight is hardly academic, because the state's answer to the loss of farmland is likely to be somewhat in proportion to the extent of the problem. Meanwhile, until agreement can be reached on the mapping guidelines, the future of farmland is likely to remain in a highly volatile condition.

PESTICIDE USE

Farmers need pesticides almost as much as they need water. If irrigation gives crops sustenance, pesticides shield them from harm. But there are two ways of looking at the pesticide question. Although these modern chemicals increase food supplies, many are potentially harmful to humans. If pesticides are left uncontrolled, toxic residues can be found on crops, in the land, or in the water we drink. It should not be surprising that, as the nation's breadbasket, California farms consume more than 10 percent of all the pesticides used in the United States. Because of the controversy surrounding these farm aids, government regulation "is more persuasive and complex in California than anywhere else in the nation."[37]

Pesticide control in California falls under the jurisdiction of the state Department of Food and Agriculture (DFA). Caught between organized farmers' complaints of overregulation and environmentalists' demands for tougher standards, the DFA has taken a "go slow" approach of the use of pesticides. This attitude stands in contrast to the past.

Before the 70s the DFA basically allowed farmers to determine the proper role and uses of pesticides. Changes took place, however, with the environmental movement and the Jerry Brown administration. In 1976 Attorney General Evelle Younger issued an opinion holding that counties, traditional agencies for pesticide permits, must act in accordance with the California Environmental Quality Act because of the potentially damaging effects of pesticides.[38] This meant, according to Younger, that an Environmental Impact Report (EIR) would have to be filed for each of the state's 50,000 pesticide permits each year. Farmers saw nothing but bureaucratic red tape facing them as insects chewed up their profits. Yielding to pressure, the legislature enacted a 2 year moratorium exempting pesticide use from environmental controls. In 1978 a second 2 year delay was passed with the stipulation that the state formulate a comprehensive pesticide policy. Secretary of Agriculture and Services Rose Bird created a forty-member Environmental Assessment Team (EAT) in 1978 to comply with the new law.

When the EAT completed its work in November 1979, the task force concluded that existing pesticide procedures were a menace to public health. The EAT found little documentation regarding permits, a defective toxic monitoring system, and a pesticide industry concerned more with growing crops than human lives.

Needless to say, agriculture was not pleased with the report. One journal, *California Farmer*, editorialized that the report "comes as close to death sentence for California Agriculture as anything we ever had. . . . It is jampacked with unworkable, unrealistic regulations by people who don't know agriculture, yet seem bent on destroying it."[39] And so the fight between agriculture and environmentalists shifted into high gear.

After long and hard negotiations in 1980 the legislature approved the new pesticide program advocated by the EAT. However, the new law contained another 2 year moratorium on Environmental Impact Reports as well as any other pesticide legislation so that the new regulations would have a chance to work. The end of the most recent moratorium coincided with the 1982 general elections.

En route to gubernatorial victory, candidate George Deukmejian made his position on pesticide use in California clear: "Modern agriculture is heavily dependent on a broad array of necessary pesticides. . . . We must have a reasonable and safe pesticide program, but those pesticide regulations which are not statutorily authorized and which are not essential to the protection of the public will be abolished" he said. Promising not to impose "impossible or foolish standards upon our farmers," Deukmejian signalled a shift in the state's oversight of pesticide use."[40]

Regardless of current administration attitudes, pesticide use continues to cause concern in California. When the Mediterranean fruit fly invasion struck Santa Clara County in 1980, Governor Jerry Brown hesitated to use a pesticide spray, malathion, because of environmentalists' prediction of widespread harm to hundreds of thousands of people. Instead the medfly invasion spread so that by the time the state's delayed malathion program was completed, crop losses amounted to more than $500 million.[41] As for Brown, his reluctance to act at any early point in the crisis may have helped undo his efforts for the United States Senate in 1982.

Planning for Tomorrows

Fundamental issues like land and water never go away from California politics. They may subside, but the controversies surrounding them prevent anything but temporary answers. Defeat of the Peripheral Canal was a momentary response to an ongoing problem in the state. Even some of the "opponents" actually wanted the canal, but on their terms. Moreover, the demand for more water in the central and south state area remains as strong today as ever.

The major questions about land and its use are also continuing issues in California politics. The needs of big farmers and the demands of agricultural labor clash head on from time to time, for as much as these two interests have in common, they have just as many issues driving them apart.

In many ways the middle 1980s represent more of a return to past ideas than an advance to new ones. Yesterday's proposals, previously ridiculed, are in vogue once again. Take the question of water. Even though the voters defeated Proposition 9 by nearly two to one, the state's policymakers seem to be moving toward another water transfer system. Governor Deukmejian's new director of the Department of Water Resources, David Kennedy, is former assistant general director of the massive Metropolitan Water District of Southern California. Aware that the canal alternative conjures up bad memories, Kennedy has proposed an expanded State Water Project transfer system that would move water south through, rather than around, the Delta. As with the Peripheral Canal, environmentalists oppose the idea. In water politics old ideas are churning once again.

The struggles over land are much the same, too. Although millions of acres are cultivated courtesy of transported water, their viability remains ever tentative because of uncertain future supplies. As long as land has multiple uses in California farmers will weigh whether it's worth the many struggles to work it or better to sell their land to developers. For the past decade farmers have maintained their position, although publicly brooding over their treatment by the Agricultural Labor Relations Board and, in some instances, the Department of Food and Agriculture.

With the new gubernatorial administration the state has moved full circle, downplaying farmworkers and recognizing farmers, minimizing environmentalists' concerns and favoring growers' reliances on chemicals. For the most part California's major agricultural interests are happier today in comparison with the past. The political winds in state politics have shifted toward a new direction, and that's fine wtih the big users of land and water.

Notes

1. Carey McWilliams, *California: The Great Exception* (New York: Greenwood Press, 1971), p. 318.
2. An acre-foot (326,000 gallons) is the amount of water consumed by a "typical" family of four over a 1 year period. Most water-use statistics are calculated in this measurement.
3. See *Arizona v. California*, 373 U.S. 546 (1963).

[4]Ronald B. Robie, Director, Department of Water Resources, "Agricultural Production and Food Needs as Input to Water Policy, in DWR *Statements Presented to the Assembly Committee on Water, Parks, and Wildlife on "A New Water Plan for California"* (California Department of Water Resources, Sacramento, Calif., February–April 1979), p. 1.

[5]State of California Resources Agency, Department of Fish and Game, *Restoration of Fish and Wildlife in the Sacramento–San Joaquin Estuary* (California Department of Fish and Game, Sacramento, Calif., June 1978), p. 16.

[6]George L. Baker and Tom DeVries, "Water," *New West*, June 16, 1980, p. 38.

[7]Charles Warren, "Federal Water Policies Subsidize Disasters," *Los Angeles Times*, May 15, 1977.

[8]Interview with Haydn C. Lee, Jr. and A. Terry Johnson, Staff Assistants, Planning and Policy Staff, Water and Power Resources, U.S. Department of the Interior, Washington D.C., August 20, 1980.

[9]For a thorough discussion of the *Los Angeles Times*'s role in bringing water to Southern California, see Robert H. Boyle, John Graves, and T. H. Watkins, *The Water Hustlers* (San Francisco: Sierra Club, 1971).

[10]The California Poll, Release S1166, May 12, 1982.

[11]Letter from David F. Abelson, Executive Director, Planning and Conservation League, to State Senator Ruben Ayala, Chairman, Senate Committee on Agriculture and Water Resources, April 30, 1979, p. 4.

[12]Quoted in "Canal Opponents May Be United Now . . . ," *San Jose Mercury News*, May 27, 1982.

[13]State of California Department of Water Resources, *Summary of Draft Environmental Impact Report: Peripheral Canal Project*, State of California, Sacramento, Calif., August 1974), p. 38.

[14]State of California Department of Water Resources, *Delta Water Facilities*, Bulletin 76, July 1978.

[15]Quoted in Hal Rubin, "Who Owns California?" *California Journal* 12, no. 6 (June 1981): 222.

[16]Boswell's 147,505 acres are equivalent to about 231 square miles. San Francisco (45.4), Oakland (53.4), and San Jose (152.6) total 251.4 square miles.

[17]"Knee-high Growth Is In Store For Farmers," *San Jose Mercury*, April 18, 1983.

[18]Rubin, "Who Owns California?," p. 223.

[19]Alvin D. Sokolow, "Legislative Pluralism, Committee Assignments, and Internal Norms: The Delayed Impact of Reapportionment in California," (Paper presented at the Conference on Democratic Representation and Apportionment: Quantitative Methods, Measures, and Criteria, New York, New York, November 1–3, 1972), p. 3.

[20]Ibid., p. 5.

[21]Interview with Hans Van Nes, Assistant Director of the California Department of Food and Agriculture, June 14, 1983.

[22]Quoted in Ann Foley Scheuring, "The Rising Power of the Farm Lobby," *California Journal* 13, no. 11 (November 1982), p. 412.

[23]Ibid., p. 411.

[24]Jim Churchill, "The Farm Bureau—Conservative Voice of Agribusiness," *California Journal* 13, no. 11 (November 1982), p. 414.

[25]Douglas Foster, "The Growing Battle Over Pesticides in Drinking Water," *California Journal* 14, no. 5 (May 1983), p. 177.

[26]Quoted in Scheuring, "Rising Power," p. 413.

[27]"State Farmers Cultivate Clout at Capitol," *Los Angeles Times*, May 5, 1982.

[28]"UFW's Changing Face," *San Jose Mercury News*, January 9, 1983.

[29]"State's Organized Labor Can Look Forward to Four Rough Years," *Los Angeles Times*, January 26, 1983.

[30]"California Water: What's New?" *California Forum*, aired on KQED (San Francisco), July 5, 1983.

[31]Richard Walker, University of California, quoted in "Irrigating Farmers Raise Dust," *San Jose Mercury*, May 24, 1982.

[32]Quoted in Ibid.

[33]Ibid.

[34]"The Legislative Battle Over Preserving Agricultural Land," *California Journal* 7, no. 5 (May 1976): 156.

[35]"Bill Affecting Farm Land Development Under Fire," *Los Angeles Times*, June 20, 1983.

[36]For a thorough discussion of the Farmland Mapping and Monitoring Program, see Jim Churchill, "Mapping the Present and Future of California's Farmland Resources," *California Journal* 14, no. 4 (April 1983): 153–54.

[37]Scheuring, "Rising Power," p. 413.

[38]Eric Brazil, "Climax of the Pesticide War Between Growers and Ecologists," *California Journal* 10, no. 9 (September 1979): 321.

[39]Ibid., p. 322.

[40]Quoted in Foster, "Growing Battle," p. 178.

[41]Eric Brazil, "The Political Stakes in the Medfly Infestation," *California Journal* 12, no. 4 (April 1981): 137.

12
THE WASHINGTON CONNECTION

How Many Californians Does it Take?

"How many Californians does it take to change a light bulb?"

"Twelve. One to screw in the new bulb and eleven to groove on the experience."

That affectionately anti-California joke might well apply to the way Californians operate in Washington, D.C. No other state is so heavily represented, yet the results are distinctly mixed.

With two senators and forty-five members of the House of Representatives, California has the largest congressional delegation of any state. Ronald Reagan, the first president to be inaugurated facing west, is also from California and he has surrounded himself with so many others from his home state in his administration that they are known as "the California Mafia." Well over four hundred registered lobbyists represent California's corporate and public interests, and thirty-seven California news media operate Washington bureaus.

What are all these Californians doing? They're getting their state a larger share of defense spending than any other state ever dreamt of, but they're also allowing California to pay the federal government more in taxes than it gets back in benefits. Billions of dollars are at stake in the decisions the federal government makes—money that can throw California's economy into boom or bust. But decisions about immigration, air quality control, or the distribution of water collected in federal projects also have a big impact on California.

Although some people think of California as a nation unto itself, it isn't. California is part of the federal system and to get its fair share—or more—it has to fight for it.

Californians in Congress: The Cast

"You're in your mother's arms," Democratic Congressman Phil Burton told his nervous colleagues as he redrew the lines for California's congressional

281

districts. But he told a Republican, "You're expendable. You've been bad for California, you're in trouble."[1]

Forty-five Californians—two senators and forty three congressmen—represented their state in the 97th Congress (1981–82). The House delegation was about evenly split between the two major political parties, with twenty-two Democrats and twenty-one Republicans. But population growth determined by the 1980 census gave California two additional representatives in the 1983–84 Congress and that meant the district lines had to be redrawn.

Reapportionment in California is the responsibility of the state legislature, which was dominated by a substantial Democratic majority. Willie Brown, the Speaker of the Assembly and the state's most powerful legislator, left it to his San Francisco ally, Congressman Phil Burton, to draw up the new congressional districts and, not surprisingly, Burton drew them to the advantage of other Democrats. Although Burton's districts were remarkably equal in population—none varied more than 223 people from the constitutionally ideal 525,698—he manipulated boundaries (also known as gerrymandering) to pack as many Republicans as possible into as few districts as possible, forcing four incumbent Republican congressmen into two districts. Other districts were especially designed for liberal allies of Burton, including his brother John who was given a grotesquely sinuous district to ensure his reelection. If his calculations worked out, the partisan division in the California delegation would have shifted from twenty-two to twenty-seven Democrats and from twenty-one to eighteen Republicans. The Democratic congressmen were, indeed, "in their mother's arms," and several Republicans were "in trouble."

Unfortunately for Burton and his friends, serious political trouble soon developed. Trying to strengthen his brother John's neighboring district, Burton had given up some of his own reliable supporters and set himself up for his most serious electoral challenge in years. To make matters worse, brother John then dropped out of his own race. But the heaviest blow came when the Republican party, foreseeing disaster, launched a drive to put repeal of the reapportionment scheme on the ballot. With President Reagan signing the first petition and an investment of hundreds of thousands of dollars in a mail petition campaign, they succeeded, and the voters rejected Burton's plan in the June 1982 election.

At the same time, however, the voters were electing a congressional delegation from the districts designed by Burton. The California Supreme Court had ruled that, pending the vote on the initiative, the existing districts would operate. So while the voters were rejecting Burton's plan, they were also bringing it to fulfillment. In November, they elected not twenty-seven but twenty-eight Democrats and only seventeen Republicans, a better ratio than even Burton had hoped for.

The Republican party had put another initiative on the November 1982 ballot to take responsibility for reapportionment away from the state legislature and put it into the hands of an independent commission. This initiative failed; the state legislature, much to the delight of the Democrats, retained responsibility for redrawing the lines rejected by the voters in June. This they swiftly did in order to get Democratic Governor Jerry Brown's approval before his replacement by Republican George Deukmejian in January 1983. In essence they tidied up the lines and got rid of some flagrant gerrymandering, but they kept Burton's fundamental scheme, which will define the shape of the California congressional delegation for some time to come. An initiative launched in 1983 by Republican Assemblyman Don Sebastiani would have repealed the Democratic plan and replaced it with one far more favorable to Republicans. Sebastiani collected more than enough signatures to put his scheme before the voters, but it was tossed out by the State Supreme Court on the grounds that the state constitution prohibited reapportionment more than once every ten years. The only dissenter on the court was its lone Republican justice.

THE DELEGATION

If state congressional delegations pull together, they can exercise considerable clout in the bargaining that shapes most legislation. Pennsylvania, New York, Michigan, and Texas have reputations for doing just that. The Frostbelt states of the Northeast and Midwest have even formed a coalition to pursue their region's interests.

But even with 10 percent of the votes in the House of Representatives, the largest single delegation, California has failed to attain such clout. "On any given day," one observer wrote, "the delegation fractures as readily as a fake diamond."[2] Sacramento Bee reporter Leo Rennert wrote, "California may be a giant among states; but it's a sleeping giant. Rudderless, without clear leadership or purpose, it's almost totally adrift."[3] This condition was partly due to the kind of people California elects—Rennert called them "lackluster and maladroit"[4]—and partly due to the way they are organized. The delegation as a whole rarely meets, though sometimes they get together with major state interest groups like the California Medical Association or the California Bankers Association. Generally, the Democrats and Republicans function as separate delegations, with minimal unity and organization even within the partisan factions.

THE REPUBLICANS

The seventeen Republicans (sixteen men and one woman) are particularly disorganized, with little leadership and few outstanding legislators among them. Their ranks were badly depleted by the 1982 election. Several Republican congressmen dropped out to run for other offices. Others, including Don Clausen, the delegation's senior member, and John Rousselot, its shrewdest strategist, were defeated. Although they remain the largest Republican delegation from any one state, they hold few crucial committee or leadership positions in Congress. That's partly because they lack seniority—only three of the California Republican congressmen have been in the House for more than two terms, and Carlos B. Moorhead, the delegation's senior member, was first elected in 1972. Moorhead is the nominal leader of the delegation, but his colleagues consider him weak and passive. "Carlos is perceived not as a mental giant," a Democratic colleague said.[5]

Congressmen Jerry Lewis, Bill Thomas, and Robert Badham, all of Southern California, are more respected leaders, and some younger members of the delegation show promise. Ed Zschau, who was elected in 1982 from the Silicon Valley, swiftly became a spokesman for the electronics industry and got a key appointment to the Committee on Foreign Affairs, where he can look after high-tech international trade interests.

Ideology is another factor that limits the Republicans' influence. Journalist George Baker wrote that "the newer Republicans, especially, belong to the Herbert Hoover wing of the party and believe they are waging a personal crusade to restore morality to America."[6] Another reporter declared, "the Republicans have no moderate wing. To the extent that California is represented here, it's really by the Democratic delegation."[7]

THE DEMOCRATS

The Democratic delegation of twenty-eight (including two women, three Hispanics and four blacks) also has its problems. Some, like Ron Dellums of Berkeley, are so far to the left as to be what a colleague called "voices in the wilderness, without the interest or skill in organizing to carry other votes." Others are merely mediocre. But the Democrats do have some real stars and at least the rudiments of an organization. Being part of the majority party in the House of Representatives helps.

For a decade the most powerful single individual among California's House Democrats was Phil Burton of San Francisco, "a smoldering volcano of political intrigue and the most feared and respected member of the lot."[8] Liberal Burton built up a formidable record of legislative accomplishments, including protections for farmworkers, coal miners, civil rights, and the environment. Because of his power as chairman of the House Subcommitee on Territories and Insular Affairs, he was known as the "virtual emperor of Puerto Rico, the Virgin Islands and Guam,"[9] but his most notable triumph was passage of the biggest parks program ever, including California's massive Redwoods Park.

Burton was interested in power as well as policy, and he made his big play in 1976, when he sought election as majority leader, the second most powerful post in the House of Representatives and the heir apparent to the Speaker. He lost to a Texan by one vote. At least four Californians deserted their home-state colleague, either because they disliked him or because they had cut a better deal with his opponent. These defections illustrate the "kamikaze tendencies" of the delegation,[10] as they tossed away California's chance at leadership and handed it over to a Texan, Jim Wright. "Ever since," Leo Rennert laments, "California has been out in the cold. . . . the Northeast and Texas are calling the shots—while Californians are excluded from powerful committee posts and left to squabble over scraps."[11] Burton's power waned after 1976, but his 1982 reapportionment scheme brought in six new Democratic House members, more than any other state and all indebted to Burton for their districts. It appeared the 56 year old congressman's last hurrah had yet to be shouted when, in April 1983, he died, leaving a void in the California Democratic delegation. He was replaced by his wife, Sala.

If Burton was its fiery star, San Jose Congressman Don Edwards is the dean of the California delegation and its quiet mentor. A staunch liberal, Edwards is the second-ranking Democrat on the Judiciary Committee and chairs its Subcommittee on Civil and Constitutional Rights. He guided the Equal Rights Amendment and its extension through Congress and was essential in defending and extending the Voting Rights Act. His vigilance in the protection of civil liberties earned him the title "the Congressman from the Constitution," and he used his power to "stall, snag and otherwise impede the political agenda of the New Right," including his arch-conservative colleagues from California.[12] As subcommittee chairman, Edwards blocked antibusing, antiabortion, and school prayer legislation. He manages to take considerable heat for this and still have the respect of his opponents, because he is from a safe district and because he is well-liked. He's also effective at lining up votes.

His work made him a hero to liberals, feminists, and minority groups, but being "the Congressman from the Constitution" didn't necessarily do much for California. Edwards operated more as a national politician than a California delegate until he became chairman of the California Democratic delegation in 1981. Since then, he has become more attentive to California's needs and has helped make the delegation more effective.

Long dominated by a couple of old-time heavy-hitters, and "chaired by a Rip van Winkle,"[13] the delegation's Wednesday morning meetings had become so trivial that junior members were skipping them, saying they had better things to do. Under Edwards, the representatives work more closely with one another on state-related issues and make their joint positions known through press releases and conferences. Edwards persuaded the members to pool their resources so the delegation could hire its own professional staff for the first time. They've provided analysis of the impact of various bills—jobs, housing, Medicaid, and others—on California. Campaign assistance is also available to members of the delegation, a good way of building loyalty. These changes were not, however, solely due to Edwards. Younger members of the delegation were instrumental, and the successes of Ronald Reagan and the Republican party in 1980 provided a stimulus for organization.

Burton and Edwards were congressional heavyweights for a long time, but California also has several rising stars in its delegation. Norman Mineta of San Jose is already a part of the House leadership as a Democratic whip, and Leon Panetta of Monterey, according to one Congress-watcher the "smartest" member of the delegation, is a member of the House Budget Committee and leads the delegation on fiscal issues along with Sacramento Congressman Vic Fazio. Tony Coelho of Fresno is a leading advocate of water projects, something dear to California's huge farm industry. Coelho also is chairman of the Democratic Congressional Campaign Committee, a position sure to win friends. A staunchly partisan Democrat, Coelho is a skilled organizer with considerable political acumen. With Burton gone, Coelho's influence has increased, both in the delegation and in the House of Representatives. Coelho's opposite might be liberal George Miller of Contra Costa, who leads emerging opposition to water projects and is a spokesman for organized labor.

By now a regional division between the parties must be apparent—most of the Republicans and their leadership come from Southern California and most of the Democrats and their leadership come from Northern California. That was true for a long time, but things have been changing in recent elections as a significant block of very able Democrats from Southern California emerged. Henry Waxman of Hollywood was elected in 1974 and has quickly built up influence on health and energy issues. Waxman ousted a more senior congressman as chairman of the House Subcommittee on Health and the Environment with the support of Cesar Chavez, Edward Kennedy, Ralph Nader, and the

AFL-CIO. He also laid out campaign contributions to committee members who elect their chair. The *California Journal* says he may turn out to be "the biggest winner" in the 1982 election because four close allies of his were also elected to Congress.[14] One of them is Howard Berman, a highly skilled political operator whose brother Michael worked with Phil Burton in drawing the reapportionment map. The Waxman-Berman alliance is likely to inherit a good deal of Burton's power.

All of the comers—Coelho, Miller, Mineta, Panetta, Fazio, Waxman, and Berman—share the characteristics of pragmatism and willingness to get involved in the nitty-gritty of legislative work. Because they are less ideologically committed and electorally secure than Edwards or Burton, they pay closer attention to the needs of California, if only to keep their constituencies and key special interests content.

THE DELEGATION'S COMMITTEE ASSIGNMENTS

Much of what Congress does takes place in its numerous committees, so the clout of any state delegation is determined in large part by committee assignments. But only eight of forty-five Californians have been in Congress since before 1974, so the delegation hasn't had a lot of time to build up seniority or expertise. When Burton lost the 1976 leadership contest, his supporters also found themselves at a disadvantage in getting key committee posts.

Aside from Edwards on Judiciary and Waxman on Health, California lacks the clout such a large delegation should have in House committees. Incredibly, the state held no chairmanships. On the Armed Services Committee—important for a state so heavily dependent on military spending—California had only three of forty-four seats, less than its share; and the one Democrat was Ron Dellums, who was on the committee as a gadfly, not to advocate California's economic interests. On the other hand, Californians were heavily represented on committees such as Government Operations, House Administration, the Post Office, and the District of Columbia. These positions are of little value to the state and indicate the weakness of the delegation and the propensity of its mediocre members to the less-than-crucial committees.

California did, however, have a sizable membership on the Interior Committee (seven of forty-two, more than its share), reflecting the state's interest in water and conservation. Californians were also well represented on the Agriculture Committee and on the Budget Committee. Still the committee clout of California was not what it should have been, given the size and significance of the state.

CALIFORNIANS IN THE SENATE

While Californians constitute 10 percent of the House of Representatives, the state has only 2 votes out of 100 in the Senate and that's California's biggest disadvantage in the upper house. This limitation has been exacerbated by California's habit of electing senators of limited ability and by replacing them before they could gain experience, seniority, or power. California's fickle voters also have a habit of electing one senator from each party, so they cancel out one another's votes on many issues.

That was the case from 1976 to 1982, when California was represented in the Senate by Democrat Alan Cranston and Republican S. I. Hayakawa; it continues with Hayakawa's replacement by former San Diego Mayor Pete Wilson, also a Republican, in 1982. Hayakawa was particularly inept, so during the years they shared responsibilities, Cranston was the more important representative for California.

Senator Cranston was elected in 1968 and has been reelected twice since then. He's known as a cautious liberal who works through compromise and rarely leads on issues. As minority whip, Cranston holds the second-ranking position in the Democratic leadership in the Senate. He seems to operate more as a national politician than a California advocate. When he ran for the Democratic presidential nomination in 1984, he was no favorite son to ten of California's congressional Democrats who preferred Minnesotan Walter Mondale. "Alan has never been too interested in the delegation," one of them said. "He's kind of a cold fish."[15]

But when push comes to shove, Cranston comes through for the home state. While often critical of defense spending, he helped get jobs for Californians by supporting Lockheed loan guarantees and the B-1 bomber. When formulas for gas rationing penalized auto-dependent California, Cranston took the leadership in scuttling them. His aides call him "California's Number One Environmentalist," citing his advocacy of park expansion in the Redwoods, Big Sur, and Point Reyes, as well as his work for wilderness and desert protection and, somewhat contradictorily, for skiers. Although usually antagonistic to agribusiness' beloved water projects, at one time Cranston supported exemptions to acreage limitations for eligibility for cheap, federally subsidized water.

Pete Wilson, a Reagan supporter and moderate Republican, joined Cranston in the Senate in 1983. His choice of committees—Agriculture and Armed Services—suggests a keen awareness of the primary needs of his home state, but his performance thus far has been lackluster. He votes with the White House except on rare occasions, such as the immigration bill which he opposed as a loyal spokesman for California agribusiness.

What California Gets: Water, Guns, and Money

California's congressional delegation hasn't always been disorganized and weak. There was a time in the 1950s and 1960s when the delegation pulled together on certain issues, and the work they did helped build up key sectors of the California economy. Water and military projects, as well as highways—all of which benefited individual congressmen's districts as well as the state as a whole—united the delegation for most of two decades.

Early in the 1950s, Bernie Sisk, John McFall, and Harold T. "Bizz" Johnson, all from the Central Valley, were elected to Congress. Each served over 20 years in Congress, building seniority, gaining key committee positions, and exercising leadership in the California delegation and in the Congress. These three men built an empire of water projects that made the agricultural and urban development of California possible. From their powerful committee positions they played a formidable game of pork barrel politics, rewarding other districts and states in return for support for the projects they wanted for California.

During the same period California, led by Southern Californian Chet Holifield, hustled military spending. The state had been doing well in this area as a legacy of the defense plant buildup in World War II. But New England, which had been pushing for a share of the spoils with some success, mounted a large lobbying campaign in 1957. The Los Angeles Chamber of Commerce, a major voice for Southern California, grew concerned and pushed the California congressional delegation for more aggressive action. Governors Earl Warren and Edmund G. Brown, Sr., backed up the delegation. Their efforts helped retain and expand California's share of military and aerospace contracts. At one time California got 25 percent of all federal defense spending.

But by the mid-1960s the consensus and efficacy of the California congressional delegation began unraveling. Those years of political turmoil seem permanently etched on the delegation, and many of its contemporary divisions date from that time. The civil rights, antiwar, and environmental movements produced younger representatives, who differed substantially from their elders. Ideological and partisan differences within the delegation appeared and deepened. By the early 1980s, the delegation frequently divided along strict partisan lines: Republicans supported President Reagan and opposed social programs (such as legal services for the poor or unemployment compensation), civil rights legislation (such as extension of the Voting Rights Act), and control of corporations. Democrats voted their liberal ideology—opposing Reagan's budget and favoring social programs, civil rights legislation, control of corpora tions, and even more controversial items like federal health insurance payments for abortions.

Although these partisan differences are considerable, neither party displayed ideological unanimity. On the *Congressional Quarterly*'s ideological voting index, some Republicans like Robert Lagomarsino achieved a 96 percent conservative score, whereas Pete McCloskey scored only 44 percent. Democrats like Don Edwards and Ron Dellums were over 90 percent anticonservative, but others like Tony Coelho and Leon Panetta scored in the 50s,[16] evidence of their pragmatic politics.

As partisan and ideological differences were increasing, the delegation's consensus on water and military projects was weakening. A new generation challenged the values and policies of the old. Conflict increased within the delegation, weakening it in relation to other, more cohesive state delegations.

WATER

The first serious slippage occurred on water projects, as urban liberals and environmentalists began challenging the programs of Sisk, McFall, and Johnson. An aide to a Bay Area congressman said water conservation was his best issue: "It's very popular; we don't have to do more than get out of bed in the morning to get 30 percent of the vote on water issues." Genuine differences between sections of the state emerged. Northern California learned that it paid with its environment for water to develop Central and Southern California, and members of Congress began voting accordingly. By the 1980s a block of votes against water projects had emerged. All were urban, liberal Democrats. The most consistent were northern Californians, but they were sometimes joined by a few Southern Californians. Sometimes as many as fourteen members of the delegation were mustered in opposition to a water project, perhaps the starkest evidence of how the delegation has changed historically.

Still the bulk of the delegation continued to support water projects, and when push came to shove, even members of the antiwater block deviated. Don Edwards, for example, overcame his usual antagonism to water projects to vote for one in his own district. And in a 1982 vote increasing the eligibility of large farmers for cheap water from federal projects, only four California representatives dissented (Democrats Phil Burton, Edwards, Waxman, and Roybal). Agribusiness lobbied the delegation heavily and effectively; their lobbyists include several former aides or members of Congress. Congressman George Miller, normally the most outspoken opponent of water boondoggles, caved in on this one, admitting that "what you have is a streamroller. . . . There's a lot of muscle on one side of this issue."[17]

GUNS

Consensus on military projects also began to dissipate in the 1960s. No state gets as much of the federal defense dollar as California, although the percentage declined from a high of 25 percent to about 20 percent in 1981. New York got 7.4 percent and Texas 8.6 percent. California received 38 percent of the funds for missiles and aerospace, 33 percent for aircraft, 30 percent for research and development, 26 percent for electronics and communication equipment, and 43 percent for weapons. California also was awarded 45 percent of the National Aeronautics and Space Agency's budget. One-third of the country's top defense contractors are located in California, and well over half a million Californians are employed in defense or aerospace related industries.[18]

With that much at stake, you'd think the California congressional delegation would unify on defense spending, but it doesn't. The antiwar movement in the 1960s produced a group of liberal congressmen who vote against virtually all military spending. Several members of this antimilitary block also oppose most water projects. Core members of the group in the 97th Congress were the Burton brothers, Edwards, Dellums, Stark, and Miller of the Bay Area and Beilenson of Beverly Hills, all liberal Democrats. A few others join them occasionally, and all but three California Democrats voted against the MX missile in 1981.

As with water projects, however, the pattern broke when certain home state industries were affected and when the pressure was on. In 1971, Lockheed, the nation's biggest defense contractor and a California-based company, got into financial difficulties and laid off 9000 workers. The repercussions of the collapse of Lockheed for California and thirty-four other states where Lockheed had operations were so enormous that President Nixon, himself a Californian, urged Congress to provide loan guarantees up to $250 million. The proposal squeaked through the Senate by one vote and the House of Representatives by just three. Both California senators supported the bail out; but seven of California's then thirty-eight–member House delegation voted against it.[19] Except for Dellums, all were arch-conservatives voting against government meddling, not defense spending. Other traditionally antimilitary voters like Burton and Edwards went along. Even on an issue of such immediate interest to the state, unanimity was impossible and slippage of just two more California votes would have lost the day.

Another tough test of the cohesion of the delegation was the B-1 bomber, a controversial new airplane, which supporters believed was needed to modernize America's bomber fleet and opponents believed was made redundant by the use of missiles. The B-1 was to be built in Southern California by Rockwell International, and that company along with the Air Force was its chief advocate. But President Carter scrapped the project in 1977, and congressional action to refund it failed by three votes. Seventeen California congressmen voted to kill the B-1, putting 5000 people out of work. Of those voting against the B-1, all but one were Democrats, and all but four were from Northern California. "Military spending just doesn't sell in our district," smiled the aide of a Bay Area congressman. With Southern Californians and Republicans supporting the project, it was clear that ideology and the wishes of the home district overrode loyalty to the state as a whole.

The B-1 was revived when Californian Ronald Reagan became president and, though his secretary of defense, another Californian, was originally leery of the B-1, included the new bomber in his first budget. This time eight Californians, all Democrats (five Northern and three Southern), opposed funding. Many who voted against the B-1 in 1977 switched in 1981, leaving only the hardcore antimilitary block in opposition.

In addition to major controversies like the Lockheed loan guarantee and the B-1 bomber, another factor sometimes altered the delegation's votes on military projects. "Defense is powerful pork," as one reporter put it, and when a project means jobs and money for a congressman's district, the vote is usually there. Edwards, for example, was a solidly antimilitary vote. But Lockheed is a major employer in his district and he supported the bail out. Mineta voted against the B-1 in 1977. But he supported an infantry carrier of dubious utility that was manufactured in his district.

Important as military spending is to California, the delegation was never unanimous and in fact put little effort into these projects, as illustrated by the state's considerable underrepresentation on the Armed Services Committee. With its senior and most powerful water and defense advocates retired or defeated by 1980, California's clout in this area of major self-interest was minimal, and disagreement within the delegation gave representatives of other states ample reason to vote against California projects.

MONEY

Both water and military projects were part of the traditional "pork barrel" style of federal spending—"specific projects for specific states."[20] But defense contracts and grants for specific projects are only one form of federal aid.

Additional billions are distributed as "fund transfers" from national to state and local governments. California alone gets over $9 billion a year. This money is for social services like welfare, health, housing, education, and other programs including highways and transit. Instead of contracts and grants, fund transfers are distributed by formulae usually based on population, but sometimes also taking into account need, tax effort, and other factors. To get its share, or more, a state needs to be sure that these formulae are favorable to its interests. It's not just a matter of hustling projects, grants, or contracts because once the formula is written, it usually remains fixed for years.

California hasn't played this formula game well. The basic conflict is between the declining, older states of the Northeast and Midwest (the Frostbelt) and the richer, growing states of the South and Southwest (the Sunbelt). Delegations from Frostbelt states have been more conscious of formula distribution of funds for urban aid, revenue sharing, assistance to low income people in paying energy bills, and other programs. In 1974 eighteen Frostbelt states organized to increase their share, forming the Northeast-Midwest Congressional Coalition and its research arm, the Northeast-Midwest Institute. The bipartisan organization keeps members informed of what's at stake in budgetary formulas for the region. A congressman from California who serves on the House Budget Committee admitted that a week after President Reagan's second budget was published, the Northeast-Midwest Institute had an analysis ready for its members. A couple of California congressmen pooled their staffs to do a rough version of the same thing, but it took a month before the Californians had reliable information. That put the Frostbelt representatives ahead in the hot contest for funding.

In 1983 Democratic Congressman Vic Fazio of Sacramento, a member of the House Budget Committee, urged his fellow Californians to "wake up" to the fact that California was a "loser" on non-defense programs. Fazio's analysis of the budget revealed that with 11.4 percent of the nation's unemployed, California got only 7.3 percent of federal anti-recession funds; with 10 percent of the population, California got 5.8 percent of the grants for maternal and child welfare services, 2.6 percent of the funds for low-income weatherization and 2.9 percent of rural water and sewer loans.[21]

Whereas California once got back billions of dollars more than it contributed in taxes, by 1979 the state paid in a billion dollars more than it got back and today it barely breaks even. But California's problem is not only the result of divisions within its congressional delegation. Long seen as economically invulnerable, other states feel little sympathy for California and because of the state's affluence, representatives have not felt the need to fight for urban development programs and social services. Prosperity may have weakened the delegation. Californians just weren't used to scrambling for bucks, and when they were, it was for pork barrel bucks, not formula-distributed funds. California's voters also did something to weaken the state in the formula-funding sweepstakes when they cut their property taxes by voting for Proposition 13 in 1978. The reduction in property taxes decreased their federal income tax deductions and so increased federal taxes paid by Californians by an estimated $4 billion.[22] Their action instantly reversed the relationship between taxes paid and benefits received to a net loss. Increasing reliance on formula distribution by the federal government has only exacerbated California's problems.

The congressional delegation was unable to recoup the loss. An aide to Senator Cranston said, "the feeling here in Washington was, if you were crazy enough to do it, that's your problem. We're not going to help you." A spokesman for the Californian in the White House had no sympathy, pointing out that "Detroit is possibly the most depressed big city in the nation. They raised taxes. [Californians] are just going to have to do it."[23]

EMERGING UNITY

Once in a while California manages to defend its interests. Congressman Henry Waxman, for example, was able to put together a bipartisan coalition to stop a revision in a formula for health care funds that would have hurt the state. In 1980 only two members of the delegation opposed the hazardous waste superfund, and only one Californian cast a vote against the Refugee Assistance Act, a program much needed in the state with the most refugees. Secretary of the Interior James Watt's proposals for offshore oil drilling brought about a rare alliance between conservative Republicans and liberal Democrats in 1982. Under Don Edwards's leadership and with the assistance of its new professional staff, the Democratic delegation is making a greater effort to analyze the impact of legislation on California and to act as a bloc to protect the state's interests.

Californians in the White House: The "California Mafia"

Of course there have been Californians in Washington other than in Congress. California was blamed for Richard Nixon and his henchmen, though the state did not benefit greatly from his tenure in office. Nixon rose to national prominence on a base of Southern Californian right-wing, anticommunist votes—very much a product of the state's wide-open, media-oriented political system. Though the state rejected him as governor in 1962, he won its vote as a presidential candidate in 1968 and 1972 in campaigns that were models of

California public relations techniques. And he took to the White House with him a number of Californians who were more political operatives than policy-makers, an orientation that may have produced Watergate.

But the public relations experts weren't the only Californians Nixon brought to Washington. David Packard, founder of one of California's biggest electronics firms and a major defense contractor, was deputy Secretary of Defense for Nixon, and Caspar Weinberger became Budget Director and Secretary of Health, Education and Welfare. He returned to California to head the Bechtel Corporation, one of the largest firms in the country and a major government contractor.

Although Nixon was less loyal to his home state than Lyndon Johnson was to Texas, he furthered the careers of several other Californians and aided the state's defense industry. He came "to the rescue" when Lockheed needed its loan guarantee, used the powers of his office to urge the Japanese to buy from Lockheed and, in return, probably won the company's support for his reelection campaign.[24]

While Georgian Jimmy Carter was president, California was on the outs. Carter owed Californians little for his election and was generally viewed as anti-West. His administration rarely consulted the California governor's representative in Washington or the leaders of the California congressional delegation. Still California was big enough to supply a half dozen of Carter's top administrators. Warren Christopher, a prominent California attorney, was deputy Secretary of State; Donald Kennedy, later president of Stanford University, was Director of the Food and Drug Administration; and Harold Brown of Cal Tech became Secretary of Defense. But the Carter presidency, though not solely responsible, spanned the years when Californians began paying more federal taxes than they got back in benefits. California's share of military spending also declined for the first and only time in its history; it was Carter who scrapped the B-1 bomber.

It was not until Ronald Reagan became president that Californians really came into their own in the executive branch, packing the White House and holding positions of power in every department and agency. Three of the four men closest to Reagan and of greatest influence served him both as governor and in the White House. Michael Deaver remains there as Deputy Chief of the White House staff, but Ed Meese, who was White House Counsel, moved on in 1984 to succeed Californian William French Smith as Attorney General. William Clark resigned from his position as Associate Justice of the California Supreme Court to become first Deputy Secretary of State, then the President's National Security Counsel, and finally, Secretary of the Interior, succeeding the controversial James Watt in 1983. In addition to Meese, Deaver, and

Clark, Reagan's press and political affairs directors were always Californians, and an additional two dozen held other key White House jobs.[25]

Reagan also appointed over seventy Californians to top positions in every department and agency. At the cabinet level, Meese and Clark joined Caspar Weinberger, the third Californian in succession to hold the post of Secretary of Defense, and George Shultz, Secretary of State. Weinberger and Shultz both served President Nixon, then worked for the Bechtel Corporation, a California company and the largest in the nation under private ownership. Bechtel is also a major government contractor in the United States and the Arab states, a relationship that critics felt might influence American foreign policy.

What difference does the California Mafia make for its home state? Although they're thought to be a "brighter, sounder bunch than the Georgians were,"[26] they don't seem to have done much for California. They consult with congressional leaders and the governor's representative more than the Carter people did, but one of those consulted wonders whether their "input has much impact." California's Republican congressmen "assumed that we would properly be afforded an instantaneous response from the White House," Representative Robert Badham said, but "such has not been the case." Congressman Jerry Lewis complains "You can't even get them to return your phone calls." But White House Political Director Edward J. Rollins says that's because there are no outstanding leaders among the California Republicans.[27]

Relations with California's liberal Democrats in Congress are worse. Democratic analysis of Reagan's proposed 1983–84 budget showed it would bring in $1.6 billion less for California than the Democrats' proposed budget. "Sometimes it seems like those Californians running this administration—Reagan, Ed Meese, William French Smith and others—have forgotten where they came from," said Congressman Don Edwards.[28]

It's clear that Reagan has no intention of showering goodies on his home state like Texan Lyndon Johnson did. California was hard hit by Reagan's budget cuts and his tilt to formula distribution of funds caught Californians off guard. Cuts in refugee assistance seem also targeted to punish California, which hosts half of the country's refugees. Actions by James Watt, Reagan's right-wing secretary of the interior, appalled California conservationists and unified the congressional delegation. These policies, of course, did not hurt Reagan's affluent, conservative political base. In fact, they hurt mainly those who opposed him. Conveniently, they dumped the social problems of the state into the lap of Jerry Brown, the Democratic governor, just as he was running for Senate. One of Reagan's political operatives explained that they didn't want "a senator from the President's home state sitting here nit-picking the President on everything he does and playing it back to his home state."[29] There were even allegations that Reagan's Environmental Protection Agency administrators held up a grant to clean up a toxic waste dump in California because they thought it might help Brown's senatorial candidacy. Brown's defeat and the election of Pete Wilson and George Deukmejian, both Reagan supporters, could, however, improve California's influence in the White House.

If Reagan hurt California in some ways, he helped in others. His 1983–84 budget included $192 million for California water projects and millions for research and development projects that will be done in Califonia. Although California is losing social service funds, Reagan has been increasing the state's share of defense spending, which had been declining. When he took office in 1980, it was 20 percent; by 1983, it was 23 percent and by 1986 it could be as high as 30 percent. The B-1 bomber, revived when Reagan took office, will be a special boost for California, and the $15 billion air transport contract awarded to Lockheed will be a further boon.

Nevertheless, the impact of the California Mafia on federal policy is general, not of specific benefit to California. If military contractors and Bechtel benefit, it is because of a broad commitment to spending for the sort of work they do, not an interest in paying off California corporations. The Californians in the administration brought an attitude to Washington that went well beyond the old pork barrel politics in the interest of the home state. Veteran presidential reporter Hugh Sidey described the Reaganites as "self-made rich men whose strong wills have produced wonders in a society that constantly shifted . . . lived a long way from the world . . . [and] still vaguely believe that American will has the power to work magic in the globe, as it did to California."[30] They are taking California to the nation, not the nation to California. If what they do is good for California, that's because of their general attitude, not an urge to get benefits for their home state. If California businesses benefit, that's because business in general (but especially the defense industry) benefits.

California's Lobbyists: The Real Delegation?

While the California congressional delegation is often divided and the Reagan administration seems unconcerned, there's another group of men and women in Washington who are unwavering advocates of the state's interests. They are the lobbyists who hustle defense contracts, water projects, tax breaks, and municipal grants; if California has benefited from federal largesse, they deserve a great deal of the credit.

Over 400 California-based interest groups and corporations retain permanent, sometimes numerous, representatives in Washington. Forty-nine of these lobbying operations represent California's public sector, including seven state agencies, seven counties, twenty-one cities, nine water districts, and five other special districts. A handful of lobbyists also represent public interest groups like Common Cause, Friends of the Earth, and the Sierra Club, the largest, with 10 advocates. But the bulk of the lobbyists from California represent private interests, including seventeen of the nation's largest defense contractors and dozens of California-based energy firms. Agriculture, land development, electronics, banks, railroads, water, and timber interests are also well represented. Many retain one or more prestigious Washington law firms as well as their professional lobbyists. Half a dozen of California's top law firms have branches in Washington, with the number growing substantially when Ronald Reagan became president and lawyers from California followed him east.

PUBLIC INTERESTS

California has more public sector lobbyists representing the state and its local governments than any other state, though their staffing is minimal. Los Angeles, for example, has just one lobbyist who acts as a link between his employer and the seventeen members of Congress from the Los Angeles area, keeping them informed of the city's needs on issues like revenue sharing, housing, transportation, harbor dredging, and airport construction. "Most of what cities do," the Los Angeles lobbyist observed, "has a federal dimension, so representation in Washington is essential." In the past the work dealt with winning specific grants, but increasingly the focus is on funding formulas.

In addition to the forty-two local government lobbyists, seven state agencies, including universities, have offices in Washington. The state itself has long had a Washington office directed by the governor. Under Governors Warren and Brown, Sr. it worked well with the congressional delegation on specific California projects. Under Governors Reagan and Brown, Jr. the relationship deteriorated, and some observers believe that the office became the center of the national political operations of these governors. Less attention was paid to the needs of the state or to working with the congressional delegation. Governor Jerry Brown was even blamed for lack of cohesion in the delegation.[31] A reporter said the office suffered from "low visibility" and was not used to pursue the state's interests, partly because Brown used it for his own ends and partly because "the state has never perceived its own interests clearly. New York State and New York City are far more effective." A California congressman who served on the budget committee said he rarely heard from the office.

But Governor Brown's man in Washington denied that his staff of ten functioned merely as political operatives. They worked on issues of keen interest to

California, including pesticide regulation, the agricultural budget, the distribution of transportation money, and the clean air and water acts. Brown took a special interest in aerospace and electronics, and his office in Washington was particularly active on these issues, advocating tax credits for research and development for high-technology industries and legislation on energy and telecommunications. They also took a special interest in federal assistance for refugees, and they became increasingly active in the formula distribution of funds, something Proposition 13 and Ronald Reagan forced onto their agenda. On the latter issue they began meeting more frequently with key members of the congressional delegation in 1982.

Brown's representative argued that his office's low profile was typical of any canny lobbyist and reflected their work with individual members of Congress only on specific issues depending on committee membership. They also lobbied representatives from other states. On the issue of offshore oil drilling, for example, the governor's agent said "we won twenty–fifteen in committee with all three California delegates voting against us because we worked with representatives from other states." Although some states, like Texas, have no representation at all, California's chief lobbyist felt his staff of ten was at a disadvantage in trying to represent so large a state with such diverse interests against such formidable competition as the Northeast-Midwest Coalition.

Both the Los Angeles and state of California lobbyists deny "helping corporations get contracts" and say they rarely advocate the interests of specific California industries. Although Governor Brown endorsed the jobs-rich B-1 bomber project, his Washington office said they "never got into it." That may sound surprising given the enormous share of military spending that California received, but it seems these industries are quite capable of taking care of themselves.

The role of the governor's representative in Washington under Republican Governor George Deukmejian had yet to be clearly defined after his first year in office, although Leo Rennert has criticized Deukmejian for paying "scant attention to the impact of federal spending during the first months of his administration."[32]

PRIVATE INTERESTS

All of California's major military, aerospace, and electronics manufacturers have substantial representation in Washington. While most public sector and public interest lobbies have offices, the corporate sector invests more lavishly in professional representation. TRW, a major defense contractor, has thirteen registered lobbyists. FMC has eight and keeps three major law firms on retainer. Lockheed has six lobbyists and two law firms. The American Electronics Association has two lobbyists and two legal counsels Bechtel employs five advocates plus legal counsel. Rockwell International, the company that will build the B-1 bomber, retains four lobbyists, two law firms and a consultant.

These corporations also rely heavily on the "revolving door" for employees with good contacts and information. According to Senator William Proxmire, as of 1979, 2124 former high-ranking military officers were employed by the top 100 defense contractors. Over half worked for just 20 companies, topped by Lockheed with 210.[33] Bechtel has employed a current member of the United States Senate, Reagan's deputy secretary of energy, and the secretaries of state and defense, as well as two former CIA directors.

When campaigning for a contract, these lobbyists target not only key members of Congress, but also the White House and the Pentagon. In addition, Rockwell International's effort to sell the B-1 involved extensive public relations activity, organizing stockholders, employees, and subcontractors to lobby their congressmen.[34] The Pentagon also lobbied vigorously for the project. The same sort of collusive campaign was underway in 1982, as Lockheed and the Pentagon tried to sell Lockheed's air transport plane over Boeing's. Additional support comes from companies that get subcontracts on major projects (Fairchild in the case of the air transport) and from the congressional representatives of the home districts of the subcontractors. One congressman said "the big corporations use subcontracting like the old pork barrel, to pick up votes in key districts. They don't need or rely on the California delegation. They can take care of themselves."

The newest California connection to Washington is that of the electronics industry. For years, high-tech industries were content to go their own way, but recently they've found they need government for more than just defense-related contracts. Apple Computers lobbied Congress for a year to get a tax break for donating computers to schools. The "Apple bill" was rejected by the Senate, but its time may yet come. In addition to individual companies, high-tech is also represented by umbrella organizations like the American Electronics Association. They lobby for tax breaks for capital investments and are especially active on foreign trade issues, trying to contain Japanese competition and avoid limits on sales of electronic equipment to the Soviet Union, which some legislators wish to limit for defense reasons.

By 1982 the electronics representatives had made *high-tech* a political buzzword, as politicians turned to the relatively new industry as a savior for the nation's faltering economy. Governor Jerry Brown and some other neoliberals caught on to the issue first and won the label "Atari Democrats." With the 1982 election of Senator Pete Wilson and Silicon Valley's Congressman Ed Zschau, electronics gained two potent Republican spokesmen. By 1983 President Reagan had climbed on the bandwagon, declaring himself "an apostle of high-tech."[35]

Rarely do the hundreds of California lobbyists operate in coalition, but there is one body that brings many of them together. The Golden State Round Table is a group of about fifty corporate and twenty public sector lobbyists who meet for monthly luncheons also attended by members of Congress and their aides. One lobbyist said the round table "drives the delegation," but most other observers dismissed that notion, saying it functioned mainly as an informal communications network. Occasionally, the participants coalesce on a particular issue, but if they could agree more often, they could be a formidable force that could, indeed, "drive" their fragmented delegation.

Still More Californians

California leads the Republican party through President Reagan, but it also leads the Democratic party. Charles Manatt, a Los Angeles attorney, came to Washington in 1980 to chair the Democratic National Committee. Manatt's prestigious law firm, with an ex-senator as a partner and offices in Los Angeles and Washington, has solid connections with banking and political interests. Manatt became party chairman by his organizing skill and fund-raising ability. Being from California helps. As one journalist wrote, "In politics, all roads lead to California,"[36] not only for votes and media-coverage, but also for money. Hollywood is part of this, with entertainers able to raise massive amounts of money, but California has plenty of traditional fat-cats, enough to be called "the Wall Street of campaign politics."[37] Manatt's fund-raising contacts made him a sensible choice for the party.

One journalist takes a sinister view of Manatt, calling him "a lawyer for hire, a fixer," but most observers approved of his pragmatic style. He tightened the party's organization and expanded its operations, introducing more sophisticated campaign techniques developed in California. He worked with Senator Cranston and Congressmen Phil Burton (on reapportionment) and Tony Coelho (on congressional campaigns), bringing these Californians more into the mainstream of national Democratic politics. He helped bring the 1984 Democratic convention to San Francisco, hoping it would help the party develop a Western strategy. Manatt's party chairmanship has given California

a greater part in the national Democratic party, after years of leadership from
Texas and the Northeast.

With all these Californians in Congress, the administration, the lobbies, and
the political parties, it should come as no surprise that there is a large contin-
gent of Californian journalists in Washington to report on their activities—
more than from any state besides New York. Eighteen California newspapers,
and nine radio and ten television stations have news bureaus in Washington.
Most employ only one correspondent, but the *Los Angeles Times* bureau has
twenty-five, plus editors. Only one of the *Times* Washington reporters is
assigned to the California "beat," however. The *Sacramento Bee, Riverside
Press*, and *San Jose Mercury*, with far smaller bureaus, pay more attention to
the impact of national politics on California. But with Reagan in the White
House and tightening budgets both in Washington and back at home, the
California press delegation has begun focusing more on how what happens in
the nation's capital affects the home districts. This tendency could give greater
focus to the congressional delegation simply by ensuring that their constituents
know what they're doing (or not doing) and what difference it makes.

The Helter-Skelter Delegation

Not long ago, the presidents of the top universities in California invited the
entire congressional delegation to a reception to talk about the needs of their
institutions. Seven members of Congress showed up, leading one university
president to lament the lack of support from the state's representatives and
wonder what they could agree on, if not education.

The episode illustrates the problems California has making its voice—or
voices—heard in Washington. With the largest delegation in Congress, California should have great clout, but numbers aren't enough. California loses out
because of better organization and cohesion among other states and regions like
the Frostbelt, with its Northeast-Midwest Coalition. As Leo Rennert, the
closest journalistic observer of Californians in Congress, puts it, "in looking at
the rising curve of California setbacks, it's obvious that growing competition
from other states is a major factor."[38] But as his colleague, George Baker,
points out, California's problems are also internal: the delegation was "riddled
. . . with petty jealousies, mediocrity, ideological intransigence, grinding
ambitions and ineffectual leadership."[39] But these journalists may have been
too hard on the delegation, whose problems may be explained partly by the fact
that it accurately represents the state and partly by certain conditions that may
have been only temporary.

Differences within the delegation mirror genuine differences within the state. The districts these men and women represent are wildly different—from liberal, urban Berkeley to conservative, suburban Orange County and the rural districts of the Central Valley. Their interests are disparate and they differ as much ideologically as their representatives do. As California grows in population, the districts grow smaller and have more insular concerns; the representatives reflect this. California's weak political parties and wide-open politics also fragment the delegation. Republican Congressman Bill Thomas complained that "Texans relate to each other as Texans because they know the party helped to get them elected. We, by and large, got there by ourselves. We're a bunch of feudal lords and we relate to each other when we deign to."[40]

These characteristics of the state make problems for the delegation inevitable, but events in the 1970s exacerbated them. The 1974 election brought an upheaval in California politics and in the congressional delegation, sweeping a whole new generation into power. The old pork-barrel politicians were replaced by ideologues, reformers, media-made candidates, and sometimes pragmatists. Whatever their talents, they lack all-important seniority and experience in Congress. With their arrival, the old consensus within the delegation on water and military projects dissipated, a change that was probably overdue if only because California itself was divided about them. Voices of dissent that had arisen in California were finally heard in Washington.

But being new and diverse aren't the only problems. Leo Rennert dismissed these arguments as "an excuse—an alibi for cautious, do-little politicians to justify their puny objectives and even smaller accomplishments."[41] Nobody denies that California has more than its share of mediocre representatives. They also suffer from lack of leadership. Senator Cranston and Congressman Edwards, until recently, focused their energies on national issues rather than California concerns. Phil Burton did the same, and his attempt to win a position of leadership in the House of Representatives, which might have served California well, was sabotaged by other Californians.

There are signs, however, that the delegation is tightening up. Reforms in the House seniority system moved some competent junior members into positions of influence more quickly than would have been possible in the old days. These "new breed" politicians like Mineta, Panetta, Fazio, Waxman, and Berman are less ideological and more pragmatic than their colleagues, traits that may improve California's position. Don Edwards is making greater efforts to lead the delegation, and reapportionment will increase the clout of California Democratic delegation, which, under pressure from the Reagan victory and an insurgent Republican party, is already cooperating better.

Some observers wonder whether delegation unity is all that desirable any-way. Newer members feel that the absence of discipline gives them a chance to advance in the House without going through an autocratic state delegation leader as would once have been necessary. And a monolithic state delegation might also mute genuine differences that exist between the interests of the home districts. Not everybody in California agrees that military contracts and water projects are such good things. And when they have to, the delegation is increasingly capable of pulling together. A Republican member's aide said, "It's not sensible to even attempt consensus. Where the state's interests as a whole are at stake, the delegation acts cohesively. The California delegation is cohesive when it chooses to be."

Concerns about California's helter-skelter delegation have probably been exaggerated. As we have seen, the state still gets plenty, and the problems of the delegation reflect legitimate divisions within the state itself. As we have also seen, the state is well represented by hundreds of men and women besides the congressia delegation. Finally, California is too important to the nation to be overlooked: It is too big, has too many voters, and is the forerunner for much that happens in the nation.

Notes

[1] Rian Malan, "Boss," *California*, November 1981, pp. 90, 97.
[2] George Baker, "Our Men in Washington," *New West*, October 20, 1980, p. 53.
[3] Leo Rennert, "Lair of the California Lightweights," *California Journal* 11, no. 1 (January 1980): 7.
[4] Ibid., p. 8.
[5] *Los Angeles Times*, March 22, 1983.
[6] Baker, p. 53.
[7] This and all other unnoted quotes were derived from in-person interviews.
[8] Baker, p. 53.
[9] Malan, p. 96.
[10] Leo Rennert, "For Californians, The House Is not a Home," *California Journal* 8, no. 1 (January 1977): p. 7.
[11] Rennert, "Lair of the California Lightweights," p. 7.
[12] *San Jose Mercury*, May 1, 1982.
[13] Baker, p. 54.
[14] Michele Willens, "Wee Henry Waxman, The New Power in the House," *California Journal* 13, no. 8 (August 1982): 269.
[15] *San Jose Mercury*, May 14, 1983.
[16] *Congressional Quarterly*, January 9, 1982, p. 52.
[17] *San Jose Mercury*, September 25, 1982.

[18]Department of Defense, *Prime Contract Awards by State, Fiscal Year 1981*, December 1981, and Joseph Wahed, "Good Growth Ahead for California Aerospace-Electronics," *Business Review*, Wells Fargo Bank, September-October, 1981, pp. 1–2.

[19]See Robert Shaplen, "Annals of Crime, The Lockheed Incident," *The New Yorker*, January 23, 1978, pp. 48–74; and January 30, 1978, pp. 74–91.

[20]Baker, p. 55.

[21]Leo Rennert, "Does California Need Uncle Sam?" *California Journal* 14, no. 7 (July 1983): 279.

[22]*San Jose Mercury*, January 21, 1982.

[23]Ibid.

[24]Shaplen, "Annals of Crime" (January 23, 1978), p. 58.

[25]Martin Salditch, "Don't Call Them the California Mafia," *California Journal* 13, no. 4 (April 1982): 113.

[26]Salditch, "Don't Call Them," p. 113.

[27]*Los Angeles Times*, March 22, 1983.

[28]*San Jose Mercury*, April 8, 1983.

[29]Salditch, "Don't Call Them," p. 114.

[30]Hugh Sidey, "Styles of Political Mafias," *Time*, July 12, 1982, p. 25.

[31]Baker, p. 65.

[32]Rennert, "Does California Need Uncle Sam," p. 279.

[33]William Proxmire, *Report from the Wasteland* (New York: Praeger, 1970), pp. 153–54.

[34]William Proxmire, *The Fleecing of America* (Boston: Houghton Mifflin, 1980), p. 127.

[35]*San Jose Mercury*, January 27, 1983.

[36]*San Jose Mercury*, September 7, 1982.

[37]Rennert, "Lair of the California Lightweights," p. 8.

[38]Ibid.

[39]Baker, p. 53.

[40]*Los Angeles Times*, March 22, 1983.

[41]Leo Rennert, "Lair of the California Lightweights," p. 8.

13

THE MEXICAN CONNECTION

California's Foreign Policy and Minority Politics

Just across the border, Mexican Highway 1 climbs a hill as it meanders south from Tijuana. If you look north, you see the sprawling, sparkling affluence of San Diego; if you look south, you see the tin shacks and grinding poverty of Mexico. Put the two together and you have a picture of the unique relationship between California and Mexico.

Few states boast their own foreign policy, but California has one. Much of the state's trade is international. California has a relatively new bond with Japan, but all through its history, California has had a special relationship with Mexico. That relationship began when California was a part of Mexico and it has remained important ever since. Mexico is a major trading partner for California and a magnet for California investors. Mexico supplied California with its largest minority group and has always been a source of workers for California industry, especially agriculture. California and Mexico share the waters of the Colorado River. Recent discoveries of huge oil reserves in Mexico have further excited California's interest.

California wants and needs what Mexico offers, but racism and condescension have twisted what should be a positive relationship. In recent years that relationship has been altered by the emergence of Mexican-Americans as a political force in the United States and especially in California. Battles over federal immigration laws illustrate not only this changing relationship, but also how important California and Mexican-Americans have become in shaping national policy.

Immigration Policy

America is a nation of immigrants, but periodically those who are already here grow concerned about those who are arriving. California led the nation in imposing limits on Chinese and Japanese immigration and played a prominent part in immigration controls established by the Progressives in the 1920s.

The 1970s saw a new movement for immigration control, which can be traced to several elements. Various international crises led the United States to accept thousands of refugees from Southeast Asia, Cuba, Central America, and Afghanistan. The lack of any cogent policy for reacting to these situations caused increased concern about overall immigration policy. Simultaneously, the economy was in recession, and some people worried that legal and illegal immigrants were taking jobs away from Americans as well as providing a pool of low-wage workers. Some state and local government officials also worried about the cost of providing social services to refugees and illegal aliens. America faced an era of limits. As Paul Ehrlich, a leader of Zero Population Growth, put it, concerned citizens were asking "If we are limiting our family sizes so that our children can inherit a better nation, why should we throw open our doors to over-reproducers. . . . However desirable each individual immigrant may be, he or she increases the number of Americans."[1] A 1981 national opinion poll showed that 80 percent of Americans wanted immigration reduced.[2]

These relatively practical concerns were inflamed by an element of racism because many immigrants were from the Third World and especially from Mexico. Demographers were projecting a Third World majority in California in the near future, and to some, this was a "message of fear."[3] Former CIA Director William Colby declared that "the swelling population of Mexico, driving millions of illegal aliens over the border, is a greater threat to the United States than the Soviet Union."[4] The increasing political assertiveness of Mexican-Americans may have contributed to these fears.

The threat of an alien tidal wave was "fomented," according to a Mexican-American scholar, "by politicans, the INS [Immigration and Naturalization Service], and certain organized interests."[5] The INS played a significant part by releasing startling figures estimating that there were 8–11 million illegal immigrants costing the taxpayers $13–16 billion annually in public services. Critics of the INS allege that the numbers were "made up" to sensationalize the problem and "make a fuss" in order to get attention and win bigger budget allocations.[6] Recent data suggest that these critics were correct and the INS was indulging in a classic case of bureaucratic expansionism by scare tactics.

Although California is probably the single state most affected by immigration, Californians contributed little to the growing movement for tighter controls. Only former Senator Hayakawa and Congressman Dan Lundgren, both Republicans, were active restrictionists.

Nevertheless, immigration policy was on the national agenda throughout the 1970s. Presidents Ford and Carter unsuccessfully attempted to expand funding for the INS border patrol and established special commissions to study the problem. Congress held hearings and in 1976 passed legislaton limiting immigration from any one country to 20,000—a quota that failed to recognize Mexico's special relationship with the United States and probably only encouraged illegal immigration.

In 1981 the Commission on Immigration Policy appointed by President Carter recommended sweeping reform, including tightened border controls, penalties for employers who hire illegal immigrants, an identification card for American workers, and an amnesty for those who had immigrated illegally before 1980, allowing them to stay without penalty. "The first priority," the commission declared, "is bringing undocumented illegal immigration under control."[7] The commission's recommendations formed the basis for the Simpson-Mazzoli bill.

Alan Simpson is a Republican senator from Wyoming and Romano (Ron) Mazzoli is a Democratic congressman from Kentucky. It's ironic that legislators from states that are minimally impacted by immigration are the prime movers in immigration reform, but perhaps that's precisely because their constituencies have no interest in the policy and so they are under little pressure. As chairmen of the Senate and House committees on immigration, Simpson and Mazzoli introduced their legislation and held public hearings in 1982.

The legislation they proposed set an annual immigration limit of 425,000, made it illegal to hire an "unauthorized alien" subject to a penalty of up to $1,000 and 6 months in jail, and mandated national identity cards for workers. To compensate for loss of workers, their program allowed for a limited system of temporary workers when the attorney general certified that American workers were unavailable. Finally, the Simpson-Mazzoli bill proposed an amnesty for those who immigrated illegally before 1980.

According to Mazzoli, the purpose of the bill was "to reform outmoded and unworkable provisions of the present immigration law and gain control of our national borders. We intend," he declared, "to close the back door on illegal immigration so that the front door on legal immigration may remain open."[8] Senator Simpson solemnly concurred: "The first duty of a sovereign nation is to have control over its own borders."[9]

THE PROBLEM

The current immigration policy allows for 270,000 legal immigrants each year, with no more than 20,000 from any one country, but it's a policy that doesn't work. Since 1975, for example, the United States has allowed over 450,000 Indochinese to enter the country as refugees. But the worst abuse of the policy comes on our southern border with Mexico.

The 2,000 mile border is weakly guarded by the INS and highly permeable. Much of it runs through desert. The American and Mexican sides are indistinguishable and sometimes divided only by rusty barbed wire. In other places there are electronic sensors and border guards, but with only 2,100 border patrol agents, of whom 400 are on duty at any one time, even the "guarded" sections are permeable. The INS apprehended 49,511 immigrants in the 60 mile Chula Vista section of the California-Mexico border in just one month in 1983, and they estimate that they catch only 25 percent of the illegal entrants. Perhaps half a million or more sneak across the California border every year, according to the INS. By 1980 they were estimating a total of more than 12 million illegal immigrants in the United States.

These numbers probably inflate the problem because most Mexican illegal immigrants do not come to stay and many of those apprehended are repeaters. The 1980 census found only 2 million illegal immigrants in the United States, half of whom were Mexicans. The Census Bureau admits, however, that it may have missed as many as 20 percent of the illegals and that it is virtually impossible to count workers who come for short visits to do seasonal work. Taking these factors into account, the most realistic estimates put the number of illegal immigrants at about 3 million—a lot less than the INS figures, but still enough to cause concern.

About two-thirds of these immigrants chose California.[10] Known in Mexican mythology as "Aztlan," or the "bright land to the north," California is just that to many Mexicans. What's called the "push-pull" phenomenon is operating. Mexicans are pushed out of Mexico by dire economic straits, with unemployment at 40–50 percent, and pulled to the United States by job opportunity. California is heavily dependent on these workers. Studies in 1983 found that 100 percent of the pole tomato workers in the San Diego area, 80 percent of the Santa Cruz strawberry workers, and 75 percent of the fruitpickers of the Central Valley were undocumented.[11] But many urban workers are also illegal immigrants. Eighty percent of the garment workers of Los Angeles are of Mexican descent, and most are illegals. "If the illegal aliens were thrown out of California today," former Senator S. I. Hayakawa observed, "three-fourths of the restaurants would close tomorrow morning."[12] Wayne Cornelius of San Diego's Center for U.S.-Mexican Studies says, "It's very difficult to identify a single element of the economy in California that is not dependent on Mexican labor."[13]

These workers provide cheap labor for businesses, but they may take jobs American citizens could have and keep wages low. Studies of the problem are inconclusive. Cornelius, the leading expert, argues that Mexican illegals take mostly disagreeable jobs that United States citizens don't want. A systematic review of a number of studies concluded that only two of ten jobs taken by Mexican undocumented workers would otherwise be filled by Americans. Still that adds up to 300,000–600,000 jobs, a significant number in times of high unemployment.[14]

The data are also mixed on another big concern about illegal immigrants: the use of social services. Cities and counties, especially in Southern California, complain that illegals consume a major share of public health and education services. As a consequence, Los Angeles County stopped free medical care to undocumented persons in 1983, and a 1982 court ruling, giving children of illegals rights to education, was expected to cost the county $415 million. Most studies, however, find that illegal immigrants pay more in taxes than they take back in services. Many do not stay in the United States long enough to use available services; others are afraid to apply precisely because they are here illegally. "In terms of tax dollars paid versus social services consumed," one analyst concluded, "undocumented Mexicans are overwhelmingly in the black."[15]

The evidence suggests that the number of illegal aliens was inflated by the INS and that their impact on jobs and social services may be minimal. But the evidence is not conclusive, so the debate on the Simpson-Mazzoli bill still centered on these issues. What was never in doubt was that existing immigration law was being violated and that many of the violators were members of a racial group that some people didn't want to see grow.

TAKING SIDES

The preceding issues defined support and opposition for the Simpson-Mazzoli legislation. Support came from the INS and the Reagan administration, as well as members of the Carter administration and the commission Carter had appointed to study immigration. The chairman of that commission, Father Theodore Hesburgh, returned to support Simpson-Mazzoli as co-chair of the National Citizens Committee for Immigration Reform. He emphasized the need for stronger border patrols and "demagnetizing the magnet" of jobs by introduction of employer sanctions and employee identification cards.[16] Another citizens group, the Federation for American Immigration Reform (FAIR), complained about the impact of illegal immigrants on employment for Americans. A few Republican congressmen from Southern California also voiced concern about job displacement as well as the use of social services by illegals. Americans for the Rights of Citizens expressed the same concern, citing the costs of educating the children of illegal immigrants. Further support for the new legislation came from the Alliance for Immigration Reform, a group of multi-national corporations including Xerox and Ford. Two traditionally liberal groups also supported Simpson-Mazzoli. The AFL-CIO and NAACP both argued that illegal immigrants took jobs away from Americans, especially minorities and women. Lane Kirkland, president of the AFL-CIO, predicted "explosive" social disruption unless the threat to jobs of Americans was diffused.[17]

Supporters of the legislation were divided, however, about one of its components. Currently, about 118,000 temporary foreign workers are permitted in the United States each year under the "H-2 Program." They are allowed only when employers prove American workers aren't available. The Simpson-Mazzoli bill included an expansion of the H-2 program, but the AFL-CIO opposed any form of guest worker program while California Congressman Dan Lundgren, a spokesman for agribusiness and a supporter of Simpson-Mazzoli, favored a substantial expansion of the system so that California growers could continue to enjoy a supply of cheap labor.

The opposition to Simpson-Mazzoli was a similar mix of traditionally conservative and liberal organizations that rarely found themselves in alliance. Among the conservative opposition were some growers and the U.S. Chamber of Commerce, which argued against penalties for employers of illegals. These sanctions, they argued, would constitute a burden for employers already subject to too much bureaucratic regulation.

The American Civil Liberties Union (ACLU), the Catholic Bishops Conference, and liberal politicians like Senator Edward Kennedy objected to the mandatory identification system for workers. The ACLU declared the ID cards a "de facto domestic passport" adding to the national data bank on individuals and encroaching on civil liberties.[18] Democrat Don Edwards, the dean of the California congressional delegation, concurred, arguing that the legislation constituted over-reaction to inflated figures resulting from repeat immigrants and better enforcement by the INS. Furthermore, he insisted, Simpson-Mazzoli would jeopardize relations with Mexico by destabilizing political and economic conditions there.[19]

The GI Forum, the League of United Latin American Citizens (LULAC) and the Mexican-American Legal Defense Fund (MALDEF) opposed employer sanctions and the ID system on grounds that both would lead to discrimination against persons of Hispanic descent. Employers, they said, would be reluctant to hire anyone with an accent or dark skin. "The INS," said one of the leaders, "has traditionally been . . . the enemy of the Hispanic, with no mercy, participating in indiscriminate raids of the workplace, participating in the separation of families, and also participating in the selective enforcement of the immigration laws."[20] MALDEF's Vilma Martinez dismissed the plan for "scapegoating the undocumented worker for the economic ills of our country."[21] To the Hispanic leaders, Simpson-Mazzoli was little more than "a WASP plot to keep down the dark-skinned races or . . . a pretext for racial discrimination."[22] Senator Simpson, however, denied any racial motivation, declaring that the intent of the legislation was "to send a signal to the world that we are going to get control of our own borders . . . and do it in a way that is not tinged with racism, as has been an evident factor in almost every single immigration reform in our past."[23]

DEATH OF A BILL

When Simpson-Mazzoli came to a vote in the Senate in August 1982, both California senators voted against it. Democrat Alan Cranston did so on civil libertarian and antiracist grounds; Republican S. I. Hayakawa, normally a restrictionist, voted "no" because of employer sanctions. Despite opposition from the senators representing the state that is most affected by illegal immigration, the bill passed the Senate. California's two votes were swamped by the votes of senators from other states.

Within a few months, however, Simpson-Mazzoli was dead. Increasing opposition from organized interest groups, good timing, and the clout of the California delegation killed Simpson-Mazzoli in the House of Representatives as the congressional session ended in December. Civil libertarians lobbied against the identification system, labor unions lobbied against the guest worker program, growers and business leaders lobbied against employee sanctions, and Hispanics lobbied against the whole thing. Almost all of these groups put forth amendments to the bill to change what they didn't like. Thus, before a vote on Simpson-Mazzoli could be held, the amendments had to be disposed of. But Christmas was coming and the congressional session was almost over. With other pressing legislation before Congress, time was on the side of the opposition.

California's congressional delegation took the lead; every California Democrat but one was opposed to Simpson-Mazzoli. Fresno Congressman Tony

Coelho, a dynamic emerging force in Congress, spoke for the growers of the Central Valley, pointing out that Californians in general are not so paranoid about immigration as the rest of the nation because Californians are accustomed to it and even rely on it. Republican Dan Lundgren, a supporter of immigration controls, introduced amendments for an expanded guest worker program so growers could retain a supply of cheap labor. Bay Area Congressman George Miller articulated labor's opposition to even the guest worker program included in Simpson-Mazzoli. Black Congressman Augustus Hawkins of Los Angeles broke with the NAACP to express opposition to the legislature for its racism. San Jose's Don Edwards, whose district is heavily Hispanic, brought up civil liberties issues. But it was Edward Roybal, a ten-term congressman from East L.A. and the senior Hispanic in Congress, who administered the coup de grace. Roybal blitzed Congress by adding 200 amendments of his own to the 100 already introduced by others.

All these amendments threatened a long struggle before a Congress eager to adjourn. The House leadership chose not to force the issue, and Simpson-Mazzoli died a quiet death in December 1982 without ever coming to a vote. Congress went home and United States immigration policy went unchanged— the problem still unresolved.

California and Mexico

California's unofficial state policy on immigration, journalist Ed Salzman has observed, is "to maintain an open border."[24] The actions of California's congressional delegation support Salzman's thesis. To understand that attitude, we must understand the historical relationship between California and Mexico.

Although California began as part of Mexico, for most of its history California has treated Mexico as its colony. Hispanic dominance of the state lasted for only 70 years, but those early settlers made contributions that shaped the future. The Spanish and Mexicans first introduced agriculture and irrigation to California. Anglos were unfamiliar with farming the sort of land they found in much of California, so they learned from these predecessors. The first miners were also Hispanic. The New Almaden Quicksilver Mine near San Jose was important not only for introducing mining, but because quicksilver was used in processing gold and silver, which soon became one of California's major industries. It was also during this era that California's pattern of landownership was established with the big Spanish and Mexican land grants. Hispanic culture, from cuisine to architecture, dates from this time and remains an integral part of California today.

Hispanic dominance came to an abrupt end in the 1840s when the Mexican population was overwhelmed by Yankee immigrants. America lusted for the land Mexico held and the Mexican-American War soon opened it up. America added huge territories, including all of Texas, New Mexico, Arizona, Utah, Nevada, and California and parts of Colorado and Wyoming when it defeated its weaker neighbor to the south. That war set the tone for United States-Mexican relations, and it's never changed much. Mexico has had good reason to mistrust the United States.

The Mexican-American War was ended by the treaty of Guadalupe-Hidalgo, which ceded the lands and also guaranteed the rights of Mexican citizens residing in the conquered territories. These rights included property ownership and Spanish as an official language. Of course the land grants were soon subject to legal challenge, and Spanish was deleted as an official language in California's constitution of 1879. Still the unique relationship survives. Carey McWilliams points out that compared to other American ethnic groups, Mexican Americans are "more like the typical minority in Europe. . . . Mexicans were annexed by conquest, along with the territory they occupied, and, in effect, their cultural autonomy was guaranteed by a treaty."[25] This unique heritage, plus proximity to their homeland and its culture, has made Mexican-Americans the slowest minority to assimilate—to adopt American culture—and has affected attitudes about immigration ever since, because Mexicans have always viewed California as, to some extent, theirs.

Conversely, Californians have long treated Mexico as a colony for exploitation. In the 1880s the Los Angeles Chamber of Commerce proposed annexing Baja California. The chamber's leaders, like Harrison Gray Otis and the Chandler family, owned huge tracts of Mexican land. California and Arizona have also eagerly claimed most of the water of the Colorado River, which ends in Mexico though its source is in the United States. Colorado River water makes the Imperial Valley bloom, but by the time the water gets to Mexico it's too salinated to be useful. Mexico has long objected to this, and only in recent years has the United States agreed to desalinate the water and give Mexico its share.

Mexico also has oil that America wants. Exploration by American companies began in the 1890s, and Californians like Edward L. Doheny were deeply involved. When civil war broke out in Mexico early in this century, Californians saw it as an opportunity to break Baja California free. A band of Americans and Mexicans invaded in 1910 but were not successful in their liberation attempt. In 1914 concern about American investments in Mexico led President Woodrow Wilson to send troops to occupy Vera Cruz and Tampico, the center of Mexico's oil industry. Wilson later sent troops across the border in pursuit of Pancho Villa. Although American soldiers were soon withdrawn, the double invasion gave Mexico further reason to mistrust its interfering northern neighbor.

WORKERS

As important as water and oil are for California, the state has always relied most heavily on Mexico as a convenient source of workers. The first big Mexican migration to California came in the 1880s, as anti-Chinese agitation reached its peak and agriculture, mining, and railroads needed to replace Chinese workers. Mexican laborers harvested most of California's crops for the next half century. Between 1900 and 1930, an estimated 1.5 million Mexicans—10 percent of that country's population—came to work in the United States. Agriculture in California was intensifying—clearing new fields, irrigating, shifting over to labor-intensive crops like tomatoes. More workers were needed and American citizens weren't interested. But with a civil war and economic chaos at home, Mexicans were desperate for employment. They were also ideal for employers: "They were close by, worked hard, accepted low wages and poor working conditions and would take seasonal employment and move on when it terminated."[26] Employers sent agents to border towns and into the interior of Mexico, recruiting "by enticement, inducement, advertising, political pressure, vagrancy laws" and other means.[27] Mines and construction projects also relied heavily on Mexican labor during this time and 70 percent of the railroad laborers between 1900 and 1920 were Mexicans.[28] The state and federal government cooperated by providing only a few dozen border patrol officers. It wasn't until the 1920s that Congress increased the border patrol to 450, still grossly inadequate for a 2,000 mile frontier. That suited western employers and politicans, however.

By the 1920s the Mexicans were making a contribution to California culture that wasn't so welcome—they were organizing trade unions on the farms. That movement was soon quashed, however, when the Depression hit and Mexican farmworkers were replaced by Okies and Arkies, the Dust Bowl migrants. Californians turned against Mexicans as they had against the Chinese and Japanese. Southern California was the center of this racial antagonism, which made little distinction between illegal immigrants and Mexican-American citizens. Trainloads of Mexicans were deported and those who lived here were subject to violence and discrimination. The Zoot Suit Riots in Los Angeles in

1943 were perhaps the peak of this xenophobic hysteria. California's political leaders mostly acquiesced in the anti-Mexican activity, but President Roosevelt was embarrassed when the Mexican ambassador made a formal protest.

During World War II America needed good relations with Mexico, and Roosevelt wanted Mexican help with the war effort. Mexican oil was particularly important, and because the Mexican government had expropriated foreign oil holdings in 1938, America needed the cooperation of the Mexican government. Once again California also needed Mexican farmworkers, because by then the Dust Bowl immigrants had left the farms to work in the war industries of the cities and to enlist in the armed forces. The Mexican government took advantage of the situation to demand a more formal system for immigrant labor with protection for workers, so the *bracero*, or "strong arms," program was worked out in 1942. The agreement provided a sanctioned system of temporary workers on condition that domestic workers weren't available and American wages wouldn't be depressed. The program was popular with growers because they were ensured of a supply of cheap labor that went away when the work was done. By 1959, 400,000 workers were imported. Many developed roots and stayed, so the program was never as "temporary" as intended.

Nor did it halt the flow of illegal immigrants. In 1953 the border patrol caught 865,318 illegal entrants,[29] enough to create a mild state of panic and launch "Operation Wetback." In 1954 INS agents conducted raids throughout the Southwest, detaining many Mexicans and prompting others to flee across the border. Despite the crackdown, the bracero program and the movement of illegal immigrants went on, and agribusiness continued to depend on Mexican workers. In 1962, for example, Mexicans were 90 percent of the workers in tomatoes, 71 percent in lettuce, and 82 percent in lemons.[30]

Nevertheless, the bracero program was allowed to end in 1964. Congress failed to reenact the legislation mainly out of concern for American money being drained from the country by foreign workers. They may also have been responding to liberal protests about the way farmworkers were treated and by organized labor, which felt the bracero program stymied efforts to unionize farmworkers and took jobs from Americans. The growers survived the change by increasing mechanization and their reliance on illegal immigrants. Large numbers of "permanent resident aliens" holding "green cards" also maintained a ready work force for the farms. The farmworkers did ultimately manage to unionize in California, but agribusiness and other California industries including electronics and garment manufacture, still depend heavily on illegal Mexican immigrants.

SHIFTING THE BALANCE

In the 1970s and 1980s the relationship between California and Mexico began to change as Mexico became economically stronger and more politically assertive. California woke up to the fact that Mexico is a major market as well as a source of workers. The third largest trading partner for the United States, Mexico is particularly important for retail sales in Southern California. A million people live in Tijuana. Many of them cross the border legally each day to work and shop. The San Diego Chamber of Commerce estimates that Mexican citizens spend $1 billion a year in their city. San Diego recognized this special relationship when in 1981 it built the "Tijuana Trolley," a light-rail transit system running between downtown San Diego and Tijuana. Heavy ridership made it an instant success. Just beyond the border there are also over a hundred American-affiliated manufacturing plants lured by cheap workers and special Mexican tax breaks.

If the oil reserves discovered in Mexico in the 1970s are as big as some people think they are, Mexico could be another Saudi Arabia. Already, it's the fourth largest oil producer in the world. These discoveries made the United States very friendly toward Mexico. Governor Jerry Brown was among the first to perceive Mexico's new potential. As a consequence he radically altered California's foreign policy with regard to Mexico. He began courting the president of Mexico and the governor of Baja California, who was present for Brown's inauguration. He negotiated an agreement for California and proposed a North American "Common Market." President Reagan jumped on the bandwagon by holding his first meeting with a foreign head of state with the Mexican president on the border and suggesting a new "North American Accord."

But now that they've got oil and a little more confidence, the Mexican government is a bit more demanding. President Lopez Portillo called Reagan's proposal an "energy grab,"[31] and expressed resentment about American immigration policy. Mexico knows that illegal immigrants take some of the pressure off their shaky economy and bring home money, but it resents low legal immigration quotas, exploitation of workers, and unilateral immigration policymaking. Lopez Portillo has protested the tightening of borders as an insult to Mexico and demanded that the United States open up markets for Mexican goods to generate more jobs in Mexico and decrease the temptation to immigrate for work. Mexico has also been a thorn in the side of American foreign policy in Central America, taking the side of Nicaragua, Cuba, and the El Salvador guerillas. Economic difficulties in the 1980s including 38 percent unemployment and an inflation rate of 116 percent may tone down Mexican assertiveness, but it's unlikely that Mexico will ever be as passive as it was in the past.

This changing balance was recognized by some California congressmen, who argued that immigration policy needed to take Mexican national interests into account.

Mexican-Americans in California Politics: The Sleeping Giant

If Mexico itself has become more assertive, so have Mexican-Americans, although this huge minority still is called "the sleeping giant" because it has yet to fully assert itself politically.

Hispanics, most of whom are Mexican-Americans, are the largest and most rapidly growing minority in California and the second largest in the United States. By 1970 the Hispanic population of California was over 3 million, or 15 percent of the state's population; by 1980 it was 4.5 million, or 19.2 percent. By contrast blacks were 7.7 percent, native Americans were .9 percent, and Asians were 5.3 percent. The latter figure soared in the 1970s with the arrival of 200,000 Indochinese refugees—one-third of the Indochinese in the United States and California's newest minority.

The Mexican-American population is distributed throughout the state; no congressional district contains less than 5 percent, but the major concentrations of Mexican-Americans are in the Central Valley and Southern California. As early as 1945 Los Angeles was second only to Mexico City in Mexican population, and it remains so today with over 1.5 million Mexican-Americans and perhaps half a million illegal Mexican immigrants. The city of Los Angeles is 28 percent Hispanic, and Los Angeles County is the home of 45 percent of the Hispanics in California. If Hispanics are combined with other minorities, Los Angeles had a Third World majority in 1980—only 48 percent of the city's residents were white. Imperial County, on the Mexican border, was 58 percent Hispanic by 1980. Asians are more likely to concentrate in the north, where San Francisco's population is 22 percent Asian, while blacks were 13 percent of the population in Los Angeles County and 18 percent in Alameda County in 1980.

Economically, Mexican-Americans are less well off than other minorities as well as their Anglo neighbors. They are the youngest, poorest, most unemployed, and least educated. The average age is 21, while the national average is

30, and 20 percent of Hispanics are under 5 years old. Of the students in Los Angeles schools in 1983, 49 percent were Hispanic, 21 percent were black, 21 percent were white, and 7.6 percent were Asian. But only 49 percent of those of age have attained a high school education. The median income of Hispanic households in 1980 was $11,825, $5,345 less than the California average. A third of the population of Los Angeles speaks a language other than English at home. That includes Asians and other foreign-born residents, but the most common language by far in this group is Spanish.

These figures suggest two contradictory messages: By sheer numbers Mexican-Americans should have a lot of political clout, but socioeconomic disadvantages limit that clout. Probably the biggest limitation is that 43 percent of Mexican-Americans are still too young to vote. Time is on their side though. Eventually, inevitably, the sleeping giant will awaken when these Mexican-Americans come of age.

MEXICAN-AMERICANS IN CALIFORNIA'S PAST

Mexicans ruled California until 1846, but their influence soon dwindled and it's been reasserted only in the past decade. Seven of the forty-eight delegates to California's first constitutional convention were native-born and the influence of the Mexican population was sufficient to ensure that the constitution and future legislation were published in both Spanish and English. In the 1850s Mexicans had some political success, electing legislators from Santa Barbara, a judge in Los Angeles, and two state treasurers. Romuldo Pacheco was elected lieutenant governor and served as governor in 1875 when his predecessor moved to the United States Senate. His party denied Pacheco its nomination for another term, but he went on to be elected to Congress in 1876.

In 1879 the second state constitutional convention deleted Spanish as an official language. For almost a century after Pacheco, Mexican-Americans were an invisible political minority. Much of this was due to Anglo nativism and antagonism to all "foreigners"—even those who arrived in California long before the Anglos themselves. In 1894 the state initiated an English literacy test for voter registration. This remained a requirement until it was struck down by the California Supreme Court in 1970. Los Angeles, with the largest concentration of Mexican-Americans, didn't elect an Hispanic to its city council until 1949. It took until 1962 to elect an Hispanic to Congress and until 1973 for the first Mexican-American to be elected to the California Senate.

Anglo racism wasn't all that held Mexican-Americans back. Many Mexican-Americans in California hadn't acquired citizenship, so it's natural that they didn't vote. Others were intimidated by registration requirements. Also, like immigrants from other countries, Mexicans lacked a strong tradition of civic participation. Fatalism and acceptance of authority are, to some extent, part of Hispanic culture. It takes time to overcome these characteristics, just as it did for immigrants from other similar cultures. To add to the problem, assimilation of Mexicans is slower because they're so near their homeland. Perhaps more than other immigrants, Mexican-Americans hang onto the old culture and adopt American ways slowly. As the Los Angeles Times put it,

> The largest immigrant group in the U.S., Mexicans have one of the lowest rates of naturalization. Without clear incentives to become citizens, Mexican immigrants maintain a marginal political existence in their adopted country, an issue of growing concern among politically active Mexican-Americans anxious to translate rising numbers into political clout.[32]

Many Mexicans hope to return to Mexico once they've made it economically, and Mexican law limiting property ownership to Mexican citizens discourages naturalization in the United States. They're also proud of their Mexican heritage.

When Mexican-Americans overcame these burdens and began participating, they found that gerrymandering limited their influence and electability. Hispanics have traditionally voted Democratic, and Democratic politicians took advantage of this. They divided Hispanic-populated areas to maximize Democratic voter registration in as many districts as possible but avoided creating predominantly Hispanic districts that might elect Hispanics. The fact that representation in the state Senate was based on counties rather than population until 1966 also kept heavily urbanized Hispanics underrepresented.

Finally, voter turnout among Hispanics is notoriously low. It's the biggest problem Hispanic candidates have, even in Hispanic districs. A 1982 ABC exit poll of voters found only 2 percent (nationally) were Hispanic, compared to the 6 percent possible. It's not unusual for Hispanic precincts to score voter turnouts around 40 percent, whereas Anglo and black precincts hit 60 and 70 percent.

By contrast, although blacks are a much smaller minority, they've had more electoral success in California. Several state legislators, including the Speaker of the Assembly, are black. Mervyn Dymally and Wilson Riles were elected to statewide office, and several other blacks have won the nomination of their parties for statewide office. Hispanics have not achieved similar political goals. Anglo voters may be less antagonistic to blacks, but black voters turn out in higher numbers than Hispanics and are more likely to vote as a bloc. The high degree of politicization of the black churches, especially during the civil rights movement, also played an organizing role that the Catholic church has, until recently, eschewed in the Hispanic community. State Senator Art Torres points out that "blacks have been more successful in electing public officials for one very important reason. They are citizens to start with, so they can register to vote."[33]

AWAKENINGS: THE FARMWORKERS AND CHAVEZ

Sal si puedes—"get out if you can"—is what they called the barrio in East San Jose. It was full of run-down little houses, and until recently the dusty streets had no curbs or sidewalks. Sal si puedes was home to thousands of Mexican-Americans who worked in San Jose's canneries or went off to the fields at harvest time. One of them was Cesar Chavez, born in Arizona in 1927 to a family of migrant farmworkers. Chavez met a community organizer named Fred Ross and joined his Community Service Organization (CSO). He worked with CSO from 1954 to 1962, learning to organize. He then set out on his own to organize California's farmworkers. Eventually the organization he formed merged with an AFL-CIO farmworkers union and formed the United Farm Workers (UFW) with Chavez as leader.

Chavez is a quietly charismatic man, a proponent of nonviolence. He built a large following among farmworkers, church leaders, and urban liberals during a long strike—*la huelga*—against grape growers begun in 1965. The UFW strikers were supported by a national boycott against nonunion grapes, a tactic Chavez repeatedly used to force growers to capitulate. Chavez also dramatized the cause by fasting and leading a long march on Sacramento, calling it a "pilgrimage of a cultural minority who have suffered from a hostile environment and who now mean business."[34] Chavez built his organizing effort into a social movement (*la causa*) that went far beyond the farms and fields. Coming at the peak of the civil rights movement and other liberal, cause-oriented movements, Chavez put the rights of farmworkers on the national agenda, raising consciousness about Mexican-Americans at the same time. When Chavez initiated a national lettuce boycott, Senator Edward Kennedy won cheers at the 1972 Democratic National Convention by addressing his speech to "delegates and fellow lettuce-boycotters." The alliances Chavez formed with the AFL-CIO, church leaders, liberals, and politicians like Kennedy and Jerry Brown helped move Mexican-Americans into the political mainstream.

By 1970 the UFW was winning contracts from Central Valley growers and the farmworkers union was a reality, but the struggle went on. Through it all Chavez understood that the battles couldn't be fought only in the fields. He kept the UFW active in California politics, supporting sympathetic politicians with funds and volunteers. Among them was Jerry Brown, who was elected governor in 1974 with farmworker support. He repaid them with the swift enactment of California's Agricultural Labor Relations Act in 1975. Farm-workers were given the right to secret ballot elections for union representation and the Agricultural Labor Relations Board (ALRB) was set up to supervise the process. Shortly after that the UFW reached an agreement with the Teamsters Union, which had tried to muscle in on their turf, giving the UFW exclusive rights to organize field workers and the Teamsters a monopoly in the canneries.

Having survived these battles and gained a firm foothold, the union faced new problems as it struggled to define itself. "We don't want to model ourselves on the industrial unions," Chavez said. "That would be bad. We want to get involved in politics, in voter registration, not just in contract negotiation. The trouble is that no institution can remain fluid. We have to find some cross between being a movement and being a union."[35] Chavez faced dissent within the UFW as union staff members began to demand better pay and more security, moving away from Chavez's traditions of volunteerism and a virtual vow of poverty for union workers. In the fields the UFW faced problems with growers who responded to unionization by increasing mechanization and im-porting more illegal aliens. This led Chavez to call for tighter border controls and to oppose temporary worker programs. Chavez also increasingly found himself in conflict with other Mexican-American political leaders. The elec-tion of Republican Governor George Deukmejian caused further problems for the UFW, because Deukmejian was pro-grower and as governor has the power to appoint members and some staff of the ALRB. Deukmejian's 1977 proposal for a military base stretching along 14 miles of the California-Mexico border is indicative of his attitude about illegal immigration.

Although the struggle in the fields is far from over, its significance cannot be doubted. Chavez built his organizing effort into a social movement that went far beyond the fields. As John Gregory Dunne points out, "the ultimate impact . . . will be felt not so much on the farm as in the city," taking the shape of "ethnic and social pride." It is the movement, Dunne wrote, "not really the union, that is breaking up the whole social structure of the Valley," and perhaps of California.[36]

MEXICAN-AMERICAN POLITICIANS

As Chavez built *la causa*, the idea of *la raza*, "the race," emerged as an expression of ethnic pride and a new political assertiveness. This movement coincided with legal reforms providing bilingual ballots and forbidding literacy tests, poll taxes, and discriminatory gerrymandering. The reforms stimulated a huge increase in voter registration among Mexican-Americans and electoral success for a number of Hispanic politicians.

California sent its first Hispanic in this century to Congress when Edward Roybal was elected in 1962. Roybal, whose Spanish ancestors settled in New Mexico almost two centuries ago, was also the first Hispanic in this century to be elected to the Los Angeles City Council as a result of a 1949 voter registration drive organized by the CSO and Fred Ross, the mentor of Cesar Chavez. But Roybal stood alone for a long time. No Hispanic has yet succeeded him on the L.A. Council, and it wasn't until the 1970s that Mexican-Americans really broke into state politics.

Before that time a few Hispanics had won election to city councils and school boards. But soon they were winning control of city councils in small Central Valley towns like Parlier, Mendota, Orange Cove, and Sanger. By 1980 there were 216 Hispanic council members in 126 California cities and 359 members of school boards.

Los Angeles began electing Hispanics to the state Assembly in the 1960s and in 1973 sent Ruben Ayala, the first Mexican-American in 60 years, to the state Senate. He made his loyalties clear at his swearing in: "Mi corazon y mis pensamientos siempre estaron con el pueblo Mexicano." (My heart and my thoughts will always be with the Mexican people.)[37] Others followed; by 1983 there were seven Mexican-Americans in the California legislature and three in the California congressional delegation.

Mexican-Americans got to be a big enough voting bloc that they were regularly courted by statewide and national candidates. Jerry Brown, in particular, sought these votes and forged a close alliance with Cesar Chavez. In his 1978 reelection bid Brown picked up 82 percent of the Hispanic vote. He repaid this constituency by appointing more Hispanics to state office than any governor in California history. Most notable among them were Mario Obledo, Brown's secretary of health and welfare, and Cruz Reynoso, the first Mexican-American to sit on the state Supreme Court. Brown made so many liberal as well as Hispanic judicial appointments that when Cesar Chavez expressed his fears that Governor George Deukmejian would harm the farmworkers, Brown reassured him by saying "the courts I appointed will be around long after Deukmejian is gone."[38] Chavez showed his loyalty to Brown with a $250,000 contribution to his unsuccessful 1982 campaign for the United States Senate.

Hispanics traditionally vote for Democratic candidates like Brown, but in recent years they've been splitting their votes more like California voters generally. In 1976, for example, Republican presidential candidate Gerald Ford picked up 36 percent of the vote in Ed Roybal's congressional district. Ronald Reagan won 35 percent of the vote there in 1980 and 25 percent of the statewide Hispanic vote. In 1983 he was already courting Hispanic votes for his 1984 reelection campaign. The Republican-affiliated Hispanic Council had 2000 members in California. Hispanics showed increasing discernment in supporting Democratic candidates when Chavez and other leaders sat out the 1982 gubernatorial race because the Democratic candidate, Los Angeles Mayor Tom Bradley, repeatedly called for "balance" on the ALRB, refusing to take a straight pro-farmworker position. When Bradley won only 64 percent of the Hispanic vote, a UFW leader said his "narrow defeat showed that any minority candidate seeking statewide office without the active support of the farm workers is begging to get beat."[39] Some analysts believe these changes indicate that Hispanics hold the balance of power in California politics.

Brown's loss in the Senate race, however, was a setback for Mexican-Americans. So was Mario Obledo's disastrously unsuccessful run for the Democratic nomination for governor, which served only to offend Tom Bradley and demonstrate disunity among Hispanic leaders and voters. And despite their numbers, Hispanics were still unable to elect one of their own to the Los Angeles School Board or City Council. Voter turnout continues to be a problem. While statewide turnout was 71 percent in 1982, key Hispanic precincts voted at a rate of 54 percent.

Still there were victories. Cruz Reynoso, the first Mexican-American on the California Supreme Court, was confirmed by the voters, although his victory was narrower than those of his black and white colleagues on the same ballot. Thanks to reapportionment, which consolidated Mexican-American voters in more districts than usual (ethnic gerrymandering was still a problem in some areas), the number of Hispanics in the California congressional delegation was increased from one to three. Hispanics held their own in the state legislature, with seven representatives, but at least two of these were emerging as significant leaders.

Assemblyman Richard Alatorre gained stature in the Assembly because he supported Willie Brown, the winner in the race for Speaker. Brown put Alatorre in charge of reapportionment, a power he used to strengthen Hispanic districts. Alatorre's support for Brown, however, alienated him from an old ally, Cesar Chavez, who supported Howard Berman for Speaker. The two Mexican-American leaders had worked closely in the past. In fact, it was Alatorre who authored the Agricultural Labor Relations Act in 1975. By 1983, however, they had mended fences. Alatorre joined Chavez in criticizing Governor Deukmejian's appointments to the ALRB and introduced legislation prohibiting guest workers, which pleased organized labor. Alatorre was making good connections, and he was only 40 years old in 1983.

Art Torres, another rising star in California politics, was even younger. Once an attorney for the UFW, Torres was elected to the Assembly in 1974. Like Alatorre, he split with Chavez to support Willie Brown in the contest for Speaker of the Assembly, but in 1982 he crossed Chavez again by running against State Senator Alex Garcia. Such a challenge of one Mexican-American politician by another was unheard of, although it was widely acknowledged that Garcia was incompetent. Chavez, other Hispanic politicians, and the Senate leadership backed Garcia, but Torres won, declaring it progress because voters got a choice between two Hispanics. Los Angeles Times columnist Frank del Olmo concurred, saying Garcia shouldn't have been "supported merely because of his ethnic background. . . . The days are past when community activists supported a Latino public official simply because he was Latino."[40] In the same election Torres' former aide and ally, Gloria Molina, won the seat he vacated to run for Senate, becoming the first Latina state legislator. Torres emerged from the 1982 election as a new and independent leader, a fact that was reiterated by his endorsement of a veteran Anglo councilman over an Hispanic challenger in a Los Angeles district that was 75 percent Hispanic.

Alatorre and Torres join senior Hispanic leaders Edward Roybal and Cesar Chavez. Meanwhile, another Chavez is making his mark on California politics. In 1983, Fernando Chavez, a 33-year old San Jose attorney and the son of Cesar, was elected president of the Mexican-American Political Association (MAPA), the largest Hispanic political group in California. MAPA bills itself as nonpartisan, but its much sought-after endorsements usually go to Democrats. New leadership could give it new energy and enhanced influence. The sleeping giant is awakening.

RETURN OF SIMPSON-MAZZOLI

This increasing clout was soon put to the test. Edward Roybal and the California delegation managed to defeat the Simpson-Mazzoli immigration reforms in 1982, but the following year Senator Simpson reintroduced the legislation, declaring that "the first duty of a sovereign nation is to have control over its borders and we don't."[41]

As the legislation came to a vote in the Senate, the INS conducted a series of raids on work places to drive home its point that illegal immigrants were taking jobs from citizens at a time of high unemployment. They caught forty-one illegals at a Levi Strauss plant in one California city and more at a tortilla factory in the same community. The INS recruited Indochinese workers to replace the illegal Mexican immigrants at the tortilla factory, thus heightening tension between two minority groups.

Hispanic leaders protested the raids, but by the time the INS called them off they had served their purpose. The Senate approved the legislation 76–18, with both California senators in opposition. At the behest of California growers, the state's new Republican senator, Pete Wilson, had tried to eliminate penalties for those who employ illegals, but he failed.

The House Judiciary Committee okayed similar legislation over the objections of California Congressman Don Edwards, but the final verdict awaited a vote of the House of Representatives. Opponents, led by the Hispanic Congressional Caucus, tried to delay a vote, as they did in 1982, but it seemed inevitable that Simpson-Mazzoli would win House approval before the session ending in 1984 unless the electoral clout of Hispanics is too intimidating for the politicians in an election year.

Mexico, California, and Mexican-Americans

The battle over immigration policy illustrates significant changes in California politics. Mexico, once treated as a colony, is now seen more as an equal. The discovery of huge oil reserves and the economic interdependence of California and Mexico contributed greatly to that change. But the biggest factor in the change is the rising influence of Mexican-Americans in California politics. Still far from meeting their full potential, they've become a force to reckon with and the sleeping giant is on the minds of Ronald Reagan, George Deukmejian, and other politicians. Men and women like Edward Roybal, Cesar Chavez, Cruz Reynoso, Richard Alatorre, Art Torres, and Gloria Molina have already made their mark. Their power is growing and so is that of Mexican-American voters.

Notes

[1] Paul Ehrlich, Loy Bilderback, and Anne Ehrlich, *The Golden Door* (New York: Wideview Books, 1981), Preface, p. vii.
[2] "Closing the Golden Door," *Time*, May 18, 1981, p. 43.
[3] Antonio Rios-Bustamente, *Mexican American Immigrant Workers in the U.S.* (University of California, Los Angeles: Chicano Studies Center Publications, 1981), p. 5.
[4] Ehrlich, Bilderback, and Ehrlich, *Golden Door*, p. 190.
[5] Rios-Bustamente, *Mexican American Immigrant Workers*, p. 26.
[6] Ehrlich, Bilderback, and Ehrlich, *Golden Door*, pp. 178–80.

[7]U.S. Select Commission on Immigration and Refugee Policy, *U.S. Immigration Policy and the National Interest*, Washington: U.S. Government Printing Office, 1981, p. 3

[8]U.S. Congress, House, Committee on the Judiciary, "Immigration Reform and Control Act of 1982," H.R. 6514, 97th Congress, 2d session, Report no. 97–890, September 28, 1982, p. 30.

[9]*San Jose Mercury*, February 19, 1983.

[10]*San Jose Mercury*, November 1, 1981.

[11]*San Jose Mercury*, April 4, 1983, and May 1, 1983.

[12]"Closing the Golden Door," *Time*, May 18, 1981, p. 44.

[13]*San Jose Mercury*, November 1, 1981.

[14]Harry E. Cross and James A. Sandos, *Across the Border* (Berkeley: Institute of Governmental Studies, 1981), pp. 91, 95.

[15]Gerald P. Lopez, "Undocumented Mexican Migration," *UCLA Law Review*, April 1981, p. 636.

[16]Joint Hearings before the Subcommittee on Immigration, Refugees and International Law of the House Judiciary Committee and the Subcommittee on Immigration and Refugee Policy of the Senate Judiciary Commitee, 97th Cong., 2nd sess. on H.R. 5872 and S. 222, *The Immigration Reform and Control Act of 1982*, held April 1, 1982 and April 20, 1982, 40 (Washington, D.C.: U.S. Government Printing Office, 1982), p. 424.

[17]Ibid., p. 410.

[18]*Congressional Quarterly*, April 10, 1982, p. 10.

[19]*San Jose Mercury*, April 4, 1983.

[20]Joint Hearings, p. 188.

[21]*The Economic Democrat*, September 1981.

[22]Arthur Corwin, *Immigrants—and Immigrants* (Westport, New York: Greenwood Press, 1978), p. 73.

[23]Joint Hearings, p. 180.

[24]Ed Salzman, "Unofficial State Policy: Open Border with Mexico," *California Journal* 10, no. 2 (February 1979): 44.

[25]Carey McWilliams, *North from Mexico* (Westport, New York: Greenwood Press, 1968), p. 207.

[26]Robert Jones Shafer and Donald Mabry, *Neighbors—Mexico and the United States* (Chicago: Nelson-Hall, 1981), p. 55.

[27]Ibid., p. 57.

[28]Ibid., p. 5.

[29]Ibid., p. 92.

[30]Cross and Sandos, *Across the Border*, p. 40.

[31]*The Guardian*, June 8, 1981.

[32]*Los Angeles Times*, January 1, 1983.

[33]*San Jose Mercury*, December 4, 1980.

[34]*Los Angeles Times*, March 19, 1979.

[35]John Gregory Dunne, *Delano* (New York: Farrar, Strauss, 1967), pp. 174–75.

[36]Ibid., pp. 198, 175.

[37]*Los Angeles Times*, February 18, 1974.

[38]Cesar Chavez, speech to the Southwest Labor Studies Conference (San Jose, Calif.), April 29, 1983.

[39]Tony Castro, "The Chavez Cloud on Senator Torres' Political Horizon," *California Journal* 14, no. 2 (February 1983): 56.

[40]Frank del Olmo, "Sophistication Changes Political Picture for Latinos," *Los Angeles Times*, January 14, 1982.

[41]*San Jose Mercury*, February 18, 1983.

14
CALIFORNIA CONNECTIONS

Past and Future

California politics is a complex, sometimes confusing and bewildering phenomenon. Its parts can seem fragmented, each independent of the others, adding up to nothing. To compound the frustration, many of our stories have yet to have their endings written. That's California and that's California politics. It *is* fragmented and it can be bewilderingly difficult to comprehend. But like Dorothy in Oz, we had to complete our journey before we could understand where we've been and where we're going. Now, looking back, we can perceive certain themes in our stories. They provide the basis for understanding California politics—past, present, and future. They are the California connection.

Constant Change

The first rule of California politics—and everything else about California—is change. Nothing stays the same for long. "California," Carey McWilliams observed, "has not grown or evolved so much as it has been hurtled forward, rocket-fashion, by a series of chain-reaction explosions."[1]

A major cause of this explosive change has been the constant waves of refugees from other states and nations that have hit California in succession with amazing regularity throughout its history. From the Spanish and Mexicans to the European ethnics, the Yankees, Chinese, Japanese, Okies and Arkies, and blacks, a decade hasn't passed without a significant new group to complicate California's already diverse population. Nor do they arrive in a trickle; they come in tidal waves that can't be resisted or ignored. The latest arrivals are refugees from Southeast Asia, a group that has already become socially and economically significant, but whose political impact has yet to be felt. They add to the state's burgeoning minority population, which may constitute a majority by the turn of the next century.

Waves of immigrants have changed California, but economic and techno-logical development also has repeatedly transformed the state. In fact, the immigrants would never have come if California's expanding economy hadn't provided the jobs to attract them. Farming, mining, oil, timber, commerce, movies, manufacturing, high-tech, tourism—these major components of California's economy have drawn more people and added to the state's diversity. Each of them is in some way dependent on government, so each economic development has also had political repercussions.

These massive forces of change impose a constant need to adapt, and that means political change. The political system has been used to resolve conflict among immigrant groups and economic interests, to protect some and deny others.

But if constant change keeps California politics in a perennial state of flux, it also makes political change easier. Because the state's population and economy are so diverse, there is no single, perceived "correct" way of doing things. Because change occurs with such regularity, little becomes stable. The only tradition is change. "The future always looks good in the golden land," novelist Joan Didion wrote, "because no one remembers the past. Here is where the hot wind blows and the old ways do not seem relevant."[2]

Californians are perpetually willing to try something new, exhibiting great inventiveness in experimenting with government structure and public policy and a willingness to elect highly individualistic, sometimes eccentric leaders. As two Englishmen observed, "California's culture is super-absorbent, syn-cretic."[3] Nothing is fixed or defined in rootless California. There is no ortho-doxy. Things change too fast for that. The only thing fixed is change, which means adapting to the new, or absorbing and synthesizing new cultures, im-migrants, and industries.

When Californians don't like the way something is working, they change it. Sometimes they change things just because something new seems interesting. Sometimes they change things by changing leaders, often going from one extreme to another. That's most apparent in their choices of governors in the past three decades. In other cases Californians haven't always waited for their leaders to remedy perceived problems, so they take it upon themselves to bring about change. Whether it's the Workingmen's party or the Progressives or the taxpayers' revolt, change is brought about with relative ease.

More than most other places, change is produced by altering governmental institutions. Californians have endless faith in structural change and great willingness to try new things. Voters in California cities have gone back and forth from district to at-large elections, trying to find a system of representation that suits their changing needs. The California Constitution has been amended hundreds of times. At virtually every election, voters consider structural changes in government, thanks to one of the biggest structural changes of all, the initiative. The idea of the public making policy through the initiative process is itself a manifestation of Californians' faith in change and impatience with traditional legislative and electoral channels that operate in most other states, often slowing or denying change.

All this can be confusing, but it's also exciting and it's a major part of California's vitality and success. California hasn't settled into a routine. It survives on its own diversity—absorbing the new, adapting, and moving on rather than resisting and stagnating.

Weak Institutions

As a consequence of all this change, another pattern in California politics becomes apparent: weak institutions and political structures. In many states entrenched institutions and structures define and limit politics and policies. They are the means by which change must occur. But California has institutionalized change by the very weakness of its political structures.

Parties, for example, have never been as important in California as they are in most other states. Party loyalty is weak among voters and sometimes even among political leaders. When political parties aren't providing what is needed, Californians have no qualms about organizing new parties, like the Workingmen's party, or organizing to take over existing parties, as they did with the Progressive movement, End Poverty in California (EPIC), and the California Democratic Council (CDC). The Progressives, in their zeal to destroy the railroad's political machine, saw to it that the political parties were so debilitated that they couldn't be easily taken over or controlled by machines. This was accomplished by structural reforms including direct primaries, cross-filing, nonpartisan local elections, and state regulation of parties.

The weakness of California's political parties extends to and affects institutions of government, many of which are also weak. Executive authority in California is fragmented by the election of a governor and six other executives. It's rare for one party to capture all seven executive offices, and even if it did, the weakness of the parties wouldn't guarantee a unified executive. Leadership in the legislature is also weakened by an absence of party discipline, which enabled the incumbent Democratic Speaker of the Assembly to gain office by soliciting Republican support.

Thus, California's political free-for-all is extended to the government institutions themselves. But weak institutions and fragmentation seem to suit Californians. They reflect the soil of place California is. Perhaps they're an inevitable and good adaptation to a diverse and rapidly changing state. They seem to govern reasonably well, and anyway, when Californians don't like the way they work, they can change leaders or structures or make new policies themselves.

The Politics of Personality

"California politics," says *Los Angeles Times* columnist Art Seidenbaum, "have almost always been pulled by political animals, a strange assortment of maverick creatures who tugged right and left and never attended obedience school in either party. . . . The player is more important than the team."[4] Because of an undisciplined political party system and overlapping, poorly defined responsibilities in the state's major elective offices, power rarely moves along predictable paths. Instead officeholders shape their power as extensions of their personalities.

Hiram Johnson and Earl Warren are outstanding examples of men who rose above party politics to lead the state like father figures for long periods of time. State Senator H. L. Richardson has made himself and his supporters an independent force within the Republican party. Assemblyman Tom Hayden and his Campaign for Economic Democracy (CED) have done the same in the Democratic party. The blessings of the party and its leadership are far from essential to win nomination for office in California. It's more important to have a personal organization. In fact, it's imperative, because the parties are too weak to deliver much support themselves.

Once elected, some politicians manage to make more of their positions than others. In the early 1970s, Secretary of State Edmund G. Brown, Jr., converted a traditionally impotent, record-keeping office into a watchdog agency for campaign records, tax law enforcement, and political reform solely through his own interpretation of the office's functions. Much the same happened in the treasurer's office, where Jesse Unruh forged new respect through his vigilant watch over the state's deficit, even though the office itself allows the treasurer no such formal authority. State Senator David Roberti has elevated the position of Senate President Pro Tem from relative obscurity to prominence and significance. Supreme Court Chief Justice Rose Bird has, perhaps unintentionally, pushed the court into the forefront of state politics.

Sometimes exploitation of such offices makes them a stepping-stone to still higher office, as in the case of Jerry Brown. Unruh is still mentioned as a gubernatorial candidate and Roberti may be positioning himself as a contender.

Even if personal advancement isn't the goal, the politician who can accrue such power gains influence over public policy.

If personalities are important in determining the power of officeholders, they can also give those who do not hold public office great power. Lobbyists like Artie Samish and James Garibaldi and leaders of movements like Howard Jarvis and Cesar Chavez also have had a major influence in the shaping of public policy in California.

But it would be naive to suggest that it is simply personality that gives these indiiduals power. That's part of it, but political success also requires organization, good media relations, and money. Richardson, Hayden, and Chavez, for example, are organizers whose personal followings give them power. That's still personality politics to the extent that their organizations might or might not survive without their unique leadership.

The media are also important to California politicians. For decades the major newspapers in the state had great success in pushing their candidates and were probably a more important political force than the parties were. In recent years their power has declined as television superceded them as a means for politicians to reach the voters, either by making news or buying advertising time. And television is the perfect medium for personality politics because it feeds on images and rarely achieves the in-depth analysis that the print media offer. Television also enables politicians to go directly to the voters, without a reporter as intermediary.

Along with personal organizations and good media—or as an alternative to them—politicians need money for their campaigns. This enables them to build a popular base to gain or maintain their power. Any number of California politicians have used this means to win office against the will of other state leaders, inside and outside political parties. But campaigns cost an enormous amount of money. As they become more important, campaign contributors, whether they're individuals or organizations, gain in power.

The politics of personality, then, is not founded solely on charisma. It also takes organization, good media, and access to campaign funds. But whatever its base, it seems to suit California voters. They like strong individuals who tickle their imagination, people who suggest opportunities, like Jerry Brown and Howard Jarvis. But they're also pragmatic, choosing leaders who they think suit their needs at a given moment. They'll retreat from the rainbow every now and then, opting for duller, safer politicians like George Deukmejian and denying Jerry Brown a seat in the United States Senate.

One of the drawbacks of the politics of personality—at least for the politicians—is its unpredictability. There are no long-term guarantees, no rules. The state's power holders can find themselves sinking in quicksand. Leo

McCarthy learned how fast things can change when he nearly had the Assembly speakership snatched away from him. Successful politicians today can be powerless tomorrow or whenever they can no longer hold together what it takes to stay in power. It's a volatile sort of politics, but that volatility reflects the sort of place California is.

Grassroots Possibilities

The openness and absence of rigid structures and traditions in California politics provide opportunities not only for individual politicians, but also for grassroots movements. The Workingmen's party, the Progressives, Upton Sinclair's EPIC, and the California Democratic Council are examples of grassroots movements that have left a mark on state politics.

The goals of these organizations were broad, but other grassroots efforts with narrower interests reiterate the possibilities. They have managed to influence public policy by various means. John Serrano, Jr., challenged the constitutionality of education spending in California in the courts and changed the system. Cesar Chavez managed to organize farmworkers into a union after decades of struggle, winning the support of the legislature and the governor despite the objections of agribusiness, one of the greatest powers in the state.

California's initiative and referendum system gives interest groups and the general public a policymaking mechanism that has been used extensively. With Proposition 9 in 1974 post-Watergate reformers succeeded in getting voter approval of laws requiring extensive disclosure of campaign contributions and lobbyist activity. Environmentalists managed to enact regulations on development of the California coast and restrictions on the damming of wild rivers, and helped stop the construction of the Peripheral Canal. Howard Jarvis and Paul Gann tapped voter resentment of high taxes in 1978 with their Proposition 13, and the repercussions of their tax revolt are still being felt. Minority, neighborhood, and labor activists managed to change the system of representation in local government in San Jose, San Francisco, and other California cities.

Stable Forces of Power

Despite the opportunities California politics provide individual politicians, organizations, and the grassroots, power is far from evenly distributed. Individual politicians may rise like stars, but they still have to contend with long-established forces. Grassroots movements may win victories, but such victories are often fleeting because the entrenched powers can outlast them.

These persistent forces are almost exclusively economic. Ownership of resources like gold, silver, timber, and oil has provided great power for certain individuals and corporations. Landownership is a perpetual source of power in California politics. Constant battles over water and development suggest that the great landowners don't always get what they want, but in the long run, they usually get what they need. The media are another stable force in California politics. Although a handful of family-owned newspapers no longer exercises as much power as they did in the first half of this century, they remain important in state politics. Other components of California's diverse eocnomy—banks; insurance companies; the aerospace, defense, and high-technology industries; and labor unions like the Teamsters—have their own interests to pursue and do so with efficiency and persistence.

Not since the days of the railroad political machine has any one of these interests clearly dominated the state. California's ever-increasing economic diversity prevents such dominance, but so do the state's open political structures and traditions. Probably more than in most other states, these big, vested interests actually lose battles. The railroad was eventually brought to heel; agribusiness had to accept unionization; and real estate interests had to come to terms with controlled growth.

Nevertheless, they remain forces with which California politicians must contend. Their power persists because they are genuinely important in California and also because they have money. Money sustains them through grassroots insurgencies. Money enables them to employ skilled lobbyists in Sacramento and Washington. Money pays for the campaigns of the politicians. As campaign costs soar, dependence on monied interests increases, however much politicians resist it and reformers try to contain it.

The grassroots may challenge these elites, but the impermanence of popular movements can't match the permanence of money. For all that may be written about the openness of California politics, these great powers persist and must not be underestimated.

The Serial Continues

If California politics have been turbulent in the past, there's no sign of a letup in the future. Every issue and every story we've examined have yet to be completely resolved and new ones will undoubtedly emerge.

Figuring out new ways of winning votes and getting elected goes on as California leads the nation in the development of clever new campaign techniques and at the same time debates ways of regulating campaigns through such reforms as public finance. Interest group power continues unabated, as does the power of the media.

Republican Governor George Deukmejian must find a way to get what he wants and deliver what he promised while sharing power with Democrats in the executive branch and with Democratic majorities in both houses of the legislature. Assembly Speaker Willie Brown and Senate President Pro Tem David Roberti will work to hold on to and consolidate their power. Supreme Court Chief Justice Rose Bird and her activist colleagues must deal with conservative opponents and a public that remains restive regarding the role of the courts.

Local government faces a seemingly endless budget crisis, continued debate over growth, and increasingly assertive minorities, especially where minorities are becoming majorities in cities like Los Angeles. Representation is likely to continue as a key issue.

California's congressional delegation, now more strongly Democratic and somewhat more unified, must continue to pursue favorable federal policies, especially for defense and water projects, although immigration and foreign competition for California's high-tech industries now rank with water and defense as policy priorities.

The tax revolt may be in recess, but there's no sign that a reversal is about to occur. More likely, resistance to tax increases will continue and the state will face a long struggle just to maintain existing services. In education the search for equality goes on and becomes more difficult because of limited revenues. Undoubtedly a new chapter is yet to be written in the Peripheral Canal story, because water is never very far from the minds of California's economic interests.

There's been one big change, however, in the context in which all these battles are fought. California has recently learned it is not economically infallible. State and local government services are suffering not only because of the taxpayers' revolt, but also because of economic recession. In 1983 unemployment exceeded 10 percent in California. After a long period of prosperity and optimism, Californians were shocked to be reminded that their economy is intertwined with that of the nation. Some politicians turned to the high-tech industries as a savior, but even as President Reagan was declaring himself an "apostle of high-tech,"[5] the manufacturing operations of many of these corporations were being moved to other countries. Now the politicians are scurrying to save the savior.

So although the old issues play themselves out and new ones arise, the conditions on the field of play have changed. Californians must now contend with increasingly limited resources. Difficult decisions will have to be made and that means some tough political battles are ahead. That's nothing new for California politics.

The California Connection

It should be apparent by now that all these issues and forces are connected to one another. But their connections go well beyond the borders of the state. What happens in California—from the taxpayers' revolt to innovative campaign techniques—usually happens elsewhere as well. Besides, California is too big and important to be ignored, even when the Golden State falls on hard times. Relationships may change, but the California connection remains a crucial one, for the nation and the world.

It may seem unique—just kooky California—but often California is the harbinger of things to come elsewhere. California is unique, but it's not an isolated case. In a way California is the future and that, ultimately, is the California connection.

Notes

[1]Carey McWilliams, *California: The Great Exception* (Westport, New York: Greenwood Press, 1971), p. 25.
[2]Joan Didion, *Slouching Towards Bethlehem* (New York: Penguin, 1974), p. 20.
[3]Jeremy Tunstall and David Walker, *Media Made in California* (New York: Oxford, 1981), p. 10.
[4]Art Seidenbaum, *This is California: Please Keep Out* (New York: Wyden, 1975), p. 154.
[5]*San Jose Mercury*, January 27, 1983.

Acknowledgments

Material on page 58 from interview with Gerald P. O'Hara, Legislative Representative, California Teamsters Public Affairs Council, reprinted with permission.

Excerpt on pages 59–60 from letter from Larry J. Kurbatoff, Assistant Legislative Representative, California Teamsters Public Affairs Council, reprinted by permission.

Excerpt on page 61 from letter from State Senator Jim Ellis, reprinted with permission.

Excerpt on page 61 from letter from State Assemblyman Louis Papan to the *Los Angeles Times*, January 10, 1980, reprinted by permission.

Excerpt on page 66 from "Sacramento Lobbyists Still Have Their Clout" by Steve Wiegand, from *San Francisco Chronicle*, November 27, 1981. © 1981 by *San Francisco Chronicle*. Reprinted by permission.

Excerpt on page 89 from "Something New for Oakland" by Joseph Lyford from *Columbia Journalism Review*, January-February, 1981. Excerpt reprinted with permission.

Material on page 90 from interview with Leo Rennert reprinted by permission.

Excerpt on page 262 from letter from David F. Abelson, Executive Director, Planning and Conservation League, to State Senator Ruben Ayala, reprinted with permission.

Material on page 268 from interview with Hans Van Nes, Assistant Director of the California Department of Food and Agriculture, reprinted with permission.

Material on pages 88, 145, 149, 257, and 267 from the *California Journal* reprinted with permission of The California Center.

Index